THE COALITIONS PRESIDENTS MAKE

Cornell Modern Indonesia Project

A series edited by Eric Tagliacozzo and Thomas B. Pepinsky

A list of titles in this series is available at cornellpress.cornell.edu.

THE COALITIONS PRESIDENTS MAKE

Presidential Power and Its Limits in Democratic Indonesia

Marcus Mietzner

SOUTHEAST ASIA PROGRAM PUBLICATIONS

AN IMPRINT OF CORNELL UNIVERSITY PRESS   ITHACA AND LONDON

Copyright © 2023 by Cornell University

All rights reserved. Except for brief quotations in a review, this book, or parts thereof, must not be reproduced in any form without permission in writing from the publisher. For information, address Cornell University Press, Sage House, 512 East State Street, Ithaca, New York 14850. Visit our website at cornellpress.cornell.edu.

First published 2023 by Cornell University Press

Library of Congress Cataloging-in-Publication Data

Names: Mietzner, Marcus, author.
Title: The coalitions presidents make : presidential power and its limits in democratic Indonesia / Marcus Mietzner.
Description: Ithaca [New York] : Southeast Asia Program Publications, an imprint of Cornell University Press, 2023. | Includes bibliographical references and index.
Identifiers: LCCN 2023023899 (print) | LCCN 2023023900 (ebook) | ISBN 9781501772641 (hardcover) | ISBN 9781501772658 (paperback) | ISBN 9781501772665 (pdf) | ISBN 9781501772672 (epub)
Subjects: LCSH: Executive power—Indonesia. | Presidents—Indonesia. | Democracy—Indonesia. | Coalition governments—Indonesia. | Indonesia—Politics and government—20th century. | Indonesia—Politics and government—21st century.
Classification: LCC JQ771 .M54 2023 (print) | LCC JQ771 (ebook) | DDC 320.4598—dc23/eng/20230606
LC record available at https://lccn.loc.gov/2023023899
LC ebook record available at https://lccn.loc.gov/2023023900

Contents

List of Figures and Tables	vii
Preface and Acknowledgments	ix
Glossary	xiii
A Note about Names	xvii
Introduction: Presidents, Coalitions, and Indonesia	1
1. The President	31
2. The Parties	55
3. The Legislature	77
4. The Military	98
5. The Police	120
6. The Bureaucracy	140
7. Local Governments	161
8. The Oligarchs	182
9. Muslim Organizations	205
Conclusion: Drivers and Contexts	226
Notes	247
References	251
Index	271

Figures and Tables

Figures

0.1. V-Dem Liberal Democracy Index, Indonesia, 1900–2021   17

0.2. V-Dem Liberal Democracy Index, Latin America, 1900–2021   23

Tables

0.1. Stability Indicators of Coalitional Presidentialism in Selected Countries, 2004–2021   20

0.2. Presidents, Parties, and Non-Party Actors in Selected Countries, 2021   22

1.1. Organization of the Presidential Palace, 2021   44

1.2. Composition of Presidential Coalitions, 2004–2019   51

2.1. Indonesian Parties, Party Types, and Participation in Coalitions, 2021   62

2.2. Party Nominations and Cabinet Inclusion in Second Widodo Government, 2019   67

3.1. DPR Structure and Brokerage Network, 2021   89

4.1. The Military's Territorial Structure versus the Civilian Administration   102

5.1. The Police's National Network versus the Civilian Administration   124

Preface and Acknowledgments

This book is the result of more than twenty-five years of studying the political behavior of Indonesia's presidents. As an exchange student in Indonesia in the 1990s, I was fascinated by long-time president Suharto's ability to engineer what seemed to be his eternal hold on power. When he eventually fell, I was equally intrigued by the chaotic but also highly dynamic years of the democratic transition, which stretched from 1998 to 2004 and witnessed the presidencies of B.J. Habibie, Abdurrahman Wahid, and Megawati Sukarnoputri. Living in Jakarta for most of these years, I constantly feared missing out on the newest developments as parties emerged and disappeared, communal conflicts escalated and ceased, and presidents came and went. The presidency of Susilo Bambang Yudhoyono marked the end of this high-speed and often unorderly transition, gradually stabilizing the country's socio-economic infrastructure. Yudhoyono's first term is now widely viewed as the high point of Indonesian democracy—both in terms of its stability and its continued dynamism. Slowly but steadily, however, the democratic liveliness that had characterized the first decade of the post-Suharto era dissipated, and a sense of stasis and almost mechanical stability took root instead. Yudhoyono served out his second term without much enthusiasm—a feeling shared by many Indonesians at the grassroots. During my frequent visits to Jakarta in that period, the citizens' longing for something different—either a revitalization of the reform project or a return to the predictability of strongman rule—was palpable. Joko Widodo, who ran for the presidency in 2014, offered the former and won, but it did not take long for him to replicate the routines of power maintenance that Yudhoyono had entrenched.

When I wrote this book, more than two decades after Suharto's resignation, the Indonesian presidency was in a curious place. It was more stable than during the transition years, with Yudhoyono and Widodo serving a decade in power each, in contrast to the three immediate post-Suharto presidents who had ruled for a total of six years. The post-transition presidential regime was also more competitive (and contested) than any of its predecessor polities, despite frequent accusations that Widodo had allowed neo-Suhartoism to infiltrate his rule. Yet the Indonesian polity of the early 2020s had lost the democratic promise that had been so celebrated, both domestically and internationally, in much of the 2000s and early 2010s. It was now widely accepted that democratic quality in Indonesia was on the decline, the continued functionality of the country's democracy notwithstanding. On the one hand, then, presidential rule in Indonesia appeared remarkably stable, both in comparison to its peers around the world and its experience during the transition. On the other hand, its democracy was backsliding while still being far away from the sort of autocratic rule that Suharto had practiced. To get a better analytical grip on how Indonesia's presidency consolidated so remarkably and yet let its democratic aspirations slip so profoundly is this book's central aim. It finds, ultimately, that the two trends are intrinsically linked, and that Indonesia's post-2004 presidents have managed to stabilize their regimes through sophisticated mechanisms of coalitional presidentialism that consumed democratic substance without ending democracy per se.

Many people have been essential in the production of this book. My biggest gratitude goes to Indonesian presidents, both former and incumbent. I have found Indonesian politicians to be extraordinarily generous with their time, and presidents have been no exception. Without their perspective, it would have been impossible to write this book. It is one thing to observe the president's behavior from the outside, and many valuable lessons can be learned from such observations. But it is different to hear from the actors themselves about why they do what they do, however self-serving such explanations may be. Being allowed to watch the inner workings of the presidency is another experience without which this book could not have been written. Among the pre-2004 presidents, Wahid gave me the widest access to him and his staff. Megawati, while never agreeing to a sit-down interview, gave me permission to attend many of the congresses of her party, from the first post-Suharto event in 1998 to the most recent in 2019. Both post-2004 presidents, Yudhoyono and Widodo—the main subjects of this book—have been very helpful in my research. Yudhoyono agreed to a five-hour interview in 2014 (with my colleague Edward Aspinall), and Widodo allowed me to accompany him on the campaign trail. The access that these presidents gave me ensured that their viewpoints were considered in the overall narrative, thus integrating a voice often missing from other coalitional presidentialism case studies.

I am also indebted to many presidential aides and government officials who helped me understand the way the Indonesian presidency works. Most of these sources requested anonymity in order to speak frankly, and their openness allowed me to paint a picture of the presidency largely drawn from insiders' accounts. But one source was always happy to speak openly and without anxiety over the possible consequences of what he conveyed to me: Luhut Binsar Panjaitan, the man widely described as Widodo's most important aide. I first met him in 2013 and have since engaged in regular and lively discussions with him. These discussions have been combative at times but always remained cordial.

He invited me to accompany him on an insightful trip to Papua in June 2016, during which I could observe him in action as the president's main troubleshooter. Obviously, his willingness to speak frankly and fearlessly stems from the natural self-confidence of a man with great power and wealth—Luhut had been minister under Wahid and then became a businessman, Widodo's first chief of staff, and finally senior minister in two key portfolios. But his outspokenness is also often ascribed—stereotypically but rather accurately—to his ethnicity as a Batak, and Luhut enjoys this identification. This book critically assesses the disproportional role wealthy elites play in presidential governance, but this does not diminish my gratitude to Luhut for telling me his side of the story and granting me a view of top-level presidential politics I otherwise would have been unable to get.

Many political observers in Indonesia have assisted me by sharing their knowledge and analyses. These include Sidney Jones, Douglas Ramage, Philips Vermonte, Sunny Tanuwidjaja, Jeffrie Geonavie, Saiful Mujani, Rizal Sukma, Hana A. Satriyo, Clara Joewono, Sandra Hamid, Julian Bowen, Tom Coghlan, Monty Pounder, and John McBeth. Academics in Australia with whom I have had productive discussions about presidential politics in Indonesia include Dirk Tomsa, Vedi Hadiz, Jacqui Baker, Ian Wilson, Ross Tapsell and Dave McRae. In the United States, I thank Tom Pepinsky, Dan Slater, Allen Hicken, Margaret Scott, and Bill Liddle. The latter has worked on his own book on Indonesian presidents and thus has been particularly interested in my study. He has been both supportive and critical of my work—he deeply dislikes the use of the term "oligarch," both in my book and more generally. We agreed to disagree, as so often in our very fruitful exchanges. In Europe, I am indebted to Aurel Croissant, Henk Schulte Nordholt, Jürgen Rüland, Michael Buehler, John Sidel, Ward Berenshot, Andreas Ufen, and Marco Bünte. In Japan, I am grateful to Masaaki Okamoto from the Center of Southeast Asian Studies at Kyoto University (where I was based in 2018/19 for a visiting fellowship) and Jun Honna from Ritsumeikan University, where I put the finishing touches to this book in early 2023. These colleagues have had a tremendous impact on my thinking, but they bear no responsibility for any shortcomings that readers might find in this book.

The Department of Political and Social Change at the Coral Bell School of Asia-Pacific Affairs within the Australian National University has been my intellectual home since I started my PhD studies there in 1997. My colleagues and students in the department have given me the best possible environment in which to research and write about Indonesia. Greg Fealy, Edward Aspinall, Robert Cribb, Eve Warburton, Sally White, and Sana Jaffrey have made the department the site with the world's highest concentration of scholars of Indonesian politics outside of Indonesia, and I have learned from them every day. My students have been equally inspiring and resourceful. Dominic Berger, Liam Gammon, Tom Power, Bayu Dardias, Usman Hamid, Chris Morris, and Burhanuddin Muhtadi have pursued fascinating research projects that I have had the privilege to supervise. Of course, Burhanuddin Muhtadi has been much more than a student: as the head of Indikator, one of Indonesia's leading polling institutes, he has been an unlimited source of data and political information. No visit to Jakarta is complete without a number-crunching session at Burhanuddin's office in Cikini. His polling data have made or broken the careers of many a politician in Indonesia, and party leaders and presidents often desperately wait for their release. Burhanuddin has become a treasured co-author and colleague, and my discussions with him have been invaluable in shaping my view of Indonesian politics.

The research undertaken for this study was primarily funded by an Australian Research Council (ARC) Discovery Project grant titled "Presidential Power and its Limits in Post-Authoritarian Indonesia" (DP150104277). I am very appreciative of this support. Other financial assistance was provided by smaller grants from the Australian National University, as well as through stipends from Kyoto University and Ritsumeikan University. The Center of Strategic and International Studies (CSIS) in Jakarta hosted me during a longer stay surrounding Indonesia's 2014 elections, providing me with office space, facilities, and a very productive environment for discussions. I hope that the institutions that supported me so generously over the many years of my studies will find this book an adequate return on their investment.

Kyoto, February, 2023

Glossary

APEKSI: Asosiasi Pemerintah Kota Seluruh Indonesia (Association of Indonesian Municipality Governments)

Apindo: Asosiasi Pengusaha Indonesia (Indonesian Association of Entrepreneurs)

APKASI: Asosiasi Pemerintah Kabupaten Seluruh Indonesia (Association of Indonesian District Governments)

APPSI: Asosiasi Pemerintah Propinsi Seluruh Indonesia (Association of Indonesian Provincial Governments)

Babinsa: Bintara Pembina Desa (Non-Commissioned Officers Supervising Villages, lowest unit in the military hierarchy)

Bamus: Badan Musyawarah (Consultative Agency)

Bappenas: Badan Perencanaan Pembangunan Nasional (National Development Planning Agency)

Bareskrim: Badan Reserse Kriminal (Criminal Investigation Agency)

barokah: blessings

Bawaslu: Badan Pengawas Pemilu (Election Supervision Board)

Baznas: Badan Amil Zakat Nasional (National Zakat Agency)

Berkarya: (Partai) Berkarya (Working Party)

Bhabinkamtibnas: Bhayangkara Pembina Keamanan dan Ketertiban Masyarakat (Supervisory Officer for the Security and Order of Society, village-level)

BKN: Badan Kepegawaian Nasional (National Civil Service Agency)

BLK: Balai Latihan Kerja (Vocational Training Centre)

BNP2TKI: Badan Nasional Penempatan dan Perlindungan Tenaga Kerja Indonesia (National Agency for the Placement and Protection of Indonesian Migrant Workers)

BNPT: Badan Nasional Penanggulangan Terorisme (National Agency for the Management of Terrorism)

BPUPKI: Badan Penyelidik Usaha-Usaha Persiapan Kemerdekaan Indonesia (Investigating Committee for Preparatory Work on Indonesian Independence)

DAK: Dana Alokasi Khusus (Special Allocations Fund)

DAPZ: Dienst voor Algemene Personele Zaken (Service for General Personnel Affairs)

DAU: Dana Alokasi Umum (General Allocation Fund)

DBH: Dana Bagi Hasil (Revenue Sharing Fund)

demokrasi gotong royong: mutual assistance democracy

Densus 88: Detasemen Khusus 88 (Special Detachment 88)

DPD: Dewan Perwakilan Daerah (Region's Representative Council)

DPP: Dewan Penasehat Presiden (Council of Advisers to the President)

DPR: Dewan Perwakilan Rakyat (People's Representative Council)

Forkopimda: Forum Koordinasi Pimpinan Daerah (Regional Leadership Co-ordination Forum)

FPI: Front Pembela Islam (Front of Defenders of Islam)

GBHN: Garis-Garis Besar Haluan Negara (Broad Outlines of State Policy)

Gerindra: (Partai) Gerakan Indonesia Raya (Great Indonesia Movement Party)

Golkar: (Partai) Golongan Karya (Functional Group Party)

Hanura: (Partai) Hati Nurani Rakyat (People's Conscience Party)

HIPMI: Himpunan Pengusaha Muda Indonesia (Indonesian Association of Young Entrepreneurs)

HTI: Hizbut Tahrir Indonesia (Party of Liberation, Indonesia branch)

ICW: Indonesian Corruption Watch

Inpres: Instruksi Presiden (Presidential Instruction)

JI: Jemaah Islamiyah (Islamic Congregation)

Kadin: Kamar Dagang dan Industri Indonesia (Indonesian Chamber of Trade and Industry)

KASN: Komisi Aparatur Sipil Negara (State Civil Service Commission)

Kepres: Keputusan Presiden (Presidential Decision)

KNPI: Komite Nasional Indonesia Pusat (Indonesian Central National Committee)

Kodam: Komando Daerah Militer (Regional Military Command, province-level)

Kodim: Komando Distrik Militer (District-level Military Command)

Koramil: Komando Rayon Militer (Subdistrict-level Military Command)

Korpri: Korps Pegawai Republik Indonesia (Indonesian Civil Servants Corps)

KPK: Komisi Pemberantasan Korupsi (Corruption Eradication Commission)

KPU: Komisi Pemilihan Umum (General Elections Commission)

KSP: Kantor Staf Presiden (Office of the Staff of the President)

LAN: Lembaga Administrasi Negara (State Administration Institute)

Lemhannas: Lembaga Ketahanan Nasional (National Resilience Institute)

LGBTI: Lesbian, gay, bisexual, transgender and intersex (persons)

LKMS: Lembaga Keuangan Mikro Syariah (Institute for Syariah Mico-Finance)

LPDP: Lembaga Pengelola Dana Pendidikan (Agency for Education Fund Management)

madrasah: Islamic school or college

MPR: Majelis Permusyawaratan Rakyat (People's Consultative Assembly)

Muspida: Musyawarah Pimpinan Daerah (Regional Leadership Discussion Forum)

Muslimat: women's organization of NU

musyawarah mufakat: deliberative discussion until consensus is reached

Nasdem: (Partai) Nasional Demokrat (National Democrats Party)

NGO: Non-governmental organization

NTT: Nusa Tenggara Timur (East Nusa Tenggara)

NU: Nahdlatul Ulama (Revival of the Religious Scholars)

PAN: Partai Amanat Nasional (National Mandate Party)

Pancasila: The five principles of state ideology (belief in one God; humanitarianism; Indonesian unity; popular sovereignty; social justice)

Paspampres: Pasukan Pengamanan Presiden (Presidential Security Troops)

PD: Partai Demokrat (Democratic Party)

PDI: Partai Demokrasi Indonesia (Indonesian Democracy Party)

PDI-P: Partai Demokrasi Indonesia Perjuangan (Indonesian Democracy Party—Struggle)

Perindo: Partai Persatuan Indonesia (Indonesian Unity Party)

Perpres: Peraturan Presiden (Presidential Regulation)

Perpu: Peraturan Pemerintah Pengganti Undang-Undang (Government Regulation in lieu of Law)

PKB: Partai Kebangkitan Bangsa (National Awakening Party)

PKI: Partai Komunis Indonesia (Indonesian Communist Party)

PKS: Partai Keadilan Sejahtera (Prosperous Justice Party)

Polda: Kepolisian Daerah (Regional Police, province-level)

Polres: Kepolisian Resor (Police Resort, district-level)

Polsek: Kepolisian Sektor (Police Sector, subdistrict-level)

PPHN: Pokok-Pokok Haluan Negara (Fundamentals of State Policy)

PPKI: Panitia Persiapan Kemerdekaan Indonesia (Preparatory Committee for Indonesian Independence)

PPP: Partai Persatuan Pembangungan (Unity Development Party)

PSI: Partai Solidaritas Indonesia (Party of Indonesian Solidarity)

RKP: Rencana Kerja Pemerintah (Government Working Plan)

santri: pious Muslim

Setgab: Sekretariat Gabungan (Joint Secretariat)

UKP4: Unit Kerja Presiden Bidang Pengawasan dan Pengendalian Pembangunan (Presidential Working Unit for Development Monitoring and Control)

A Note about Names

A note on the use of names is in order. In Indonesian, there is no standard for the use of names, especially as far as the identification of the "main" name is concerned. In many cases, usage even changes over time. In the late 1990s, for instance, it was common to refer to Susilo Bambang Yudhoyono as Bambang, but as he rose to more political prominence, he'd be more often referred to as Yudhoyono, no doubt partly because of the influence of the international press. (He also created a catchy acronym for his campaigns—SBY—that is widely used). This leaves a lot of room for subjectivity in the use of names, and this book is no exception. It follows a personal feeling of what is most useful rather than what is most systematic. For instance, it refers to "Megawati" rather than "Sukarnoputri", but to "Wahid" instead of "Abdurrahman". Some readers may find this dissatisfying, but this is an area in which trying to achieve conformity would do more harm than good.

THE COALITIONS PRESIDENTS MAKE

Introduction

PRESIDENTS, COALITIONS, AND INDONESIA

At the crack of dawn on March 2, 2000, I entered the presidential palace in Jakarta to interview Abdurrahman Wahid, who had become head of state only four and a half months earlier. The visit was arranged by Djohan Effendi, who would later serve as Wahid's state secretary, and the president's Australian biographer, Greg Barton, who sat in on my interview with him. Despite being hooked to a dialysis machine for the entirety of the interview, Wahid was typically flamboyant and combative. In breathless speed, Wahid told me which ministers he planned to fire, and how he would replace the current military leadership. Although many of the details of his predictions never came to pass, he did not misrepresent his intentions to create havoc in his ministry. In his twenty-one-months presidency, between October 1999 and July 2001, he replaced ministers more than two dozen times, with cabinet reshuffles becoming unremarkable events. The rapid hiring and firing produced a predictable outcome: the parties whose ministers Wahid threw off the presidential bandwagon united against him and impeached him after a highly contested process. Wahid's long-suffering vice president, Megawati Sukarnoputri, replaced the president (who had to be escorted out of the palace by his daughter as he initially refused to leave) for the remainder of his term. Megawati subsequently lost her re-election bid, making way in 2004 for the fifth president in six years. It seemed that Indonesia was on the path to a revolving door presidential regime, with near-certain political and socio-economic instability.

None of this surprised political scientists who subscribed to the Linz school of "perils of presidentialism" (Linz 1990). Linz argued that presidential systems are unsuitable for emerging democracies for various reasons, and that a multi-party system (such as Indonesia's) was a particularly poor institutional fit for presidential rule. Indeed, numerous examples exist of unstable presidential systems from the 1980s and 1990s, when Linz developed his theory—and cases of chaotic presidential impeachments continue to be widespread today. In April 2022, Peruvian president Pedro Castillo raced back to his country by car from a visit to neighboring Ecuador because failure to cross the border by midnight would have given his parliamentary opponents a pretext to impeach him (in Peru, legislators grant presidents travel authorization, the violation of which is an impeachable offense). Castillo had every reason to be concerned; one observer noted in 2020 that "every [Peruvian] president elected since 1985—with the exception of one interim leader who served for just eight months—has either been impeached, imprisoned or sought in criminal investigations" (Quigley 2020). Indeed, Castillo—after surviving the initial impeachment attempt—was removed from power in December 2022. Outside of Peru, Brazil and South Korea saw successful presidential impeachments in 2016, while other presidents—such as the chief executives of Bolivia in 2019 or Ukraine in 2014—fled the country amid popular protests that accompanied impeachment attempts. Thus, Wahid's experience appeared to fit into a broader pattern that existed then and persisted.

Yet two decades after Wahid's fall and Megawati's electoral demise, Indonesia has emerged as the opposite of a weak, unstable presidential democracy with high incumbency turnover. In its post-2004 polity, based on constitutional amendments agreed upon in 2002, there has not been a single attempt at presidential impeachment; two presidents completed their constitutionally allowed two terms, easily winning re-election each time; and cabinet reshuffles have been rare and orderly affairs. With two presidents in two decades, Indonesia has presented itself as an anchor of stability in a Southeast Asian region prone to frequent changes in government, whether through coups, intra-regime machinations, or electoral dynamics. As Indonesia's president Joko Widodo approached his last full year as president in 2023, he was the longest-serving democratic incumbent in Southeast Asia, and had been longer in office than any Asian or Latin American democratic leader in that year.[1] At the same time, the stability of the presidential system did not automatically translate into consolidated democratic gains. Most observers agree that Indonesia has witnessed a slow but noticeable decline in democratic quality since the early 2010s (Power and Warburton 2020). This democratic erosion, which followed trends elsewhere, has left Indonesia's presidential democracy still functional, but dramatically falling short of its once-cherished goal of moving toward a liberal democracy—which some activists and observers thought was achievable when long-time autocrat Suharto fell in 1998.

This book, then, deals with two inter-related puzzles associated with the post-authoritarian journey of Indonesia, the world's second-largest presidential democracy. The first relates to Indonesia's remarkable turnaround from an unstable presidential regime in the early post-Suharto period into one of the world's most resilient. How does one explain such a sudden yet profound transformation? How have post-2004 presidents in Indonesia not only managed to steer clear of the sort of impeachment attempts that plagued many of their counterparts in other presidential systems but also to win comfortable re-election victories? In other words, how could Indonesia's contemporary presidents circumvent the perils of presidentialism that led to the fall of three of their predecessors between 1998 and 2004? To find solutions to this first major puzzle, we have to embed an analysis of Indonesia's post-2004 presidential system within comparative literature that highlights, against Linz, that presidential regimes in multi-party systems can—despite all risks—be effective and stable. But why did, in the Indonesian case, the stabilization of presidential democracy not lead to a strengthening of democratic quality? Why did it, on the contrary, produce democratic decline? In resolving this second puzzle, we must explore the link between the increased stability of competitive presidential systems and eroding democratic substance. Indeed, we need to ask whether the same factors that led to a more stable presidential democracy also caused a concurrent loss of democratic capacity over time.

To understand how minority presidents in multi-party systems establish well-functioning administrations against all odds, we turn to the work of scholars who developed the concept of coalitional presidentialism. Coined by Chaisty, Cheeseman, and Power (2017), but building on the studies of others (Shugart and Carey 1992; Ames 2001; Amorim Neto, Cox, and McCubbins 2003; Amorim Neto 2006), the idea of coalitional presidentialism emphasizes coalition-building by minority presidents not as an emergency fix but as a productive strategy. At the heart of their concept is the "presidential toolbox" available to chief executives when trying to court and co-opt potential coalition partners in the legislature. This toolbox consists of five main instruments: first, the president's legislative powers, that is "the formal legislative prerogative of the executive branch that enhances the influence of the president over the agenda of the elected assembly" (Chaisty, Cheeseman, and Power 2017, 86); second, partisan powers, describing the control a president typically exercises over his or her party; third, cabinet authority, which is essentially the power of appointment to ministries; fourth; budgetary authority, which denotes the president's role in "the formulation and execution of public spending priorities with a view to obtaining targeted political support" (Chaisty, Cheeseman, and Power 2017, 87); and fifth, exchange of favors, including financial or other material inducements to attract coalition partners. I argue it was the successful usage of this toolbox of coalitional presidentialism that is to no small extent responsible for the significant stabilization of Indonesia's post-2004 presidential system.

Chaisty and colleagues exclusively focus on the relationship between presidents and legislatures, continuing a long tradition of presidentialism scholarship going back to Linz (1990). To be sure, this arena is central to presidential coalition-building and power maintenance, as the loss of support from legislators can lead to policy deadlock and presidential impeachment. Analytically, the focus on presidential-legislative relations also allows for a maximum extent of conceptual sharpness and consistency. But as this book argues, and as the case of Indonesia shows, presidents in systems with high levels of power dispersal not only require the support of legislatures and its parties. They also need to build informal coalitions with other actors. These actors can include state agencies with long records of assertively striving for political privileges and autonomy (such as the military, the police, the bureaucracy, and local administrations), as well as non-state organizations (such as oligarchs or religious groups). These non-party and non-legislative actors are crucially important in stabilizing presidential rule and require the same courting, persuasion, and co-option strategies as parties and legislators. In many cases, presidents can even use them to balance the influence of parties and legislators, especially when the latter threaten to withdraw their support. Thus, it is important to expand the concept of coalitional presidentialism beyond the traditional forums of parties and legislatures, and to study how presidents integrate other players in their broad coalitions to strengthen their administrations.

Therefore, this book explores how Indonesian presidents have successfully deployed coalitional presidentialism to build broad-based coalitions of both parties and non-party players. Borrowing from Chaisty, Cheeseman, and Power, the book analyzes how the toolbox of coalitional presidentialism is utilized in the Indonesian context, but it extends significantly the range of actors they investigated. This approach brings a new perspective to presidentialism studies and the use of the coalitional presidentialism paradigm. Studying in detail how presidential coalition-building works in Indonesia, the book investigates how successive post-democratization chief executives have interacted with—and made offers of cooperation to—the country's political parties; the legislature; the armed forces; the police; the bureaucracy; local governments; the oligarchs; and Muslim organizations. This approach is better suited for a country such as Indonesia, where the legislature operates differently from other polities (Sherlock 2012), and in which much residual power continues to rest with security forces and informal actors. Without support from these actors, presidential rule can be unstable, even if presidents possess large majorities in the legislature. Hence, amending Stephen

Skowronek's (1997) call to focus on "the politics presidents make," this book underscores the need to scrutinize "the coalitions presidents make" in both the legislative arena and in other equally important fields of politics.

Importantly, in addressing Indonesia's declining democratic quality as the stability of its presidential system increased, this book also adds to existing coalitional presidentialism studies by connecting them to debates on democratic quality. While Chaisty, Cheeseman, and Power are mostly concerned with the effectiveness of technical governance (even if achieved through ugly bribes), the discussion in this book reflects on what a power balance established through coalitional presidentialism means for the prospect of deepening democratization. The picture resulting from this analysis is mixed. On the one hand, "successful" coalitional presidentialism creates stability that allows young democracies to strengthen and avoid democratic reversals. Given the current trend of global democratic breakdowns (Daly 2019; Diamond 2021), this effect of coalitional presidentialism should not be belittled. On the other hand, that same stability can also be blamed for lack of democratic progress and democracy's subsequent decline; in other words, coalitional presidentialism might breed stagnation and, in some cases, trigger populist counter-reactions by a public dissatisfied with too much inter-elite stability (as in Brazil, for example). This is because broad coalitions are often purchased by stalling policy initiatives that could threaten the vested interests of one of its members. The more members such a coalition has, the less likely ground-breaking democratic reforms become. Indonesia, whose presidential coalitions include a wide range of actors, is a prime example of this phenomenon.

The remainder of this introduction will lay the conceptual and empirical foundations for the book's architecture. It begins with an overview of the discussion of presidentialism since the Juan Linz controversy in the early 1990s. It then proceeds by introducing in some detail the concept of coalitional presidentialism, and the way it has been applied thus far. Subsequently, the case study of Indonesia is briefly introduced, followed by a comparative contextualization of the country within a broader coalitional presidentialism and democratic decline context. It will become clear from this discussion that analyzing Indonesia both confirms and, importantly, challenges some of the assumptions of existing coalitional presidentialism studies, and that there is much benefit in broadening the latter in order to make it applicable to more countries. Based on this insight, the subsequent section offers a revised definition of coalitional presidentialism that includes a larger range of actors and takes its applicability beyond the limitations of the executive-legislative arena. Finally, after some short remarks on methodology, the chapter overview explains the rationale behind the structure of the book.

Presidentialism

Let us first define what is meant by "presidentialism." There are two main dimensions of this definition. The first is the *functional* aspect of how presidential systems work (Mezey 2013). In presidential systems, the head of the executive (that is, the president) and the legislature are elected separately, although in many cases these elections occur on the same day. The election of the president is direct by popular vote, with the legislature playing no role in it other than holding nomination rights in some countries (in Indonesia, for instance, the right to nominate presidential candidates is tied to the number of seats or vote share achieved by parties in the last legislative election). The president's tenure is fixed, with almost all democratic presidential systems imposing term limits. Typically, legislatures cannot use policy disagreements or a change in the composition of presidential coalitions to seek the premature removal of the president (Mezey 2013, 7). Thus, presidents can be driven from power only under extraordinary circumstances; in most cases, this involves legal proceedings (by the legislature or courts) to prove violations of the law and the constitution, or popular uprisings that convince the president to resign. In other words, in presidential systems, the executive nominally does not need the support of a legislative majority to exist (Cheibub 2007, 35). In practical terms, however, presidents are in a stronger position if they control a majority in the legislature, allowing them to pass laws and budgets more smoothly. At the same time, most democratic presidential systems do not give presidents the right to unilaterally dissolve the legislature, establishing separated spheres between the executive and legislative branches.

But as Mezey (2013, 8) pointed out, presidentialism is not simply a functional or constitutional category. Rather, it also describes a set of *normative* and *informal* propositions. To begin with, "presidentialism is characterized by a broadly shared public perception that places the president at the center of the nation's politics and views him (or her) as the person primarily responsible for dealing with the challenges before the country" (Mezey 2013, 8–9). Hence, regardless of the constitutional details, presidentialism is marked by a collective consensus, in both the elite and the broader population, that the president is the central figure of the nation. This is partly the result of the president being concurrently the head of state and the head of government but also a reflection of a country's particular history, often involving struggles for independence that saw strong figures subsequently emerge as presidents (such as George Washington in the United States or Sukarno in Indonesia). These historically rooted beliefs in the centrality of the president can breed tendencies toward autocratization—both from the perspective of the president, who naturally seeks to consolidate power, and from that of the population which accepts this expansion of authority. Indeed, some ambitious autocrats have created presidential systems to profit from the aura of power naturally associated with presidentialism. In Turkey, for instance, Recep Tayyip Erdoğan found that his autocratic ambitions were best served by switching from a parliamentary to a presidential system in the second half of the 2010s (Esen and Gumuscu 2018).

Given this risk of personalization and autocratization, it is somewhat ironic that one of the earliest substantive political science debates on presidentialism focused on its alleged inherent weakness and instability. In the early 1990s, emerging presidentialism discussions were mostly concerned with whether presidential systems are stable enough to guarantee effective governance. In his seminal essay "The Perils of Presidentialism," Juan Linz (1990) warned that presidentialism was not a good option for young democracies, and that parliamentarism was vastly superior. He justified this view by highlighting the dual and often conflicting democratic mandates for the president on the one hand and the legislature on the other; the unavoidable tension between the two, especially if a president did not hold a strong majority in the legislature; the winner-takes-all mechanism of presidential elections that produced much frustration among losers; and the incompatibility of the president's role as symbolic head of state with the partisanship of being chief executive. Thus, in his view, presidentialism—even in its purest form and relatively uncomplicated settings—had too many built-in flaws to make it a recommendable option for democracies, especially young ones.

The situation is more complex in systems that have both presidents and prime ministers with strong powers, and in regimes that see presidents operating in fragmented multi-party systems. In the former, which are typically called semi-presidential systems, a particularly difficult constellation can arise if presidents and prime ministers come from different parties. In France, such constellations are referred to as cohabitation and have occurred three times between 1986 and 2002 (Conley 2007). Similar semi-presidential contexts exist in Central and Eastern Europe, with many post-communist societies opting for a high level of power dispersal after decades of authoritarian rule (Elgie and Moestrup 2012). In presidential systems with multi-party systems, on the other hand, chief executives often are confronted with a constellation in which no party has a legislative majority. As Chaisty, Cheeseman, and Power (2017, 1) recognized, minority presidents in multi-party systems embody two contemporary trends at once: first, the move toward direct presidential elections in many younger democracies; and second, the shift toward ever-more diversified party systems, some of which have become atomized. In such systems, presidents constantly need to build and maintain coalitions to stay in power and govern effectively. Latin

America, East and Southeast Asia, Africa, and parts of Eastern Europe have a high contraction of such presidential systems operating in a multi-party environment.

While Linz's claims accurately captured the challenges and complexities of presidents working in difficult institutional terrain, his conclusions met with significant opposition. Most importantly, many authors argued that he exaggerated the notion of the unworkability of presidentialism. In a first substantial response, Mainwaring (1993) remarked that Linz's criticisms were only valid for a specific form of presidentialism: that is, a polity in which the president faces a highly fragmented multi-party system. Consequently, presidents operating in stable two-party systems, such as the United States, were unlikely to face the problems Linz described. According to this critique, presidents who hold legislative majorities in low-fragmentation multi-party systems were also shielded from major executive-legislative fallouts.

In the next step of de-problematizing presidentialism, authors began to question whether even presidents in severely fragmented multi-party systems fared as badly as Mainwaring and others suggested. Significantly, this included presidents far from holding a legislative majority. While Chaisty, Cheeseman, and Power eventually developed this approach into the concept of coalitional presidentialism, they credited others for introducing the ideas that a) power-sharing can occur under presidentialism and b) that it happens in the form of multi-party presidential coalitions more often than initially thought. Concretely, they pointed to Shugart and Carey (1992) and Cheibub, Przeworski, and Saiegh (2004), who demonstrated that Linz's rigid separation between winner-takes-all presidentialism and coalition-building parliamentarism was misguided, and that presidents can deploy power maintenance strategies normally ascribed to parliamentary systems. One stream of this literature went further and argued that not only did coalition-building occur in presidentialism and parliamentarism alike, but that it produced comparable excesses in both systems. Drawing from the work of Katz and Mair (1995) on competition-limiting party cartels in Western Europe's parliamentary systems, these authors pointed to similar patterns in Latin American and Asian presidentialism. In their work on Bolivia and Indonesia, Slater and Simmons (2012, 1366) revealed "powersharing arrangements [that] prove so encompassing as to make a mockery of putative partisan differences, and even to wipe out political opposition entirely by bringing every significant party into a 'party cartel.'" In short, not only does coalition-building occur in presidential systems, its ramifications are similar to those found in parliamentary regimes.

The important work by Slater and Simmons has been part of a trend to revisit the "perils of presidentialism" paradigm, but in different ways than initially intended by Linz. The latter believed that presidentialism was essentially ineffective and prone to collapsing through inter-institutional conflict. By contrast, contemporary critics of presidentialism emphasize that it is the absence of such conflict that can be the problem—either because presidents pursue successful autocratization projects or because they build coalitions that reduce political competitiveness. These critiques are useful correctives to the coalitional presidentialism model designed by Chaisty, Cheeseman, and Power, which remains largely silent on the possible implications of minority presidents' successful coalition-building for a country's democratic trajectory. Nevertheless, the notion of coalitional presidentialism has been a breakthrough in the study of presidentialism, forming a significant part of the foundation for this book.

Coalitional Presidentialism

Chaisty, Cheeseman, and Power (2017, 14) define coalitional presidentialism as "a strategy of directly elected minority presidents to build stable majority support in fragmented legislatures, specifically via the coordination of two or more legislative parties by the president." At the core of their analysis are the specific mechanisms through which presidents achieve such majority support; however, they base the notion of coalitional presidentialism on seven propositions established by other authors between the 1990s and 2010s. First, the size of the president's party determines how much political capital a president has to invest in gaining a majority in legislature. In this view, the closer a president's party gets to the magic 50-percent mark in the legislature, the fewer instruments of coalitional presidentialism are typically deployed. As we will see later, the size of post-2004 presidential parties in Indonesia has been relatively small (holding around a quarter of legislative seats), which partly explains the strong impetus for coalitional presidentialism in the country. Second, the extent of constitutional powers at a president's disposal decides the strength of the bargaining position he or she has in negotiations with potential coalition partners. These powers vary from country to country and shape the specific type of coalitional presidentialism a polity develops (Carey and Shugart 1998). Third, the level of cabinet discipline is linked to the proportionality of seat allocations in cabinet (Amorim Neto 1998). The more ministries are allocated strictly based on a party's result in the legislative election, the higher the level of cabinet discipline a president can expect. By contrast, if presidents allocate cabinet seats based on other principles and preferences, they risk defections and acts of disloyalty.

The fourth proposition ties the presence of non-party cabinet members to a president's willingness to act unilaterally, and thus outside of the traditional arena of coalitional presidentialism. The more non-party ministers (such as technocrats) operate in a cabinet, the more likely it is for a president to rule by decree. By contrast, a higher proportion of partisan ministers indicates a president's preparedness to engage in the conventional dealings of coalitional presidentialism. This proposition is relevant for the Indonesian context, as the country typically has a high percentage of non-party ministers (more than half), but this is not necessarily an indication of lower levels of coalitional presidentialism. On the contrary, if we understand the concept of presidential coalition-building as not limited to the party and legislative arenas, then the inclusion of non-party actors is a sign of a broader approach to coalitional presidentialism. Fifth, the prevalence of particularistic, non-programmatic parties in a polity forces presidents to apply patronage-related strategies of coalition-building but also gives chief executives a chance to preserve a maximum amount of their policies (Ames 2001). Moreover, it leads to more flexibility in coalition-building and more frequent changes in cabinet. This may mean that presidents cannot achieve permanent coalitions, but it also allows them to play parties against each other and extract greater concessions. Sixth, rather unsurprisingly, presidential coalitions become less stable as the next election nears and parties re-align with different candidates.

Finally, Chaisty, Cheeseman, and Power (2017, 17) draw from the existing scholarship that membership of the presidential coalition or the opposition becomes a new "meta-cleavage in political life." This cleavage transcends ideological or value differences and becomes the main political identifier of parties in the legislature. This proposition has certain limits, however: if a party system includes a large number of particularistic, non-programmatic parties, coalition-building can be fluid, and the demarcation lines of this "meta-cleavage" can be re-drawn quickly, either by the president or by the parties.

Based on these seven propositions, Chaisty and colleagues introduce their set of strategies that presidents use to build majority coalitions in the legislature. We already considered their "toolbox" of coalitional presidentialism, ranging from a president's legislative powers to exchange of favors. In developing their model, they take a highly legislature-centric approach. They consolidate this preference further by defining coalitions as "floor-based" rather than based on cabinet membership. Their main definition of a coalition member is therefore "parties and legislators [who] consider themselves to be, and are seen by others (especially the formateur), as belonging to the pro-presidential bloc in the assembly on a stable basis" (Chaisty, Cheeseman, and Power 2017, 216). Although for them the distinction between floor-based and cabinet-based coalition membership is merely an issue for their quantitative calculations (they found that under the former definition, the number of presidential coalition partners was

25 percent higher across their country studies compared to a cabinet-based analysis), the differentiation is paradigmatic. If applied consistently, a cabinet-based definition of presidential coalition partners would allow for (and indeed, require) an expansion of the range of actors examined. In the Indonesian case, as in many other Asian democracies, military officers, police generals, bureaucrats, or Muslim clerics sit in cabinet. Under Chaisty, Cheeseman, and Power's definition, they are only of interest as non-partisan minsters outside of the arena of coalitional presidentialism. If they were to be situated as coalition partners similar to parties, a new arena of inquiry would open.

Empirically, Chaisty, Cheeseman, and Power focused on democracies and hybrid regimes in Sub-Saharan Africa, post-Soviet republics, and Latin America. In Sub-Saharan Africa, they studied Benin, Kenya, and Malawi; in the former Soviet Union, they looked at Armenia, Russia (until 2004), and Ukraine; and in Latin America, they investigated Ecuador, Brazil, and Chile. This is an admirably wide range of countries, but it misses the insights from another world center of presidentialism: East and Southeast Asia. For instance, South Korean or Taiwanese presidents have often had a minority position in their respective legislatures, and Philippine presidents have been model "artists" of coalitional presidentialism; like in no other country, Philippine presidents typically turn minorities into supermajorities within weeks after winning elections. And then there is Indonesia. Emerging from fifty years of authoritarianism in 1998, Indonesia built a democratic system in which presidents have a strong constitutional position but have to share power with the legislature and other actors. This has led to notoriously large "rainbow coalitions" (Diamond, 2009) and complaints by presidents that Indonesia's polity resembles a semi-presidential or semi-parliamentary system. Consequently, presidents often rely on other actors than parties to stabilize their rule. Thus, Indonesia is a major Asian example of coalitional presidentialism and provides a great opportunity to test whether Chaisty, Cheeseman, and Power's legislature-centric approach can be fruitfully expanded to include other players. At the same time, Indonesia's slow democratic decline offers the chance to explore to what extent this erosion is connected to the practices inherent in its contemporary coalitional presidentialism.

Indonesia

In addition to its broad suitability as a case study, there are more specific reasons why Indonesia is a near-perfect laboratory to explore the dynamics of coalitional presidentialism. The country adopted a presidential system when declaring independence from the Dutch colonial power in August 1945, and presidents thus have been at the center of political affairs since the beginnings of Indonesia as a nation. Importantly, too, Indonesia experienced various manifestations of presidentialism throughout its history. The first phase, *executive presidentialism* amid the conflict with the Dutch, only lasted until November 1945, when power effectively shifted to the provisional parliament and its prime minister. Founding president Sukarno stayed in office, but had his powers significantly curtailed (Kahin 1952). This constellation remained in place after the end of the war and the proclamation of a new provisional constitution in 1950, which created a *ceremonial presidency* placed on top of a parliamentary system (Feith 1962). With the help of the army, Sukarno grabbed power from parliament in 1959 and reinstated the 1945 constitution, resurrecting presidential supremacy (Lev 1966). With his 1959 coup, Sukarno initiated four decades of *autocratic presidentialism*, in which the country's supreme legislative body nominally elected the president (and thus, strictly speaking, operated in a hybrid system). But the autocratic character of Indonesia's presidentialism meant that the legislative institutions simply rubber-stamped the president's election and decisions, making him the most powerful actor in a regime created by him. Suharto, coming to power after an alleged communist coup attempt in 1965, further entrenched autocratic presidentialism. Indeed, Suharto became the embodiment of Indonesians' notions of an all-powerful president, both as a symbol of the state and as executive ruler (Elson 2001).

After Suharto's fall in 1998, the new democratic leaders decided to amend, rather than replace, the 1945 constitution that had underpinned autocratic presidentialism (Horowitz 2013). This approach initially produced a *hybrid and transitional presidentialism* that was inherently unstable. Until 2004, the president was not elected directly but by the People's Consultative Assembly (MPR) which, in turn, consisted of members of the legislature—the People's Representative Council (DPR)—as well as appointed delegates representing regional and functional groups. Indonesia's first post-authoritarian president, Abdurrahman Wahid, was elected this way. But his chaotic presidency (1999–2001) showcased that the old constitution lacked the necessary ingredients for a modern presidential democracy. Most importantly, there was no clear mechanism for presidential impeachments, leading to a trial-and-error process that removed Wahid from office in 2001. Consequently, one year later, the Indonesian elite established a detailed catalog of regulations on the presidency. Through the final round of constitutional amendments in 2002, it was stipulated that the president would be elected by popular vote from 2004 on; impeachment procedures were clarified in a way that made presidential removal difficult; presidents retained full ministerial appointment powers, but the legislature received confirmation authority for some non-cabinet positions (such as judges); and, as in the past, the president and the legislature were situated as co-legislators, although the overall transformation of the DPR from an authoritarian rubber stamp body into an autonomous institution meant that the legislature's role in lawmaking would significantly increase (Crouch 2010).

Based on Mezey's definition, therefore, it was not until 2004 that Indonesia witnessed the arrival of full democratic presidentialism—that is, a system in which the president and the legislature are elected separately and democratically. Not coincidentally, 2004 also marked the beginnings of an institutionalized regime of *coalitional* presidentialism. The three presidents before 2004 had built semi-coalitional cabinets, but they had done so amid irregular circumstances unlikely to be replicated in post-amendment presidentialism. B. J. Habibie, Suharto's vice president in 1998 and his constitutional successor, was allowed to rule ad interim by a broad elite consensus (Elson, 2013). Once Habibie signaled ambitions to re-contest the presidency in the MPR in 1999, however, the elite removed him from competition by rejecting his accountability report. Wahid, for his part, falsely believed that he was unimpeachable; for him, coalition-building was only an instrument of gaining power, not a precondition for maintaining it (Mietzner 2001). Firing ministers one month into his presidency, he quickly self-destructed. When his vice president, Megawati Sukarnoputri, replaced him, she was given elite assurances—similar to those granted to Habibie—that she would be allowed to serve her term without disruptions until 2004 (Crouch 2002). In other words, Habibie and Megawati did not need continued coalition support to rule during their terms because they had received alternative (albeit temporarily limited) guarantees, and Wahid erroneously thought he did not require such support at all. None of these transitional presidents, then, made use of strategies of coalitional presidentialism to develop and, especially, sustain presidential coalitions over time. If they reached for the coalitional presidentialism toolbox, this was done for short-term gains.

In consequence, this book focuses on the presidencies of Susilo Bambang Yudhoyono (2004–2014) and Joko Widodo (2014–2024) to illustrate the workings of coalitional presidentialism in Indonesia. They were the first to operate under the new presidentialism put in place with the 2004 elections, ending the transitional arrangements in both formal and substantive ways. Moreover, both men started out as minority presidents and ended up ruling with large legislative majorities; both sustained broad presidential coalitions over a decade, doing so first with a view toward re-election and then toward securing their presidential legacy as well as dynastic continuity; both expressed fears of impeachment to justify incessant compromising with their coalition partners, despite the strong safeguards against such impeachment in the amended constitution; and both were convinced that non-party actors were as important to the architecture of their presidential power as political parties and the legislature. Accordingly, Yudhoyono and Widodo were agents of coalitional presidentialism par excellence, with their re-elections and high approval ratings demonstrating that they understood how to use its tools effectively over extended periods. At the same time, the trend of democratic decline beginning in Yudhoyono's first term and accelerating during the Widodo presidency provide important insights into the potentially damaging side effects of coalitional presidentialism for the democratic fabric of young post-authoritarian societies.

In addition to having a rich and turbulent history of presidential regimes, Indonesia is well suited as a case study of coalitional presidentialism because of its moderately stable party system, and the relative strength of some of its parties if compared to, for instance, the Philippines or South Korea (Croissant and Völkel 2012). In the Philippines, parties are little more than shells that individual leaders appropriate for presidential runs or other electoral purposes. With few exceptions, parties are often abruptly founded, merged, and disbanded, depending on the needs of politicians in specific electoral contexts. This constellation has made it easy for incoming presidents to pull legislators on their side, even if the former controlled only a minimal share of legislative support at the time of the election. In Indonesia, by contrast, parties hold a stronger bargaining position vis-à-vis presidents and thus pose a more significant challenge to the latter to deploy carefully crafted strategies of coalitional presidentialism. To be sure, parties have gradually weakened in Indonesia, too, largely because of the country's shift to personality-based rather than party-centered elections since the mid and late 2000s (Mietzner 2020). But some parties remain deeply rooted in specific socio-ideological constituencies, and they retain a loyal voting base. For example, Indonesia's leading party, the Indonesian Democracy Party—Struggle (PDI-P), originated in the nationalist movement of the 1920s, with the daughter of the initial founder—Sukarno—still chairing it at the time of writing in 2023. Other parties are less institutionalized, and their orientation is more catch-all in nature, but overall the Indonesian party system has shown a level of stability that makes tracing the impact of coalitional presidentialism more useful than in systems dominated by short-lived parties.

This book's situating of the post-2004 Indonesian polity as a case of coalitional presidentialism, and its suggested focus on party as well as non-party actors, builds on the important work of other authors. Dan Slater, for instance, analyzed the phenomenon of oversized presidential coalitions in Indonesia since the Wahid and Megawati cabinets of the early 2000s. He used the paradigm developed by Katz and Mair to describe Indonesian presidential coalitions as party cartels guided by the collective interest of its members to avoid accountability, seek access to patronage, and sustain a system of collusive democracy (Slater 2004, 2018).

Usefully, Slater viewed the military as part of the Wahid and Megawati era cartels—but he did so largely because the generals still held unelected seats in the legislature and the MPR at the time. Slater's work—further developed by Ambardi (2009)—was crucial in advancing our understanding of how oversized coalitions function, and how they can damage democratic quality. As I explained elsewhere (Mietzner 2013), I believe that the cartelization approach overstates the extent of collective unity of purpose among party elites; misses the continued ideological divisions between parties; and understates the role of the president in managing coalitions. This book, in response, proposes that the coalitional presidentialism approach is better equipped to grasp the centrality of the president in forming and disciplining coalitions; capture the significance of material and ideological tensions between coalition partners; explain how these conflicts allow presidents to play coalition partners off against one another; and highlight the equal importance of non-party actors in coalitions.

Some authors have previously used the coalitional presidentialism lens to study aspects of Indonesian politics. The most advanced of these studies has been that of Dirk Tomsa (2018). One of his particularly valuable contributions has been to introduce non-party players as part of presidential politics—but he stopped short of positioning them as members of presidential coalitions. Instead, he classified them as "strategic groups [that] are defined here as extra-electoral veto actors with significant power resources whose support or lack thereof can make or break a president" (Tomsa 2018, 274). For Tomsa, these groups include oligarchs, the military, and conservative Islamic groups. As extra-coalitional veto actors, however, they remain outside of the coalitional presidentialism strategies that presidents normally would apply to political parties and legislatures. This book will show that non-party groups and their interactions with presidents should be analyzed in the same way as parties, given that both are represented in cabinet and have similar rights and obligations. Another instructive finding of Tomsa's study was "the important role of political ideas and narratives that constrain presidents just as much as interests and institutions" (2018, 267). This emphasis draws our attention away from the almost ubiquitous focus on patronage as the guiding motive of politicians in Indonesia and beyond. While indeed a key motivation of politics, patronage and rent-seeking are often intertwined with major conceptual and ideological debates over what orientation the state should take, both in terms of the extent of its democratic liberties and the role given to religion. These conflicts, as those related to access to funds, often play out within the specific parameters of a polity's type of coalitional presidentialism.

A rich body of literature exists on the informal politics that feed and frame such intra-elite conflicts, in Indonesia and elsewhere. These studies informed my conceptualization and empirical assessment of coalitional presidentialism in Indonesia. For example, Aspinall's seminal 2010 article on the "irony of success" in Indonesia touches on many aspects covered in this book: the appeasement of veto powers that kept them from sabotaging the polity; the concessions made to them that made this outcome possible; and the damaging effects these deals have had on the prospects of consolidating democracy (Aspinall 2010). In many ways, this book expands and conceptualizes Aspinall's approach by explaining in detail the mechanisms of this veto power accommodation through coalitional presidentialism—and how the informal politics of patronage have become increasingly formalized. This book also borrows from the work of Hadiz and Robison (2004), who have established the political economy approach to studying contemporary Indonesian politics. While not fully sharing their view of the dominance of oligarchic forces in Indonesia's polity (as this relegates all other actors, including the president, to puppets of the wealthy elite), this book's discussion benefits from their insights into how political power is exercised behind the scenes. It also finds strong similarities between their stress on the elite's predatory interests and the coalitional presidentialism literature's emphasis on the exchange of favors as a crucial element of the president's toolbox to control leading political actors.

In the context of such elite accommodation dynamics, this book is also concerned with the link between consolidating coalitional presidentialism arrangements and declining democratic quality. Again, Indonesia offers a unique opportunity to study this relationship. Since the mid-2010s, much has been written on Indonesia's democratic stagnation and, subsequently, regression (Tomsa 2010; Power 2018). It suffices here to briefly establish some fundamental evidence for this erosion. To begin with, leading democracy indexes recorded a slow but significant decline in democratic quality in Indonesia—in line with patterns in other countries. This decline occurred after the country reached its democratic peak between 2004 and 2008. Freedom House, for instance, upgraded Indonesia to "free" status in 2006, giving it its highest point score in 2008, but downgrading it again to "partly free" in 2013.[2] Similarly, as shown in figure 0.1, the Liberal Democracy Index designed by Varieties of Democracy (V-Dem), which covers the period from 1900 to 2021, points to a democratic peak between 2004 and 2008, and a descent from thereon. To be sure, none of this means that Indonesia has crossed over into non-democratic territory. It means that a young, defective democracy stopped improving after 2008 and lost some of the democratic substance it had accumulated after 1998. Indonesia, then, remained an electoral democracy at the time of writing in 2023, but one with increasing illiberal tendencies in the elite and society at large.

PRESIDENTS, COALITIONS, AND INDONESIA 17

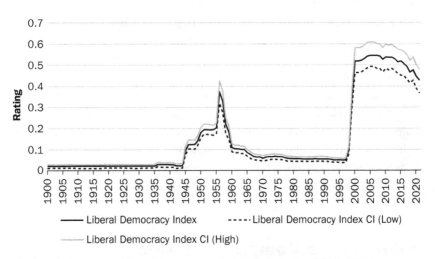

FIGURE 0.1 V-Dem Liberal Democracy Index, Indonesia, 1900–2021

Indonesia's democratic decline has been visible on many fronts. The first signs of democracy receding emerged in the second half of the 2000s in the arena of religious and political minority rights protections. Increasing attacks on non-orthodox Muslim sects or non-Muslim houses of worship, tolerated by the state, highlighted an expanding influence of Islamist groups on senior politicians (Bush 2015). From 2009 on, there were also growing concerns about the rise of vote buying in elections (Muhtadi 2019), the shrinking of political space for small parties (Mietzner 2020), and fewer choices in presidential elections (in the latter, the number of candidates decreased from five in 2004 to three in 2009 and just two in the 2014 and 2019 elections). Internal party democracy (which had been weak from the beginning) further eroded, with oligarchs having the best chances of capturing party leaderships. Executive illiberalism (that is, the tendency of power holders to use autocratic tools against opponents) became prominent in Widodo's first term and a common feature in his second (Power 2020). There were also open calls to rethink electoral democracy as a whole, with some floating the idea of withholding voting rights from poorer citizens (in local elections) and others demanding that presidential elections be returned to the MPR. Conceptually, these trends were framed in what Warburton (2016) called the "new developmentalism" of Widodo's era, which unapologetically subordinated democratic values to the need for economic development. This approach echoed that of the former autocrat Suharto, who had justified repression by his successful delivery of economic growth and the political stability required for it.

Indonesia, therefore, promises to deliver important insights into the practice of coalitional presidentialism and its correlation with democratic decline. This is not only because of Indonesia's importance as the world's third-largest democracy and its fourth most populous nation; rather, it exhibits all the features of coalitional presidentialism and democratic dynamics that make it a fruitful case study for a broader phenomenon. Indeed, as the next section shows, while Indonesia sits at the top end of stability in terms of its coalitional presidentialism regime, many other polities have exhibited similar patterns, both in terms of the tendency towards building broad-based coalitions as well as the erosion of their democratic quality.

Indonesia in Comparative Context

At the outset of this book, we noted Indonesia's striking transformation from a feeble presidential regime in 1998–2004 into an exceptionally stable polity after the country's 2002 constitutional amendments were put in place. We also observed that Indonesia's stability stood out from many of its peers internationally, and indicated that the country's full adoption of coalitional presidentialism practices after 2004 was the main contributor to that outcome. Part of Indonesia's adoption of coalitional presidentialism was the inclusion of a wide variety of non-party actors into its coalitions—the importance of which has been understudied so far in conventional coalitional presidentialism studies. We also acknowledged that Indonesia's democratic quality decreased as the stability of its presidential strengthened—and that by doing so, it followed a global democratic recession trend. In the following discussion, we must test these hypotheses against measurable data. Hence, we have to compare Indonesia against other presidential systems, especially those widely considered to also practice coalitional presidentialism, albeit in country-specific forms.

The selection of the countries to which Indonesia is compared in this section was guided by literature-based, institutional, and regional factors. Including some of Chaisty, Cheeseman, and Power's case studies ensures that this book communicates directly with theirs. Kenya, Chile, and Brazil are discussed here because they were important examples of coalitional presidentialism in their work (Chaisty, Cheeseman, and Powers 2017, 43). But to broaden the regional focus of our comparison, additional countries—which also conform to the institutional profile of coalitional presidentialism—were included. From the Asian continent (which was not covered by Chaisty, Cheeseman, and Power), we look at South Korea and the Philippines; and from Latin America, we add Peru and Bolivia (Julcarima Alvarez 2020; Albala 2021), which recorded some particularly dynamic processes in their presidential coalitions in the last few years. Overall, then, we have cases from three continents and some sub-regions within them, providing a good geographical spread. As for the investigated timeframe, we focus on 2004 to 2021, the period in which Indonesia's current arrangements of coalitional presidentialism are investigated in this book.

We begin by testing the stability component. The stability of presidential systems can be measured in many ways, but some core indicators seem to be especially suitable for comparison. The first and second relate to the incidence and success of impeachment proceedings against a sitting president. Impeachment attempts point to cracks in the presidential coalition, while successful impeachments deliver clear evidence of its breakdown. Thus, we will separately list the occasions in which impeachment processes were officially launched (as opposed to simply being talked about) and cases of actual impeachments. The third broad indicator is a president's loss in his or her fight for re-election. Although multiple factors may cause incumbency losses, one key determinant is usually the level of the president's ability to keep his or her coalition together, both during the term and in elections. Coalitions that fall apart as presidents face re-election challenges indicate severe problems in that coalition, making it hard for a president to return to office. Conversely, incumbency wins suggest that coalitions worked effectively and that voters rewarded such effectiveness. Some countries have one-term presidencies, and this will be noted accordingly. Fourth, we look at possible legal prosecutions of presidents after they leave office (Helmke, Jeong, and Ozturk 2019). Such prosecutions highlight acts of post-coalitional revenge, which in most cases involve the opposition and other actors who felt slighted by the president. In combination with the other three, this indicator gives us a good hint at problems in the coalition, especially if one-term presidencies prevented a run for re-election.

Table 0.1 showcases that Indonesia sits at the high end of the coalitional presidentialism stability scale. It recorded no attempted or successful impeachment between 2004 and 2021, saw no president losing his bid for re-election, and witnessed no prosecution of a former president either. This all points to a tightly knit elite that seeks affiliation with presidents while in office and is ready to protect them after they leave it. It also suggests relatively high levels of public satisfaction with the arrangements put in place; at least voters returned the practitioners of coalitional presidentialism to office every time. In the other assessed countries, stability indicators are more mixed, or even highlight great instability. Three of the seven non-Indonesian countries examined here experienced at least one attempted impeachment; four had successful impeachments; and five charged at least one of their former presidents, with two committing suicide to escape imprisonment. One country (Peru) recorded multiple successful

TABLE 0.1. Stability indicators of coalitional presidentialism in selected countries, 2004–2021

COUNTRY	ATTEMPTED IMPEACHMENT	SUCCESSFUL IMPEACHMENT	INCUMBENCY LOSS	POST-OFFICE PROSECUTION
Indonesia	x	x	x	x
Kenya	x	x	Election re-run (2017)	x
Chile	Pinera (2019)	x	One-term presidency	X
Peru	X	Kuczynski (2018), Vizcarra (2020), Merino (2020, resigned)	One-term presidency	Toledo (2016–2020), Humala (2017), Kuczynski (2019), Garcia (2019, committed suicide), Vizcarra (2021)
Brazil	x	Rousseff (2016)	x	Da Silva (2017)
Bolivia	x	Morales (2019, resigned)	x	Áñez (2021)
Philippines	Arroyo (2005–2008), Aquino (2014)	x	One-term presidency	Arroyo (2012–2016)
South Korea	Roh (2004)	Park (2016)	One-term presidency	Roh (2009, committed suicide), Lee (2018), Park (2018)

impeachments, and two (Peru and South Korea) launched criminal proceedings against various ex-presidents. Peru is at the bottom of the stability index, with impeachment and other forms of presidential removal the norm rather than an exception. After seemingly going down a similar path between 1998 and 2004, Indonesia took the opposite direction, with presidents taking office having a good chance of securing re-election, finishing their terms, and staying out of legal trouble during their post-presidential careers.

This does not mean, however, that Indonesia's example is extreme and incomparable to other cases of coalitional presidentialism. Kenya, for instance, has seen few attempts to remove sitting presidents—its instability problems are more related to ethnically charged, violent, and disputed elections (Klaus 2020). Similarly, the Philippines recorded no serious challenges against presidents Benigno Aquino and Rodrigo Duterte. Indeed, in the latter's case, his total dominance over the political system, including the legislature, became a source of concern (Kasuya and Teehankee 2020). Chile also enjoyed relative stability, with only one failed impeachment attempt in 2019—the first in over six decades. (That attempt was largely symbolic, as it targeted an outgoing president who was not eligible to seek re-election after two non-consecutive terms.) Hence, while the exceptional stability of Indonesia's post-2004 presidential regime is intriguing, it can be integrated effectively into a cluster of other cases with similar arrangements for comparison and contrast.

In the next comparative step, we need to ask how Indonesia is situated vis-à-vis other systems of coalitional presidentialism in terms of the broadness of their coalitions. Is Indonesia an outlier with its systematic inclusion of non-party actors as equal partners in presidential coalitions? Or do we find similar patterns elsewhere? We look at four indicators in our seven non-Indonesian comparison cases to assess this. The first is the strength of the president's party in parliament (more specifically, the lower house). Presidents whose parties hold a majority in parliament have become increasingly rare, putting them under pressure to consolidate their alliances inside and outside parliament. Regardless of the strength of the president's party, however, the president might not have a strong position in his or her own party (Indonesia being a prominent example). Thus, we take as our second indicator of coalitional dynamics whether a president is the chairperson of his or her party. The third indicator examines the size of the presidential coalition in parliament, giving us a sense of whether presidents seek to build supermajorities or are content with gathering a 50-percent-plus-one majority. Fourth, and crucially for our context, we assess the percentage of cabinet positions held by non-party actors. Taken together, these criteria (all of which reflect the state of affairs in late 2021, for reasons of consistency in cross-country comparison) will point us to either a case of Indonesian exceptionalism or common patterns of broad coalitions integrating non-party actors—or something in between.

Table 0.2 highlights that presidents whose parties control only a small minority in the lower house are most likely to build oversized legislative coalitions well beyond the 50-percent mark, and are also somewhat more likely than others to include a large proportion of non-party actors in their cabinets. Indonesia, Brazil, and the Philippines have seen constellations in which presidents have built bloated coalitions in the lower house, although their parties were far from an absolute majority and thus faced a tougher challenge to achieve majority status. At the same time, they also heavily turned to non-party figures to fill their cabinets. It appears, then, that at the heart of a president's drive to create oversized party and non-party alliances is a sense of insecurity overcompensated by the production of unnecessarily big coalitions. As this book demonstrates, this fear was certainly a motivator for post-2004 presidents in Indonesia. In Peru, President Pedro Castillo did not have a legislative majority at all, but he, too, integrated a high percentage (more than half) of non-party actors into his cabinet. Evidently, both large party coalitions and the inclusion of non-party figures (either in combination or separately) can serve as insurance policies for presidents

TABLE 0.2. Presidents, parties, and non-party actors in selected countries, 2021

COUNTRY	SIZE OF PRESIDENT'S PARTY (% OF SEATS IN LEGISLATURE)	SIZE OF PRESIDENTIAL COALITION (% OF SEATS IN LOWER HOUSE)	PRESIDENT AS CHAIRPERSON OF HIS/HER PARTY	PERCENTAGE OF CABINET SEATS HELD BY NON-PARTY ACTORS
Indonesia	22	82	No	55
Kenya	49	49	Yes	57
Chile	44*	44	No	30
Peru	28	39	Yes	53
Brazil	10**	59***	No	61
Bolivia	58	58	No	0
Philippines	20	87	Yes	70
South Korea	56	59	No	53

* Chile Vamos, alliance of four parties.
** President left his party in 2019.
*** 302 legislators who voted for president's candidate for speakership in February 2021.

concerned about their rule's stability. We can conclude, therefore, that the pattern of Indonesia's coalitional presidentialism—which rests on these two pillars—is not a phenomenon exclusive to this country but shared by others.

To be clear, the blunt assessment of the presence of non-party cabinet members tells us little about their backgrounds and why they were included. Some presidents may appoint non-party technocrats to "secure expertise" and "to avoid agency loss that comes with surrendering a key portfolio to a coalition partner," as Chaisty, Cheeseman, and Powers (2017, 229) speculated. Given the lack of concrete comparative data on this matter, in-depth country studies are necessary to fully understand the extent and political significance of non-party participation in presidential coalitions. As we will see in the Indonesian case, presidents also include non-party members with a clear-cut political calculus of recruiting the latter's groups into the coalition. Indeed, integration into cabinet is only one element of coalition-building, with additional material and policy concessions typically cementing the deal. The prominence of the phenomenon of strong non-party representation in cabinets built on coalitional presidentialism principles (when in the United States, for instance, non-party ministers are extremely rare) again suggests that the analysis of coalitional presidentialism needs to go beyond the arena of presidential-legislative relations, and must take a much closer look at what happens in the non-party space. Not doing so might overlook trends that could be decisive for a president's fate: Bolivia's Morales, for example, was not removed from office only by parties or the legislature; ultimately, the military and the police told him to go.

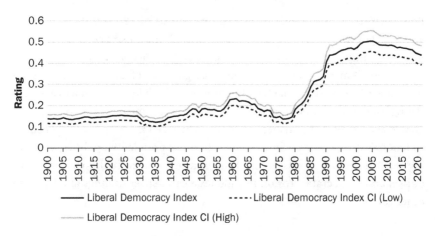

FIGURE 0.2 V-Dem Liberal Democracy Index, Latin America, 1900–2021

Finally, we need to test whether Indonesia's democratic decline—while developing coalitional presidentialism as the organizing principle of its presidential regime—is an anomaly or part of a broader pattern. To achieve this, we can use a composite of democratic decline trends in Latin America as a proxy. This is because Latin America exclusively exhibits presidential systems and is the focus of coalitional presidentialism studies outside of Eastern Europe. As a result, V-Dem's Liberal Democracy index for Latin America can serve as a useful guide for tracing the democratic quality curve in the continent's presidential regimes. As figure 0.2 demonstrates, Latin America and Indonesia followed similar trends—at least after 2004, which is the period that concerns us most (obviously, the third wave of democratization began earlier in Latin America than in Indonesia, but this is of little relevance for this book). Importantly, in both cases, the indexes note a peak in the middle of the 2000s at above the 0.5 mark, with a subsequent decline in the early 2020s to about 0.45. Thus, the trend of democratic decline we identified in Indonesia is similar in other countries with coalitional presidentialism regimes, both in terms of the extent and timing.

In sum, the comparative contextualization of the Indonesian case has shown that the country scores high in the stability of its coalitional presidentialism system; the size of its presidential coalition in the legislature; and the level of integration of non-party actors in cabinet—but not to the extent that would make it an incomparable outlier among its peers. On the contrary, the detailed analysis of Indonesia's coalitional presidentialism patterns undertaken in this book can deliver important hints toward areas of investigation that need to be deepened in other countries. For example, studying how coalitional presidentialism outside of Indonesia accommodates the vested interests of militaries (relevant in

Bolsonaro's coalition), police forces (highly influential in Bolivia), bureaucracies and local governments (essential in all countries), the oligarchy (powerful even in high-quality democracies such as Chile), or religious organizations (revered across Latin America and Africa) would be a good start for a comparative study of presidential coalitions that base themselves on both legislative majorities and strong backing by key non-party veto actors. At the same time, the comparative analysis has identified statistical similarities between the broad development of Indonesia's democratic decline and that in other presidential polities, suggesting that this book's investigation of the linkage between coalitional presidentialism and democratic erosion in Indonesia can deliver findings applicable to other countries.

Coalitional Presidentialism Redefined

Based on the conceptual, empirical, and comparative considerations outlined thus far, this book proposes to amend the definition of coalitional presidentialism developed by Chaisty, Cheeseman, and Power to better fit systems in which presidents not only seek to build stable majority support in fragmented legislatures but also to integrate non-party actors into their coalitions to stabilize their rule. The countries where this occurs are mostly younger democracies with security forces, bureaucracies, and religious groups that play key political roles and thus require courting by the president. Many Latin American and African countries fall into this category, and some Asian presidential systems, too, have long histories of non-party veto players that became part of a president's support infrastructure. Against this background, this book defines coalitional presidentialism as a *strategy by presidents in multi-party systems to build stable majority support in the legislature and integrate influential non-party actors into their governing coalitions.* These broad coalitions are designed to fend off potential attempts at presidential impeachment and allow for more effective governance. The non-party actors included in presidential coalitions can be veto players but do not have to be. Tsebelis set a high bar for this status by defining them as "individual or collective actors whose agreement (by majority rule for collective actors) is required for a change of the status quo" (Tsebelis 1995, 298). Under our definition of coalitional presidentialism, it is sufficient for a non-party actor to have the potential to develop into a veto player to be included in the list of actors a president might wish to include in his or her coalition.

Broadening the scope of coalitional presidentialism means connecting the concept to different streams of political science literature that have so far been excluded from it. In the case of the military as a potential presidential coalition partner, this makes the existing civil-military relations literature highly relevant. In Indonesia, the number of former military officers in cabinet has roughly remained constant throughout the post-1998 polity (at about four or five in each ministry), despite the fact that the armed forces lost their non-elected seats in the legislature and the MPR in 2004. This suggests that presidents continue to view offering the military direct political participation as crucial to their rule, as generals might assume a key role in political crises. The civil-military relations literature posits such an approach as an appeasement strategy (Croissant 2013, 271). By integrating military representatives into the presidential apparatus, executive leaders hope to purchase the armed forces' endorsement of the democratic system in general and the incumbent president in particular. Presidents might also choose to apply other strategies—such as monitoring, sanctioning, appointing loyalists, creating splits in the ranks, and so forth—but granting political and material concessions to the armed forces by privileging them with equal status to coalition parties is a favorite approach by presidents who are keen to avoid open confrontation with the military. Under such an arrangement, the military remains nominally subordinated to the president, but the former can extract rewards from the latter for acquiescing to his or her rule.

In the case of the bureaucracy, situating it as a part of presidential coalitions links it to the extensive literature on politicized bureaucracies. This politicization can occur in the form of the executive trying to subjugate civil servants to its partisan interests (Alemendares 2011) or the bureaucracy—as a corporate actor—attempting to defend its vested interests at the cabinet table or other government forums (Aberbach, Putnam, and Rockman 1981). In Indonesia, President Yudhoyono experienced the latter phenomenon in 2013 when he tried to push for extensive civil service reform but was opposed by senior bureaucrats who feared their privileges could be at risk. Ultimately, Yudhoyono backed down and endorsed a much watered-down version of the reform. The campaign against the reform initiative was driven by the head of the civil service organization (Korpri), who was also the secretary-general of the Ministry of Home Affairs. This meant that the target of reform sat at the table when the executive discussed it, and could undermine it both from within and through external mobilization. The tradition of the Korpri headship being held by a senior Ministry of Home Affairs official has continued, integrating the civil service into the presidential power apparatus it is supposed to neutrally serve. Since Yudhoyono's experience, no further major administrative reform was launched, with key bureaucrats able to pre-empt such moves at their inception.

Similarly, the analytical inclusion of oligarchs into the study of coalitional presidentialism can draw from a large body of literature on oligarchic influence in new and old democracies. This influence is typically exerted through donations to politicians and subsequent demands for rewards, funding of lobbying groups that push for specific policy initiatives favoring the wealthy, or direct participation in party politics and presidential cabinets (Winters 2011). In Indonesia, all these forms of influence have manifested themselves (Robison and Hadiz 2004), but there is little need to uncover its deeper, hidden layers as oligarchs have actively and visibly engaged in politics. Oligarchs have been party chairpersons and ministers, with the second Widodo cabinet initially featuring five oligarchs in cabinet and several ministers representing parties chaired by oligarchs. The way these actors have promoted oligarchic interests has been anything but subtle. In 2020, the coordinating minister for economic affairs, an entrepreneur chairing a large party, oversaw the passing of a major package of deregulation measures that cut benefits for laborers and reduced environmental protections that businesses had for long complained about (Lappin 2020). President Widodo approved this package, partly because he hoped it would accelerate economic growth but also because such concessions to oligarchic interests constituted an integral element of coalitional presidentialism. Oligarchs who fund presidential campaigns and operations—and the many aides presidents require—are a main pillar of this power constellation.

The integration of religious actors into presidential cabinets has also been analyzed within a literature that has so far remained distinct from that exploring the dynamics of coalitional presidentialism. Although not necessarily members of parties or the legislature, representatives of influential religious movements can be useful additions to presidential coalitions for several reasons. They can give the president a devout image and thus help him or her penetrate particularly conservative segments of the electorate; they can handle religious conflicts that other state officials find difficult to manage; and they can reach out to extra-parliamentary actors from the religious right that might threaten the president's rule. In return, religious actors recruited into cabinet or other presidential institutions can access state funds to support their various communities, and lobby for legislation and government regulations promoting their religious needs. These phenomena are typically discussed by a literature focusing on how secular leaders diffuse the repercussions of rising religious conservatism, with a particular emphasis on Islamism. In this literature, strategies of both accommodation and repression are investigated (Mustafa Şen 2010), and both approaches have been present in Indonesia. Facing a major threat from an Islamist mass mobilization against his government in 2016 and 2017, Widodo accommodated the more centrist of the Islamic conservatives and repressed the most radical Islamist margins (Fealy 2020). As a result, a conservative Islamic cleric who had initially endorsed the 2016/17 movement became Widodo's vice president in 2019, while more hard-line Islamist leaders were penalized.

Despite its broadening, an integrated model of coalitional presidentialism can still focus on the five main instruments contained in the presidential toolbox that Chaisty, Cheeseman, and Power described. Constitutional-legislative authority, partisan powers, cabinet appointment rights, budgetary authority, and exchange of favors are not only key presidential assets to ensure the loyalty of political parties, but they are also deployed to keep non-party coalition partners in check. However, as this book will show, the specific character of each actor requires slightly adapted presidential strategies that reflect the actor's power, status, and constitutional setting. For instance, when designing strategies to deal with the military, presidents have to weigh their constitutional authority in military oversight against both the institutional strength of the armed forces and the possibility of generals going rogue by challenging the executive in unconstitutional ways. Thus, the armed forces need to be managed with adjusted tools that align with this context (for example, through the president's grooming of loyalist officers). The police, bureaucracy, and Islamic groups also require presidential approaches that are in line with, but modified versions of, the five conventional toolbox instruments. This book's detailed analysis of how these instruments are used in each context delivers a portrait of what Indonesian presidents can do to establish effective governance—and what the limits of their powers and coalition-building efforts are. Importantly, this portrait also showcases the potentially damaging effects that using the instruments of coalitional presidentialism—whether applied successfully or unsuccessfully—can have on a country's democratic quality.

The picture that emerges is one in which presidents are neither all-dominant figures nor puppets of vested interests. Rather, they are tasked with balancing the presidency and its coalition partners in a way that serves the agenda of both sides in equal fashion. Indeed, it is this carefully calibrated balance that best describes the power distribution in stable cases of coalitional presidentialism. (By implication, unstable or failed cases typically produce either autocratization or impeachment of the president, depending on which side is advantaged by the imbalance.) In the Indonesian context, which has witnessed remarkably stable coalitional presidentialism arrangements since 2004, such an assessment corrects analyses that have viewed President Widodo alternatively as a reincarnation of Suharto (Maulia 2020) or a weakling struggling for agency (Muhtadi 2015). Under coalitional presidentialism, Indonesia has neither crossed the line into autocracy, nor have presidents been fully overpowered by their allies. In an effort to sustain the coalition's balance and the general stability of the polity, however, the practice of coalitional presidentialism has led to democratic stasis and decline, raising questions about whether the quest for stability (which was Linz's primary concern) is itself the source of democracy's decay.

Methodology and Structure

Chaisty, Cheeseman, and Power (2017, 42) used a small-N comparative approach that relied on a data set of coalition and cabinet membership in their case study countries and on survey data gathered from legislators across the respective polities. These data were enriched by qualitative analyses of actor behavior in various country settings. This methodology revealed important patterns that applied throughout multiple countries and set up a useful comparative scale for the intensity of presidential power and coalitional presidentialism. However, this book uses a different method. While it contextualizes the Indonesian case within the criteria defined by Chaisty, Cheeseman, and Power, it relies much more on in-depth qualitative analysis than they did. The reason for this lies in the significantly broadened spectrum of analyzed actors. Whereas the Chaisty, Cheeseman, and Power approach is focused on presidential-legislative relations, and makes heavy use of quantitative indicators such as the effective number of parliamentary parties, the seat share of the presidential party, or an "index of coalitional necessity," this book enters more diverse arenas. As indicated above, Indonesian presidents have built oversized coalitions well beyond the threshold of an absolute majority, and they added a wide range of non-party actors, formally and informally. To capture the motivations and practices that drive these oversized coalitions, both from the president's and his or her partners' perspectives, the value of quantitative data analysis is not as high as in a narrow presidential-legislative relations examination.

Accordingly, this book offers a fine-grained analysis of presidential politics in Indonesia that investigates how executive leaders integrate political actors into their coalitions. Quantitative data are used when necessary, but the main emphasis is on understanding why and how actors engage in coalitional presidentialism, and how the oversized coalitions resulting from it operate in practice. Hence, a qualitative methodology based on semi-structured interviews, process tracing, and participatory observation is best suited for this book (de Walt and de Walt 2011). The book draws from twenty-five years of research on Indonesian presidents and their partners. During this time, about 150 interviews were conducted with presidential aides, party officials, legislators, Muslim leaders, military and police officers, and bureaucrats. Interviews with presidents Yudhoyono and Widodo provided insights into what motivates presidential coalition-building, and observing them during travel and campaign rallies added much to my understanding of how they interact with other actors. Having spent time at the presidential complex and in key ministries in Jakarta, I was able to observe the operations of the president's staff office and how it manages cabinet members. The same applies to the legislature, where I watched many key events of post-Suharto presidential politics unfolding since 1998, from the election of Wahid in 1999 to the passing of the constitutional amendments in 2002 and important votes in the 2010s. Similarly, I attended party congresses at which presidents were either celebrated or ostracized by their parties, depending on their relationship at that moment in time.

The book also bases its examination on documents and regulations issued by the presidential office, ministries, political parties, and other actors involved in presidential coalitions. Analyses of media coverage and social media accounts are integrated into the investigation, too, as they help us understand how actors use public communications to position themselves in political negotiations with the president and others. Finally, while I did not conduct targeted surveys of elite actors—given the breadth of the actor spectrum covered in this book, this would have been impractical—I have used opinion survey data collected by the Indonesian Survey Institute (LSI) and other survey institutes I have worked with on several projects between 2017 and 2020 (Mietzner and Muhtadi 2018, 2019, 2020; Mietzner, Muhtadi, and Halida 2018; Fossati and Mietzner 2019). These surveys contain popular and elite views, among others of the presidency as an institution as well as the performance of specific presidents. Analyzing such surveys allows us to gain a comprehensive perspective of how the post-Suharto Indonesian presidency has been reflected in and shaped by public and elite views. In combination, these documents, media analyses, and surveys—explored using the standard techniques of critical discourse analysis (Widdowson 2004)—add substantively to the interviews and direct observations of elite actor behavior.

It is important to note that the book's qualitative approach to in-depth analysis complements—rather than replaces or challenges—that offered by Chaisty, Cheeseman, and Power. It goes deeper where a small-N study comes to its limits and brings to life political processes that appear rather abstract in quantitative analyses. But it pursues the same aim: that is, to highlight how presidential coalitions are built and run, and to underline that they are—contrary to what Linz claimed—now a main staple of politics. In fact, they are now so common that we need to consider their unintended side effects, especially as they relate to the potential "perils of stability."

The expanded definition of coalitional presidentialism, and the methodology applied, also informed the structure of this book and its chapters. The book begins with an overview of the presidency, discussing its historical development, constitutional powers, organizational set-up, and coalition-building strategies. The second chapter looks at political parties and how they have interacted with Indonesian presidents, both in supporting and opposing them. The third chapter separately examines the role of parliament in presidential coalitions—this is necessary because individual legislators often act outside of their parties' mandate and thus require special attention from presidents who want to secure legislative support. Reflecting the broadened paradigm of coalitional presidentialism that looks beyond presidential-legislative relations, the subsequent chapters focus on the military, the police, the bureaucracy, local administrations, oligarchs, and Muslim organizations. In each of these chapters, the discussed actors are considered key members of presidential coalitions, equal to parties and legislators. Each chapter explores the constitutional and material leverage actors have in dealing with the president and what leverage the latter holds over the former. In negotiating these competing powers, typically an equilibrium is reached in the form of a specific arrangement under which an actor participates in presidential coalitions. The conclusion highlights the structural patterns of coalitional presidentialism in Indonesia, places it in a comparative context, and points to its stabilizing and damaging effects on democracy. It substantiates the hypothesis that while coalitional presidentialism helps to explain Indonesian democracy's endurance, it also caused and sustained many of its defects.

1

THE PRESIDENT

Any discussion of the dynamics of coalitional presidentialism in a particular country must start with a detailed analysis of the role presidents play in the larger political landscape of that nation. The powers entrusted to a president vary widely from country to country, even in systems typically described as purely presidential. Presidents can have different appointment and decree powers; their authority to initiate legislation is strong in some countries and weaker in others; they may or may not have significant veto powers; and their budgetary authority can differ substantially (Metcalf 2000; Bradley and Morrison 2013). Moreover, as Mezey (2013) reminds us, the role of a president is not only the sum of his or her functional powers. Rather, it reflects how a nation's population perceives the president and the extent to which citizens expect a president to embody their collective aspirations. These perceptions and expectations, in turn, are born out of a nation's specific history and the contribution of presidents to it. In the United States, for instance, leagues of presidential historians are routinely commenting on how the performance of a sitting president compares to that of prior presidents and how the incumbent conforms to or violates historically grown standards of presidential conduct or policy (Beschloss 2007). In France, presidents are seen as continuing a national history that predated the creation of the presidency (Derfler 1983), with the official presidential residence, the Élysée Palace, having been used by Napoleon Bonaparte, Louis XVIII, and the presidents of the Second Republic. Thus, the public perception of the French presidency is drawn from a rich history that began in the early nineteenth century.

From the early beginnings of the Indonesian republic, the president has formed the key pillar in the country's institutional and ideological architecture (McIntyre 2005). Although this primacy of the president was disrupted for about a decade from the mid-1940s to the mid-1950s, since then the centrality of presidentialism has remained unquestioned. As briefly alluded to in the introduction, presidents have ruled during both autocratic and democratic periods, and although our analytical interest in coalitional presidentialism directs our focus to the latter, there is no doubt that the specific manifestation of presidential coalitions in Indonesia owes much to the legacy of previous authoritarian experiences. Many contemporary Indonesians' view of the country's presidency has been shaped by the ways through which founding president Sukarno and longtime autocrat Suharto—who were in office a combined fifty-three years until 1998—carried out the functions of the office. In a survey conducted in February 2020, 24 percent of Indonesians listed Suharto as their favorite president; Sukarno was only slightly behind, at 23 percent; and the incumbent, President Widodo, was at level with Sukarno (Adinda Putri 2020). These results not only suggest that many Indonesians approve of strongman presidents but also that they expect the presidency to be the central organ of power. The poll also indicates that any incumbent president has to both respond to the specific political constellation of the day and measure himself or herself against historical expectations of presidential behavior set by Sukarno and Suharto.

It is important, therefore, that our discussion of coalitional presidentialism in post-Suharto Indonesia is based on a sound understanding of the historical origins and development of the presidency. The first section of this chapter provides sketches of the discussions on the 1945 constitution; the changes to presidential power made in late 1945 and again in 1949 and 1950; the rise of autocratic presidentialism in 1959; its further consolidation under Suharto; and the adaptation of the presidential system to the new democratic context after 1998. Subsequently, the chapter explains the current powers of post-authoritarian presidents as enshrined in the constitution, which was amended through four rounds of revisions between 1998 and 2002 (Horowitz 2013). These powers keep evolving and are constantly fine-tuned through laws and government regulations, but the broad outlines of presidential authority can be presented as the constitution has not changed since 2002 (Butt and Lindsey 2002). The third section then illustrates the organizational arrangements that guide the operations of the presidency. This discussion explains the inner workings of the palace administration itself as well as the political and formal functions of its three main support bodies: the state secretariat, the office of the cabinet secretary, and the office of the chief of staff of the president. Finally, the chapter highlights some of the main approaches through which post-2004 Indonesian presidents have built coalitions to stabilize their rule. These general descriptions of coalitional presidentialism strategies provide the background for the much more detailed analyses in the remaining chapters of the alliances built with each actor.

Historical Origins

In the first half of 1945, the Japanese military administration—which had occupied the archipelago since 1942—allowed selected Indonesian leaders to meet and discuss ideas as to how best prepare for independence (Anderson 1972). As the Japanese military position was dire, it was clear to everyone involved that decisions had to be made quickly. Thus, when the Investigating Committee for Preparatory Work on Indonesian Independence (BPUPKI) met for the first time in late May 1945, many issues of fundamental importance were only touched upon rather than deeply deliberated. However, there seemed to be broad agreement that Indonesia's political system needed to be governed by a strong leader. In one of the first BPUPKI sessions, prominent legal expert and future minister of justice, Soepomo, explained that "a head of state has to be able to lead all people. The head of state has to stand above all groups and must have the attitude of [wanting to] unite the state and nation. Whether this head of state will be positioned as king [*raja*] or president or . . . as Führer is not directly relevant to the principle of government arrangements" (Sekretariat Negara 1995, 41–42). Some BPUPKI members justified this call for a strong leader with stipulations in Islamic scripture, while others viewed it as the logical consequence of the independence struggle and the need for unity. Hence, there was no lengthy discussion on weighing up the alternatives of parliamentarism, which the Dutch colonial power practiced, and presidentialism. During the discussions, the term "president" was adopted to replace the more general "head of state" used in earlier discussions. After the explosion of the atomic bomb in Hiroshima on August 7, 1945, the debates on the constitution were accelerated further, independence was declared on August 17, and the final version of the constitution was passed the following day.[1]

Under this 1945 constitution, the president was to be elected by the MPR (Article 6-2). The MPR consisted of the legislature (DPR) and an unspecified number of representatives from regional and functional groups (Article 2-1). No stipulation existed on how the composition of the DPR was to be decided, or how regional and functional groups should be appointed. Theoretically, therefore, the DPR did not have to be democratically elected, and other MPR members could be non-elected delegates as well. These regulations appear to have been the result of the impracticality of holding elections in the near future (as it turned out,

Indonesia would be waging war against the returning Dutch between 1945 and 1949). But the vagueness of constitutional rules surrounding the composition of the MPR and DPR stayed in place until the end of the Suharto era. One of the core elements of the original 1945 constitution even survived the post-1998 transition: that is, the positioning of the president and the legislature as co-lawmakers. Neither the president nor the DPR could make laws without the agreement of the other (Articles 5, 20, and 21), which forced both into a relationship of mutual dependence and established incentives for informal consensus building. Outside of lawmaking, however, the president enjoyed a high level of autonomy: the appointment of ministers did not require approval from the legislature (Article 17); the president was the commander in chief (Article 10); and he or she could declare a state of emergency (Article 12).

But opponents of Sukarno and the executive presidency enshrined in the constitution managed to effectively suspend the latter through a series of moves in October and November 1945. Many of these anti-presidential activists had been excluded from the BPUPKI, which was dominated by "senior civil servants and nationalist politicians who had worked for the Japanese military administration" (McIntyre 2005, 7). Consequently, after the declaration of independence, the non-BPUPKI elements forced a fresh and intensified parliamentarism versus presidentialism debate on Sukarno, emerging as temporary winners. Their campaign was assisted by the fact that Indonesia, now facing the challenge of having to gain international recognition from major powers such as the United States and the Soviet Union, needed leaders who had not collaborated with the defeated Japanese. Sutan Sjahrir was the leader of this faction, and he succeeded in extracting major concessions from Sukarno, one of the collaborators (Mrázek 1994). First, in mid-October the legislative powers of the MPR and DPR, which a provisional stipulation in the constitution had given to the president before these two bodies could be formed, were transferred to the new Indonesian Central National Committee (KNPI), making it a quasi-parliament. Second, in early November the government allowed the formation of political parties. Third, in mid-November Sukarno agreed that the KNPI could form a cabinet responsible to it rather than the president, and that Sjahrir could act as cabinet formateur. Sjahrir was ultimately installed as Indonesia's first prime minister, marking the beginning of a parliamentary interregnum that would last, with some interruptions, until 1957.

After the war between the Dutch and the Indonesian republic ended in December 1949 with a negotiated settlement, two new constitutions were passed in quick succession (Soepomo 1964). The first was the 1949 Constitution of the Federal Republic of Indonesia (RIS), which came into force when the Dutch handed over full sovereignty to the RIS on December 27, 1949. In prior peace negotiations between the Dutch and the Indonesian republic, the former colonial power had insisted that the new Indonesia adopt a federal system. While the Indonesian side had grudgingly agreed, it did so in the knowledge that it would be able to subsequently overturn this concession. In the meantime, Indonesia adopted a RIS constitution that retained the roles of president and prime minister; gave the federal states power to select three cabinet formateurs; and established both a House of Representatives and a Senate. Under this arrangement, Sukarno's vice president Mohammad Hatta was prime minister, as he had been during the war on several occasions when the KNIP was paralyzed. But by May 1950, Sukarno was already in negotiations with the federal states about the dissolution of the RIS and a new constitutional framework. In these discussions, it was agreed that once Indonesia returned to its status as a unitary republic, it would not restore the original 1945 constitution. Instead, a temporary constitution would be adopted in which Sukarno remained president; the parliamentary system remained in place; the president would not be allowed to establish a non-parliamentary cabinet (Feith 1962, 96); and a Constitutional Assembly would be set up to pass a new permanent constitution. In August 1950, the RIS was disbanded, and the new temporary constitution of 1950 (UUDS 1950) was enacted.

Between 1950 and 1957, Indonesia's parliamentarism reached its peak, with the ceremonial president Sukarno watching from the sidelines as legislative cabinets exercised power (Legge 1972, 242). Importantly, however, Sukarno remained in the public's eye as the nation's symbol and charismatic figurehead. In extensive international travel, he represented the new nation abroad, and the 1955 Bandung Conference—which he organized, assembling many leaders from post-colonial states—positioned Indonesia as one of the key players in the African-Asian movement (Shimazu 2014). This image of Sukarno as the embodiment of the nation, at home and overseas, put him in a position in which he was likely to profit from any crisis of the parliamentary system. This crisis set in around 1956, only one year after the country's first parliamentary elections. Regional rebellions began to cripple the central government; the Constitutional Assembly, elected in 1956, was hopelessly deadlocked; and incessant corruption scandals ate away at the legitimacy of the parties and legislature. To be sure, Sukarno fueled these anti-party sentiments, and in the background he negotiated with the military over terms to return to the 1945 constitution. In March 1957, martial law was declared, followed by Sukarno's appointment of a presidential cabinet—despite the stipulations against such a move in the UUDS 1950 (Lev 1966, 22). After two more years of crisis, on July 5, 1959 Sukarno dissolved the Constitutional Assembly and declared Indonesia's return to the 1945 constitution. It did not concern Sukarno that neither of these acts was allowable under the UUDS1950. Indonesia's autocratic presidentialism had been born.

Sukarno's regime, which he called Guided Democracy, revived the executive presidency that had been envisioned in the 1945 constitution but only practiced for a brief moment. Crucially, however, Sukarno went beyond the spirit of the constitution, exploiting its vagueness to cement his autocratic rule. For instance, he disbanded parliament in 1960, replacing it with an appointed legislature that accommodated parties and groups that had pledged loyalty to his rule, including representatives from the armed forces (Feith 1963). As discussed earlier, the 1945 constitution did not specify how the DPR was to be elected, opening the door to Sukarno's operation. He also banned parties opposed to Guided Democracy—again, he profited from the absence of any mention of parties in the constitution. In 1963, the provisional MPR appointed Sukarno president for life, and while this exceeded the five-year terms set by Article 7 of the 1945 constitution, the supporters of his anointment could justify their motion with the MPR's near-unlimited powers. But in political terms, Sukarno's regime depended on the continued support of the military and the Indonesian Communist Party (PKI), and as the relationship between these two actors became increasingly tense, the foundations of Guided Democracy began to crumble by 1964 (Roosa 2006). Against the background of deteriorating economic conditions and political uncertainty, the military quelled what it claimed was a PKI-led coup attempt on September 30, 1965; gradually removed Sukarno from office between 1966 and 1968; and installed General Suharto fully in the presidency by 1968. Unsurprisingly, the new regime decided to stick with the 1945 constitution.

One of the reasons why Suharto's military-backed government opted to retain the 1945 constitution despite its close affiliation with Sukarno was the fallen president's careful autocratic re-interpretation of the initial document. For instance, Sukarno decided in 1959 to have Soepomo's president-centric elucidations of the 1945 constitution declared an integral element of the constitution itself. In these elucidations, which were re-confirmed by the new government in a provisional MPR decree in 1966, Soepomo had laid out the principles of state organization in a clearer fashion than the constitution itself (Nurtjahyo 1997). Among others, Soepomo had declared that "all state power" rested with the MPR, but that the president was its sole "agent" [*mandataris*]. Further, he specified that the president was the highest government official, and he added—in rather awkward English—that the "concentration of power and responsibility [are with] the President." Soepomo also clarified that the president did not report to the DPR—and neither did his or her ministers. Nevertheless, the president needed to get approval from the DPR for laws and the state budget. For Suharto, even more so than for Sukarno, this meant that control of the MPR was the key to further expanding the already extensive presidential powers enshrined in the 1945 constitution. Such control over the MPR, it appeared to him, was easy to accomplish as the constitution did not regulate the exact composition of the body, making it vulnerable to manipulation by whoever exercised real executive power. In post-coup Indonesia, power was firmly in the hands of Suharto and his military, and so they would determine how the MPR was assembled and what it would decide.

Suharto perfected his control of the MPR, and all other state organs, in a systematically and patiently pursued campaign between 1966 and 1973. In the late 1960s, he developed the military-backed Functional Group (Golkar) alliance as the regime's electoral machine, which won heavily manipulated elections in 1971 (Suryadinata 1989). Two years later, he forced the nine non-Golkar parties that had participated in the 1971 polls to merge into one nationalist party—the Indonesian Democracy Party (PDI)—and one Islamic party, the Unity Development Party (PPP). Tightly controlled, they formed a pseudo-opposition to the most senior regime (Aspinall 2005). In subsequent elections, Suharto—as president, the most senior leader of Golkar, and supreme commander of the armed forces—had the right to screen all Golkar, PDI, and PPP candidates for the DPR for possible security concerns and disqualify anyone who raised red flags. Thus, all members of the DPR were pre-approved by Suharto, regardless of the outcome of the elections held every five years (the military, for its part, was given a quota of non-elected seats). Additionally, Suharto signed off on the regional and functional representatives that made up the rest of the MPR. In other words, every MPR member was directly or indirectly appointed or approved by Suharto. Based on this artfully crafted system of presidential control, the MPR would re-elect Suharto every five years, perpetuating him in office until 1998. In that year, the Asian Financial Crisis caused much economic damage to Suharto's regime (Pepinsky 2009), triggering popular unrest and intra-regime splits that forced him to resign.

Initially, most post-authoritarian heirs of Sukarno's and Suharto's presidential system believed that they could continue operating within its framework while democratizing some of its key components. For instance, early post-Suharto leaders were confident that conducting democratic elections for the DPR would solve the main problem of the missing link between the MPR and popular accountability (Crouch 2010, 52–55). They also thought that a two-term limit on presidents, imposed through a 1999 constitutional amendment, was sufficient to prevent another Suharto-style autocratic presidency. Some politicians raised the possibility of a direct election of the president in the constitutional debates of 1999 (Yusuf and Basalim 2000, 160), but powerful actors argued against it. Among them was Megawati, Sukarno's daughter and the most popular politician in that period, who wanted to maintain as much as possible of the system that her father had created (McIntyre, 2005). But the idea of reconciling the pressures of a new democratic era with a presidential system misused by two successive autocrats was doomed from the beginning. As mentioned earlier, it needed Wahid's presidency, which came crashing down in his 2001 impeachment, to convince the elite that cosmetic changes to the constitution were inadequate. As a consequence, the fourth round of amendments in 2002 produced a new regime of presidentialism, based on direct elections and a re-arranged power balance between the president and other state organs. It was under this reformed system that coalitional presidentialism became fully practiced after 2004, replacing the transitional regime that had proved unsustainable.

Indonesia's turbulent history of presidentialism produced important legacies that continued to echo in the post-2004 polity. Most importantly, the 1945 revolution had situated the president as the nucleus of national political life, and while that role was challenged in the immediate post-independence period, it was permanently entrenched by two autocratic presidencies after 1959. At the same time, the political contestation of the 1940s and 1950s highlighted that other forces outside of the presidency sought accommodation, and that incumbents had to deal with them either by co-optation or repression (or a combination of both). The fact that both autocratic presidents, who had prioritized repression, were ultimately overthrown suggested to their post-1998 successors that co-optation of potential veto actors might be the smarter option as Indonesia democratized, setting the scene for coalitional presidentialism. Finally, with Habibie effectively removed by the MPR, Wahid impeached, and Megawati losing her bid for re-election in 2004, the presidents operating in the post-amendment environment had much to ponder in terms of what they could do better than both their toppled autocratic predecessors and the short-lived transitional presidents ruling after Suharto's fall. In many ways, then, coalitional presidentialism was a concept that amalgamized the experiences of all Indonesian presidents since the nation's inception. It recognized both the president's vulnerabilities and the strengths inherent in the office, combining them into a strategy that balanced the two in a stabilizing fashion.

Constitutional Powers

Studying presidential powers in any country is obviously dependent on the time period examined. For our context, investigating the powers of Indonesian presidents means discussing their post-2004 authority that can be leveraged to shape the contours of coalitional presidentialism and the alliances necessary to sustain it. Pre-2004 presidents either had no need to build formal coalitions because they were autocrats (Sukarno and Suharto), or they relied on elite guarantees given to them in the chaos of the post-Suharto transition that saw the constitution constantly changing under their feet (Habibie, Wahid, and Megawati). These presidents were precursors to, but not actors of coalitional presidentialism, and for these reasons, the detailed study of their powers in their respective periods is not essential. Rather, our focus is on those powers that presidents have had access to, and have deployed, since 2004. The individual chapters explain the powers presidents possess vis-à-vis each actor, but it is important to start our discussion with a general overview of the political assets handed to post-2004 presidents by the amended constitution.

To begin with, post-2004 Indonesian presidents enjoy high levels of popular legitimacy, which is a significant resource in their negotiations with other state and non-state actors (Fukuyama, Dressel, and Chang 2005). This legitimacy is bestowed on them through a direct popular vote, which replaced the previous mechanism of indirect election through the MPR. In 1999, Abdurrahman Wahid won the presidential elections in the MPR despite the weakness of his party, which had gained only 12 percent of the votes in the preceding legislative elections. The party of his opponent, Megawati, had obtained almost three times as many votes. Entering into several backroom deals with the military and other parties, Wahid prevailed (Mietzner 2000), but his lack of a clear popular mandate, and his misguided belief that the legislature and MPR could not disrupt his presidency, predisposed him to impeachment. By contrast, post-2004 presidents can point to their direct election to fend off challenges to their rule. This legitimacy is strengthened through the run-off mechanism, by which candidates who do not win an absolute majority in the first round of the elections will face the second-placed nominee in the final round. This sets Indonesia apart from the Philippines and the United States, for instance, where presidents can win office with a minority vote share. In Indonesia, an additional stipulation seeks to prevent candidates from concentrating their campaign on the most populous island of Java, where about half of the country's citizens reside. Successful candidates must win at least 20 percent of the votes in at least half of the provinces. Both Yudhoyono and Widodo won compelling victories between 2004 and 2019, and polls showed that about 70 percent of the population accepted them (Octaviyani 2019).

Indonesian presidents can also rely on constitutional arrangements that make presidential impeachment unlikely (Santika 2019). Any impeachment process must start in the DPR, in which a relevant motion has to receive a two-thirds majority in a session attended by at least two-thirds of its members. Effectively, this means that the absence from the House of a little more than one-third of MPs supportive of the president can stop an impeachment proceeding early on. Should an impeachment motion get the necessary number of votes, the motion is then assessed by the nine judges of the Constitutional Court (a body created by the 2002 constitutional amendments). In their deliberations, the judges (three of whom are appointed by the president, three by the DPR, and three by the Supreme Court) must establish whether the president has committed a "legal offense in the form of treason, corruption, bribery, or other serious criminal code violations or reprehensible acts." Only if the judges affirm this can the motion against the president be submitted to the MPR for a final vote that must be attended by at least three-fourths of its members. Again, the absence of one-fourth-plus-one members of the MPR—which since 2004 consists of the members of the DPR and the senate-style Region's Representative Council (DPD)—can foil the impeachment. If more than three-fourths of MPR members attend the impeachment vote, two-thirds of them have to vote in the affirmative for the president to be removed. Between 2004 and 2021, not once was the first stage of this process initiated. As noted, this contrasts sharply with some Latin American and East Asian presidential systems that have a high incidence of impeachments.

The introduction of direct elections and high impeachment thresholds reflected a broader pattern of post-2004 presidents benefitting from a substantial disempowerment of the MPR (Sorik and Aulia 2020). No longer the body that elects presidents, other powers were taken away from the MPR as well. Most crucial among them has been the MPR's previous authority to issue Broad Outlines of State Policy (GBHN). These GBHN bound elected presidents to a set of policy principles that they subsequently had to implement during their five-year term. The GBHN were abolished after 2004, giving presidents greater authority to set policies and change them quickly should circumstances demand. In the late 2010s and early 2020s, conservative politicians, including Megawati, raised the idea of re-instating the GBHN (later repackaged as Fundamentals of State Policy [PPHN]), in an effort to restore some of the powers party leaders had lost through the 2002 amendments. Initially, President Widodo spoke out strongly against this initiative, arguing that the restitution of the GBHN would unduly constrain presidents and make it impossible for them to respond to sudden policy crises (Syahrul 2019). He later softened his stance, however. At the time of writing, the constitution has not been amended again, leaving presidents free of the obligation to follow guidelines set by the MPR. Similarly, MPR decrees—which in the past were issued on matters of great importance and were legally superior to laws—have no longer been issued in the post-2004 period. While some old MPR decrees remain in place and retain their legal validity (Wicaksono 2013), new ones have not been added, giving presidents more leverage in designing laws and implementing policies.

In the post-2004 polity, Indonesian presidents have maintained their co-legislative powers, a major instrument in their interactions with parties, legislators, and other actors. Unlike in other presidential systems where the executive's co-legislative authority is regulated through a complicated mechanism of vetoes and counter-vetoes (Hoff 1991; Alemán and Schwartz 2006), Indonesian presidents must give their approval in joint deliberations with the DPR for a law to be passed. Indeed, formal legislative deliberations cannot begin if the president refuses to appoint an executive representative (most frequently, a minister) for these discussions. In a final DPR session, legislators vote on a bill, and the president's representative simultaneously expresses approval. Subsequently, the president has to sign the new law within thirty days, but it comes into force even without such a signature. In some cases, presidents used this staged process to blame the legislature for the passing of controversial bills—when, in fact, their governments had approved them. In 2014, Yudhoyono's home minister endorsed—in the president's name—a bill abolishing direct elections for local government heads. Yudhoyono expressed his opposition to the bill but struggled to explain why his government had formally supported it in the relevant DPR session, and he finally was forced by a public outcry to issue an emergency decree in lieu of law to overturn it. Five years later, Widodo did not sign an unpopular revision to the anti-corruption law that his government had agreed to in joint talks with the DPR. Unlike Yudhoyono, however, he did not overturn it, indicating that his refusal to sign the law was primarily designed to shift responsibility for the initiative from the executive to the legislature.

The instrument of an emergency decree that Yudhoyono used in 2014 to overturn a law is one of many weapons in the president's regulatory arsenal. Formally called a Government Regulation in Lieu of Law (Perpu), this emergency decree becomes law from the time the president issues it until the DPR has a chance to vote on it in its next session. DPR rejections of a Perpu are rare; for example, in 2008 the DPR refused to endorse a decree on financial regulation but also did not formally reject it. Instead, the DPR asked the president to submit a new bill, leaving the Perpu in place (Harsono 2010). Below the Perpu, presidents can also issue Government Regulations (PP). These regulate details of governance typically not spelled out in laws. Given the significant frequency with which laws stipulate that further detail will be specified by government regulations, the authority over the latter gives presidents leeway to partially rule by executive orders. Further below government regulations, there are Presidential Regulations (Perpres), Presidential Decisions (Kepres), and presidential Instructions (Inpres). These are used for different purposes (Husen 2019), with Perpres often laying out political and development strategies, ratifying international agreements, and detailing the inner workings of ministries; Kepres formalizing the appointment of teams and their officials; and Inpres giving instructions to the executive on how to coordinate policies. While these regulatory instruments give Indonesian presidents a strong position, they do not allow them to fully rule by decree. Decrees can be challenged in court, and the DPR can demand changes to laws that would subsequently override the contents of government and presidential regulations.

The Indonesian president also has extensive budgetary powers. The president prepares the budget proposal, formally presents it to parliament through a speech (typically a few days before Independence Day on August 17), and subsequently passes it with the DPR in the form of a law. While the DPR has the authority to request changes and often does so, its "scrutiny tends to focus more on detailed line items than overall budget policy and strategic priorities" (Blöndal, Hawkesworth, and Choi 2009, 24). This is largely due to the primary interests of legislators in gaining access to patronage resources for themselves and their constituencies (Farhan 2018). This tendency, combined with the president's constitutional budgetary powers, leaves the executive much room for shaping the general size and direction of the budget while entering into compromises with individual legislators and parties over its details. As a result, although there have been occasional threats by the DPR to withhold endorsement of the budget—which, according to the constitution, would allow the president to apply last year's budget—post-2004 presidents have seen their budgets approved without major incidents. Any conflicts related to the budget are normally resolved behind closed doors by the give-and-take practices of coalitional presidentialism before it reaches the floor. Afterward, "it is almost impossible to track the history of a particular budget item or to understand why its allocation has decreased or increased" (Farhan 2018, 52), pointing to the often-discreet nature of coalitional presidentialism operations and the predatory behavior they enable.

As Chaisty, Cheeseman, and Powers (2017) indicate, presidential appointment powers are particularly important for heads of state to exert influence and attract coalition partners. This is no different in the Indonesian case. Presidents directly appoint ministers, executives of state-owned enterprises, some judges, the chiefs of staff of the army, navy, and air force, and the heads of state agencies; nominate the commanders of the military and police as well as ambassadors; have influence over civil service appointments; and can—in special circumstances—appoint replacements for governors, district heads, and mayors. Later chapters discuss in more detail the exact appointment authority and other powers Indonesian presidents hold over each coalition actor. But the brief sketch presented above already gives us some glimpses into the strong politico-constitutional position of post-2004 presidents. They are better protected from impeachment than many of their global counterparts, and the unique form of their co-legislative powers makes it impossible for the legislature to promulgate laws without presidential consent. Similarly, extensive budgetary and appointment rights give the presidency unrivaled political influence. Conversely, presidents have many incentives to engage a broad range of actors into their coalitions, given that they need the legislature's consent for their own bills and budgets, and that other actors—such as the military, the police, local administrations, or the bureaucracy—have either retained or gained significant powers in the post-2004 environment. Before analyzing in subsequent chapters how Indonesian presidents have managed such actors as part of their coalitions, the next section looks briefly at how the presidential office is organized to deal with this challenge.

The Palace

The way presidents operate within administrative structures is often an indication of their ability (or the lack thereof) to set their political and strategic agendas (Patterson and Pfiffner 2001). As is the case with other bureaucratic institutions, presidential organizations consist of a complex and entrenched network of pre-existing structures that can constrain and even dominate incoming presidents. Long institutional traditions and their defenders frequently aim to transform a presidential newcomer into an executor of the status quo, and more often than not, they are successful in that endeavor. However, some presidents come to office with a determination to shape the institutional infrastructure around them instead of being shaped by it. In most cases, a mixture between the new and the old emerges, with few presidents managing to completely reform the institutions administering the presidency but most leaving their individual mark on the set-up of their office. In Indonesia, for instance, President Widodo established the Office of the Staff of the President (KSP) at the beginning of his first term in 2014, addressing long-standing calls for a more efficient presidential administration. Yet he was unable, or unwilling, to realize more wide-ranging plans developed by some of his supporters for a complete restructuring of the presidential institutions left over from Suharto's three-decade rule. As we will see below, the fact that Widodo only managed to institute half-hearted reforms had to do partly with the strength of the existing structures, but also with interventions by coalition partners, his own uncertainty about what exactly he wanted, and his self-imposed physical isolation from the offices designed to assist him.

Since Widodo's post-2014 limited reform, the presidential administration consists of three main institutions, all located within the complex of the president's palace in the capital Jakarta. They are the State Secretariat, led by a minister; the Office of the Cabinet Secretary; and the abovementioned Office of the Staff of the President (see table 1.1). The State Secretariat has traditionally been the

TABLE 1.1. Organization of the presidential palace, 2021

PRESIDENT		
STATE SECRETARIAT	**CABINET SECRETARIAT**	**OFFICE OF THE PRESIDENT'S STAFF**
• Presidential Secretariat • Vice Presidential Secretariat • Military Secretariat • Ministry Secretariat	• Special staff of the president	• Deputy I (Infrastructure, Energy, Investment) • Deputy II (Human Development) • Deputy III (Economy) • Deputy IV (Information and Political Communication • Deputy V (Politics, Law, Defense, Security, and Human Rights)

most powerful of these offices, and it remains so today (Pangaribuan 1995). The State Secretariat assists the president with carrying out all of his or her functions as head of state and as head of government. That means preparing and scrutinizing bills, formalizing decrees to be signed by the president, managing media relations, overseeing the relationship with other state bodies, and a whole range of protocol tasks. The State Secretariat is the largest of the three presidential offices, and it has the Presidential Secretariat, the Vice Presidential Secretariat, the Ministry Secretariat, and the Military Secretariat under its coordination.[2] The minister leading the State Secretariat is usually a close confidant of the president, giving him or her not only formal but also immense informal influence. During Yudhoyono's second term, the position was held by Sudi Silalahi, who had known the president since 1971, when they began serving in the military together. Widodo, for his part, chose Pratikno, a fellow graduate from Yogyakarta's Gadjah Mada University. Thus, presidents recruit State Secretariat ministers mostly from non-party figures, whose main assets are discretion, loyalty, and competence rather than independent political clout. In the dynamics of coalitional presidentialism, they often deal with the non-party actors in the presidential alliance.

Sudi and Pratikno have given similar accounts of their role and the qualifications needed for it. According to Silalahi, "the less visible you are, the better. You must be seen as loyal but without own political interests. Then the president believes in you, and his partners also trust that you deliver messages without manipulating them in any way" (interview, Jakarta, September 8, 2014). As a former military general, he felt he had better access to the non-party side of the presidential coalition: "parties are not really my domain, I mostly leave that to others." Pratikno, who succeeded Silalahi when Widodo ascended to the presidency in 2014, similarly highlighted that in addition to the formal business of the presidency, the minister heading the State Secretariat "needs to handle a lot of the actors who seek access to the president and have particular requests; in order to do that, these actors must view me as a loyal aide to the president, and nothing else. And I think [Widodo] chose me partly because he knows that I don't have political ambitions or other masters. I'm just an academic" (interview, Jakarta, September 13, 2016). Like Silalahi, Pratikno initially did not view the interactions with the political parties as his main priority: "that's not my world. Pram [Cabinet Secretary Pramono Anung] is mostly in charge of that." In later years, however, Pratikno increasingly dealt with parties as well. One insider, describing the situation in 2023, observed that "whenever the president wants to tell party leaders that he can't meet a particular demand they made, he sends Pratikno to convey the bad news. When Pratikno comes, party leaders know it's official (confidential interview, Semarang, February 15, 2023).

Within the State Secretariat, the Military Secretariat has a special role in the president's efforts to build close relations with the security forces. In functional terms, the military secretary assists the president in carrying out his or her function as the supreme commander of the armed forces, especially when it comes to the appointment of the military chief and the chiefs of staff of the army, air force, and navy. The secretary also coordinates with the military in regard to the president's security arrangements. But more importantly, the office is a political link between the president and the military, and its holder has a good chance of subsequently being promoted to higher positions. For instance, Hadi Tjahjanto, who was the secretary from 2015 to 2016, became military chief in 2017. In that post, Tjahjanto was crucial in ensuring continued military support for Widodo, including in his re-election year of 2019. Under the coordination of the military secretary are the presidential adjutants, recruited from both the military (usually colonels) and the police (typically at the chief-commissioner level).[3] These adjutants carry out mundane assistance jobs, but just like the military secretary, they possess enhanced career prospects. For instance, Widi Prasetijono, Widodo's adjutant from 2015 to 2016, was promoted to the chief of staff position in the military's Central Java command in 2020 and as its commander in 2022. Another presidential adjutant, police officer Jhonny Edizzon Isir (2017), became deputy police chief of North Sulawesi in 2021. The Military Secretariat's personnel, then, solidify the president's ties with the military and (to a lesser extent) the police and are groomed by the president for future leadership roles.

The Cabinet Secretariat, as the name implies, deals more specifically with the management of the cabinet. This includes preparing cabinet meetings, holding briefings on particular policies and, in cooperation with the State Secretariat, analyzing and synchronizing bills. In the political and administrative hierarchy, the cabinet secretary sits below the minister heading the State Secretariat but holds considerable power because of his or her closeness to the president. Presidents have filled the position in different ways. Yudhoyono put loyal nonparty administrators in the post (before becoming State Secretariat minister, Silalahi was cabinet secretary), while Widodo first appointed Andi Widjajanto, the son of a politician of his party (PDI-P), to reward him for running much of his 2014 election campaign. However, Widjajanto had a tense relationship with Megawati, the PDI-P leader, and she ultimately demanded his dismissal. Thus, Widodo replaced him in August 2015 after less than a year in office. In his stead, he selected Pramono Anung, a former PDI-P secretary-general, who was a smooth operator and known to be close to both Megawati and Widodo. After his appointment, the relationship between Megawati and the president improved significantly, pointing to Anung's politically shrewd use of the Cabinet Secretariat as an operational bridge between Widodo and his party. On many occasions, Anung was able to resolve tensions between the president and PDI-P on policy or personnel issues before they erupted into the open (interview, Denpasar, August 8, 2019). As a party politician, he was well suited to interact on the president's behalf with "my friends, the other party leaders in the coalition" as well.

The Cabinet Secretariat also coordinates the special staff of the president. Special staff are hired to advise the president on specific matters, such as policy on the troubled provinces of Papua, or carry out certain tasks, such as preparing speeches or media summaries. The number of special advisers varies, but in 2019, twelve were appointed. The coordinator of the team was Ari Dwipayana, an academic close to State Secretariat minister Pratikno and a member of a team that had prepared Widodo's candidacy and advised him during the 2014 campaign. Another member of that campaign team, Sukardi Rinakit, also became a special staff of the president. The inclusion of presidential confidants into the structure of the palace bureaucracy helps presidents to establish a routine not dominated by the existing civil servants but by what the president wants. This process of entrenching presidential staff in an environment shaped by previous presidents and their bureaucracies often takes a long time. According to Rinakit, "it was difficult at the beginning. Most staff we had to deal with were from the Yudhoyono period, and because of bureaucratic rules, we could not easily shift them. In that context, having staff that the president already knows is very helpful. But even then, this process of adaptation is very slow—much of the first year [of the Widodo presidency] was spent on finding our feet" (interview, Jakarta, April 20, 2016). In short, the facility of special staff gives presidents a way to reward political assistants but also to circumvent the established civil service apparatus.

The Office of the Staff of the President (KSP) operates outside of the State and Cabinet Secretariats, and was only established in 2014 (Suyadi 2018). It grew out of an earlier office created by Yudhoyono in 2009, the so-called Presidential

Working Unit for Development Monitoring and Control (UKP4). The latter had the task of supervising the government's priority programs and submitting evaluations to the president, including on the performance of ministers. The head of UKP4, the tough-talking bureaucrat Kuntoro Mangkusubroto, had assembled a team of young, energetic experts, and by most accounts, delivered critical reports. The problem was, as Kuntoro admitted, that, "sometimes we would have liked the president to pay more attention to them" (interview, Jakarta, December 5, 2013). As a consequence, when Widodo took office in 2014, he dissolved UKP4 and set up the KSP. As the first chief of staff, whose position was designed to resemble the White House chief of staff in the United States, Widodo picked Luhut Pandjaitan, a retired general, entrepreneur, and former Wahid minister. Widodo and Luhut had owned a joint furniture business since 2007, and Luhut was instrumental in organizing and funding his 2014 campaign. Luhut initially used his private resources to get the office running, pointing out that "I even brought staff and some furniture from my old business office" (interview, April 29, 2015). He moved into an enormously sized office in the Bina Graha Building that had been used by Suharto but was subsequently shunned by all post-1998 presidents. Luhut recruited five deputies with different responsibilities, setting KSP up as the kind of executive office that previous presidents lacked.

But the KSP did not develop into such an office. Over time, it evolved into a body that fulfilled think tank and trouble-shooting functions but did not act as the president's main institution for political strategy. Judging from his personnel decisions, Widodo himself seemed unsure about the role he wanted KSP to play. After Luhut had shaped KSP in its early stages, Widodo replaced him as chief of staff in September 2015, moving him to a key ministry (Vice President Jusuf Kalla, among others, had complained about Luhut's increasing power). As his replacement, Widodo appointed Teten Masduki, an anti-corruption activist whose persona was the opposite of Luhut's—he had few private resources and political connections. Under him, KSP managed important crises spots; in 2018, for instance, the office's special staff Ifdhal Kasim helped resolve a sensitive land conflict in Ambon, where thousands had died in religious violence in the late 1990s and early 2000s (interview, Ambon, February 2, 2018). But senior staff criticized Masduki for not developing the KSP's full power potential. One of the five deputies at the time lamented that "we are not the office that we could and should be—we're mostly a think tank. We are not what the president and Luhut wanted us to be" (confidential interview, Canberra, September 17, 2016). Apparently taking the concerns seriously, Widodo removed Masduki in January 2018 and again put a Luhut-style figure into the chief of staff position—the former armed forces chief Moeldoko, an ambitious and resourceful general. During Moeldoko's tenure, KSP regained some of the clout it had under Luhut, but it did not emerge as the kind of presidential office that some Latin American presidents possess.

Finally, the physical architecture of presidential institutions also shapes the way presidents operate. Close proximity to the president is crucial for officials to ensure an effective administration of presidential tasks, but it can also make presidents feel controlled by bureaucrats. In Indonesia, none of the three presidential institutions managing the presidency are located in the presidential palace itself—officials of all bodies have to take walks of varying distances through the presidential complex to get to the president. Moreover, they mostly do so only when called. This means that even leading officials often have little knowledge of what the president does at any given time, as he or she works in the palace with only the closest advisers. This sense of distance has been intensified by the fact that neither Yudhoyono nor Widodo lived in the palace, and that the latter only irregularly conducted business there. Yudhoyono lived in his private residence in Cikeas on the outskirts of Jakarta, while Widodo opted for the secondary presidential palace in Bogor, about sixty kilometers to the south of the capital.[4] Over time, Widodo shifted much of his presidential operations there (Firmansyah 2015). As indicated above, this physical isolation has had advantages and drawbacks: on the one hand, presidents could escape attempts by the palace bureaucracy to appropriate him or her; on the other hand, the presidential administration often worked without direct leadership from the president. Politically, this physical set-up increased the importance of informal networks outside of the official presidential administration that Indonesian presidents can use to communicate with actors involved in their coalitions. These informal networks are specific to each actor and will be analyzed in later chapters.

The historical, constitutional, and institutional scene described in this chapter so far has equipped Indonesian presidents with a strong sense of their power but also with an acute awareness of its limitations. As we have seen in the last segment, presidents have under them an apparatus that they nominally control but are also suspicious of, forcing them to rely heavily on pre-presidency confidants to bend the presidential institution and its bureaucrats to their will. With this, the organizational portrait of the presidency is a mirror of its politico-constitutional evolution, showcasing both its resourcefulness and constraints. Flowing from this simultaneous sense of power and vulnerability is the determination of post-2004 presidents to secure their position through coalition-building. Against this background, we can now turn to the broad outlines that guide the building of such coalitions. As the later chapters deal with this alliance formation and maintenance in detail, the following section can limit itself to a brief sketch of post-2004 coalitions that will help to put this detail into a broader context.

Coalition-Building

The strong commitment of post-2004 presidents to the logic and practices of coalitional presidentialism is simultaneously predictable and surprising. It is predictable because this is what the coalitional presidentialism literature tells us they would do, and Indonesia's history and constitutional settings provide enough examples of presidential vulnerabilities for incumbents to be justifiably worried about their status. Both Yudhoyono and Widodo were minority presidents facing a fragmented legislature, and Widodo was not even in charge of his own party (indeed, he was not included in its leadership structure at all). Building a coalition to gain a majority in the legislature made sense to get bills passed and budgets approved. But it is also surprising in terms of the obsession they both displayed over the possibility of impeachment, and in terms of the size of the coalitions they assembled. Not only did Yudhoyono and Widodo build coalitions that held vast majorities—in fact, supermajorities—in parliament, but they also opted to integrate a wide range of non-party actors into their coalitions. Thus, they designed coalitions that were larger, and broader, than conventional coalitional presidentialism studies would deem necessary.

Yudhoyono and Widodo took very different pathways to arrive at their conclusion that large presidential coalitions were compulsory. Yudhoyono had been a senior minister under Wahid and was tasked with fending off the latter's impeachment. This experience had a profound impact on his views on his own presidency. "Almost every night," he recalled, "I told [Wahid] that we really didn't have the strength to confront the legislature. He would say, 'no, no, we're strong.' I told him that sometimes we have to give and take" (interview, Cikeas, December 2, 2014). Although impeachment regulations were subsequently changed, Yudhoyono retained his conviction that Indonesia's democracy was not only "multiparty but semi-presidential and semi-parliamentary." In this context, "it was my interest to ensure the continuation of government, so that it doesn't fall mid-term [di tengah jalan]. That allowed me to do many things, including economic development." In his analysis, presidents cannot rely on the popular mandate that the electorate has given them—"in my case, I was elected with 61 percent, but these voters turn into passive cells after the election. The battle then moves into parliament" and other arenas of society that also need to be prevented from creating "chaos" [kegaduhan]. At the beginning of his presidency, Yudhoyono faced exactly the kind of "chaos" he was so fearful of. Opposition parties held a majority in parliament, and they briefly blocked all of his initiatives. The situation was only overcome when his vice president took over the Golkar Party (then the largest in the DPR) two months into his term (Tomsa 2006). This gave Yudhoyono and Kalla a legislative majority, which Yudhoyono later enlarged further by integrating more party and non-party actors, securing the government's stability.

In contrast to Yudhoyono, Widodo initially believed that he would be able to rule effectively as a minority president. Indeed, his 2014 campaign was based on the premise that Yudhoyono had given too many concessions to his coalition partners, and that he—Widodo—would not repeat this mistake (Muhtadi 2015). Interviewed briefly before his inauguration, Widodo insisted that he did not need a majority. "If the DPR opposes me, I'll let the people know," he said, indicating that he might mobilize his voters against elite initiatives to obstruct his presidency (interview, Jakarta, September 15, 2014). Asked what he would do if the DPR rejected his budget, he smiled and said that "I would just use last year's budget, no problem at all." Brushing aside all doubts about the viability of this approach, he told the interviewer to "just watch me." But Widodo changed his mind very quickly. One experience was particularly important in triggering this change. When he put together his first cabinet, he included Maruarar Sirait, a PDI-P politician who had been one of the first in the party to call for Widodo's nomination. Megawati had felt slighted by Sirait's rapid support for Widodo, and she thus refused to endorse him for a cabinet seat. If Sirait was still included, she threatened, PDI-P would withdraw its support from the president (confidential interview with a Widodo adviser, Jakarta, April 28, 2015). In shock, Widodo canceled Sirait's planned appointment at the last minute. The event was a watershed in his presidency; from then on, Widodo took steps to enlarge his coalition, and within two years, he turned a 37 percent minority into a 69 percent majority in the legislature. As Yudhoyono, he was now convinced that he needed a large coalition to be safe from impeachment and—in his case—to increase his independence from his own party.

In their composition, therefore, the Yudhoyono and Widodo cabinets look strikingly similar. Table 1.2 shows the actors that were given seats in each of the cabinets built by Yudhoyono and Widodo between 2004 and 2019. The first thing one recognizes is a large number of non-party cabinet members—more than half were typically not affiliated with parties. Much of the presidentialism literature suggests that a high number of non-party ministers is a sign of the president's strength and his or her ability to prevent agency loss through the appointment of persons more loyal to the chief executive than to their various parties (Gallardo and Schleiter 2015). This book proposes an alternative interpretation. While the Indonesian case also features technocratic appointments that fit into Gallardo and Schleiter's explanation (in table 1.1, these are captured in the category "others"), it is clear that presidents also appoint non-party ministers to broaden their coalitions beyond the legislative arena. As becomes evident in the table, certain groups are integrated into presidential coalitions with great

TABLE 1.2. Composition of presidential coalitions, 2004–2019

	PARTY	MILITARY (NON-PARTY) *****	MILITARY (PARTY)	POLICE	LOCAL GOVERNMENTT	BUREAUCRACY	OLIGARCH (NON-PARTY)	OLIGARCH (PARTY)	MUSLIM GROUPS	OTHERS	TOTAL**
Yudhoyono I (2004)*	17	2	2	1	0	3	0	0	1	14	38
Yudhoyono II (2009)	17	3	2	2	1	3	1***	0***	2	12	41
Widodo I (2014)	14	3	1	1****	0	3	2	0	1	17	41
Widodo II (2019)	17	3	2	3	0	2	2	3	1	12	40

* All data in this table are drawn from the cabinets initially announced at the beginning of a presidential term; reshuffles are not considered.

** The number of cabinet portfolios varies based on which portfolio was included in the president's cabinet announcement.

*** One more party-affiliated oligarch (Aburizal Bakrie) and one non-party oligarch (Chairul Tanjung) were included in later reshuffles.

**** A second police officer was appointed to a cabinet-level position early in Widodo's first term.

***** Both active and retired officers are included.

consistency—that is, retired military officers, police, the bureaucracy, oligarchs, and Muslim groups. In regard to the latter, the number of its representatives is even higher than the formal figures suggest. This is because two parties are closely tied to the country's two largest Muslim groups: the National Awakening Party (PKB) is the political wing of Nahdlatul Ulama (NU), and the National Mandate Party (PAN) is affiliated with Muhammadiyah. Hence, many representatives of Muslim groups in the cabinet are hidden in the table's party category. As for local government leaders, whom this book posits as members of presidential coalitions but who do not seem to record significant cabinet representation, our later discussion will show that their link to the presidential coalition is built via their interest groups and through party links as well.

The overview presented in table 1.2 allows us to trace nuanced but important changes in presidential coalition-building over time. For instance, the data confirm the narrative on the trajectory of Yudhoyono's and Widodo's thinking on coalitional presidentialism mentioned above. The low number of party appointees in Widodo's first cabinet reflects his then still existent—but already weakening—belief that he could rule without a large legislative coalition. In his second term, he had let go of this conviction, returning to the level of party representation in the Yudhoyono cabinets in 2004 and 2009. Yudhoyono, therefore, was more stable in his appointments; he recognized the need for large party coalitions from the beginning. Indeed, he even named Golkar ministers in his first cabinet announcement although the party only came under the control of his vice president two months later. In the overview, we also see changes that emphasize momentous shifts in the power held by non-party groups: the police and oligarchs, in particular, have gained political influence since the mid-2000s, and that is reflected in their increased cabinet representation. It is essential to recall, however, that cabinet representation is only one dimension of how coalitional presidentialism is put into practice—albeit a very important dimension. As the rest of this book will demonstrate, Indonesian presidents have used many other formal and informal avenues to integrate the country's key socio-political actors into their coalitions.

Post-2004 presidents have been embedded in the country's history, constitution and institutional structures in ways that have shaped their understanding and practice of coalitional presidentialism. Historically, the country's founders put the president into the center of politics, drawing from notions of strong leadership in times of anti-colonial struggle and the idea that someone needed to serve as a symbol for the unity of the nation. Sukarno, the informal leader of the independence movement, was the natural choice for that position. At the same time, the suspension of executive presidential rule between late 1945 and 1959 gave the nation a sense of the importance of non-presidential actors. While parliamentarism ultimately collapsed in 1959, it subsequently served as a source of inspiration, and aspiration, for marginalized pro-democracy groups living under four decades of presidential authoritarianism between the late 1950s and late 1990s (Bourchier and Legge 1994). The democratic presidentialism emerging after 1998, and especially after 2004, combined ideas of strong presidential leadership and the desire for powerful legislative institutions into a new, post-authoritarian concept of modern presidentialism. In this concept, presidents and the legislature have to find, and constantly maintain, an equilibrium that allows the government to work effectively but concurrently prevents the emergence of another autocracy.

But the legacies of Indonesia's long periods of presidential autocracy remain powerful today, and they even neutralize some of the new constitutional arrangements put in place in the early 2000s. Sukarno's approach of integrating the military into legislative and executive positions—and Suharto's massive upgrading of that practice—is echoed by the consistent allocation of cabinet seats to retired military officers more than two and a half decades after democratization began (Aminuddin 2017). Similarly, Sukarno recognized the centrality of Indonesia's largest Muslim organization, NU, and made it the centerpiece of his appointed parliament in 1960 (Fealy 1998). To this day, every Indonesian president has to include a number of NU representatives in the cabinet, both party and non-party, in order to sustain the support of this group. Indeed, Widodo made the spiritual leader of NU his running mate in the 2019 elections. Thus, Indonesian experiences with autocracy delivered a number of unwritten rules to post-1998, and especially post-2004, presidents that appear nowhere in the constitutional regulations governing its reformed presidentialism. These rules lead presidents to include actors that may not have a great impact on their position in the DPR but can stabilize government outside of it.

This historical context has produced a constellation in which even the tight, post-2004 impeachment rules have not strengthened presidents' self-confidence in their position. Despite the fact that one-third-plus-one of DPR members would be sufficient to stop any impeachment process, presidents have aimed at securing at least two-thirds majorities in the legislature. Having secured that, they did not stop: they enlarged their broad coalitions by adding non-party actors. These broad coalitions are managed by a presidential administration apparatus that is only partially equipped for this task. As we have seen, the president can use the Military Secretariat at the palace to build bridges with the armed forces and fill the military's ranks with loyalists. In Widodo's case, he also utilized the Cabinet Secretariat to maintain good relations between himself and his party.

But outside of that, presidents lack a proper support network; in fact, presidents tend to isolate themselves from the existing civil service force in the palace, in fear of being controlled by it. This requires the president to resort to many informal mechanisms to balance and sustain his or her coalitions. The following chapters will analyze these informal mechanisms, as well as the formal ones, to highlight how presidents manage each actor in their coalition. In combination, these chapters will demonstrate how Indonesian heads of state try to stay on top of the coalitional presidentialism game by playing groups off against each other without risking the coalition's breakdown.

2
THE PARTIES

In much of the coalitional presidentialism literature, political parties are considered legislative entities that are vitally important to presidents for gaining and maintaining a majority in parliament. This focus, while conceptually grounded, has blurred the definitional demarcation lines between parties and legislatures, as it views parties primarily as negotiators with presidents over legislative support or opposition. With most examples examined by coalitional presidentialism scholars concerning presidents who augment "their parliamentary bloc upon taking office" (Chaisty, Cheeseman, and Power 2017, 216), concentrating on the legislative dimension of parties often seems justified. The Indonesian case is more complex, however. Political parties have more functions than supporting or opposing the president in the post-election legislature. In Indonesia, parties hold the right to nominate presidential candidates—and because the threshold for such nominations is high, incumbent presidents and other candidates have to collect support from several parties to run. Moreover, given the size of the country and the limited resources of candidates, much of presidential campaigning is outsourced to nominating parties' legislative candidates. After elections, parties rooted in key constituencies are expected to shield the president from attacks by extra-parliamentary movements. At the same time, the parties' control over their legislators is not as strong as in other presidential systems, creating the necessity for Indonesian presidents to lobby parties and legislators as separate entities. Thus, we need to treat parties and legislatures as distinct elements, requiring different sets of focused analysis.

While the Indonesian case alone would justify adjusting the way parties and legislatures are posited in coalitional presidentialism studies, evidence suggests that other countries witness comparable trends. Chaisty, Cheeseman, and Power (2017, 216) concede that Chile is a case in which pre-electoral alliances between presidents and parties matter greatly. Others highlighted similar patterns across Latin America (Freudenreich 2016; Kellam 2017; Borges and Turgeon 2017). In the Indonesian case, presidents view parties that supported their candidacy differently from those that did not. The former enjoy preferential treatment in cabinet formation, obtaining a higher number of seats and more strategic portfolios than those considered latecomers. In 2004, for example, Yudhoyono appointed Yusril Ihza Mahendra, the chair of a tiny Muslim party (it obtained 2.6 percent of the votes in the legislative elections) to the key post of State Secretariat minister because his party had been one of only a few that nominated Yudhoyono in the first round of the presidential ballot. Conversely, Widodo gave PAN, which joined his coalition long after the 2014 elections, only one marginal cabinet portfolio, despite its medium-size status and access to an important segment of the Muslim community. He took that seat away from PAN after it declared its support for Widodo's challenger in 2019, although it had promised continued legislative support to Widodo until the end of his term. In short, what parties do before and after elections, both inside and outside of legislatures, is key to a full understanding of the dynamics that shape the formation and operations of presidential coalitions.

This chapter starts with an overview of the powers political parties hold vis-à-vis the president. Outside of legislative support, they lie in nominating authority, provision of campaign support, and political protection in times of extra-parliamentary crises. The second section outlines the president's instruments to groom, reward, and punish parties. These instruments are mostly drawn from the conventional presidential toolbox outlined in the coalitional presidentialism literature, but include others as well. Among the latter are the offer to parties to benefit from a president's popularity (in elections, this comes in the form of a promised coattail effect) and the unique ability of Indonesian presidents to decide the outcome of intra-party conflicts. The third section delivers a general portrait of how coalitions between parties and presidents are built and maintained. Although there have been a few differences between the Yudhoyono and Widodo periods, some organizing principles have remained the same—such as that nominating parties receive a larger share of the spoils and that presidents only in extreme cases penalize coalition parties. Finally, the fourth section offers a case study of the power play between presidents and parties. The case presented is the nomination of Ma'ruf Amin as Widodo's running mate in the 2019 elections. This case is ideal for showcasing how both the president and the parties deploy their powers—and how settlements are achieved through negotiations that allow both sides to protect their interests but often stymie political reform.

Party Powers

One of Indonesian parties' most consequential powers over the president is the right to nominate presidential candidates. Parties equipped themselves with this power in the 2002 constitutional amendments to compensate for losing the authority to elect the president in the MPR (Crouch 2010). For the 2004 elections, a transitional arrangement was put in place by which parties that held 3 percent of the DPR seats or had gained 5 percent of the votes in the preceding legislative elections could make a presidential nomination. This increased to 20 percent of the seats or 25 percent of the votes in 2009, and stayed at that level for the 2014 and 2019 elections. For the latter, there was much discussion on revising the threshold because, for the first time, the legislative and presidential elections were held on the same day in that year (Gobel 2019). This meant it was difficult to uphold the logic of drawing a threshold for presidential nominations from the parties' performance in the preceding legislative elections (which in 2004, 2009, and 2014 had taken place a few months before the presidential ballot). Nevertheless, the high threshold was left in place for 2019—it was now based on the result of the legislative elections held five years earlier. The high threshold for presidential hopefuls has the advantage for parties that every candidate typically needs to lobby several parties to get nominated, which reduces the possibility of nominees running on—and implementing—an anti-party agenda. For incumbent presidents seeking re-election, high thresholds limit the number of potential challengers. It was no surprise, then, that most parties and Widodo agreed to keep the threshold high.

In practice, the high nomination threshold allows parties outside the president's own to join a pre-electoral alliance and participate in the distribution of spoils after victory (Slater 2018). As noted, parties of the pre-electoral coalition can expect more of these spoils than those that seek access to the presidential alliance at or after inauguration day. This power of parties to force their way into a nominating coalition is particularly relevant given the traditionally small size of the president's nominating party and his or her sometimes-weak role in it. In 2004, Yudhoyono's Democratic Party (PD) won a mere 7.5 percent of the votes, and could only make a nomination because of the transitional threshold regulations. For his re-election in 2009, Yudhoyono could have relied on a sole nomination by PD (it had won 26 percent of the seats), but many parties rushed to co-nominate the president as polls predicted his win. Widodo's PDI-P was just below the nomination threshold in 2014 and 2019, requiring additional parties to file his candidacy. In Widodo's case, nomination by non-PDI-P parties served his interests, as it compensated for his weakness in his party. In 2014, it was public knowledge that PDI-P chair Megawati had nominated Widodo—the leader in the polls—only because her own chances to win were slim and because no other member of the Sukarno family stood ready to replace her. To be sure, Widodo's enthusiasm for PDI-P was equally limited.[1] In this situation, the existence of other parties in his nominating coalition was advantageous to the parties as well as the nominee and future president.

Beyond their formal nomination authority, parties typically offer their grassroots campaign networks to presidential candidates in exchange for later, postelectoral rewards. As Aspinall and Berenschot (2019) showed, local executive and legislative elections in post-Suharto Indonesia are won mainly by candidates employing an effective network of brokers and grassroots campaigners. These networks organize events, make material promises to specific communities, and frequently distribute cash. In presidential elections, however, this system is unworkable for a national campaign. With a population of 275 million, an archipelago stretching over 3,200 miles from west to east, and no effective campaign financing mechanisms, Indonesia makes it impossible for a single presidential campaign to set up an apparatus that could replicate what has proven successful at the local level. Hence, presidential candidates are forced to shift much of the campaigning to the about 250,000 legislative candidates that parties nominate in local legislative races. This army of nominees, it is hoped, will add promotion of the presidential candidate to the campaign for their seats. This hope was particularly high in 2019, as presidential and legislative campaigns took place concurrently. As could be observed on the ground, candidates did not necessarily implement the orders from their party headquarters to put the presidential candidate's image on their campaign posters, especially in areas where the latter was unpopular (Mietzner 2019). Despite these frustrations, most presidential hopefuls and incumbents still believe that the support by party and local candidate machines remains crucial to their campaigns.

After elections, parties can leverage the legislative powers of their members in the DPR to gain concessions from the president (Sherlock 2012). These legislators can support or oppose bills and budgets, approve or reject the president's nominations for key positions, and either attack or praise government representatives when appearing at parliament. Whether implicitly or explicitly, parties promise the support of their legislative caucuses for the president if given cabinet representation and other benefits in return, while presidents expect that parties' membership in the government will convince them that it is inappropriate to vote against its policies in the legislature. In practice, the picture is less clear-cut. Parties do not exercise full control over their legislators, and at times, party leaders are divided among themselves over how to direct their caucuses on specific issues. Yudhoyono, for instance, tried unsuccessfully in 2009 and 2011 to codify the voting behavior of his coalition parties in the DPR through a written contract. However, this failure to enforce the loyalty of legislators by contractually binding their party chairpersons did not lead him to dismiss the importance of the parties altogether. Rather, he—and Widodo after him—developed a dual strategy by which party leaders and legislators had to be courted in parallel; this approach recognized that party chairs played an important role in filling senior leadership positions in the DPR but also acknowledged that the presidential apparatus had to work with individual legislators to secure specific deals. In his presidential memoirs (or, more precisely, a voluminous collection of thoughts on his presidency), Yudhoyono concluded that despite the unreliability of parties, including them "in a political coalition still makes our politics way more stable" (SBY 2014, 39).

Another asset of parties in their negotiations with presidents is their ability to bestow legitimacy during and after elections. This legitimacy capacity is particularly useful when presidents come under attack on issues of identity or faith (Aziz 2020). In such circumstances, Islamic parties can protect the president with their religious credibility and connections in the Muslim community. Except for Wahid, a Muslim cleric, all Indonesian presidents since 1945 have been mainstream nationalist figures—that is, Muslims who may practice some elements of their faith but otherwise lead what can be described as secular lifestyles. Thus, they have been vulnerable to questions about their devoutness. In the 2014 elections, Widodo had to confront false rumors spread by his opponents that he was a secret Christian of ethnic Chinese origin. As part of his pre-electoral coalition, the traditionalist Muslim party PKB took it upon itself to run a campaign in Islamic boarding schools to counter this smear. In one such school in Bogor, the party distributed pamphlets that showed pictures of Widodo performing the hajj (notes by the author, Bogor, June 7, 2014). Two years later, when the Widodo government came under siege from a mass mobilization of Islamists—which protested against alleged blasphemy on the part of the Christian and ethnic Chinese governor of Jakarta, Basuki Tjahaja Purnama, who was a Widodo ally—the Muslim parties in the president's coalition were again called upon to act as a buffer against notions that Widodo was lacking in faith. Hence, some political parties play the same legitimacy-producing role as large Muslim organizations that, as separate entities, are also part of presidential coalitions.

Indonesian parties, then, hold important constitutional, institutional, and cultural powers that presidents have to manage. These powers can either act as stabilizers of presidential rule or be used against it. From our discussion above, it is clear that presidential management of parties goes well beyond the need to secure a legislative majority. For that, a simple 50-percent-plus-one formula would be sufficient. Instead, presidents have sought to include a much wider range of parties that not only deliver votes in the legislature but also offer other services. The explanation for this pattern partly lies in the broad party powers. Presidents are interested in benefitting from a variety of party functions, from electoral support to crisis protection and leverage in order to balance difficult relationships with their own parties. And above it all towers the permanent fear of presidents that parties not integrated into the coalition could create "chaos" in the legislature and society at large. As Yudhoyono expressed it, every party brought into the coalition is one party less to worry about in terms of its potential to trigger discontent and instability. Yudhoyono was well aware of the efficiency losses inherent in oversized coalitions: "convincing all these parties in the coalition is not easy, and in probably 30 percent of cases, I had to accept the reality [that I could not prevail with my policy]" (interview, Jakarta, December 2, 2014). But, he asserted, building such broadly inclusive party coalitions meant that 70 percent of his policies could be adopted, and—as remarked in his memoir—stability could be secured. As later chapters will demonstrate, many critics would view Yudhoyono's assessment of his success rate as overly optimistic.

Presidential Assets

While we have noted the many assets that parties can use to extract concessions from the president, it is important to begin the discussion of presidential strengths vis-à-vis the parties by recognizing one of their key weaknesses. Remarkably, since the presidency of Megawati Sukarnoputri, long-established parties have been unable to produce competitive candidates for presidential elections from their leadership ranks. In every presidential ballot after 2004, competitive candidates have been political outsiders who quickly established personalist parties with the sole goal of running for president, or figures whose role in parties was marginal but who commanded high poll ratings. The first category of candidates includes Yudhoyono and Prabowo Subianto, both former military generals who gained name recognition through their military service under Suharto (indeed, Prabowo was married to Suharto's daughter). Yudhoyono established PD before the 2004 elections (Honna 2012), while Prabowo—who unsuccessfully but competitively ran in the 2014 and 2019 elections—set up the Great Indonesia Movement Party (Gerindra) in 2008. Neither party has strong institutional or ideological roots, which was highlighted by the fact that Yudhoyono handed over the leadership of PD to his son Agus Harimurti in 2019. In the second category is Widodo, who rose to political prominence by having been mayor of the Central Java town of Solo from 2005 to 2012 and governor of Jakarta from 2012 to 2014. Mostly inactive in PDI-P, he was the only alternative for the party if it wanted to stand a chance in the 2014 elections. Post-2004 presidents, therefore, have benefitted from the incapacity of established parties to challenge them at the ballot box.

In addition to the inability of traditional parties to groom presidential hopefuls from their leaders, most of the personalist parties that sprung up between the late 2000s and late 2010s have not made their patrons competitive either. The National Democrats Party (Nasdem), founded by media tycoon Surya Paloh in 2011; the People's Conscience Party (Hanura), established by former armed forces chief Wiranto in 2006; and the Indonesian Unity Party (Perindo), created by billionaire Hary Tanoesoedibjo in 2014, are all examples of parties headed by rich but unpopular figures whose ambitions to become president were strong but unfounded. After coming to terms with that reality, they discovered that their best opportunity to stay engaged in politics below the level of the presidency was to align with a popular presidential candidate who, in case of victory, could offer them ministries. Thus, the Indonesian party landscape after 2004 has been populated by two types of parties, as table 2.1 shows. The first type consists of more conventional, historically grown ones appealing to a specific socio-political community, and the second comprises personalist vehicles set up for presidential candidacies. Importantly, most parties in both categories have been reduced to endorsing the presidential campaigns of outsiders to gain access to post-election patronage. Having gained office with the very popularity that most political party leaders lacked, post-2004 presidents have paraded their political capital with great self-confidence. In his memoirs, Yudhoyono devoted an entire chapter to the argument that popularity cannot be bought—a not-so-subtle swipe at those party leaders who had tried exactly that (SBY 2014: 363–366).

This post-2004 separation between party politics featuring unpopular operators and presidential races dominated by outsiders is not unusual in presidential systems (Carreras 2012). However, it came as a disappointment to many Indonesian party leaders. They had hoped that the party-based nomination threshold would allow them to maintain their control over who could run in presidential elections and who would win (interview with former Golkar chairman Akbar Tandjung, Jakarta, February 11, 2008). Instead, the focus of presidential competition shifted from the party arena to figures whose main asset was popularity in the polls and who only needed party support to get nominated and gain a campaign network. One of the main reasons for this split between the

TABLE 2.1. Indonesian parties, party types, and participation in coalitions, 2021

PARTY*	CHAIR	PARTY TYPE	STANDING OF CHAIR IN PRESIDENTIAL POLLS	PARTICIPATION IN PRESIDENTIAL COALITION
Indonesian Democratic Party of Struggle (PDI-P)	Megawati Sukarnoputri	Socially rooted (targeting nationalist-pluralist voters)	Poor	Yes (Widodo 2014–2024)
Functional Group Party (Golkar)	Airlangga Hartarto	Socially rooted (targeting voters prioritizing development)	Very poor	Yes (Yudhoyono 2004–2-14, Widodo 2014–2024)
Great Indonesia Movement Party (Gerindra)	Prabowo Subianto	Personalist	Good	Yes (Widodo 2019–2024)
National Awakening Party (PKB)	Muhaimin Iskandar	Socially rooted (targeting voters affiliated with NU)	Very poor	Yes (Yudhoyono 2004–2014, Widodo 2014–2024)
National Democrats Party (Nasdem)	Surya Paloh	Personalist	Very poor	Yes (Widodo 2014–2024)
Prosperous Justice Party (PKS)	Ahmad Syaikhu	Socially rooted (targeting conservative, urban Muslim voters)	Very poor	Yes (Yudhoyono 2004–2014)
Democratic Party (PD)	Agus Harimurti Yudhoyono	Personalist	Poor	Yes (Yudhoyono 2004–2014)
National Mandate Party (PAN)	Zulkifli Hasan	Socially rooted (targeting voters affiliated with Muhammadiyah)	Very poor	Yes (Yudhoyono 2004–2014, Widodo 2016–2018, 2022–2024)
Unity Development Party (PPP)	Soeharso Monoarfa	Socially rooted (targeting conservative, rural Muslim voters)	Very poor	Yes (Yudhoyono 2004–2014, Widodo 2014–2024)
Indonesian Unity Party (Perindo)	Hary Tanoesoedibjo	Personalist	Very poor	Yes** (Widodo 2019–2024)
Working Party (Berkarya)	Tommy Suharto	Personalist	Very poor	No
Indonesian Solidarity Party (PSI)	Giring Ganesha	Socially rooted (targeting liberal, urban voters)	Very poor	Yes** (Widodo 2019–2024)
People's Conscience Party (Hanura)	Oesman Sapta Odang	Personalist	Very poor	Yes (Widodo 2014–2019)

* Includes all parties that received more than 1 percent of the votes in the 2019 legislative elections.
** Parties received deputy minister positions.

party and presidential arenas has been the trend within parties to appoint chairpersons whose sole task is to secure the party's funding (Mietzner 2015). This pattern has been obvious for personalist parties—in which the wealth of the "owner" is often the only reason the party exists—but it has also affected the socially rooted parties. In the absence of a functioning party funding system (with private donations low and state financing minuscule), party chairs are chosen primarily based on their ability to supply operational funds. As one senior party functionary conceded, "we would love to put people in the position of party chair who are popular and could win the presidential elections for us. But that is not how it works. The first question on our mind, when evaluating candidates for party chair, is: can this person pay our party's bills?" (confidential interview, Jakarta, December 7, 2019). Hence, structural changes in party development have put faceless party financiers in charge, weakening the parties' standing in presidential ballots.

Closely related to electoral power as a key element of presidential political capital is the anticipated ability of a popular candidate to increase the legislative vote of the parties that nominated him or her. This so-called coattail effect is both expected by parties and promised by presidential incumbents and nominees. In Indonesia, Golkar nominated Widodo for re-election in 2016, three years before the election and long before his own party did. Golkar's secretary-general, Lodewijk Freidrich Paulus, was open about the reason for this move: "we hope that nominating [Widodo] so early will help our legislative candidates. That's why we did it" (Mardiansyah 2019). As in the case of presidents' hopes that their nominating parties' networks will mobilize their resources for the presidential campaign, the coattail effect for the parties is often less pronounced than desired. In 2019, only PDI-P and Gerindra seemed to benefit from the candidacies of Widodo and Prabowo, respectively, while other nominating parties stayed largely flat (Golkar lost votes compared to the 2014 elections, when it did not nominate an incumbent president). Nevertheless, the theory of a coattail effect continues to attract interest and support within party elites, allowing presidents or candidates leading in the polls to use it as leverage. This was proven again in October 2022, when Nasdem nominated the popular Jakarta governor Anies Baswedan as its candidate for the 2024 presidential race, openly explaining this early choice within an expected coattail effect.

Another asset that Indonesian presidents can deploy in negotiations with parties is their authority to determine the outcome of intra-party conflicts. In Indonesia's legal system, parties have to register the composition of their central boards with the president's Ministry of Justice and Human Rights (Rahman 2016). Only if the latter certifies this registration is the leadership board deemed legitimate. This certification, in turn, allows the party to submit legislative candidates to the General Elections Commission (KPU), replace its MPs in the DPR, or seek access to state subsidies. Therefore, the president—through his or her minister—can decide which claimant in a party leadership dispute is the officially legitimated representative allowed to engage with the state. While Yudhoyono was reluctant to use this power and largely left intra-party conflicts to the courts to decide, Widodo was not so hesitant. In 2015 and 2016, his government's meddling in the internal affairs of Golkar and PPP led to the removal of their respective party leadership boards that had nominated Widodo's rival Prabowo Subianto in the 2014 elections (Mietzner 2016). In their stead, two rival leadership boards loyal to the president were installed and received government confirmation. This shift in Golkar and PPP allowed Widodo to broaden his party coalition in the DPR, taking it from minority to majority status. Consequently, parties have to consider the risk of executive interference in their affairs should they oppose the president, giving the latter a useful power instrument when dealing with parties inside and outside their coalitions.

Indonesian presidents also possess important patronage distribution capacities from which parties seek to benefit. Chaisty, Cheeseman, and Power describe three of these patronage powers contained in the presidential toolbox: cabinet appointment authority, budgetary powers, and the exchange of favors. To begin with, cabinet posts are essential for parties to channel money into their underfunded organizations. Ministers representing a party in a coalition are not only expected to defend the party's policies but also to make their ministry's resources available to the party. Under Yudhoyono, for instance, PKS officials used their hold over the agriculture ministry to demand kickbacks in return for granting beef export quotas; the party's president, one recipient of the funds, was arrested in 2013 (Kramer 2014). In the Widodo period, the social affairs minister, who was also the PDI-P deputy treasurer, diverted money from the COVID-19 social assistance budget into the party's coffers.[2] The president's authority to draft the state budget is of interest to parties, too. Presidents can negotiate with parties over individual budget items that might benefit a party's leaders or its main voting base. One example was a project to produce new identity cards for all citizens—most parties were believed to have pocketed funds siphoned off from the project budget, with the then Golkar chairman going to prison in 2018 for his role in the affair. Finally, presidents can hand out informal favors to parties; for instance, presidents often contribute, directly or through allies, to the funds necessary for holding a party congress, especially if they have an interest in potential decisions emerging from that congress.

The final two elements of the conventional presidential toolbox—namely, the president's legislative and partisan powers—are also relevant for Indonesian presidents' relations with parties, but in slightly different ways. Recall that in Indonesia, of the president and the legislature must jointly promulgate laws. This equips presidents with powers superior to standard package or partial vetoes but also forces them to seek consensus with party-affiliated legislators. However, most of these negotiations occur in the legislature's caucuses or committees rather than at the party leadership level. Only key issues are brought into a rare forum between the president and coalition parties. Accordingly, discussing the process through which presidents negotiate with party-based MPs over legislation and vice versa must concentrate on parliament as its main arena and thus will be dealt with in the next chapter. As for partisan powers—which refer to the control of presidents over their party—the experiences of Yudhoyono and Widodo were decisively different. Yudhoyono was the de facto founder and sole patron of his party. While he faced occasional internal strive over personnel matters (Honna 2012), the party elite accepted his supremacy in the policy domain. By contrast, Widodo had no partisan powers, given his marginal role in PDI-P. Significantly, however, this lack of partisan power drove him to build stronger ties to other parties to leverage the latter against of the influence of PDI-P. Thus, while Yudhoyono's "ownership" of his party was an advantage for him, Widodo turned his weakness in this field into a political strength by mastering the art of coalitional balancing.

We have now reviewed both the powers Indonesian political parties hold vis-à-vis the president and the assets that the latter can bring to bear in order to lobby, reward, and punish the former. The picture that emerged from this discussion is one of great leverage on both sides. On the one hand, parties recognize the powers of the presidency, and so they seek to capture or align with it to gain resources and policy influence. On the other hand, presidents need parties to receive support for nominations, campaigns, and post-electoral governance. This constellation provides an ideal breeding ground for coalitional presidentialism—an arrangement from which both sides benefit. The next section offers a portrait of how this arrangement typically takes shape in the Indonesian context and explains its endurance as the foundation of president-party relations in post-2004 Indonesia.

Balancing Party Coalitions

As noted, Indonesian party coalitions take shape before an election and are subsequently modified as post-election alliances. In much of the coalitional presidentialism literature, this distinction between pre-electoral and post-election coalitions is downplayed (Chaisty, Cheeseman, and Power 2017, 216). But the Indonesian case shows that the difference is significant. Pre-electoral coalition parties gain more of the share of the cabinet seats, and they are typically ideologically closer to the president. Indeed, it is possible to speak of a two-phase model of presidential coalition-building: in the first phase, parties often side with the candidate closer to their politico-ideological orientation, while in the second, some parties from the losing side are integrated, receiving a lower ministry share as a result. Thus, despite a growing body of literature on the irrelevance of ideology in Indonesian party politics (Ambardi 2009), important ideological traces remain in pre-electoral coalition-building. The main cleavage is between those who promote a stronger role for Islam in state organization and those who support the pluralist mandate of the constitution. In the 2004 and 2009 elections, Yudhoyono—whose party adopted the descriptor "nationalist-religious"—portrayed himself as more religious than his main rival Megawati, and the parties supporting them in the elections divided roughly along those lines. In the 2014 and 2019 ballots, Widodo took the mantle of the pluralists, while Prabowo was supported by conservative Muslim parties and groups (Power 2019). There were some shifts and exceptions over time, but in broad terms, this cleavage persisted.

Even after elections, these ideological tensions continue to influence the broader coalitions built to secure the president's hold on government. PDI-P remained outside of Yudhoyono's government for the entirety of his rule, and so did Gerindra, Hanura, and Nasdem. Conversely, PKS and PD did not join any of the Widodo coalitions. Personal animosities played a role in these decisions as well. For example, Megawati's legendary grudge toward Yudhoyono (she felt that he had not properly informed her of his intention to run against her in 2004, although he was in her cabinet) led her to prevent her party from entering Yudhoyono's coalition and PD from joining Widodo's. It is true, of course, that ideological lines blurred considerably in the process of putting together postelection party coalitions. But as table 2.2 demonstrates, the support of a party toward a president in the election continued to matter greatly in determining if or how many cabinet seats were given to the said party. The table's analysis of the composition of the second Widodo cabinet shows that the only non-nominating party to be included in the ministry in 2019 was Gerindra, and that the latter was the only cabinet party to receive a lower cabinet seat share than its seat share in the DPR would indicate.[3] All other parties in cabinet obtained a ministry seat share significantly larger than their DPR seat share. Other non-nominating parties received no representation in cabinet. This suggests that the cost of being outside of a president's nominating coalition remains high, despite the chance of being integrated into the post-electoral alliance.

While ideological default lines are visible in electoral coalitions, it is important to emphasize that the overall mechanics of coalitional presidentialism in

TABLE 2.2. Party nominations and cabinet inclusion in second Widodo government, 2019

PARTY	NOMINATION OF WIDODO	DPR SEATS (%)	MINISTRY SEATS (%)***
PDI-P	Yes	22	29
Golkar	Yes	15	18**
Gerindra	No	14	12
PKB	Yes	10	18
Nasdem	Yes	10	18
PKS	No	9	0
PD	No	9	0
PAN	No	8	0
PPP	Yes	3	6
PSI	Yes	0	0*
Perindo	Yes	0	0*

* Received deputy ministry positions.
** Luhut Pandjaitan was a Golkar member but was appointed outside of the party quotas; if included, Golkar's ministry share would increase to 22 percent.
*** Percentage calculated against the total ministry allocation to parties in the broader coalition (17).

Indonesia remain non-ideological. Ideological polarization tends to occur during elections (hence its influence on a president's electoral coalition), but periods between elections are mostly marked by patronage deals that integrate former electoral opponents into the alliance (albeit with reduced privileges) and dispense some limited benefits to the remaining opposition. The inclusion of Gerindra into the second Widodo ministry (with the president's rival in the 2014 and 2019 presidential elections Prabowo Subianto becoming minister of defense) is an example of integrating former adversaries. Oppositional figures staying outside of cabinet, for their part, are typically accommodated through arrangements made in the legislature (more about this in the next chapter). Ideology, then, should neither be fully dismissed nor overstated in its significance for presidential politics. It does play a role in the early formation of alliances that are subsequently formalized in a nominating coalition in presidential elections, but it is not the organizing principle of day-to-day coalitional presidentialism. Furthermore, it is common for some actors to change their ideological positions for practical reasons—Prabowo, for instance, eventually abandoned the Islamists who had supported him in 2014 and 2019, hoping to build a more inclusive platform for his anticipated bid in 2024. Therefore, the technical aspects of coalition management remain our analytical priority.

When managing their coalitions, presidents can use reshuffles (or the threat of reshuffles) to punish parties deemed disloyal. Indeed, threats are more common than actual wide-ranging changes to cabinet. During Yudhoyono's and

Widodo's rule, only once was a party's cabinet seat share reduced, and only once was a party expelled from cabinet. In 2011, Yudhoyono took away one of the four cabinet seats PKS had held, penalizing it for voting against the government in the DPR. Widodo, for his part, removed PAN from his cabinet in 2018 when the party nominated Prabowo Subianto for president in the 2019 elections.[4] Despite the rarity of such punishing reshuffles, the mere mention of their possibility has a disciplining effect. According to Luhut Pandjaitan, one of the president's closest aides, "cabinet reshuffles are the only thing that keeps parties in line. Even if the president just mentions the word 'reshuffle,' parties get nervous and hold emergency meetings" (interview, Jakarta, June 15, 2016). Although the prospect of reshuffles might prevent open dissent and coalition collapse, it often fails to produce the kind of full-time loyalty presidents seek. In the case of PKS, the party continued to take steps Yudhoyono and other coalition parties viewed as hostile. Despite being threatened with expulsion from the cabinet again in 2012 and 2013, PKS retained its remaining ministries until the end of the president's term in 2014. Andi Mallarangeng, a former Yudhoyono minister, recalled that the president told him that he did not remove PKS from the cabinet because that would have increased the power of other parties, especially Golkar (interview, Jakarta, June 20, 2022). Hence, presidents judge the cost of removing parties from cabinet to be higher than that of tolerating minor acts of disloyalty.

The management of Indonesian party coalitions is poorly institutionalized but for different reasons in each presidency. Yudhoyono tried to create a coalition council to coordinate policies and enforce binding discipline rules but largely failed in that effort. Irked by what he saw as a lack of discipline among coalition parties in his first term, he created a Joint Secretariat (Setgab) for his alliance at the beginning of his second term in 2009. But this institution proved to be ineffective. In April 2012, a meeting of the Setgab—under the leadership of Yudhoyono—decided that PKS had (again) violated the code of ethics all parties had agreed to in 2009. But no sanctions were imposed. Widodo, by contrast, opted not to establish a council. During his presidency, meetings of the party chairpersons occurred rarely and irregularly. In fact, Widodo deliberately tried to reduce such meetings to a minimum and instead preferred dealing with party leaders individually. As one of his assistants explained, "it is normally during joint meetings when the party chairpersons put forward collective demands that the president then finds difficult to refuse. In one-on-one negotiations with parties, the president can balance the positions of the various parties better, and he can exploit differences between them" (confidential interview, Jakarta, February 8, 2017). Although neither president faced serious threats to their presidencies from their party coalitions, Widodo's strategy was overall more successful in preventing parties from voting openly against government policies. Despite occasional friction, he pushed through some controversial government programs with a striking level of coalition unity (Setijadi 2021).

Widodo's divide-and-rule approach to his party coalition was the key to improving his own standing vis-à-vis his own party. At the beginning of Widodo's first term, his relationship with PDI-P was poor, with some of its leaders calling for the president's impeachment (Rastika 2015). At a PDI-P congress in Bali in April 2015, Megawati lectured Widodo in front of the party crowd, telling him that a president is supposed to implement the directives given by his party and that thus far, he had failed to do so (notes by the author, Denpasar, April 9, 2015). In what was seen as the ultimate punishment, the president was not allowed to speak at the congress—a highly unusual incident. One local branch leader felt that Widodo "does not want to serve the party that nominated him, and if he continues this way, we will try to get rid of him" (interview, Denpasar, April 10, 2015). As noted, Widodo subsequently broadened his coalition. Supported by more parties, he was able to change the power balance with PDI-P. The most important strategy in this regard was asking other parties to take a public stance against an idea endorsed by PDI-P but rejected by him. This enabled Widodo to inform his party that there was resistance to the PDI-P policy, and that the government therefore could not adopt it. As a senior Golkar official reported, "Widodo is smart. He often asks us to take a stand against this or that because he feels he can't reject a request by Megawati and PDI-P directly" (confidential interview, Jakarta, December 9, 2019). The changed power balance was on display at the next PDI-P congress in Bali in August 2019. This time, Megawati was much softer in her approach to the president, Widodo was invited to speak, and there was no talk of impeachment (notes by the author, Denpasar, August 9, 2019).

But PDI-P's new politeness toward Widodo could barely mask its deep-seated disappointment over the president's success in emancipating himself from his party. In the leadership's internal accountability report circulated at the 2019 congress, the party lamented that there still was "no correlation between the elected president and vice president and the party that nominated him" (PDI-P 2019, 4). Excerpts from Megawati's 2015 speech were re-printed and underlined in the report, suggesting that the party had not given up on its self-proclaimed right to control the PDI-P-nominated president—but also that it now grudgingly accepted that it could not exercise this control. Much to PDI-P's dismay, Widodo had managed his presidential coalition in a way that served his interests more effectively than those of PDI-P. This again highlighted that partisan powers are not necessary for a president to run a party coalition, and that their absence can produce shifts in the alliance that disadvantage the president's party. PDI-P's secretary-general Hasto Kristiyanto conceded this in 2022 when he defined firmer control over the next president as one of the party's main goals for the 2024 elections (interview, Jakarta, June 28, 2022).

Broad party coalitions, then, put presidents at the center of managing a multi-actor contest for resources and policy influence. Maintaining an alliance with so many parties, based on a sense of mutual dependence, carries benefits and risks for the president. The more parties are included, the higher the opportunities for the president to use one party against another and to fend off requests that he or she deems inappropriate. However, the danger for presidents lies in parties forming a collective stance against the head of state. Such issues could relate to the interests of the political class as a group or parties as organizations. Faced with a united front, presidents are often forced to give in—turning the inclusiveness of the coalition from an asset into a liability. Thus, party-based coalitional presidentialism—especially if it comes in the form of oversized coalitions, as in the Indonesian case—is both durable and prone to stagnation. It is durable because it profoundly satisfies both the parties (which can express their ideological preferences in elections while retaining the chance of joining government if defeated) and the president (who can benefit from the parties' resources and neutralize their potential threats, as well as play individual parties off against each other for even greater advantage). Naturally, such juggling of multiple interests comes at the cost of bold reformist policy initiatives. Filtered through various layers of presidential or party interests, initiatives for major change are at risk of foundering or being watered down. In the next section, we explore a case study that showcases both the reasons for the durability of broad party coalitions and the stagnating impact it can unfold.

The 2018 Vice Presidential Nomination

As we have seen, coalitions between Indonesian presidents and political parties have settled into an equilibrium that is carefully balanced through a set of unwritten rules (such as that pre-election partners are privileged) and a mutual understanding of the costs of a possible failure (which leads presidents to rarely punish parties through reshuffles and parties to refrain from seriously pursuing the president's impeachment). This balance, which allows both sides to survive without excluding or destroying the other, forms the basis for the party dimension of coalitional presidentialism in Indonesia. To illustrate how the broad outlines of this equilibrium manifest themselves in practice, the discussion below analyzes the negotiations through which Widodo and his pre-electoral coalition arrived at the choice of the vice presidential running mate for the incumbent in 2018. This process led to frustrations on both sides but still sustained the conviction that all involved actors benefitted. As such, the episode is an appropriate metaphor for Indonesian party coalitions per se.

Selecting a vice presidential running mate is an important moment in any presidency (Kamarck 2020). Especially for incumbents up for re-election, picking a running mate without outside interference is a test of their power. While first-term presidents often have to accept deputies recommended by their sponsors, incumbents are expected to have accrued enough political capital to choose the person they think is best suited to assist in the campaign and when in office. In 2014, Widodo's coalition of nominating parties had imposed a running mate on him. Jusuf Kalla, who had also been Yudhoyono's vice president in his first term, was the preferred choice of Megawati and other party leaders. They had looked for someone who was both useful and non-threatening, as they did not want to select a candidate with prospects of gaining the presidency on his or her own. Kalla fit the bill: at the time of the 2014 election, he was seventy-two years old, had lost the chairmanship of Golkar in 2009, and was an experienced administrator. As such, he was a politician well beyond his prime and without an independent power base but still a safe choice as far as his governmental expertise was concerned. Because of the existing term limit, Kalla could not be nominated again for the 2019 elections. Accordingly, a new vice presidential nominee had to be recruited. After having expanded his coalition and his presidential power in his first term, Widodo appeared to be in a better position this time to make his own choice.

The golden standard of a smooth and self-determined vice presidential pick, and thus the model for Widodo to follow, was Yudhoyono's selection of Boediono in 2009. During his first term, Yudhoyono had grown tired of Kalla's autonomous political maneuvers. Instead of the powerful and wealthy Kalla (who was still chairman of Golkar at the time of the 2009 election), Yudhoyono wanted someone more low-profile: that is, a loyal assistant administrator rather than a self-confident politician. Boediono was a perfect match. A rather bland technocrat and academic, Boediono had been in several ministerial roles before the 2009 elections but had no connections to party politics. At sixty-six years of age and with non-existent popularity ratings in the polls, he also appeared unlikely to be a candidate in the 2014 elections. Boediono's profile suited the leaders of Yudhoyono's coalition parties, too. They accepted that in a large multi-party coalition, it was implausible for one of them to become vice president, given that this would unfairly privilege one party over the others. In this context, they were satisfied with endorsing a neutral, non-political actor who could not threaten their interests, and who made sure that in the next elections—for which no incumbent would be able to draw from government resources—all parties could push their own candidates.

But Widodo failed to replicate Yudhoyono's success, and he inadvertently turned the selection of the 2019 running mate into a major power contest between the incumbent president and his nominating parties (Fealy 2018a). To be sure, Widodo was in a slightly different position from the one Yudhoyono had found himself a decade earlier. Before the 2009 ballot, Yudhoyono had such a strong lead in the polls that he could choose a running mate without electoral considerations. Boediono, a Javanese like Yudhoyono, was not going to attract voters from outside the president's regional and ethnic core support base. Widodo, by contrast, faced a significant challenge from Prabowo Subianto, and so he had to make the potential to increase his overall electability a major criterion of his vice presidential choice. Beyond this significant difference, Widodo made a series of mistakes that Yudhoyono had avoided. Most importantly, while Yudhoyono had early on closed the door to the notion of selecting a party chair as running mate, Widodo not only tolerated the ambitions of party leaders but actively fueled them. Throughout the selection process, he allowed at least three party chairmen to enthusiastically propagate their mistaken belief that they had a chance of being selected. Golkar chairman Airlangga Hartarto, PKB leader Muhaimin Iskandar, and PPP chair Muhammad "Romy" Romahurmuziy all credibly claimed that the president had made encouraging remarks to them about their chance of becoming the vice presidential nominee.[5] Some palace sources insisted that Widodo deliberately egged them on so that he could use their competition to pick a neutral outsider.

If this was Widodo's plan, it failed badly. Even in the last week before the nomination in August 2018, all three men still believed in their chances. In the meantime, Widodo was working with his pollsters and staff on making his real pick. His main concern was a candidate's contribution to his electability and his feeling of personal compatibility. Finally, a few days before the nomination deadline, Widodo made his choice: it was Mahfud MD, the former chief justice of the Constitutional Court, who commanded high approval ratings and also had links to NU, the country's largest Muslim group. The NU connection was important as Widodo tried to gain the organization's support to challenge expected accusations from the Prabowo campaign that the president was anti-Islamic. Being presented with the latest survey numbers that showed Mahfud as the most promising running mate, Widodo looked at one of his pollsters and said, "Okay, let's do it" (confidential interview, online, August 7, 2018). But in yet another grave error, Widodo did not inform his partners in the party coalition—and neither did he discuss with NU whether Mahfud was a choice it could support. Instead, the news about Mahfud's imminent nomination leaked to the press, which is how the president's partners found out. As Mahfud began to give interviews in the press on why he accepted the nomination, a rebellion was brewing within the party coalition and NU against Widodo's decision.

The key summit between Widodo and the chairs of his coalition parties to discuss the vice presidential candidacy was scheduled for August 9, one day before the nomination deadline. On the evening before this meeting, NU leaders—including the PKB chairman—gathered at NU headquarters and threatened the president with desertion should Widodo nominate Mahfud (Detik 2018). NU made it known that it did not view Mahfud as a NU cadre, and that it had proposed to Widodo its list of four NU-endorsed figures. This list included the NU-linked party chairpersons of PKB and PPP, the NU chairman Said Agil Siraj, and its supreme spiritual leader, Ma'ruf Amin. The latter was a conservative cleric who had played a significant role in the 2016 mobilization of Islamists against the Christian and ethnic Chinese governor of Jakarta; it was his certification that the governor had committed blasphemy that justified the protests (Fealy 2018a). Following the NU gathering that threatened Widodo, assistants to the president began to inform party leaders individually that the president had picked Mahfud. In one-on-one communications with the palace, party leaders did not openly voice their opposition to Mahfud. Simultaneously, however, the elites consulted among each other. In these meetings, party leaders shared their dismay over how Widodo was about to nominate Mahfud over their heads, and that the parties needed to warn the president that he could not make such a momentous decision unilaterally. After some back and forth, the party chairpersons decided to use the August 9 meeting to reject Mahfud and nominate Ma'ruf instead (confidential interviews with party officials, Jakarta, March 7, 8, and 10, 2019).

The president arrived at the August 9 meeting unprepared. Mahfud had been told by palace assistants to wait in a restaurant nearby and expect a call to join the gathering for the public announcement. It is unclear whether Widodo was told before entering the room that the party leaders would reject Mahfud or whether that decision was only conveyed to the president in the meeting. In whatever way he was told, Widodo decided on the spot not to challenge his coalition and endorse the choice. To protect the president's public integrity, it was decided to present Ma'ruf's selection as Widodo's choice. Awkwardly, as the president and his coalition parties announced the nominee to the press, Ma'ruf was not even present, and Mahfud had been told to go home quietly. Ace Hasan Syadzily, a senior Golkar official, described the deal as a "good consensus. The parties had made their voice heard. The president listened. Ma'ruf is a respected figure, and we can live with that choice. We would have preferred our own chairman, but that's life. And there was one thing we could all agree on: the selection of Ma'ruf was the best way to leave all parties in the same position for the 2024 elections" (interview, Jakarta, March 15, 2019). As with Boediono in 2009, parties ultimately endorsed a vice president because he was too old (Ma'ruf was seventy-six and thus fifteen years older than Mahfud during the election) and not popular enough to launch his own presidential bid. Unlike in 2009, however, the parties had to force the president into this consensus, while Yudhoyono had proposed Boediono to them in a much more orderly manner.

The conflict surrounding the vice presidential nomination—which Yudhoyono and Widodo approached differently but with the same outcome—reflects the political centrality of the equilibrium between presidents and their coalition parties. This equilibrium is only rarely disturbed in a serious fashion, but the 2018 vice presidential nomination was one such rare case. On the one hand, the incumbent president was popular and on course for re-election, and the parties had no competitive alternative to nominate on their own. On the other hand, the parties held the power of formal nomination, which they felt Widodo did not sufficiently respect. In the conflict that ensued, both sides renegotiated their respective roles and eventually settled back into the power balance that benefited them both. While Ma'ruf was not Widodo's preferred pick, he could accept the selection because it kept his party coalition together and secured NU's support in an election partly fought on each candidate's Islamic credentials. For the parties, the president had given in to their demands, reassuring them that they are crucial to the sustainability of presidential coalitions. Both sides became aware that although they had considered walking away from each other, neither could follow through with such drastic action. The conflict brought into sharp focus what both sides could lose if coalitional presidentialism were to collapse: the president could have potentially lost his nominators and electoral machine network, and the parties risked their access to the spoils of government had Widodo gone on to win without some of them. Continuing their arrangement offered the least risk for both.

Recall that one of the patterns emerging from our comparative analysis in the introduction was that presidents whose own party is small tend to build oversized coalitions. We speculated that that might have to do with their greater anxiety compared to other incumbents with larger partisan bases. While this chapter has further substantiated that hypothesis (Yudhoyono directly confirmed it), the above discussion has also pointed to additional motivations. Most importantly, the benefit of a broad party coalition offers presidents the chance to reduce their dependence on their own party. But there are risks, too: if parties form a united front against the president, the parties have a high chance of prevailing. This pattern was visible in the nomination of Widodo's running mate in 2018, but it is also affecting the policy arena. In September 2019, an alliance of Widodo's coalition parties pressured the president to endorse revisions to the law on Indonesia's Corruption Eradication Agency (KPK). The KPK had been a major nuisance to the parties, with dozens of their senior officials going to prison for corruption since the agency's creation in 2003 (Blakkarly 2015). Widodo, too, felt unhappy about the KPK's wide-ranging powers, but similar to Yudhoyono before him, he had been hesitant to act against it out of fear of a public backlash. However, faced with a collective stance formed by his coalition parties, Widodo acquiesced (Warburton 2019). In such cases, the regressive effect of broad-based coalitional presidentialism is apparent: the KPK lost significant elements of its powers, undermining anti-corruption policies (Mujani and Liddle 2021). Similarly, through Ma'ruf's selection, a conservative cleric with a reputation for limiting minority rights became vice president, instead of Mahfud, a popular former chief justice who had presided over numerous democracy-supporting rulings from 2008 to 2013.

The logic of achieving maximum inclusiveness of party coalitions in post-2004 Indonesia has become so entrenched that it is hard to ascertain what the polity would look like without it. Since Yudhoyono's ascension to power, there were only brief windows into such a counter-factual scenario. Yudhoyono was confronted with a hostile majority of opposition parties between October and December 2004, and Widodo faced a similar scenario at the beginning of his term (in his case, as noted, he had proudly claimed in the preceding campaign that such a minority status would not bother him). Both Yudhoyono and Widodo were shocked by short demonstrations of the parties' powers (which consisted mostly of monopolizing DPR committees and delaying presidential initiatives) without actually experiencing consequences that could have threatened their presidencies. To be sure, governing without broad party support would be more unstable, but neither Yudhoyono nor Widodo wanted to test just *how* unstable—or what the potential benefits of smaller coalitions could be. It is worth emphasizing again that no Indonesian president operating under the post-2002 constitutional arrangements has faced an impeachment process, not even in its earliest stages. This fact indicates a tendency toward risk aversion on the part of presidents—but also shows their knowledge that implementing the broad outlines of coalitional presidentialism offers significant protections from impeachment and instability. As a result, the equilibrium generated by coalitional presidentialism has protected Indonesian democracy from destabilizing conflict, while at the same time paralyzing the polity in a state of policy conservatism.

However, political parties are only one element in the coalitional presidentialism architecture. There are others that presidents can resort to for assistance in elections and government. Including a wide range of non-party elements into presidential coalitions allows presidents to build additional safeguards against disloyalty by political parties or other non-party allies. One of these additional coalitional presidentialism actors is the legislature (as well as individual legislators). Although much of the coalitional presidentialism literature has combined parties and legislatures into one main actor presidents have to deal with, a separate treatment may be more appropriate. From a perspective of party strengths, parties hold powers as organizations that partially lie outside of their representation in legislatures (such as mobilization capacity during and between campaigns). The next chapter will showcase the other side of this equation: that is, the political weight of the DPR and its members that is unrelated to—or only loosely associated with—the parties they affiliate with. In reality, individual legislators can exercise so much power that presidents need to target them individually to secure their cooperation.

3

THE LEGISLATURE

Apart from the different functions of parties and legislatures, other reasons exist that motivate Indonesian presidents to situate the DPR and individual MPs as coalition partners distinct from parties. In Indonesia, the legislature works in a way that differs significantly from the practices in other democracies. Partly because of the unique co-legislative roles of the president and the DPR but also because of the emphasis of Indonesian political tradition on consensus-building, plenary votes to decide policy or personnel issues are uncommon (Sherlock 2010). Instead, most debates and decision-making processes occur in the DPR's committees and special bodies, often behind closed doors. Deals are being made informally between the president's representatives, pro-government legislators, and oppositional MPs, often through the mediation of the DPR leaders and the various committees and bodies. These compromises are then formalized by acclamation, first at the committee level and then in the plenary. Only in very rare cases do votes in the plenary occur, and even then the side that expects defeat tends to walk out from the proceedings rather than having its loss recorded. Unlike in many Latin American polities, it is almost impossible to ascertain how a particular legislator voted vis-à-vis the government's initial proposals, or how a particular compromise was reached (Morgenstern, Negri, and Pérez-Liñán 2008). Scholars interested in studying these processes are left with having to examine the transcripts of official DPR meetings, but these do not include records of behind-the-scenes negotiations either (Farhan 2018; Barrett 2011). Thus, the DPR conceals its inner workings rather than being a body that exhibits its political contestations in open votes and debates.

This constellation presents both problems and opportunities to Indonesian presidents. On the one hand, legislators' informality, secrecy, and committee-focused work loosens the ties between MPs and their parties. Behind closed doors, legislators often submit proposals outside of their parties' policy agenda, with the origins of such proposals subsequently becoming untraceable. This means that the president cannot rely on negotiations with top party leaders to ensure that their caucuses vote with the government. Rather, he or she needs to be in close contact with the DPR speaker, deputy speakers, committee heads, and chairpersons of key special bodies to understand who is with the government and who is not. Based on this mapping of the legislative fault lines, presidents can then ask their assistants to target individual legislators that may be persuaded with specific incentives. Alternatively, presidents may outsource this work to senior DPR leaders, who can then build special ties to the president by making themselves indispensable to the stability of government operations. As a consequence, presidents accrue a debt to these DPR operators, which has to be repaid through concessions—both in terms of material benefits and political protection. However, there are also positive implications of this pattern for presidents. The autonomy of legislators gives presidents the chance of not only keeping MPs formally in line through careful individual targeting, but they can also tie oppositional legislators to their interests, often against the wishes (and, in many cases, without the knowledge) of their party leaderships.

To be sure, it is not uncommon for presidents in other democracies to target individual legislators, especially if they hold a swing vote in tight contests (Arnold, Doyle, and Wiesehomeier 2017). In the US Congress, such campaigns occur regularly (Bolton 2021). Despite these commonalities—which again suggest that parties and legislatures deserve separate analytical treatment beyond the Indonesian case—there are key differences, too. First, in the United States and many Latin American presidential systems, presidents typically approach a handful of legislators whose support is uncertain; in Indonesia, the higher levels of individualization in the legislature mean that the problem of securing a presidential majority is much more wide-ranging and systematic. Second, while rogue senators or MPs in the United States often display their uncertainty publicly and spell out to the media the concessions they request to overcome it, their Indonesian counterparts tend to negotiate quietly with the president's aides. Hence, Indonesia's legislature is more atomized, informal, and clandestine than in other parts of the democratic world, making applying coalitional presidentialism strategies more complex. If handled carefully, however, the integration of legislators into the broader presidential coalition can be highly rewarding for the president.

This chapter starts, in line with this book's general approach, with a discussion of the powers that the legislature and individual legislators hold vis-à-vis the president. As we will see, these powers have been a source of considerable irritation to presidents, especially in the area of budgeting. The second section looks at the president's set of specific authorities in dealing with the DPR—which give the executive much leverage in enticing MPs to cooperate. In the third section, the chapter explains how executive-legislative coalitions and negotiations work in practice, both at the institutional and individual level. Key to these negotiations are brokers in the DPR's various leadership bodies and caucuses, who promise the president cooperation but gain strong concessions in return—for themselves and for the institution. The fourth section then uses a case study of Setya Novanto to show how presidents have used legislative brokers to secure the DPR's integration into the broader structures and practices of coalitional presidentialism. Novanto, the DPR Speaker between 2014 and 2015 and again between 2016 and 2017, was the epitome of the dilemmatic challenges presidents face when picking their legislative allies, and the price they have to pay for their choice.

DPR Powers

We have noted earlier that the 2002 constitutional amendments established a system in which the president holds key powers but faces a strong legislature (Horowitz 2013). This balance encourages cooperation to avoid dysfunction and has thus developed into a cornerstone of Indonesia's coalitional presidentialism. In the post-2002 constitutional landscape, the DPR possesses co-legislative powers together with the president; can overturn government regulations in lieu of law (Perpu); carries out oversight functions vis-à-vis ministries; is deeply engaged in the drafting and passing of the budget; and selects and confirms personnel for important state bodies. We had already touched on these powers in previous chapters, but to fully grasp the legislative dimension of coalitional presidentialism in the current polity, it is necessary to unpack the most important of them in some detail.

Among all its powers, the most consequential for Indonesia's political economy—and the standing of legislators—is the DPR's budgetary authority. It is also the one that presidents have most complained about. In his memoirs, Yudhoyono (2014, 34) lamented that "in the drafting and implementation of the state budget, the DPR has now the power to go as deep as the third level [with the first being the most general, and lower levels indicating a higher level of detail]. This means that [the legislature can influence] budget documents that regulate the allocation of funds per ministry/agency, sector, sub-sector, program, and activity. The DPR also has the right to withhold the disbursement of the budget, which is typically described as 'the DPR giving the budget an asterisk.' Unless this asterisk is lifted by the DPR, the budget—although it has previously been passed and turned into a law—can't be disbursed." Clearly annoyed, Yudhoyono added that "it was situations such as this that constantly disturbed the implementation of the budget as the main [driver of] economic growth and, at the same time, as a precondition for the functioning of the government." His Finance Minister Chatib Basri (2013–2014) similarly lamented that his "rational policy" often collided with particularistic interests of legislators (interview, online, November 29, 2021). The DPR's budget authority, then, does not only provide legislators with leverage against the president but also hands them ample opportunities to insert clauses into the budget that can benefit themselves or their electoral constituencies. As a result, during Indonesia's post-1998 democratization, the center of patronage exchanges and corruption moved from Suharto's executive-heavy administration to the forums of executive-legislative negotiations in the DPR.

Echoing Yudhoyono, Farhan (2018) described how the DPR can deploy its budget powers. In Indonesia, the budget process is divided into four stages: formulation, approval, execution, and monitoring. The first stage is the president's responsibility, with the Ministry of Finance setting the macroeconomic assumptions and spending limits for the next fiscal year (Farhan 2018, 46). Parallel to this, the government's National Development Planning Agency (Bappenas) develops a Government Working Plan (RKP), drawing from longer-term development agendas and government priorities. Once the Finance Ministry and Bappenas have synchronized their budget planning, preliminary budget discussions with the legislature begin. This usually happens in May, based on the fiscal policy framework and the budget priorities submitted by the government to the DPR. This is also when the DPR's powerful Budget Agency and its Commission XI, which oversees finance issues, become involved and represent the legislature in negotiations with the executive. From these discussions emerges a basic joint agreement, which is subsequently "used by ministries and government agencies to formulate a detailed annual budget and work plan" (Farhan 2018, 46). That work plan, in turn, is the basis for the 11 sectoral DPR commissions (each with at least one ministry as a cooperating partner) to negotiate with their respective ministries and agencies. As mentioned earlier, the overall budget ceiling remains mostly unchanged in these debates, but the budget line items can change dramatically—which is what Yudhoyono referred to as interference in the third level of budgeting. At this stage, legislators have the most opportunities to insert their patronage projects, and they do so until satisfied and their approval is secured.

Once a general agreement is reached between government representatives and the DPR, the president delivers the annual budget speech to the House, normally—as noted—in August. Another round of negotiations ensues before the draft is put to the DPR plenary for endorsement. This typically occurs in September or October. In the post-2004 period, all budgets were passed unanimously, indicating that sufficient concessions were made behind the scenes to satisfy all legislators.[1] But the DPR's budgetary authority does not stop with the approval of the budget. During the third and fourth stages (namely, execution and monitoring), legislators have additional opportunities for intervention. One such opportunity emerges during discussions on budget revisions and additions, which take place in the first half of each budget year. During the 2012 and 2013 revision debates, some caucuses rejected the government's proposal to cut fuel subsidies. PKS—a member of Yudhoyono's party coalition—took the same stance, which was the reason for the continued debates within the alliance over whether to expel the party for violating coalition discipline. However, such open expressions of dissent are rare, even from parties and legislators not formally part of the president's coalition. It is much more common for potential dissenters to receive quiet incentives to approve the government's proposals. This also applies to the final stage of the budget process; that is, the passing of the Law on the Responsibility for Budget Execution in the past budget year. The DPR's approval of this bill absolves the government from any potential wrongdoing in past budgetary matters, both legally and politically.

The display of power of the DPR and individual legislators in the protracted, multi-layered budget deliberations is replicated in deliberating non-budget bills. In contrast to the executive-centered early formulation of the budget, the DPR can initiate its own bills that are deliberated once the president agrees to appoint representatives for this process. The Legislative Agency in the DPR—the non-budget equivalent of the Budget Agency—coordinates which bills are discussed, determines the schedule, and oversees the deliberations. In most cases, a bill is deliberated in the DPR committee covering a bill's subject area; if a bill cuts across multiple policy arenas, a special working committee consisting of members from various committees is created. After the agreement is reached among the members and, collectively, with the government, the bill travels back through the Legislative Agency to the DPR plenary for endorsement. As in the case of the budget, approval is generally unanimous—only in rare cases is a vote taken and dissent recorded. As in the budget process, too, legislators have a lot of opportunities to make sure that their particularistic interests are accommodated in bills, explaining the low level of opposition to the final product. Many of these individual insertions to (or removals from) a bill become untraceable; in 2009, an article disadvantaging the tobacco industry disappeared from the Health Bill after it was passed, and in October 2020, a major Omnibus Law (which changed numerous laws in one step to launch a massive economic deregulation drive) was passed without anybody able to say how many pages and articles it had (Pebrianto 2020). It took days before the final version was published, but the mystery of who had inserted what and when remained unresolved.

In the arena of personnel selection for Indonesia's key state institutions, the DPR has the power to confirm the appointment of the military and police chiefs as well as ambassadors; it picks from a list of nominees to appoint members of the Supreme Court, the Supreme Auditing Board, the Judicial Commission, the Human Rights Commission, and other major agencies; and it can directly name three out of the nine judges of the Constitutional Court. These appointment powers have shaped presidential behavior in the selection processes. For instance, to narrow down the DPR's range of choices, presidents do not submit more than one candidate for the military and police chief—this leaves a potentially sceptical legislature only with the option of rejecting the president's nominee. The DPR has thus far shied away from such a move, partly because of fears among legislators that rejection of powerful military or police leaders could make them targets for future acts of retaliation. Similarly, presidents usually submit a list of candidates for positions in other state agencies that only includes nominees acceptable to the executive but gives the DPR the final say in the selection. This creates patronage opportunities for individual legislators, who rarely follow party lines in selection processes and—in some cases—have been known to accept payments for their votes (Amelia 2013).

On the surface, viewing the DPR's individualization and fragmentation as a weakness in its strategic positioning toward the presidency would be tempting. It could be argued that a united and coherent legislature (as well as strictly organized caucuses) could extract more concessions from the executive. But in Indonesia's specific context, the DPR's atomization situates its institution and members as independent actors rather than as subordinates of their parties. Were parties in stronger control over their caucuses and members, presidents could limit themselves to negotiating with party and caucus leaders—and indeed, much of the coalitional presidentialism focuses on these interactions. In Indonesia's post-2004 polity, however, the difficulty of "herding" MPs and the DPR as an institution is the source of their power, and it necessitates presidents to integrate them into ruling coalitions with strategies that are different from those applied to political parties. Moreover, the self-confidence of legislators (both vis-à-vis their parties and the president) has continued to gradually increase in the post-2004 polity. One reason for this is the growing personalization of legislative elections following the introduction of an open party list system of proportional representation in 2009 (Aspinall and Berenschot 2019). Under this system, nominees compete with members of their own parties for seats, which means that individual candidates, not parties, run and finance their campaigns. Once they reach the DPR, therefore, members view themselves as nominally affiliated with—rather than subordinated to—their parties.

The broad outlines of the DPR's powers suggest that Indonesian presidents have to manage the demands of the institution and its members if they want to secure the stability of their rule. We will see below how exactly they do this, but the fact that there have been so few instances of DPR dissent, and no serious threat of impeachment since 2004, indicates that presidents have successfully integrated the DPR and its MPs into their coalitional presidentialism arrangements. Key to this success has been the fact that presidents have significant powers that they can bring to bear. In the next section, we turn to the assets Indonesian presidents possess in interacting with the DPR, before then discussing the system of brokerage through which they ensure the legislators' support.

Presidents' Legislative Leverage

Indonesian presidents' first noteworthy asset vis-à-vis the legislature is the near-impossibility of impeachment. We already noted that presidential impeachments in Indonesia involve a cumbersome process that must pass through the DPR, the Constitutional Court, and the MPR, and that presidents can prevent its initiation by commanding a one-third-plus-one minority in the DPR. This constellation creates a different relationship between the president and the legislature than, for instance, in Brazil or Peru (Rattinger 2017). There, presidential impeachments are regular occurrences, and legislators include them in their repertoire of potential actions against the president. In Indonesia, legislators must assume that presidents serve their five-year terms and, if a first-term incumbent is popular, the likelihood of a second term is high. This fact encourages cooperation rather than fundamental opposition and prefigures a broadly inclusivist model of coalitional presidentialism. As conceded by Jazuli Juwaini, the chairman of the PKS caucus in the DPR, "although we are in opposition, we know that the position of the president is very strong. He is deliberately protected by the constitution, and we respect that. That means we are engaging with him constructively, and we try to reach a win-win solution: the best for the president but also the best for our constituents. We're in this together for at least five years" (interview, Kyoto, February 6, 2020). Thus, while presidents need to manage the DPR's strengths, they also know that they can only be removed by it in extreme circumstances.

As much as the DPR's budgetary powers aggrieved Yudhoyono, legislators depend on the president to realize their budget ambitions. The president establishes the initial budget framework through the minister of finance, and it is this framework within which legislators have to create opportunities for themselves, their constituencies, and their sponsors. In the more detailed budget discussions, legislators must secure the president's approval (however tacit) for their projects to make it into the final budget law. According to a political adviser who had helped Widodo and his running mate, Basuki Tjahaja Purnama, to win the 2012 gubernatorial elections in Jakarta, Widodo became—as governor—a master of the bargaining processes necessary to have his budgets approved by the capital's legislature. "How do you think Widodo got all of his budgets through so easily in Jakarta? He accepted that about 10 percent of the total budget is set aside for special interests of legislators, and he never questioned that practice," the adviser said, adding that Purnama felt more appalled by such patronage exchanges than Widodo did (confidential interview, Jakarta, April 17, 2014). While not confirming that he was engaging in material deals with legislators during his time as governor between 2012 and 2014, Widodo emphasized briefly before his presidential inauguration that he anticipated smooth relations with the DPR once sworn in: "I know what my role is, and I know what their role is. I have faced oppositional legislatures before, as in Jakarta, and I did well" (interview, Jakarta, September 15, 2014). Given that all of his presidential budgets passed without incident, he was proven right.

Within the broader budgetary powers of the president, the DPR has to seek approval from the head of the executive for its own budget. This budget includes important benefits for the institution and individual legislators, such as international travel, per diem payments for domestic trips, salaries for staff, and renovations for existing facilities. The negotiations surrounding this budget are controversial as the public tends to pay much attention to it—much more than to the significantly larger project budgets debated below the media's radar screen. This is because items in the DPR budget are easier to expose for the media as evidence of the extravagance of politicians than the secretly inserted vested interest items in the rest of the overall budget. In 2012, for instance, there was extended media coverage of the planned Rp 1.4 billion (US$100,000) renovation of toilets in the DPR corridors, which were indeed in a sad state (Tempo 2012). Presidents are aware of the sensitive nature of the DPR budget and tend to be restrictive in the allocations. The DPR's budget increased from Rp 2.4 trillion (US$171 million) in 2010 to Rp 3.9 trillion (US$279 million) in 2015 and Rp 5.1 trillion (US$364 million) in 2020, but these increases were below the growth rates of the total state budget. Similarly, both Yudhoyono and Widodo consistently rejected DPR requests to introduce discretionary funds for MPs, which are common in other presidential systems (such as the Philippines). Although presidents routinely agree to budget requests submitted by individual legislators, they do not wish to formalize this arrangement, which would reduce their leverage in negotiations and attract bad publicity.[2]

Another significant power of Indonesian presidents vis-à-vis the legislature is derived from the former's co-legislative authority. Based on this authority, presidents not only have the power to introduce bills but also have several options to obstruct bills initiated by the DPR. One such option is to not appoint a government representative for deliberations of the bill in question, which means that the bill cannot proceed. Under post-2004 conditions of coalitional presidentialism, this has rarely occurred, as presidents are aware that the DPR would view such defiance as a hostile act. During her presidency in the early 2000s, Megawati refused to name a representative to start deliberations on a controversial anti-pornography bill, much to the frustration of its DPR initiators (Sherlock 2009). But her successor Yudhoyono did appoint deliberation representatives, and the bill was passed into law in 2008, leading to the imprisonment of dozens of people for "transgressions" since then. While post-2004 presidents have been reluctant to use their power of legislative obstruction, they have repeatedly threatened to do so. Before the 2019 revisions to the KPK law, Widodo stated that he had yet to decide whether to agree to the deliberations, and if he were to do so, he would make his own proposals (Putratama 2019). Ultimately, he agreed to the talks, and the bill was passed quickly. Some of his proposals were accommodated—a fact he disclosed in a media conference to fend off criticism that he had given in to the DPR. Hence, although rarely used, presidential powers to prevent legislation make the DPR dependent on the president's goodwill, shaping the pace and outcome of deliberations.

DPR legislators are also attracted to the president's executive appointment powers. While becoming a member of the legislature and its leadership bodies is highly lucrative for politicians, cabinet positions remain the most coveted jobs in the Indonesian political system outside of the presidency. As a result, legislators use their relationship with the president—often built up over years of executive-legislative negotiations—to recommend themselves for a ministry. There have been eleven former DPR legislators and one former provincial legislator in Widodo's second cabinet, with previous presidential ministries showing similar patterns. Extended lobbying efforts by legislators for a cabinet post often involve adopting a softer stance toward the government in DPR forums than otherwise would be the case, delivering clear benefits for the president and his or her representatives. In the same vein, older legislators looking to retire often seek and receive ambassadorial appointments. For instance, after a seventeen-year career in the legislature, Golkar politician Hajriyanto Y. Thohari became ambassador to Lebanon in 2019. "As a member of Golkar, I am part of the coalition supporting Widodo, and I feel that I have done that job well. Now it's time to serve the president in a different capacity," Thohari explained (interview, Jakarta, January 8, 2019). As they are well paid, ambassadorships are highly competitive, with the president's allies submitting nominations and lobbying for the candidates' endorsement. The fact that the final list of presidential nominations returns to the DPR for confirmation is an additional encouragement for many legislators to seek an appointment, which then becomes part of broader presidential-legislative deal-making.

Finally, the president has broader powers of sanction that can be utilized to discipline legislators. Recall that Indonesian presidents can recognize or annul the legal standing of party leaderships and that Widodo used this authority to turn two parties (Golkar and PPP) from oppositional into pro-government parties. Given the autonomy of individual MPs, this did not mean that every legislator suddenly became a loyal supporter of executive policy, but it formally transformed Widodo's minority position in the DPR into a supermajority and made governance easier. Importantly, however, the politico-psychological impact of Widodo's intervention in internal party (and, indirectly, DPR) affairs went well beyond the Golkar and PPP cases. Other parties feared that they would experience the same fate, and some thus instructed their legislators to reduce their open criticism of the government in the DPR and outside. Even Yudhoyono's party was affected. Before the PD congress in May 2015, there were rumors that the Widodo government would use the event to encourage anti-Yudhoyono forces in the party to take over its leadership. Responding to these rumors, Yudhoyono deployed two strategies. First, he publicly called out Widodo, with whom he had a tense relationship. Yudhoyono's son and chair of the PD caucus in the DPR, Edhie Baskoro, confronted Widodo in a consultation meeting between the president and the legislature, demanding that presidential intervention in the party's internal affairs stop immediately (Prihandoko 2015). Second, Yudhoyono started a charm offensive to commit the president to attend the upcoming PD congress. The president's attendance, Yudyohono was sure, would end the conflict.

The subsequent meeting of the former and incumbent presidents at the PD congress in Surabaya put their expertise in managing coalitional presidentialism on full display. Before the event's opening, Yudhoyono told this author, "I am sure the president's presence here will demonstrate that all the rumors of possible intervention into our affairs were false. At the same time, my party can demonstrate that it holds no ill will toward the government, and that we are prepared to cooperate in the legislature and other arenas" (interview, Surabaya, May 11, 2015). Widodo, for his part, lectured the ex-president's party about the need for political stability and the necessity for harmony in the parliament in particular—something PD politicians had heard much about from their patron during his own presidency (notes by the author, Surabaya, May 12, 2015). In the end, both men got what they wanted: Yudhoyono remained in control of his party, having neutralized the potential power the president could exercise over it and its DPR legislators; and Widodo received Yudhoyono's promise that while PD would not formally be in the president's coalition, it would refrain from fundamental opposition in the legislature and other political arenas. With this, the Yudhoyono-Widodo arrangement was representative of the many day-to-day negotiations and compromises that typically occur when a president's powers are leveraged against the equally significant authorities held by legislators. And in a fashion symbolic of the presidential-legislative interaction, too, the Yudhoyono-Widodo relationship settled into a stable equilibrium in which both sides did not necessarily like each other but accepted the counterpart's existence.[3]

Managing DPR Coalitions

The discussion of the DPR's and the president's power resources suggests that both sides would have much to lose if they tried to paralyze or even destroy the other. Cooperation, by contrast, offers rewards that are not only substantial but also stable and predictable. Nevertheless, the establishment of a cooperative equilibrium is not automatic. On the contrary, it needs to be carefully managed and constantly renewed. The primary fuel that keeps the coalition between presidents and legislators running is patronage, which presidents channel to key DPR actors in formal and informal ways.

The highest-level formal channel of presidential-legislative interaction is the consultation forum. This is a rare event in which the president meets with the leaders of DPR bodies and caucuses, with the location of the gathering typically alternating between the palace and the DPR complex. In most cases, consultation forums convene when a major political issue needs to be discussed. In his first consultation meeting with the DPR in April 2015, for instance, Widodo had two items of interest on his agenda (Gera 2015). First, he needed the DPR's support to help him resolve a crisis surrounding his first appointment of a new police chief (more about this in chapters 4 and 5). This was a calamity of his own making, and he had to ask the DPR to use its constitutional power of confirmation to make the problem disappear. The second item was the spending of Yudhoyono's last budget—a topic of great interest to the president and the DPR alike. The connection between the two items, which Widodo proclaimed publicly, signaled that the president was prepared to trade concessions on the police chief issue with budgetary promises. The outcome confirmed this arrangement. Emerging from the forum, the president and the speaker of the DPR, Setya Novanto, announced that the legislature would consider Widodo's proposed plan of action on the police chief issue and that the government, in return, would involve the DPR more in the ongoing expenditure of the budget. It is important to note that at the time of the meeting, Widodo was technically still a president without a majority in parliament. Yet a simple exchange of budget patronage against the endorsement of a key post allowed him to obtain approval for the latter in the short term and, by implication, for the executive's budget in the longer term.

Below the consultation forum, formal interactions between the government and the legislature take place in the various DPR committees. There, legislators have the right to call representatives of the ministry allocated to their committee as a counterpart. These ministry delegates then have to brief the DPR on government initiatives and answer questions. As the majority of these hearings are public, they mostly serve the purpose of political pageantry. MPs want to demonstrate to their constituencies (via the press) that they take their control functions seriously, and executive leaders likewise wish to perform in a way that conforms to expected government accountability standards vis-à-vis the legislature (Rahman 2021). For legislators of government parties, these public events are an opportunity to both highlight their support for executive policies they view as useful for their constituencies and distance themselves from less popular government actions. Legislators not aligned with the president, for their part, use the chance to propose alternatives to the policies offered by the executive. While mostly perfunctory, the hearings fulfill an essential function in coalitional presidentialism by providing a public platform on which both sides can showcase their roles. This political theater suggests constitutional functionality, which is crucial to the operations and stability of the president's coalition architecture. As Yudhoyono knew from the beginning, and as Widodo learned quickly in his presidency, the projection of a stable political order is the main goal of, and reason for, the sustenance of broad-based presidential coalitions that allow the government to operate and society to avoid "chaos".

As important as the public display of functional interaction is for maintaining political alliances, the real work of keeping the necessary relationships in place happens informally. Presidents do this by building a network of contacts in the DPR, both with leaders of its bodies and with individual legislators. High-ranking DPR officials engage with the president or his representatives on specific issues, and once an agreement is reached, the former are expected to implement these deals. To the extent that caucus leaders have power over their fellow party MPs, presidents can ask the chairs of factions nominally integrated into his or her coalition to do the lobbying work. However, the chairpersons of DPR bodies often have greater influence over the members in their respective institutions, regardless of party affiliation. In persuading MPs to back presidential policies, DPR leaders distribute patronage to them, often by negotiating and then communicating executive approval for legislators' special budget requests. Indeed, it is appropriate to understand the entire DPR hierarchy as a network of brokers that trades DPR support for policies against benefits for its members (Iaryczower and Oliveros 2016). In this system, the president is both a client (who seeks DPR approval of proposals) and a patron (as a dispenser of executive favors). At the apex of this network is the DPR speaker, who is assisted by four deputy speakers (see table 3.1). Each of the deputy speakers coordinates special bodies and some of the sectoral committees. The chairs and deputy chairs of these committees, in turn, manage individual MPs belonging to them. The caucuses, for their part, are represented in the Consultative Agency (Bamus), in which decisions are negotiated between the functional DPR leaders and caucus officials.

As the most senior official in the DPR hierarchy, the speaker is typically the chief broker between the president and the other elements of the legislature whose support the executive requires. It is not a coincidence that for much of the post-Suharto era, the post of speaker has been held by a politician of Golkar—the party most known for its transactional and tactical prowess (Tomsa 2008; Saragih 2021). Although no Golkar cadre has been president since 1999, the party has had five DPR speakers: Akbar Tandjung (1999–2004), Agung Laksono (2004–2009), Setya Novanto (2014–2015, 2016–2017), Ade Komarudin (2016), and Bambang Soesatyo (2018–2019). Only on two occasions have representatives of the president's party held the speakership: PD's Marzuki Alie (2009–2014) and PDI-P's Puan Maharani, Megawati's daughter (2019–2024). Rather counterintuitively, presidents have often found it easier to form alliances with legislators and extract deals from them when a Golkar politician is in the speaker's chair. Using

TABLE 3.1. DPR structure and brokerage network, 2021

		SPEAKER			
CONSULTATIVE AGENCY	CAUCUSES	DEPUTY SPEAKER—POLITICS AND SECURITY	DEPUTY SPEAKER—ECONOMY AND FINANCE	DEPUTY SPEAKER—INDUSTRY AND DEVELOPMENT	DEPUTY SPEAKER—PEOPLE'S WELFARE
		Committees I, II and III	Committee XI	Committees IV, V, VI, VII	Committees VIII, IX, X
		Legislative Agency	Budget Agency		Internal Affairs Agency
		Plenary (575 Members)			

their wide networks and long political brokerage experience, Golkar politicians can reach agreements with MPs under them that DPR seniors directly linked to the president's party might find hard to accomplish. The only post-Suharto president who failed to appreciate this circumstance was Wahid, whose 2001 impeachment was arranged in no small part by Akbar Tandjung. According to Tandjung, "[Wahid] did not understand that he needed the DPR. I told him that I could hold the DPR together for him if he wanted to, but he did not want to listen. At the end, as I predicted, he fell" (interview, Jakarta, February 11, 2008). Post-2004 presidents have learned that lesson and generally done well in upholding the DPR's allegiance with the help of allied speakers who enjoy significant presidential patronage.

Below the speaker, a network of influential sub-brokers in committees and other DPR bodies (such as the crucial Budget Agency) ensures that individual MPs follow general agreements made with the president, and that they are sufficiently compensated for their support. Presidents also have the option of approaching sub-brokers directly, or even working with individual legislators. As one MP explained, "normally we get approached by the DPR leadership or the committee chairs. They say, 'hey, the president's team wants this or that. And they ask if there is anything they could do for us.' Then we come up with a list of requests, normally in the form of budget items or policy changes. In some cases, presidential aides go to MPs directly. That hasn't happened to me, but I know colleagues who have been called" (confidential interview, Jakarta, June 25, 2019). The key advantage of the president over other clients of the DPR brokerage network is his or her unique ability to move budgets officially and thus legally. Other clients, by contrast, have to use cash to get the DPR to fulfill their requests. These clients even include governmental institutions below the president. In 2018, Deputy Speaker Taufik Kurniawan was arrested because he had received bribes from at least two district government heads to arrange an increase in their Special Allocation Funds (DAK)—a transfer by the center to the regions that is normally set by a standardized process but can be changed through intervention (Aritenang 2020). In the case of Kebumen district, Kurniawan engineered the allocation of an additional Rp 93 billion (US$6.6 million) to the territory and received a fee of Rp 3.7 billion (US$264,000) in return. For his part, the district chief of Purbalingga sent Kurniawan Rp 1.2 billion (US$85,000) for a similar service (Galih 2019).

In trying to secure the DPR's participation in broader presidential coalitions, therefore, the most powerful instrument of the head of state is his or her budgetary power. Presidents can also use other tools from their classic coalitional presidentialism toolbox (such as the promise of appointment or endorsement of DPR-drafted legislation), but the main glue that binds presidents and legislators together is direct patronage. While other brokerage clients of the DPR—such as interest groups, oligarchs, or non-presidential state actors—have to cross into spheres of illegality by paying for expected favors, the president can remain within the formal parameters of executive-legislative relations when engaging in patronage deals. This set of arrangements forms a stable foundation for semi-permanent alliances between presidents and MPs, regardless of who is formally in the governing coalition and who is not. The relative stability of Indonesian governance after 2004, and the absence of even the slightest indication of a serious impeachment drive, are due to this patronage-based system of mutually beneficial exchanges. But while most operations that protect this status quo take place behind closed doors, the citizenry has a general awareness of the DPR as a center of corruption. The DPR routinely finishes last in opinion surveys of public trust in specific institutions (Detik 2019b). Thus, the other side of the stability coin is a major trust deficit in a critical democratic body, contributing to the overall decline in the quality of democracy in Indonesia.

The Case of Setya Novanto

No other case can better illustrate the ways DPR brokers engage with presidents—and the deals that emerge from such engagement—than the rise of Setya Novanto to the position of DPR speaker. Novanto was the archetype of a class of transactional politicians who had transitioned successfully from Suharto's regime to the democratic order (Budi 2016). Born in 1955, Novanto had built up a trading business in the 1980s and 1990s, forming a commercial alliance with Sudwikatmono, one of Suharto's cousins. He also sought the patronage of Hayono Isman, a senior Golkar politician, and Wismoyo Arismunandar, the army chief of staff in the mid-1990s. In 1999, he ran for the first post-Suharto legislature, became Golkar's deputy treasurer, and joined President Habibie's re-election team. While juggling these campaigns, Novanto became involved in the first big political finance scandal of the democratic era. Through a company that offered debt recovering services, Novanto entered into a deal in January 1999 with the boss of Bank Bali, who sought the repayment of loans from two banks then under the supervision of the Bank Restructuring Agency. Novanto, closely connected to the government, promised Bank Bali to lobby for the return of the funds but asked for a whopping 60 percent of the money as a commission. Thus, Novanto's company—which found it easy to get the funds released—obtained about Rp 546 billion (US$39 million) from the deal. Once the sum arrived at the company's account, money was sent to multiple recipients, including another Golkar deputy treasurer. While the case went to trial and one of Novanto's business partners was imprisoned, Novanto was not charged.

Electorally, Novanto entrenched himself in remote constituencies particularly prone to clientelism and patronage practices (Aspinall and Berenschot 2019). In 1999, he was nominated as a Golkar candidate in East Timor, which was then under the strong control of the Indonesian military. Novanto's deep ties with the army—which began with Arismundar and were regularly refreshed with each incoming top brass—helped him to win the election in a territory he had no pre-existing relationship with (he was born in Bandung and resided in Jakarta). But as East Timor voted for independence in 1999, Novanto's constituency was dissolved, and he moved to neighboring East Nusa Tenggara (NTT). From this basis, he easily secured re-election to the DPR another three times between 2004 and 2014. In the corridors of the DPR, it was rumored that Novanto routinely was among the top spenders in each election campaign—a tale that he seemed to have little interest in dispelling. On the contrary, the image of a man of great financial resources was exactly what he wanted to nurture. While building an increasingly wide web of contacts in Jakarta that connected the political and business worlds he operated in, he also became a major commercial player in the DPR constituency he represented. Building hotels, agrobusinesses, and power plants, Novanto treated his constituency as a business opportunity, which he exploited by facilitating additional development funds approved by the very legislature in which he worked as an MP (Seo 2014). His ability to escape the repercussions of the Bank Bali scandal gave him an aura of apparent invincibility, and he continued to test the limits; in 2003, he was involved in a scandal surrounding rice imports from Vietnam, but he once again was able to avoid legal consequences.

Slowly but steadily rising up the ranks, Novanto became chairman of the Golkar caucus in the DPR in 2009. In the following year, he engaged in a brokerage scheme that would eventually lead to his downfall; he worked with corrupt officials in the Ministry of Home Affairs, entrepreneurs, and individual legislators to pass a budget of about Rp 6 trillion (US$428 million) to produce electronic identity cards for every Indonesian citizen. The ministry had tried to get the project approved for some time, but the normal instruments of persuasion—that is, promises of special budget allocations in other areas—had not convinced the DPR to approve it. Legislators knew that there were powerful entrepreneurs who were interested in this project, as well as ministry officials who would get a cut, so DPR brokers wanted their share. Setya Novanto was the chief broker during the debates on the budget revisions in 2011, when a formula for the distribution of the project funds and fees was worked out. Of the total budget, 51 percent would be used for the actual work and 49 percent for commissions. Within the latter, 7 percent would go to ministry officials, 5 percent to legislators in Committee II (which was in charge of the project), 11 percent to Novanto and his team, 11 percent to Anas Urbaningrum and Nazaruddin (the chairman and treasurer of Yudhoyono's PD respectively), and 15 percent as profit to the entrepreneurs (Gabrillin 2017). It was a project perfectly tailored to Novanto's talents. The president—who credibly claimed he was not aware of the terms of the agreement—got a long-delayed project approved; Novanto benefitted personally; and money was flushed into the latter's patronage network.

In 2014, Novanto climbed one step further in the DPR hierarchy, becoming speaker. The regulations of how a DPR speaker was selected had changed several times during the post-Suharto period, with the position open for election in 2004 but automatically filled from the ranks of the largest caucus in 2009. In 2014, the electoral mechanism returned to the competitive model, advantaging Novanto, whose party had only finished second in the preceding legislative ballot. With Widodo's party coalition in a minority position and Golkar still outside the pro-government alliance, Novanto joined an oppositional ticket of candidates that was put up against a rival team headed by PDI-P's Puan Maharani. Realizing their imminent defeat, pro-Widodo parties walked out of the proceedings, handing victory to Novanto and his affiliated deputy speaker candidates. But Novanto had no intention of being an oppositional speaker. Instead, he was determined to make the most of his new role as the key bridge between the president and the DPR, making himself indispensable to the former and the supreme broker in the latter. He lost no time letting the president know that he was ready to cooperate. Luhut Pandjaitan, the president's incoming chief of staff, met Novanto even before his (anticipated) election. "Novanto is very friendly to us—I don't think there will be any problem with him as speaker," Luhut said then (interview, Jakarta, September 16, 2014). Indeed, the president's team believed that Novanto might be easier to work with than Puan, given that the latter had made no secret of her reservations about Widodo's rise (Mietzner 2014a). Novanto, by contrast, was a pragmatist without any grudges.

Not long after his inauguration, Novanto boasted in meetings with politicians, bureaucrats, and businesspeople that he formed a "triangle" with Widodo and Luhut, and that together, they could bring "99 percent" of policy proposals to completion (DPR 2015). On one such occasion, in June 2015, Novanto met the CEO of Freeport Indonesia, a large gold and copper company operating in Papua. Freeport, which at that time was majority owned by American investors, faced the expiry of its contract in 2021, and it was under pressure to divest shares to the Indonesian government under any new cooperation agreement. In the meeting with Freeport Indonesia's CEO, Novanto was accompanied by Reza Chalid, a businessman widely associated with shady oil deals during Yudhoyono's rule (Bareksa 2014). Novanto suggested that he could help Freeport to negotiate an arrangement with the government but indicated that he was interested in obtaining 49 percent of shares in a future electricity plant in Timika from which the company would be obliged to buy set quotas of power (BBC 2015). Chalid, for his part, proposed to the CEO of Freeport that in its divestment, it should give 11 percent of its shares to Widodo and 9 percent to Vice President Kalla. Unbeknown to Novanto, the Freeport CEO recorded the conversation and gave the tape to the reformist minister for mining and energy, Sudirman Said, who reported the case to the DPR's ethics committee in November. Ironically, Said had been appointed partly to end the government's entanglement with Chalid's oil business networks—only to encounter him again in a new role.

But the president did not show any signs that he was pleased with his minister for exposing a major political corruption attempt. On the contrary, Luhut reminded the public that Said had reported the case to the DPR without the president's knowledge. According to Luhut, it was Said's report to the DPR that had caused "chaos" and given the government "trouble" (Maharani 2015). The reason for the government's anger, it appears, was that the affair undermined the president's chief ally in the DPR. Although Novanto was again able to escape legal repercussions, the political pressure became too strong for him, and he resigned as speaker in December 2015. From the president's perspective, Novanto's sudden departure was unwelcome as he left just months after delivering on his promise to get Widodo's first budget approved without problems. Recall that Widodo had taken office in October 2014 without a parliamentary majority, and that he had defiantly declared he would use last year's budget if the DPR did not approve his submission. Although Widodo was still formally in a minority position in mid-2015 (Golkar and PPP changed their oppositional leaderships in 2016), his budget sailed through the DPR processes without a single vote of dissent. Novanto had been crucial in this effort, smoothing over any opposition by generously distributing patronage and mediating between the president's representatives, DPR bodies, and individual legislators. Novanto's replacement as speaker, Ade Komarudin, was also a Golkar politician, but he was much less experienced in oiling the patronage machine.

Widodo, consequently, helped Novanto to return to his old position as speaker in 2016. The Golkar chairman and Widodo opponent, Aburizal Bakrie, declared his willingness in late 2015 to vacate the party's leadership, expressing his frustration over the government's relentless intervention in its affairs. This triggered a race for his replacement, and Novanto—having just resigned as speaker—announced his candidacy. From the beginning, it was clear to all delegates of the extraordinary Golkar congress in May 2016 in Bali that Novanto enjoyed the president's support. Once again, Luhut—also a Golkar member—played the key operator role. Asked later about the president's and his support for Novanto, Luhut said, "we know that Novanto isn't exactly clean. But do you think the others are cleaner? We did our homework, we looked into everyone. With Novanto, the cooperation [as DPR speaker] was good" (interview, Canberra, June 9, 2016). Novanto's main rival was his replacement as speaker, Komarudin, who was backed by Vice President Kalla. Widodo had no interest in strengthening his vice president, giving him further reasons to support Novanto. On the floor of the congress, senior Golkar politicians who could read the political map collected votes for Novanto, despite their dislike for him. Agus Gumiwang Kartasasmita, who would later become a minister in the Widodo cabinet, was one of them. "We all know who Novanto is, but for Golkar's positioning vis-à-vis the government, this is the best course," he said while making calls that helped Novanto gain the upper hand (interview, Nusa Dua, May 17, 2016). Novanto won the Golkar contest, and half a year later, he reclaimed his role as speaker.

After another year as speaker, the KPK finally caught up with Novanto. The anti-corruption agency had for many years unearthed layer after layer of the electronic identity cards scandal, and was ready to make its indictment of Novanto by the middle of 2017. He clung to office until December but then resigned as speaker a second time. In April 2018, he was sentenced to fifteen years in prison for his role in the affair. While Widodo had lost Novanto again, there was no need for him to be concerned this time around. Novanto was replaced by Golkar's Bambang Soesatyo, a politician from Novanto's mold. The owner of thirteen luxury cars, Soesatyo came to office with a transactional understanding of politics similar to Novanto's, and the cooperation between the president and the DPR was as smooth under him as it had been under his predecessor. In 2019, when Soesatyo had to make way for Puan as the next DPR speaker,[4] Widodo made sure that the former remained influential, assisting him in getting elected to the position of MPR chair by acclamation. As the new DPR chairwoman, Puan inherited a well-oiled patronage machine that worked to produce majorities for the president and deliver massive benefits to the legislators running it. Eying the presidency for herself, Puan had little interest in changing this status quo, and so she continued to play her role in maintaining the post-2004 balance between the president and the legislature that has proven so profitable to both sides.

At the heart of coalitional presidentialism studies has been the challenge of presidents to co-exist with legislatures marked by fragmented multi-partyism. In most cases, this is done by creating post-election party coalitions in which the president offers cabinet representation to parties that, in exchange, order their legislators to support the government's policies when they come up for a vote. Formally, this is what happened in Indonesia. Yudhoyono and Widodo turned initial minority positions in the DPR into large majorities, and they subsequently ruled without significant interruptions by the legislature. But as this chapter has shown, Indonesian presidents have gone far beyond simply securing party support and hoping such support will translate into legislative control. Indonesian legislators are semi-independent political actors that require presidential attention and incentives on their own. In a system where legislative committees and other agencies rather than party caucuses are the central arenas of executive-legislative negotiations, legislators demand concessions that add to, and sometimes contradict, those arranged by party leaderships. Accordingly, presidents must use their powers vis-à-vis the DPR—most importantly, their budgetary authority—to persuade legislators to cooperate. Unsurprisingly, then, the main currency governing the presidential-legislative relationship is budget patronage, with the president engaging in a complex system of brokerage to deliver it to the DPR's leaders and—often through them—to its individual members.

The apparent smoothness of presidential relations with the legislature, even if compared with Latin American cases of effective coalitional presidentialism, should not mask the intense power struggles behind the scenes. For every unanimous—or in rare cases, majority—vote on a budget or bill, presidents must make hard-fought compromises that can result in bad policy at best or corrupt wastage of public funds at worst. Yudhoyono's complaints about how the DPR interfered with his government's budget—and his finance minister's description of how legislators undermined "rational policy"—are illustrative of executive frustrations in this regard. But it is equally telling that Yudhoyono accepted these sacrifices as the price for a decade of stable rule and that Widodo—despite initial protestations to the contrary—continued this tradition. The cost of the patronage-soaked negotiations with the DPR was higher than just the inconvenience of the president, however. The fact that a figure such as Setya Novanto managed to place himself at the center of the DPR's relations with the palace—and that a president not only tolerated but actively promoted such a figure—highlighted deep and worsening defects in Indonesia's democratic polity. It is hard to escape the conclusion that Setya Novanto was in the speaker's chair not *despite* but *because* of his well-known track record of corrupt dealings during the Suharto and post-1998 periods. In other words, Setya Novanto was not an accident, but the outgrowth of both the legislature's and the president's need to have a chief broker to make the deals that tie them together.

We have also noted that in some cases, even the vast resources of the presidency are insufficient to purchase the legislature's cooperation. In the case of the electronic identity cards project, the government had tried for years to gain the DPR's approval but was ignored every time. Only the intervention of entrepreneurs and rogue bureaucrats with vested interests in the project broke the deadlock and delivered the patronage impetus that legislators had been waiting for. In this instance, external actors pushed a project that enriched themselves but that the president also wanted as part of his policy plans. In other cases, third party actors promoted causes in the DPR that were not only outside of the president's agenda, but incompatible with it (such as the tobacco clause presumably removed at the request of the cigarette industry). Thus, it is important to recognize that presidents compete with other actors to pursue their legislative goals, and that it is not enough to focus on presidential-legislative relations as the sole analytical arena of coalitional presidentialism research. Presidents need to deal with non-party and non-legislative actors to prevent them from sabotaging their government. In doing so, they have to apply strategies similar to those used to get parties and legislators to cooperate. The rest of this book, consequently, explains how presidents have integrated non-party and non-legislative actors with potential veto power capacity into their broader presidential coalitions, expanding the arena of coalitional presidentialism in the process.

4

THE MILITARY

Militaries play a significant role in any polity. In fully consolidated democracies, militaries are subjected to institutionalized mechanisms of civilian control, but they are key to protecting the state from external and internal threats (Kuhlmann and Callaghan 2017). In autocracies, by contrast, militaries are typically a tool of repression used by rulers to defend their regime, constraining the armed forces' professional autonomy but also granting them the power to decide the fate of autocrats by either sustaining or withdrawing support in times of political crisis (Kovalevskyi 2022; Croissant, Kuehn, and Eschenhauer 2018). Flawed democracies such as Indonesia, which often had politically powerful militaries in pre-democratic periods, take a middle position between these two ends of the spectrum. Although militaries in these systems are no longer political hegemons, democratic rulers have to integrate them into their political infrastructure. As strong civilian control usually remains elusive (Croissant and Kuehn 2017), presidents or prime ministers have to resort to alternative methods to keep the military loyal and prevent it from undermining the polity. Some rulers choose to coerce the military into submission but risk a backlash—in some cases, even a coup. Others opt for extensive appeasement, handing the officer corps political and material compensation to tolerate democratic rule or, in some instances, even support the incumbent politically. In most cases, however, rulers of weak democracies choose a combination of these two approaches: they use their constitutional powers over the military to establish authority but also offer significant concessions to the military to ensure its cooperation (Pion-Berlin and Martinez 2017).

The interaction of militaries with presidents has thus far not been the subject of much debate in the coalitional presidentialism literature.[1] Instead, the dynamics between the executive and the armed forces have been relegated to the civil-military relations literature, an important but often marginalized sub-theme of comparative democracy studies. In the revised concept of coalitional presidentialism advanced in this book, however, the military is a central element of the coalitional presidentialism architecture. As we will see in this chapter, Indonesian presidents have applied methods to coerce and appease the armed forces that are very similar to those used to persuade parties and legislators to support their rule. This suggests there is little reason to exclude the military—and other equally powerful actors—from the study of how presidents balance a variety of groups within broad coalitions to make governance more effective and to cement their authority. In other words, the military is—in substance if not by name—a member of presidential coalitions, and an important one. In periods of upheaval (such as when the focus of politics shifts from the formal institutions onto the streets, as it did at several of Indonesia's post-1998 junctures), the military can decide to either contain the unrest or to sit back and let the ruler be engulfed by further chaos. In such situations, the power of the military exceeds that of the parties and legislators. Hence, in anticipation of such crisis points, presidents need to carefully cultivate the military to ensure its political and security cooperation when it is most required.

This chapter starts with a discussion of the powers that the military holds vis-à-vis the president. In the Indonesian case, these powers go beyond the "control of the gun" (Char 2016). As a self-perceived guardian of independence and territorial integrity, as well as a key component of the authoritarian regimes between 1959 and 1998, the military is—for many Indonesians—inseparably linked to the concept of authority. Thus, the military's leverage is significant. Nevertheless, as the second section shows, Indonesian presidents have considerable authority, which they can use to counterbalance the military's weight. The constitution positions the president as supreme commander of the armed forces who nominates the military chief and appoints the service chiefs. These appointment powers allow presidents to fill the ranks of the military with personal loyalists, giving them an effective control mechanism against potential insubordination. In the third section, the discussion demonstrates how Indonesian presidents and the military have used their powers to extract concessions from each other within the framework of coalitional presidentialism. This system has stabilized Indonesian democracy as far as the absence of coups is concerned (in stark contrast to Thailand or Myanmar, for example) but also explains some of the setbacks of Indonesian democracy from the 2010s on. The last section offers an illustrative case study of these dynamics. It outlines how the military forced

President Widodo in 2016 to abort an attempt to publicly discuss the anticommunist massacres of 1965. In return, the military supported Widodo in his early conflicts with some parties and the police, and helped him to stabilize after a weak start into his presidency in late 2014 and early 2015.

The Military's Power

The Indonesian military's effective political power (as opposed to its formal one) becomes clear only when its history is integrated into an assessment of its overall contemporary status. Between 1945 and 1949, the military was at the forefront of the armed conflict with the Dutch, who wanted to reclaim their former colony after the end of World War II (Lowry 1996). While the Indonesian army lost the fight militarily and was only saved by an intervention from Washington that forced the Dutch to negotiate, the period of struggle instilled a sense of historical entitlement in the officer corps. The generals demanded an institutionalized role in post-independence politics, believing that it had a right (and indeed, an obligation) to protect the nation from both security and political threats. Sukarno granted the armed forces such a role in 1959, and after this was deemed insufficient, they grabbed full power in 1966 (Crouch 1978; Roosa 2006). For the next thirty-two years, the military formed the backbone of Suharto's New Order regime: first as a political hegemon in its own right, and later as the palace guard for the aging president's autocracy (Schwarz 2004). Even when relegated to agent status by Suharto in the later periods of his regime, the military was able to ensure that it remained deeply engrained in the country's political psyche (Honna 2003). Military symbols and practices were idolized and reproduced in schools, universities, the bureaucracy, and daily life. After Suharto's fall, the generals could rest assured that the long-term societal power base they had built up since 1945 would not dissipate quickly—despite the protest and upheaval the military faced during the regime change in 1998 (Mietzner 2009a).

Before the operation of the post-2004 presidential system, the military sent signals of its continued power and expectation that it needed to be compensated for its loyalty. Between 1998 and 2003, severe communal violence rocked the democratic transition, with thousands of people killed in ethno-religious conflicts in Kalimantan, Sulawesi, and Maluku (van Klinken 2007). There were credible reports of the military doing little to stop the violence and, in some instances, even actively fueling it (Bertrand 2002, 81). At the national level, civilian elites were convinced that the military could do more to address the crisis if it wanted to—and if it felt more committed to the emerging democratic order. They were not wrong: as one officer confirmed, "some of my colleagues sit on their hands to force the government to make them promises" (interview with Agus Wirahadikusumah, Makassar, February 23, 2000). Consequently, post-1998 governments took several steps to appease the military and purchase its cooperation. They agreed to a significant expansion of the military's size—from a strength of 334,000 in 2001 to more than 438,000 in the second half of the 2000s.[2] The budget also increased along with the economy's growth, flushing more money into the coffers of the generals (the budget more than doubled from US$2 billion in 2001 to US$4.5 billion in 2010). Moreover, after an initial drive to reform the military institutionally and hold it to account for human rights abuses committed under Suharto, such moves slowed down in the early and mid-2000s (Honna 2018, 2019). This abortion of reformist policy initiatives suggested to the military that it could co-exist with democratic governments through arrangements with its leaders.

Pre-2004 presidents also felt the residual powers of the military in more direct ways. Habibie's 1999 bid for re-election was effectively terminated by the announcement of the then military chief Wiranto that he would not be available as his vice president. Similarly, Wahid's presidency ended in 2001 when the military refused to heed his calls to protect him from the impeachment proceedings in the DPR and MPR. Leading generals refused to implement Wahid's July 2001 decree to "freeze" parliament and ban Golkar. They also rejected his plans to conduct a major reshuffle to place more loyalists in the military hierarchy (Barton 2006). The armed forces leadership's firm stance emboldened the DPR and the MPR to execute their impeachment of Wahid. When it came to a vote, the generals (then still represented in both bodies) opted against the incumbent president. As noted, this experience profoundly impacted on Yudhoyono, who was Wahid's chief political minister at that time. Yudhoyono, himself a former general, concluded from Wahid's fall that presidents had to balance Indonesia's various forces to prevent "chaos" and stabilize governance. Thus, as the 2002 constitutional amendments put Indonesia's new presidentialism into place, and as the 2004 presidential elections marked the official start of its operations, the country's post-amendment presidents entered the new era with a full understanding of how the military could potentially destabilize their rule—or how, alternatively, they had a chance of governing calmly if the generals supported the incumbent's administration.

Partly because of its successful lobbying, the military retained substantial formal powers in the democratic polity. This was despite the fact that it lost its representatives in the DPR and MPR in 2004, and despite the separation of the police (as well as its internal security function) from the armed forces in 1999. One of the remaining military powers was drawn from the still-active 1959 Law on States of Emergency, through which the military gains special powers during civil or military emergencies and in times of war. Once a status of military emergency is declared, for example, the local military commander becomes the head of the emergency administration. In Indonesia's history, this occurred in the late 1950s and early 1960s, allowing the military to consolidate its power in the regions. Under the lower-level status of a civil emergency, the local government head remains in office—but the local military commander becomes one of his or her chief advisers, meaning that the local military command turns into the de facto political and security power center. In the post-Suharto polity, such civil emergency regimes were established for Aceh (2004–2005) and Maluku (2000–2003), and Widodo briefly considered declaring a state of civil emergency (presumably for the entire territory of Indonesia) in March 2020 to fight the COVID-19 pandemic. After a civil society backlash that warned of the potential increase in the military's power through such a declaration, Widodo shelved his plans but included numerous military officers in the COVID-19 emergency response team (Jaffrey 2020). In addition to the 1959 law, a host of other regulations and inter-agency agreements grant the military special powers, ranging from rural development roles to education in remote areas (IPAC 2016).

The military's biggest power resource in contemporary Indonesia remains its territorial command structure (Haripin 2019). This structure, developed during the regional conflicts of the late 1950s, places military units at all levels of civil administration. As a consequence, every local official, from the governor to the village head, has a military counterpart (see table 4.1). This matters greatly as many decisions at the local level are made in a Regional Leadership Forum (previously called Muspida but after 2014 named Forkopimda), which includes the head of the civil administration, the military commander, the police chief, the chief of the attorney general's office, and other important figures. Reflecting the political influence of each institution, the forum's power dynamics give particular weight to the word of the military commander. Aware of the significance of this territorial command structure to its institutional interests, the military

TABLE 4.1. The military's territorial structure versus the civilian administration

PRESIDENT	
MILITARY'S TERRITORIAL STRUCTURE	CIVILIAN ADMINISTRATION
Military Commander	Home Affairs Minister
Kodam Commander (Province-level)	Governor
Kodim Commander (District-level)	District Head/Mayor
Koramil Commander (Subdistrict-level)	Subdistrict Head
Babinsa (Non-commissioned officers, village-level)	Village Head

fought hard after 1998 to defend it. Under Wahid, there had been an initiative to disband the system, driven by a small group of officers affiliated with Agus Wirahadikusumah. Arguing that the structure was an obstacle to military modernization, Wirahadikusumah proposed to dismantle the system gradually. With this suggestion, he made many enemies within the ranks, and when Wahid tried to promote him to army chief of staff, other senior officers threatened to resign. Eventually, Wirahadikusumah was sidelined, Wahid fell, and the reform of the territorial command system was aborted. According to Wirahadikusumah, "the idea of abolishing the territorial system destroyed me, and Wahid, too. The military couldn't take it" (interview, Agus Wirahadikusumah, Jakarta, July 5, 2001). Subsequently, the system was maintained and expanded further, with four new provincial commands added between 2002 and 2016.

In providing the military with a nationwide network, the territorial command system equates to an infrastructure through which generals could potentially launch a coup. In the eventuality of a takeover, the territorial structure would allow for seamless cross-regional coordination of military units, which could then move rapidly against their civilian equivalents at each level. Though the Indonesian military is not as coup happy as its Thai or Myanmar counterparts (it even continues to deny that the 1966 takeover constituted a coup), it enjoys regular rumors about the possibility of a coup as indicators of its continued power. In late 2016, for example, Indonesian newspapers were filled with discussions about the potentiality of the military usurping power from Widodo as Islamist demonstrators took over the streets of Jakarta (Gumilang 2016). Observers at that time noted an increased frequency of presidential visits to military units, feeding speculation that Widodo was trying to fend off a coup by issuing hidden warnings to the generals (Wicaksono 2016). When Indonesian presidents make such calculations on the likelihood of a coup against them, the territorial command system is at the center of their thinking. This was the reason Wahid wanted to dissolve it. As he explained in 1999, briefly before taking office, "we need to get rid of that system. Otherwise it will come after us" (interview with Abdurrahman Wahid, Jakarta, September 15, 1999). With Wahid proven right about the military turning against him, post-2001 presidents concluded that reforming the system would increase the risk of a coup or other forms of insubordination, and hence decided not to push the issue with the generals (Kusandi and Wahono 2020).

Accordingly, the Indonesian military can bring much leverage to the table when negotiating with presidents over their interests and demands. Its monopoly on the instruments of warfare gives it an advantage over non-armed civilian actors. By agreeing to use these instruments—or deciding not to—the military can stabilize or destabilize the rule of incumbent presidents. It can also deliberately sabotage governments that it deems unsupportive of its agenda.

Moreover, the deep entrenchment of the armed forces in Indonesia's history, social life, and concepts of authority make it a source of legitimacy many politicians want to draw from. In short, there are multiple reasons why presidents can ill afford to face a hostile or just uncooperative military—and an equal number of incentives to appease and reward the generals for securing their loyalty. As we shall see, Indonesian presidents have typically acted within this incentive structure; but before explaining how exactly they have done that in the post-2004 polity, the next section explores the constitutional powers of the president vis-à-vis the armed forces. These powers, if used firmly and credibly, help the latter to design a strategy of achieving military cooperation that is not only the product of the incumbent's fear of the military and a possible coup, but also—conversely—of the respect of the armed forces towards their president and formal supreme commander.

Presidents as Supreme Commanders

Indonesian presidents' most important power resource vis-à-vis the armed forces is their constitutionally anchored position as holder of the "supreme authority" [kekuasaan tertinggi] over the army, navy, and air force. This function, first enshrined in the original 1945 constitution and maintained in the 2002 amendments, is similar to that of other presidents in Europe, the Americas, Africa, and Asia. Outside of the constitution, the Indonesian president's role as supreme commander was detailed in an MPR decree in 2000. It determined that the president appoints the military commander after gaining the approval of parliament (before 2000, no such endorsement was necessary).[3] Despite this new appointment hurdle, the president's right to pick the armed forces commander remains his or her primary instrument to control the military. It allows the president to appoint personal loyalists to discipline the rest of the officer corps, or to threaten the incumbent commander with removal should he disobey orders and work against the president's interests. Under democracy, Indonesian presidents—both before and after the 2004 changes to the polity—have made extensive use of this authority. B.J. Habibie, a civilian technocrat without a power base, established his authority over the armed forces by telling the then-commander Wiranto that he wanted to replace him. This forced Wiranto to offer the military's support to Habibie should he (Wiranto) be allowed to stay in his job (interview, Wiranto, Jakarta, October 13, 2000). Habibie agreed to the deal, with the armed forces tolerating most of his democratic reforms, including reducing the military's role in formal politics.

The control of post-2004 presidents over the top military appointment has thus far remained intact, with all nominations approved by the DPR. Only in the earliest phase of his rule did Yudhoyono struggle to get his way. Shortly before departing the presidency, Megawati (who had lost the 2004 elections to Yudhoyono) nominated the archconservative chief of staff of the army, Ryamizard Ryacudu, as the new military commander. But Ryamizard was not confirmed before the old DPR's term expired. This gave Yudhoyono, who was anxious about Ryamizard's nationalist and potentially insubordinate views, an opportunity to revisit the nomination when he took office in October 2004. As one of his first acts as president, therefore, Yudhoyono withdrew Ryamizard's nomination from parliament, insisting that the incumbent commander, Endriartono Sutarto, remain in place (interview, Endriartono Sutarto, Jakarta, June 11, 2007). The new DPR, then controlled by an anti-Yudhoyono majority, initially opposed the withdrawal of the nomination, demanding that Ryamizard attend a confirmation hearing. But using his position as supreme commander, Yudhoyono did not permit Ryamizard to visit the DPR, thus buying time until a solution could be found. This solution came in the form of Vice President Kalla's takeover of the Golkar party in December 2004. As Yudhoyono slowly built a majority in parliament, the fight over Ryamizard's nomination softened and eventually ended. Presidential control over the military in coalitional presidentialism, then, is intertwined with the broader balancing of other coalition partners.

In addition to the military commander, the president appoints the chiefs of staff of the army, the navy, and the air force. Unlike in the case of the military commander, the president does not have to seek the legislature's approval for these appointments. This gives the president significant and direct control over the personnel that leads the military in its day-to-day operations. Below the chief of staff level, the president also formally appoints all senior officers at the suggestion of the military commander. This means that the president can object to the commander's nominations and quietly propose alternatives.[4] Such interventions in the internal appointments of the armed forces are often executed through the president's Military Secretariat, which oversees his or her interactions with the generals. Importantly, the detailed organizational structure of the armed forces is determined through a presidential decree rather than through a law that would require the legislature's consent. As a result, the president can change the military structure on his or her own accord. For instance, in November 2019, Widodo signed a presidential decree to create the new position of deputy military commander. While he had not filled the position by 2023, it gave him additional options to promote officers close to him. Including the position in a presidential decree also allowed him to circumvent potential legislative demands that the position should require the latter's approval. Hence, Indonesian presidents possess crucial intervention powers in the composition and institutional set-up of the military's organization, requiring the armed forces to seek arrangements with the president to prevent his or her hostile intrusion into internal military affairs.

In addition to the president's appointment powers in regard to active military personnel, he or she can select retired officers to serve in other positions across the government infrastructure (Faishal 2017). This creates a strong incentive for high-ranking officers close to retirement to gain the president's favor and cooperation in finding an influential (and lucrative) position after leaving the military. As noted, and as explored further below, including retired military officers in cabinet is a crucial element of coalitional presidentialism in Indonesia. Furthermore, presidents can place former military officers in other leading posts. For instance, the military commander from 2013 to 2015, Moeldoko, became Widodo's chief of staff in 2018. Similarly, Endriartono Sutarto was named chief commissioner of the state oil company Pertamina in 2006, after having helped Yudhoyono to prevent the appointment of Ryamizard to the military commander post. In short, Indonesian presidents can combine their direct appointment authority vis-à-vis the military as an institution with more traditional appointment tools that, according to Chaisty, Cheeseman, and Power, are generally available to presidents to dispense patronage and bind political actors to their government's interests.

The practice that Indonesian presidents appoint retired rather than active military officers as the institutions' representatives in cabinet has historical roots. Active military officers had initially held cabinet positions from the late 1950s on. Sukarno had agreed to this concession to purchase the military's loyalty, and after Suharto's takeover in 1966, the appointment of active officers to cabinet and other government posts naturally escalated. But Suharto ended this trend after he retired from active service in 1978. Starting with the 1978 cabinet, most military officers holding ministries had to retire first; indeed, cabinet appointments became rewards for the president's retiring long-time allies in the military or, occasionally, a way of removing from active service generals he viewed with suspicion. Exceptions were sometimes made for the minister of defense, but even in this case, it was more common for the post to be held by a retired general. After Suharto's fall, democratic governments did not change this approach. As part of the reform process after 1998, laws and regulations were issued that stipulated which posts in the bureaucracy active officers can be appointed to (mostly secondments in the Ministry of Defense or the Coordinating Ministry of Political, Legal, and Security Affairs), making all others unavailable for them. This, in turn, shaped the practice of presidents to use the appointment of retired military personnel as the main instrument to cement military participation in their coalitions.

The president's budgetary powers, another tool in the toolbox described by Chaisty, Cheeseman, and Power, are also essential for the interests of the armed forces and their officer corps. In terms of formal military budget flows, presidents and their aides decide how much money they are willing (or able) to provide to the armed forces every year. As with other actors, the military typically lobbies the government (and the legislature) for overall budget increases and specific items. Of particular importance are high-cost allocations for foreign defense equipment acquisitions, which offer patronage opportunities for the responsible officers. How such budget allocations can benefit individual military members became obvious in a 2016 case involving the purchase of helicopters for the air force (Saputra 2021). The officers in charge had the helicopters included in the government's five-year strategic plan, which allowed the air force to go ahead with the purchase. Private agents affiliated with the officers signed a contract for US$40 million with the producers but charged the state US$56 million for them. The case only became public because Widodo had asked the military commander to annul the contract (the helicopters were reported to be luxury versions acquired for the president—an impression Widodo wanted to avoid). The officers, already tied up with the existing contracts, proceeded anyway, leading an angry Widodo to demand explanations. The KPK interviewed eight air force officers, but by late 2022, only one civilian had been charged, while the military police terminated the investigation of its personnel. Widodo had thus sent a warning, but the lucrative procurement system remained in place.

The Indonesian president has another equally important role in military budgeting: that is, to disrupt or tolerate the traditional off-budget fundraising of the armed forces (Rieffel and Pramodhawardani 2007). Under Suharto, it was widely believed that the military gained up to two-thirds of its operational funds from off-budget activities. Suharto viewed such off-budget financing as a privilege of the military, allowing it to raise funds, and enrich its officers, without the scrutiny of state agencies. In Suharto's eyes, the military's external search for funds made the generals more dependent on him and his financial cronies, creating another bond of loyalty between the president and the officer corps. After 1998, the practice of self-funding was gradually reduced, but it did not disappear (Mietzner and Misol 2013). Senior officers still forge extensive relationships with oligarchs who expect security protection and other services in return for their unofficial contributions to the military as an institution and its officers. The significant wealth among the top brass is testimony to this pattern. Wiranto, for instance, reported a wealth of about US$42 million in 2019, while Andika Perkasa, the commander installed in 2021, recorded US$13 million. In

Wiranto's case, this wealth allowed him to pursue a post-retirement career in politics, resulting in his funding the establishment of a party and holding a senior cabinet post in the first Widodo cabinet. For the most part, post-2004 presidents have accepted the continuation of military self-funding as something that keeps the officer corps satisfied—and as something they could threaten to end should the armed forces show signs of political disloyalty.

In sum, Indonesian presidents have much at their disposal to counterbalance the armed forces' massive political and security weight. Based on their constitutional powers, they can hire and fire military leaders; change the institutional organization of the armed forces by the strike of a pen; control official military budgets and patronage flows in the officer corps; offer non-military appointments to senior leaders looking for post-retirement opportunities; and acquiesce toward, or intervene in, the military's off-budget funding regime. In reality, they need to carefully calibrate these powers, given a possible military backlash. Consequently, the negotiation between the two sides occurs in the give-and-take framework of coalitional presidentialism, similar to the mechanisms with which presidents ensure the cooperation of—and try to prevent hostile attacks by—parties and the legislature.

Managing the Military

The attempts of presidents and the military to influence, control, and utilize each other are compellingly represented in a customary act of Indonesian political theater: the initiation of presidents into military units as titular members. In April 2015, for instance, Widodo was initiated as an honorary "citizen" of the Special Forces, the Marines, and the air force's Special Unit Corps. In front of 6,500 troops and a parade of military equipment Widodo was given military berets and combat uniforms from the units, one of which he wore while posing for pictures with the top brass. As a president without military roots, and Indonesia's first from a non-elite background, Widodo seemed to appreciate the political symbolism associated with the event. "This morning, I am very proud of wearing the historic military uniform. It should make me look more dashing than usual," the president told the troops (Teresia 2015). Moeldoko, the military commander at that time, responded with similar language, stating that "it makes us proud that you, Sir, have accepted [the unit membership] in good spirit. We, and all officers, want to show you that we are professional soldiers." With this performance, carried out in front of the media, the two actors sent each other important messages. The military signaled that it accepted Widodo as the new supreme commander of the armed forces, but also that, as an honorary member, he was expected to protect their interests. The president, for his part, assumed his function as the chief of the military chiefs, expecting obedience toward his rule while also indicating respect for the officer corps.

Beyond such symbolic events, the president interacts with the military through various formal and informal channels. As noted, the presidential Military Secretariat is the main formal link between the head of state and the armed forces. This is mainly because the Indonesian military is not institutionally subordinated to the department of defense—as is often the case in other countries (Kemenhan 2021). Both the armed forces commander and the minister of defense are cabinet members, and both report to the president. While the defense minister has some coordinating functions, the military's headquarters is the real power center of the Indonesian armed forces.[5] Dealing directly with the president, as opposed to negotiating through the defense minister, is a significant element of that power. This, in turn, hands the Military Secretariat a special role in the president-military relationship. Part of this military structure in the palace are the president's military adjutants, who are key communication bridges between the head of state and the armed forces headquarters. Adjutants are with the president almost around the clock and thus grow into personal confidants, giving the president insights into the thinking of the officer corps. Conversely, the adjutants are providing feedback to their military hierarchy as to the expectations and goals of the president. Almost invariably, military adjutants experience a rapid rise through the ranks after leaving the palace. We mentioned Widi Prasetijono before, but there have been others: Deddy Suryadi, for example, who served as Widodo's adjutant between 2017 and 2019 and became commander of the Special Forces in 2023, rising even faster than Widi.

The Military Secretariat and its apparatus, therefore, constitute an essential pool from which presidents can recruit and groom loyal military officers who then spread across the ranks and promote the president's interests. Another institution in the palace that adds to this pool is the Presidential Guard (Paspampres). Formally under the command of military headquarters, the head of the guard is as close to the president as the adjutants but significantly more senior in rank. Because of this seniority, holders of this post are more likely than the adjutants to rise to the top of the armed forces while the president is still in office. Andika Perkasa, for instance, was Widodo's first Paspampres chief (2014–2016). His successor, Bambang Suswantono (2016–2017), was appointed as commander of the military academy, a three-star post, in 2020. The next head of the guard, Suhartono (2017–2018), became commander of the marine corps in 2018, and his replacement, Maruli Simanjuntak (2018–2020), was selected as commander of the powerful Strategic Reserve in 2022. In other words, within his first term in office, Widodo had created a clique of palace loyalists that, by his second term, reached the apex of military power and was able to safeguard the interests of the president in the day-to-day operations of the armed forces. Widodo's aides pointed out that such an approach was necessary because they believed, in 2017, that "60 percent of the rank and file are supporters of Prabowo [Widodo's adversary in the 2014 and 2019 elections], so we need to at least control the upper echelons" (confidential interview, Jakarta, February 7, 2017). Hence, appointing loyalists is an important instrument of enforcing coalitional loyalty in the military, especially if lower-ranking officers without direct interaction with the president are deemed untrustworthy.

Yudhoyono even placed family members with a military background in key positions in the armed forces and his party, PD. For example, his brother-in-law Pramono Edhie Wibowo was army chief of staff from 2011 to 2013. But while such family links might ensure the highest level of loyalty from the officer concerned, they risk damaging sympathies for the president in the rest of the military. This is because the negative image of nepotism can potentially undermine—rather than strengthen—the position of such family members and, by implication, the president himself. Pramono confirmed this pattern: "Don't think that everyone respected me because I was the president's brother in-law. As a soldier, I want to be respected because of my service and my position, not because of my family. Looking back, my relations with [Yudhoyono] might have hurt me more than they benefitted me" (interview, Jakarta, April 27, 2014). His links to the president certainly did not help in his candidacy for Yudhoyono's succession in 2014, when after a lackluster campaign, he did not win the nomination of PD. Between 2005 and 2010, Yudhoyono had also put another brother-in-law, Hadi Utomo, in charge of the party. A retired colonel, Hadi was expected to hold the party together, using his military experience to impose discipline and establish links with active and retired military officers who held sympathies for the party. Hadi played this role effectively for a while but made room for a new generation of civilian party leaders in 2010.

How exactly do loyalist military officers, family members or otherwise, enforce the allegiance of the officer corps to the president in the armed forces' routine operations? Endriartono Sutarto, military commander from 2002 and 2006, has offered some insights into this mechanism. As we have seen, Yudhoyono insisted on him staying in his position in 2004 because the president wanted to prevent the appointment of Ryamizard Ryacudu, the general nominated by Megawati. This constellation forged a strong bond between Endriartono and Yudhoyono, which was tested when the president signaled his intention to negotiate a peace deal with Acehnese separatists in 2005. Conservatives around Ryamizard opposed this deal, and the task of preventing insubordination in the ranks fell to Endriartono. "There was much upheaval, with some officers saying we should oppose the government, and so forth. I told them: you are serving this government, so if you don't support what your government is doing, just resign and leave" (interview, Jakarta, June 11, 2007). Faced with dismissal or "suggested" resignations, most officers refrained from sabotaging the peace agreement signed with the Aceh rebels in Helsinki. To the surprise of many observers (and the dismay of some officers), the deal was still in place at the time of writing, approaching its twentieth anniversary.

As important as they are in keeping the military in ruling alliances, the presidents' appointment powers are not a one-way street of coalitional presidentialism. Rather, every appointment comes with the expectation that loyalty is repaid with the president's support of the military. Even if generals become part of the president's network, they are still military officers—socialized for decades in a hierarchy that instilled in them a deep devotion to the organization's agenda. Thus, loyalist officers might defend the president—but they know that the head of state must reciprocate for the institution to follow suit. This deal is embodied, among others, in the appointment of retired military officers to cabinet. These appointments are part of an informal but consistent arrangement between presidents and the military to mirror the latter's participation in the presidential coalition. The level of military participation in presidential cabinets remains, more than twenty-five years after the onset of democratization, similar to those of the early post-Suharto period (with four or five former generals generally sitting in each cabinet after 1998). Some appointees concurrently represent political parties, but most are non-party figures. Luhut Pandjaitan, who held two senior positions in Widodo cabinets after initially serving as his first chief of staff, has openly described how he brought the military into many policy areas he handled. "What's wrong if I ask the military to help if it has the capacity to do so? You in the West might think that's wrong, but in Indonesia, in many cases the military can do things that civilians can't" (interview, Canberra, June 9, 2016). Under Widodo, his approach led to an expanding web of military cooperation with civilian ministries, with the president's consent.

In addition to the inclusion of military figures in cabinet, Indonesian presidents typically agree that there are red lines they cannot cross if they want to sustain their coalitional relationship with the military. We already noted that the maintenance of the territorial command structure is one such red line, and no post-2004 president has even considered questioning it.[6] We also saw the importance of budgetary matters—the military expects a stable and gradual increase in its official budget and tolerance of its off-budget practices. Post-amendment presidents have guaranteed both. This does not mean that the military budget has increased disproportionally: official military expenditure in Indonesia remains below 1 percent of GDP, one of the lowest ratios in the region. But in US dollar terms, the budget has roughly quintupled between 2001 and 2021, giving officers enough opportunities for institutional development and patronage (Nugroho, Bainus, and Darwawan 2018). Similarly, the military's off-budget practices remain politely ignored, despite a formal handover of its businesses to the Ministry of Defense in 2009.[7] Outside the budgetary realm, the legal impunity of the armed forces is another red line. For instance, no high-ranking military officer has been jailed for human rights abuses committed under the New Order or subsequent administrations. While some officers stood trial in human rights courts in 2002 for the violence surrounding the East Timor referendum of 1999, and six of the eighteen defendants were initially convicted, all of the accused were acquitted on appeal (Cammack 2015). The 2003 trial on a 1984 massacre of Muslims in Jakarta ended with a similar outcome: all twelve defendants were acquitted on appeal. After that, only one more human rights trial against a military officer was held in 2022 (involving a 2014 case in Papua), with the accused also acquitted and critics arguing that the government had not seriously pursued the case.

With presidents respecting the red line of the military's legal impunity to protect its participation in their coalitions, some officers involved in human rights abuses even made political comebacks many years after their actions. Wiranto, for instance, who was indicted by the UN over the East Timor carnage, became Widodo's most senior security minister in 2016 (he had held the same position under Wahid from 1999 to 2000, but was dismissed by him over the accusations). Similarly, several officers aligned with Prabowo Subianto—and accused of kidnapping activists in 1998 under his direction—followed their former boss into government in 2019. Prabowo, appointed as defense minister by his two-time presidential election opponent Widodo, tapped Dadang Hendrayudha as his ministry's director general for defense potential, and Yulius Selvanus as the head of the strategic defense installations body. Both had been convicted by a military tribunal in 1999, but after an appeal, they continued their military careers. Thus, Prabowo's integration into the presidential coalition not only accommodated Widodo's archrival and neutralized the threat of him becoming an anti-government agitator, but it also sent further signals to the military that it did not have to fear legal prosecution and could rest assured that its officers had opportunities to prosper under democratic rule. Having killed two birds with one stone, Widodo began his second term with a substantially broadened and consolidated coalition. Prospects of any pro-democracy breakthroughs, however, were also much reduced.

Managing the military as part of presidential coalitions, then, requires heads of state to hold their ground by deploying their appointment powers and constitutional privileges but also to make heavy concessions to sustain the military's satisfaction with their rule. As in the case of other participants in coalitional presidentialism, this approach to the armed forces secures the government's stability—yet it also underscores executive incapacity to move against the generals' vested interests. In the next section, a detailed case study of Widodo's early presidency illustrates how Indonesian presidents have used the military to solidify their political position and calibrate the internal balance of their coalitions. It also shows, however, that Widodo had to pay a significant price in return.

Widodo, the Generals, and 1965

Widodo entered office in 2014 with an acute awareness of his lack of personal military credentials. A former furniture entrepreneur and local politician, he had faced off in the elections with the experienced military hard-liner Prabowo. To compensate for the absence of a similar military biography, Widodo surrounded himself with a clique of retired officers who had fallen out with Prabowo and thus wanted to prevent his rise to the presidency. Luhut was the leader of this clique, but it had other powerful members. A.M. Hendropriyono, for instance, had been a senior general under Suharto but cultivated close ties with Megawati.[8] His son-in-law was Andika Perkasa, who would later become military commander under Widodo. There were also Sutiyoso, the former Jakarta commander and governor, and Subagyo H.S., who had been army chief of staff in the final phase of the Suharto regime. During a television debate between Widodo and Prabowo in June 2014, the clique of retired military officers supporting Widodo sat as a bloc in the audience. "Look at us," Sutiyoso said, pointing to the ex-generals around him, "aren't we dashing? I'm sure Prabowo will be impressed when he sees us" (interview, Jakarta, June 9, 2014). Emerging victorious from the contest, Widodo appointed Luhut as his first chief of staff, Sutiyoso as intelligence chief (albeit only briefly), and Subagyo to the Presidential Advisory Council. In short, Widodo's non-existing historical ties with the armed forces had led him to integrate military figures into his apparatus from the beginning of his presidential career.

Widodo had to turn to his military allies for help earlier than he had hoped. This was because he got entangled in a political conflict with the military's main institutional rival, the police. Still finding his feet in the first few months in office, Widodo gave in to pressure from Megawati and nominated her former-adjutant-cum-confidant Budi Gunawan as the next chief of police in January 2015. But three days later, the KPK declared Gunawan a suspect in a corruption case, trapping Widodo in a dilemma: on the one hand, he had to show loyalty to Megawati and her ally; on the other hand, the fight against corruption had been a cornerstone of his campaign. Eventually, Widodo withdrew Gunawan's nomination, named a replacement, and approved Gunawan's appointment as deputy chief of police. While this appeared as an effective compromise, it infuriated Gunawan's supporters in the police. Using his association with Megawati, and his new position as deputy chief, Gunawan became the head of an informal network of disgruntled officers in the police that the president could no longer rely on. The official police chief, Badrodin Haiti, was largely seen as a figurehead, with Gunawan's patronage network entrenching itself in the police command units. In this situation, approaching the military for support was a natural choice for an Indonesian president. Since the split of the police from the armed forces in 1999, the two organizations have been involved in an ongoing competition over institutional authority, resources, and political influence (Baker 2013). Hence, once the police appeared to turn against Widodo, the president was forced to strengthen his ties with the other powerful security actor, and the military was happy to oblige.

To communicate its willingness to assist the president and take on the police in the Budi Gunawan case, the military sent subtle messages to the police and the public. For instance, it offered to second military investigators to the KPK to help the anti-corruption agency with the case against Gunawan, and it let it be known that the KPK had approached the armed forces to enforce subpoenas should internal police witnesses against Gunawan be unwilling to testify (Kemenhan 2015). Of course, these warning signs against the police came at a cost for Widodo. In June 2015, as the crisis was still ongoing, the president was given hints by the army that it expected the next military commander to be from its ranks instead of from the air force, whose turn it was if an informal post-Suharto tradition of rotating the commandership between the services was to be upheld. As the largest and most powerful of the services in the armed forces, the request of the army carried a particular weight that was difficult to ignore. A close Widodo aide recalled, "in that situation, with all that was going with the police, it would have been unwise to alienate the army. The army supported us. So it was decided to grant its wish, and the president appointed Gatot [Nurmantyo] as the military commander" in July 2015 (confidential interview, Canberra, December 15, 2015). This example demonstrates how presidents can use the balancing mechanisms inherent in coalitional presidentialism to reprimand and control a disloyal coalition member by turning to another for assistance. It also showcases, however, how such balancing forces the president into costly compromises.

Unsurprisingly, Gatot's appointment was only the prelude to more substantive concessions the president was forced to grant to the military. Gatot represented the most conservative stream within the officer corps. Unlike the military commanders in the Yudhoyono period who had been careful not to provoke the president with political commentary, he was vocal in expressing his views to the elite and the media. Having received all of his training at home (in contrast to some colleagues with extensive records of international education), he believed in the distinctness of the Indonesian military and rejected notions that the armed forces had to professionalize in line with the examples set by their peers in Latin America. He was convinced that Indonesia was encircled by adversaries (Agastia 2016), with the West accused of trying to morally destroy the country's youth and China of aiming to use the archipelago as a stepping stone for its power expansion. Above all, he claimed that Indonesia faced a continued threat from communism—despite the destruction of the PKI in 1965/66 and the failure of the left to revive some form of socialist politics after 1998. In Gatot's eyes, the PKI used pro-democracy NGOs, environmental activists, and labor unions to stage a comeback in disguise. Evidently, Widodo's promotion of Gatot in exchange for the military's counterbalancing of the police had swept a myriad of long-suppressed conservative military views and demands to the surface, voiced by its new commander.

Gatot's conservatism collided with progressive policy promises that Widodo had advanced during the 2014 campaign to attract the small but influential segment of liberal voters. This liberal segment had leaned toward Widodo not because of great enthusiasm for him but because he promised to block Prabowo's path to the presidency. To bind such voters to him, Widodo included the handling of past human rights abuses in his campaign program. The reference to "past human rights abuses" was commonly understood as a promise to revisit the state's interpretation of the 1965/66 massacres of suspected communists. Up to one million people were killed then, with the army driving the campaign in cooperation with Islamic and nationalist groups (Melvin 2018). Under Suharto, the killings were portrayed as a heroic act to save Indonesia from communism, and this narrative remained a main staple of the military, Islamic forces, and nationalist groups after 1998. But the democratic opening allowed victims and their relatives to demand justice. In their efforts, they received support from some pro-democracy NGOs—the segment that Widodo appealed to in the 2014 campaign. Thus, when he became president, there were widespread rumors that Widodo planned an apology for the killings, or at least planned to acknowledge the state's responsibility for them. The rumors were fueled by the announcement of his attorney general on several occasions in 2015 that the government planned to address the issue (Laisina and Lesmana 2015). Plans for an international tribunal on the killings in Den Haag, organized by Indonesian and international experts, added further urgency for the government and created nervousness in the military.

The military's apprehension increased exponentially when it learned that a symposium on the 1965 killings would be held in April 2016 by the National Resilience Institute (Lemhannas), a think tank linked to the Department of Defense. The governor of this institute was Agus Widjojo, a retired general whose father had been killed by the pro-communist coup plotters in 1965. Despite this traumatic experience, Widjojo was one of the most reformist military thinkers. He believed that Indonesia should emulate countries such as Cambodia, South Africa, and Germany in how they managed their past (Gumilang and Suriyanto 2017). These nations had held tribunals and truth and reconciliation processes—something the Indonesian military opposed. Worse still for the military, Widjojo indicated in interviews that his symposium had gained the president's approval (Tempo 2016). However, Widjojo also suggested that Luhut was part of the initiative, too. Luhut, who later spoke at the seminar, was more conservative than Widjojo but shared the latter's view that the nation needed closure. In his mind, the government should oversee a formal process of reconciliation and unearth some of the mass graves (Kuwado 2016a), "but after that, it must be over. We can't go on like this forever. Let's do this, and then we all move on" (interview, Jakarta, June 15, 2016). According to Luhut's plan, the process should establish a number of victims much lower than the figures found in the international scholarly literature. Against this background, it appears that Widodo believed that the event was safe from possible accusations by the military that the president betrayed one of its main interests.

But the president's confidence in his strategy was misplaced. The backlash from the active military leadership under Gatot—and from hard-line retired officers—was swift and harsh. Some retired officers held a counter-symposium in June 2016, at which speakers denounced the testimonials given by victims at Widjojo's seminar (Aritonang 2016). Following this event, Widodo immediately backed down; he declared, at a military gathering, that he had never intended to issue an apology. Gatot, however, was not yet satisfied and continued to campaign against any revision of the state's stance on 1965. In 2017, he stepped up his anti-communist rhetoric and ultimately ordered all military commands to organize public viewings of a discredited propaganda film on the events of 1965, which had been broadcast annually under the New Order but had been shelved soon after Suharto's fall. Widodo, dropping any attempt to find a new approach to 1965, joined in the military's chorus. In June 2017, he vowed that his government would clamp down on any "communist movement or thinking" still left in Indonesia (Kuwado 2016b), and in September, he attended one of Gatot's screenings. The president's turn-around was now complete: the process that the Widjojo event had intended to start was discontinued; there was no unearthing of mass graves; and the government chose to ignore the issue—just as Yudhoyono had for much of his two terms in office.

However, the story did not end there. As noted earlier, Indonesian presidents have significant appointment powers they can leverage to balance the armed forces. Widodo used his powers in this case, too: in December 2017, he dismissed Gatot and replaced him with Hadi Tjahjanto, a loyalist he had known since his days in Solo (Lowry 2017). Indeed, Gatot believed that his invitation to Widodo to watch the 1965 propaganda movie was the reason for this dismissal. It is likely that Widodo saw the invite as an act of intimidation and decided to send a signal that his readiness to compromise with the military had certain limits. But despite Gatot's dismissal, Widodo did not renew the 1965 reconciliation initiative.[9] The episode, then, highlighted the red lines on both sides of the coalitional presidentialism equation: Widodo needed the military as a counterweight to the police and was willing to give the armed forces concessions in return—but he was not prepared to accept an open show of defiance against him. The military, for its part, was ready to help the president in his conflict with the police—but expected that its red line regarding the 1965 issue would be respected. As the two stances moved dangerously toward a point of irreconcilability, the president abandoned his reconciliation project but re-established his authority by replacing the military commander. Subsequently, the equilibrium between the two sides—which marks the president's relationship with other coalition partners as well—was reinstated again.

This chapter has demonstrated that Indonesian presidents position the military as a member of their coalitions—and that the officer corps views its role and power in the same way. The armed forces receive an informal quota in cabinet formations, filled with retired officers; negotiate with the president over budget and patronage issues; grant or withhold support to the government, depending on the concessions offered; balance themselves against other members of the coalition, whether they are parties or actors such as the police; and communicate red lines to the president, the crossing of which would mean the end of coalition membership. Presidents, for their part, can use powers similar to those they hold over parties and the legislature to discipline the armed forces and ensure at least basic support for their governments. Chief among them is the authority to appoint the military top brass, which presidents have used to pressure potentially disloyal generals or to fill key posts with loyalists they had groomed during years of service in their surroundings. They can also bring their budgetary powers to bear, granting the military increased allocations and allowing it to continue its long-standing practice of informal fundraising. The appointment and budgetary powers are at the heart of what many members of the officer corps view as their main institutional and personal interest; that is, the continuation of the material privileges the military had become used to in decades of authoritarian rule. The ideological concessions extracted from the president, such as ongoing commitment to fight the (long-defeated) threat of communism, arguably serve as ideational justifications for these welfare demands.

Despite its status as a member of presidential alliances, the military differs in important aspects from other civilian actors of coalitional presidentialism. Its monopoly on warfare instruments is the most important distinction, which the military uses to increase its weight in negotiations with the president and other political actors. Similarly, its territorial command structure gives it a nationwide outreach that few other actors have (including the parties). As a consequence, to fully grasp the presence of the Indonesian military in presidential coalitions, it is appropriate, and indeed necessary, to bring civil-military relations analysis of the country—which has a long history and central place in its political scholarship (Sundhaussen 1972; Laksmana 2019)—into our coalitional presidentialism studies. We have seen many of the themes highlighted in civil-military relations debates reoccurring in the examination of coalitional presidentialism practices: the president's constant rebalancing of appeasement and confrontation strategies; presidential interest in both limiting and occasionally exploiting military intrusion into civilian affairs; and the observation of red lines drawn around institutional interests to prevent upheaval. These strategies, applied by presidents to deal specifically with the armed forces, are concurrently key to maintaining the stability of the overall coalition. Should these strategies fail, it is not only the civil-military relationship that is affected but the foundations of the presidential coalition as a whole.

In Indonesia, the outcome of the presidential-military coalition arrangement has been beneficial to both sides but has had a paralyzing effect on democratic reform. Unlike in Thailand and Myanmar, where the armed forces tend to operate outside of executive coalitions and thus often overthrow the governments they do not feel aligned with (Chambers 2021), the inclusion of Indonesia's military into presidential power-sharing arrangements has secured its allegiance to the formally democratic system. Despite frequent speculation in Indonesian newspapers and seminars, no serious attempt has been made at a military coup since 1998—a fact that should not be taken for granted. Since the introduction of full presidentialism in 2004, the mechanisms through which generals are bound to the incumbent president have been institutionalized further. This has allowed presidents to rule without significant disturbances (to begin with, they have been able to complete their terms, in contrast to some of their executive counterparts in mainland Southeast Asia), and democracy has been sustained. But the accommodation of the military's interests, and the expectation of presidents for the officer corps to assist them against their opponents in times of crisis, has helped to freeze Indonesian democracy at low to moderate levels. Under Widodo, the increasing concessions given to the military have even led to unmistakable signs of democratic decline, while the overall frame of nominal democracy remains intact (Repucci and Slipowitz 2020, 55). Consequently, presidential interactions with the military are comparable to those that presidents have developed with other actors—and they also produce a similar result.

5
THE POLICE

Like the military, the police have significant special powers that distinguish them from other socio-political actors. Just as the armed forces, the police have the authority to wield coercive instruments to enforce state policy (Zedner 2006), giving them access to resources of violence that can be leveraged in negotiations over their institutional interests. But the police hold powers that the military does not: they oversee legal investigations, command the authority to conduct arrests, and charge suspects with crimes. This set of powers is of particular importance in Indonesia's patronage-guided polity, in which many economic and political activities occur in a permanent grey zone between the legal and the criminal (Aspinall and van Klinken 2011). The power to decide what is legal and what is criminal is thus a bargaining chip that puts the police in a position where various actors seek cooperation or, minimally, acquiescence. Whether a politician wishes to conceal corrupt activities, avoid drug-related charges, or secure the authorities' aquiescence toward environmental violations committed by business cronies—the decisions taken by the police in such cases can make or break the career of many Indonesian elite actors. The president is not exempt from this pattern; the head of state, too, must keep the police satisfied with the existing status quo, for dissatisfaction within the police ranks can express itself in arrests of presidential allies or of other actors who could then threaten to review their loyalty toward the government as a result. As the previous chapter demonstrated, presidents' efforts to counterbalance the power of the police can force the latter into unsavory arrangements with other elites (such as the military), which often causes a new range of problems.

Unlike the military, the police reached the highest levels of influence in the post-Suharto polity (Muradi 2019). While the armed forces were the backbone of authoritarian regimes between 1959 and 1998, the police had played only a minor role in those periods. Institutionally, they were subordinated to the military commander, who prioritized the three military services in terms of budgetary allowances and political privileges (Aini, Muntholib, and Suryadi 2019). Given the military's dominance under autocracy, it also carried out internal security functions that were nominally the police's authority. Military officers had no difficulties conducting arrests, patrolling the streets, and disciplining critical civil society groups. But all of this changed with Suharto's fall. The police were separated from the military in 1999, giving them authority over their affairs for the first time in many decades. They also gained full responsibility for internal security, while the role of the armed forces was limited to external defense and a few other specifically listed areas of domestic emergencies. The police were also handed responsibility for managing terrorist threats, which gave them particular prominence (including internationally) after 2000, when the first Islamist bomb attacks occurred (Jones 2012). Thus, while the armed forces had to negotiate their place in the post-1998 polity from a position of overall declining influence, the police were on an upward trajectory (Baker 2012). The increase in the number of police officers holding positions in cabinet and other political institutions has been a testament to this growing political weight of the police.

This chapter discusses how post-2004 presidents have integrated the police into the broader framework of coalitional presidentialism. The first section lays out the powers of the police that the latter can bring to bear vis-à-vis the president and other political actors. In the second section, the president's authority over the police is detailed. As in the case of the armed forces, Indonesian presidents have the authority to nominate the police chief, who is then appointed after the legislature's approval has been obtained. But the conflict surrounding the aborted appointment of Budi Gunawan in 2015 demonstrated that this nomination power could attract a host of problems if the police reject the candidate, or if their preferred nominee is overlooked. The third section, then, explores how presidents deal with this challenge of maintaining the loyalty of the police, pointing to several instruments and techniques used in the process. In the final section, a case study of the rise of Tito Karnavian illustrates the gradually expanding political power of the police. Tito, who served in various key police posts before becoming the first minister of home affairs with a police background in 2019, tried to put his ideological stamp on many areas of political organization in Indonesia. The police, therefore, have used participation in coalitional presidentialism to not only strengthen their position in dealings with the president and other political elites, but also to reshape the polity along the lines of the conservative security thinking so prevalent in the force.

Police Powers

As in many other countries, the national police of Indonesia hold a wide range of coercive powers that are crucial to incumbent presidents. One of the most essential roles in this regard is controlling demonstrations (Eggert, Wouters, Ketelaars, and Walgrave 2018). Under authoritarianism, and in the early democratic period, this function was carried out mostly by the military, but since the mid-2000s, the police have been at the forefront of defending sitting governments against protests. The military is called in to help control protests, but the police manage day-to-day activist gatherings (Suliyanto 2021). In facing such protests, the police can either take a hard-line stance and stop the demonstrations (and thus help the government in suppressing opposition to its policies), or allow public dissent to spread and undermine the administration—indeed, there have been reports of apparently police-sponsored demonstrations that related to the organization own interests.[1] Consequently, the police possess a key authority that has the potential to decide the fate of governments—managing protests effectively can secure the latter's survival, while a passive or even encouraging attitude could mean their end. (To be sure, excessively violent repression of demonstrations by the police can harm governments, too.) Presidents are keenly aware of this sensitive role of the police and hence have a strong incentive to maintain the police's support for the government.

The police have also increasingly assumed the authority to contain armed communal violence and unrest (Diprose and Acza 2019). The military played the leading role in fighting ethno-religious violence from 1998 to about 2003, but as the intensity of this unrest declined, the police were put in charge of managing its aftermath. In the post-2004 polity, the police are the first to mobilize in cases of small-scale community violence, with the military becoming involved only if the police prove incapable of handling it—or if there is an active armed movement, such as in Papua. Much to the dismay of the military, the police have also obtained the authority to manage terrorism cases, which has given them a reason to ask for additional funding, including international aid (Carroll 2016). Under Widodo, the military secured the president's approval toward a greater role for the armed forces in counter-terrorism (Priamarizki 2021); however, the police's function as the primary responder to terrorist events has remained untouched. Thus, just as the military did in the early democratic transition, the police now oversee outbreaks of unrest and terrorist incidents that could destabilize the government if not handled effectively. Police leaders unsympathetic to the incumbent government could let violent episodes in the regions spread to remove the incumbent or to extract concessions from him or her. This, in turn, creates a dependency of the president on the police that needs to be considered when making broader decisions about the architecture of presidential coalitions and the resources and concessions required to sustain them.

But the police are not only a security force; they are also a law enforcement agency. As such, they are the first layer in a multi-agency process that determines whether a citizen is charged with a crime. This power makes it possible for the police to either overlook a violation or, conversely, to build a case to entangle a citizen in legal proceedings. There are numerous examples of both patterns. In July 2021, Ardi Bakrie—the son of former Golkar chair Aburizal Bakrie, who had made a deal with the Widodo government in 2016 to leave his post—was arrested on drug charges. But while other citizens have gone to prison for minor drug offenses, Ardi was put into a "rehabilitation program" recommended by the police (Detik 2021).[2] Similarly, in 2013, the son of senior minister Hatta Radjasa—Yudhoyono's brother-in-law—caused a car accident that killed two people (including a toddler) and seriously wounded three others. The police processed the case "gently," and he was only hit with a probation sentence. At the other end of the spectrum, Rizieq Shihab—the leader of the Islamist protest movement against the Jakarta governor and the government more broadly in 2016 and 2017—was sentenced to four years in prison in June 2021, ostensibly for denying that he had tested positive for COVID-19. Of course, other citizens—including cabinet members—had kept their COVID-19 infection a secret, but in Rizieq's case, the full force of the police was mobilized to pursue the case. Apparently, Rizieq's return to Indonesia in December 2020 after three years in exile created anxiety in the government that he could once again become a popular extra-parliamentary opposition leader (Fealy and White 2021). His arrest and sentencing ensured that he was unable to play this role.

Of particular importance within the police's law enforcement portfolio is the authority to handle corruption cases (Kurniawan 2021). This power gives them direct leverage over the world of politics and business. Although the creation of the KPK in 2003 shifted the responsibility for large corruption cases away from the police to the new anti-corruption agency, the police remained in charge of the bulk of the smaller cases. Over time, the police also infiltrated the KPK, and by 2019, they had succeeded in almost entirely controlling it. In the early period of the KPK, the police exerted influence over it by sending police officers to act as KPK investigators. But in 2019, a police general known for his hostility toward the KPK was elected its chairman (KPK commissioners and chairs are nominated by the president and elected by the legislature). This appointment was the culmination of a concerted effort by the political elite—which included the political parties, the president, and the police—to weaken the KPK, as it had imprisoned many of their associates. During both the Yudhoyono and early Widodo presidencies, the police had arrested KPK commissioners in retaliation whenever the latter indicted police officers (as in the Gunawan case of 2015). However, the placement of one of their own as KPK chair made such interventions unnecessary. Under Firli Bahuri (the former police chief of South Sumatra), the KPK conducted fewer operations (Yahya 2020), reducing the threat it posed to vested elite interests. With Bahuri as chair, the KPK also removed the last investigators deeply committed to the organization's independence, turning it effectively into an extension of the police.[3]

Like the military, the police have a nationwide network that runs parallel to the civilian administration (see table 5.1). Compared to the armed forces, however, the police have found it easier to justify the existence of this network as its law enforcement function requires presence at all administrative levels. Indeed, far from having to defend the system, the police have seen its network expanding massively in the post-Suharto era. Police officers at all levels have taken their seats at the local leadership forum, Forkopimda, where they mingle with other government officials to discuss key political and economic matters. Hence, the police have a national organization that is stronger than that of most civilian actors, and that can be of use to the president for intelligence, communication, and political engineering purposes. For instance, when Widodo feared in 2019 that a low turnout in the presidential elections could hurt him, the police started a campaign encouraging citizens to vote. Posters featuring the police chief (in some cases, together with the military commander) proclaimed that going to the ballot box was "cool," and local officers conveyed the message to village communities across the archipelago (Polsek Karang Bintang 2019). Partly because of this coordinated effort, voter turnout was 81 percent, 11 percent higher than in the prior presidential election of 2014, when the police had not run a similar voter mobilization campaign.

TABLE 5.1. The police's national network versus the civilian administration

PRESIDENT	
POLICE'S NATIONAL NETWORK	CIVILIAN ADMINISTRATION
Police Chief	Minister of Home Affairs
Polda Commander (Province-level)	Governor
Polres Commander (District-level)	District Head/Mayor
Polsek Commander (Subdistrict-level)	Subdistrict Head
Bhabinkamtibnas (Village-level)	Village Head

In combination, these trends of rising police power have turned the chief of police position from a marginal post under the New Order into the most sought-after domestic security job in the post-Suharto era. Whenever an active police chief approaches retirement age, parties, business actors, and other groups begin to lobby for a replacement who they think can best represent their interests. According to Luhut Pandjaitan, "the president gets a headache every time the chief of police position needs to be filled. You should see the amount of messages we receive, 'candidate A is really great, don't pick candidate B,' and so forth. This happens with few other positions we have to fill" (interview, Jayapura, June 16, 2016). Correspondingly, police officers interested in becoming chief must build political coalitions long before the appointment process begins. One of the difficulties Widodo experienced in cancelling Gunawan's 2015 nomination was the latter's formidable political network. Not only was he Megawati's confidant, but he had also developed close relationships with caucus leaders in the DPR, who would later be in charge of the confirmation hearings. One parliamentarian conceded that "[Gunawan] is a very clever operator. He always makes sure that he does favors to people—and if you're high up in the police, you can do a lot of favors to a lot of important figures. These favors are then repaid in time" (confidential interview, Jakarta, November 16, 2016). In the eyes of many ordinary Indonesians, too, the position of police chief is now among the top posts in the country's socio-political hierarchy, giving its holder high levels of name recognition. In a 2019 survey, both Gunawan and the incumbent police chief, Tito Kurniavan, had a name recognition of above 25 percent, qualifying them for consideration as presidential hopefuls (Fajri 2019).

It is important to bear in mind, therefore, that in young, defective democracies such as Indonesia, the police are neither the kind of professional, apolitical enforcer of the law that we typically associate with liberal polities, nor are they a willful instrument of executive leaders, as is often the case in autocracies. Rather, they are a politicized security agency with multiple powers and a host of institutional and ideological interests, and they are not shy in using the former to advance the pursuit of the latter. As such, the police are one of the actors with veto power potential that Indonesian presidents have to cultivate if they wish to rule without major disturbances to their day-to-day governance. As with other players, this occurs via the integration of the police into the system of coalitional presidentialism, in which the police gain representation in cabinet and other rewards that presidents can hand out to their partners. In the following section, we look at the powers that Indonesian presidents can bring to the table to discipline, appease, and reward the police and secure their active support or—at the very least—their passive tolerance.

Presidential Powers vis-à-vis the Police

The police hold a crucial position in Indonesia's socio-political landscape, but the president has numerous instruments at his or her disposal to enforce their loyalty. As noted in other cases, and as the coalitional presidentialism literature suggests, the president's appointment powers are essential in extracting support from key actors. In contrast to the military, which the Indonesian constitution directly subordinates to the president, the place of the police in the country's institutional hierarchy was not determined in the post-2002 constitution. However, the police law of 2002 situated the police under the president, based on the general understanding of Indonesia's presidential system and the similar position of the armed forces (Danendra 2012). In fact, although not constitutionally anchored, the authority of presidents over the police is more direct than their control over the military. While the armed forces have an institutional relationship with the Ministry of Defense, the police have no ministry to cooperate with, let alone report to (other than the Coordinating Ministry for Political, Legal and Security affairs, which is traditionally weak as it has fewer resources than the core departments it oversees). In 2002, and at several later junctures, there were discussions on whether the police should be placed under the Ministry of Home Affairs or a newly created police ministry. But the police resisted such a move, preferring to deal with the president directly, and presidents have also shown little interest in weakening their direct vertical oversight. Thus, in Indonesia's current political set-up, presidents have the ultimate authority over the police.

In practice, this means that the president nominates the police chief, who is subsequently confirmed by the DPR. As noted, these nominations are highly politicized and contested, but despite the tensions surrounding them, none of the president's nominees has been rejected by post-2004 parliaments. While this is testimony to the deals that presidents typically make with legislators to secure their nominations, it also underlines the president's institutional power to select the personnel serving him or her. Below the police chief, all senior appointments within the police have to be consulted with the president. This gives presidents opportunities to place officers close to them in leading positions in the police. In addition to the deputy chief of police, the politically most sensitive post in the police is the head of the Criminal Investigation Agency (Bareskrim), a three-star position. The Bareskrim chief handles all major crime investigations, making him a focal point for politicians who wish to protect themselves or people close to them from potential charges. At the beginning of Widodo's presidency, the post was held by Budi Waseso, a close ally of Budi Gunawan. As the Budi Gunawan crisis developed, Waseso created significant problems for Widodo by arresting senior KPK leaders with questionable charges

(Arnaz 2015). Widodo was able to relieve Waseso of his command after less than a year in office but had to compensate him with another important post as his links to Gunawan (and thus Megawati) remained strong. Nevertheless, Widodo succeeded in using his appointment powers to put a much less controversial—and more cooperative—officer in the Bareskrim position.

Significantly, the president's power to endorse all senior appointments in the police is a self-given right. It is neither enshrined in the constitution nor in the 2002 police law; rather, it is stipulated in a presidential act (Iskandar 2018). Article 29(1) of the Presidential Decision 70/2002 regulates that all appointments from two-star level upward require consultation with the president. In other words, this authority is rooted in a legal instrument that the president can issue without seeking approval from any other institution (such as the legislature). Embedded within the same Presidential Decision are details of the police's internal organization, as are important privileges for its leaders—Article 31(1), for instance, regulates that the police chief receives the rank, enumeration, and facilities of a cabinet minister. This ability of presidents to decree the way the police work and which hierarchical privileges they obtain highlights another tool of coalitional presidentialism: that is, legislative authority. Not only can the president promulgate laws (together with the DPR) that govern the internal rules of the police, but—similar to how the military is subject to presidential regulations—he or she can make independent calls on changes to the police's overall set-up. Against this background, there are many reasons why the leadership of the police would want to seek friendly relations with the incumbent president, lest the latter penalize them through sudden alterations to its regulatory framework and institutional decision making.

Outside of the police's own institutional arena, the president's cabinet formation powers are an attractive proposition for senior police leaders planning their post-service careers. Like their military counterparts, senior police officers need to prepare for their transition into civilian life once they reach retirement age (which currently is fifty-eight, based on a 2003 government regulation). An appointment to cabinet or a cabinet-level position is an ideal outcome for police leaders, but even positions at state-owned enterprises are much sought-after retirement bases. Budi Waseso, for example, was appointed as head of the national logistics board in 2018, overseeing the distribution of food items worth billions of dollars. Budi Gunawan, for his part, was named intelligence chief in 2016 (partly to remove him from the police), and he remained in that position after he reached retirement age in 2017. Widodo's loyalist police chief Tito Karnavian became minister of home affairs in 2019. In short, presidents can offer lucrative and influential positions outside of the police to either reward officers who served them well or to remove those that did not (with the latter often requiring specific incentives to make way without causing major disruptions). If handled effectively, this presidential privilege of handing out patronage posts is a major counterbalance to the immense power that the police possess vis-à-vis the head of state.

The president's budgetary powers are also essential to the police. After the separation of the police from the military in 1999, one of their main institutional interests has been to strengthen their institutional and budgetary independence. Gaining parity with the military in terms of state funding became a threshold by which the police assessed the success of this autonomy campaign and their standing in the rivalry with the armed forces. The president's influence on the budgetary position of the police becomes evident when comparing the allocations to the police in the second Yudhoyono term with those in Widodo's first. In the second Yudhoyono term, in the budget years 2010 to 2014, the police received on average 7.9 percent of the total funds flowing to government agencies. In the first Widodo term (2014–2019), this percentage increased substantially to 10.9 percent and rose further to 11.5 percent in 2020, the first year of his second term (Rizky 2019). These increases allowed the police to be almost at par with the armed forces, which has to divide its total budget into allocations to the army, navy, and air force. With Widodo's help, then, the police transformed from the institutional and budgetary stepchild of the armed forces under Suharto and in the early post-New Order period into a socio-political and funding heavyweight. Widodo and his loyalists in the police have helped to spread this narrative in the force; in 2017, in front of Widodo, police chief Tito Karnavian told a gathering of police troops that the president had doubled the police budget in his first three years in office (Sohutoron 2017).

Moreover, the president's hold over the state budget allows him or her to distribute favors to the police at politically opportune times. Most importantly, presidents can increase the salary for civil servants, military members, and police officers through direct government regulation. For instance, just one month before the 2019 election, Widodo announced an increase in the salary of all members of the police (CNN Indonesia 2019). Such increases are particularly important for the lower-ranking officers as they lack the lucrative patronage opportunities of their superiors. Although police (and military) members do not vote in elections, ordinary police members can influence the voting choices of their families and communities. Not coincidentally, the 2019 salary increase occurred during the police's voter mobilization campaign, which was widely seen as benefitting the incumbent more than the challenger. Outside of election times, presidents can also help the police realize programs that further their socio-political standing. In April 2021, Widodo launched the police's new TV and radio stations, offering government funding and endorsement. These channels gave the police additional instruments to deepen their entrenchment in society and shape public opinion. In his speech, Widodo made clear that he hoped that the police would repay his kindness by using the channels to fight "the disinformation of perceptions" (Yamin 2021), a reference widely understood to mean the spread of anti-government information on social media, which had—in the eyes of the president—escalated during the COVID-19 pandemic.

Accordingly, while there are many reasons why a president would fear a hostile police force, equally strong reasons exist for the police to be anxious about an unsupportive or openly antagonistic president. The last time such a mutually hostile relationship developed was under Wahid, and both actors suffered as a result. At that time, Wahid tried to appoint a new police chief against the wishes of the force (and the legislature), creating strife within the police. Wahid, for his part, was impeached, with explicit reference to his irregular attempt to install a loyalist as police chief. Evidently, the incentives for both sides to seek an accommodative arrangement are compelling. Coalitional presidentialism offers such a two-sided accommodation, in which the police stabilize the rule of the incumbent in exchange for concessions that go well beyond the compensation police forces receive in polities with apolitical security forces. In a patronage-oriented society such as Indonesia, even seemingly routine appointments and budget allocations become part of a larger clientelist deal that includes informal agreements through which cabinet seats and other lucrative posts are handed to the police's elite. In the next section, we turn to the exact mechanism through which the president and the police interact and perpetuate their institutionalized cooperation.

Managing the Police

To manage the role of the police as a member of presidential coalitions, the president has fewer formal channels available than in the case of the military. Recall that the president's formal liaison with the armed forces is the military secretary stationed at the palace. The minister of defense can also serve as a communication bridge with the officer corps. In addition, the Paspampres—the presidential guard—which stays with the president around the clock, is exclusively made up of military personnel, and its commander has typically been a direct link between the head of state and the armed forces. No such channels exist in the case of the police. Formally, the military secretary is in charge of official business between the president and the police, especially when it comes to appointments. But the military secretary, who handles both the armed forces and the police, has invariably been a member of the armed forces. This arrangement, which is a leftover from the times when the police were a part of the armed forces, is unsatisfactory for the police. Besides, because no line ministry manages the police, the president can rely only on the coordinating minister for politics, legal, and security affairs to convey formal messages to the police. But as the coordinating minister has traditionally been a retired military officer (except Mahfud MD, a civilian who was appointed in 2019), the police are generally reluctant to use this communication mechanism. Thus, many interactions and negotiations between the president and the police must take place through informal relationships and processes.

At the heart of these informal communications is the presidential adjutant from the police, both when holding this position and when moving on to higher posts in the force. Though formally under the military secretary, the police adjutant also reports up the chain of the police hierarchy. One archetypical case in this regard is Listyo Sigit Prabowo, appointed police chief in January 2021. Widodo knew him when he was mayor of Solo, while Listyo was deputy chief of the police in the city. At his inauguration as president in 2014, Widodo had Listyo recruited as his adjutant, a position he held for two years. Subsequently, Listyo rose to the post of police chief of the province of Banten, an extraordinarily fast ascent in the police ranks. In 2019, he was appointed to the crucial Bareskrim portfolio, which he used to aggressively pursue Rizieq Shihab, the president's main political opponent at that time. Throughout this period, Listyo was considered one of the police officers closest to the president. Hence, when the post of police chief became available in early 2021, few observers had any doubt that Listyo would be named. The close relations with the president helped Listyo overcome a significant obstacle that would have prevented the promotion of almost any other candidate to the police's top post: he is Christian, and some Islamic activists expressed their opposition to a non-Muslim being placed in such an influential position (Pradewo 2020). But Widodo ignored these objections and completed the rise of his protégé from their joint time in Solo and the position of adjutant to the apex of the police organization.

The institution of police adjutants in the palace is therefore both an important communication channel and a pathway through which presidents groom future loyalist leaders of the police. We had discussed earlier the difficulties Widodo faced with the police when coming to power in 2014: forced to nominate Megawati's pick for police chief, he then found it hard to overturn that nomination when it became indefensible in the eyes of public opinion. Even when he had found a solution, he still had to deal with the remnants of the powerful Budi Gunawan network in the police. Over time, however, Widodo placed more loyalists in the police, making negotiations with their leadership easier. Before Listyo, he had appointed Tito Karnavian, who turned out to be a staunch defender of the president's interests. Tito had not been an adjutant to Widodo but enjoyed a close relationship with Luhut, the president's problem-fixer (interview with Luhut Pandjaitan, Merauke, June 18, 2016). In 2016 and 2017, Tito was at the forefront of containing the fallout from the Islamist mass mobilizations, appearing personally at demonstrations to calm protesters. He also oversaw the first wave of legal cases against Rizieq Shihab that drove the latter into exile in 2017, and he visited him there to discuss terms for his possible return (Maharani 2021). At the same time, Tito stood up for police interests when negotiating with the president; as mentioned above, he credited Widodo (and implicitly, himself) with a significant increase in the police budget.

Tito was also at the center of another strategy of integrating the police into the president's coalition: that is, increasing the police's cabinet representation. Tito was appointed minister of home affairs in 2019—a position that had traditionally been held by retired military officers, bureaucrats, or party cadres. The ministry oversees the country's regional civil service members and thus holds immense power; its control by a retired police officer gave the force influence over the nationwide bureaucratic hierarchy that runs parallel to the police's (see table 5.1). Tito's appointment continued a trend of expanding police representation in cabinet that had begun in Yudhoyono's first term. In 2009, he handed the post of intelligence chief to Sutanto, the recently retired chief of police. This brought the number of cabinet-level posts for the police from one (that of the police chief itself) to two. As with the minister of home affairs, the post of intelligence chief had typically been a bastion of military officers, so its shift to the police was a remarkable gain in their rivalry with the armed forces. Tito's ministry then brought the number of police representatives in cabinet to three, making the police (together with the oligarchs) the group with the most substantive increase in cabinet participation since 2004. This, in turn, confirmed the police's increasing political weight and their recognition as a protagonist of coalitional presidentialism.

Ceremonial events—such as the one at which Tito thanked the president for budgetary increases—are important sites of negotiation over and affirmation of the police's membership in the presidential coalition. These events are even more essential to the police than to the military, as the police lack some of the formal linkages to the president that the armed forces enjoy through their entrenchment in the palace. In July 2019, for instance, Tito used the celebrations for the seventy-third anniversary of the police to ask Widodo for an increase in the allowances for police personnel (in Indonesia, allowances for government employees are a key component of the take-home pay, often constituting a larger proportion than the base salary). In a polite but firm tone, Tito remarked that "we are hopeful that you, Mister President, can lift the working allowances for . . .

police members in the next five years of your leadership to 100 percent [of the base salary]" (Batubara 2019). This request came two years after Tito had lauded the president for large budget increases, and just months after a pre-election increase in the police's base salary. Now that the president had won re-election, Tito staked the police's claim on more privileges in the president's second term, which—as Tito hinted at indirectly—the police had some role in obtaining for Widodo. The president reacted to the request by increasing some segmental benefits but did not meet the suggested 100 percent threshold. In doing so, Widodo displayed both his willingness to accommodate some of the police's expectations and, at the same time, his presidential authority as the powerful master of the purse who does not simply give in to any demand made.

In other areas of the president's relationship with the police, agreements evolve without direct negotiations. In the case of the KPK, for example, Widodo gradually adopted the police's critical view as a result of his changing attitudes toward the anti-corruption agency. The police had for a long time looked at the KPK as an usurper of their own functions (indeed, the latter had been established in 2003 because the police were considered too implicated in corruption itself). Widodo, by contrast, had pledged during the 2014 campaign to work closely with the KPK and had (unsuccessfully) favored its then-chairman Abraham Samad as his running mate. But when Widodo asked the KPK to screen his ministerial candidates ahead of his first cabinet announcement, the agency ruled out many of the nominees, creating headaches for Widodo and leading him to ignore the advice. We also noted how the KPK's naming of Budi Gunawan as a suspect produced the first crisis of the Widodo presidency. Subsequently, Widodo became more open to the lobbying of the police and other actors against the KPK. Ultimately, in September 2019 the KPK law was changed in a way that weakened the agency, and Widodo also agreed to the police's suggestion to put one of their own, Firli, in charge of it. Tellingly, Yudhoyono had undergone a similar transformation in his presidency—he was initially keen to be seen as a KPK supporter, but the arrest of a relative by the KPK in November 2008 changed the president's attitude. Toward the end of his presidency, he spoke of the KPK as an out-of-control "superbody" (Viva 2009). However, unlike Widodo, he shied away from joining the police in their determination to emasculate it.

Hence, Indonesian presidents manage the police as a key actor in their coalitions through the use of the police adjutant as a communication bridge and future presidential ally in the police leadership; delicate placements of other loyalists in the police's senior hierarchy; the careful calibration of police representation in cabinet, reflecting their grown power since the end of authoritarianism in the late 1990s; timely increases of budgets, negotiated through both private and public interactions, often involving ceremonial events; and a natural adaptation of conservative political stances by presidents over time, as their reformist impetus wanes and they become more sympathetic to the police's long-held status quo ideology. In order to further explore the dynamics of the relationship between presidents and the police, and how the interests of both are served in the framework of coalitional presidentialism, the next section details the rise of Tito Karnavian from professional police officer to presidential loyalist and, eventually, one of the chief ideologues of the Widodo government.

Tito Karnavian and Police Politics

Like many Indonesian elite actors, Tito Karnavian has often portrayed himself as coming from humble beginnings. The family's narrative has been that Tito entered the police academy, which was then part of the armed forces academy, so that his parents would not have to pay the fees for more expensive study programs (Inge 2019). But there are indications that the family held what could then be considered middle-class status—especially given the historical context of Tito's youth. Tito was born in 1964, just before the 1966 takeover by the military. Tito's father was then a state radio journalist in Palembang, the capital of South Sumatra, and he helped establish the branch of the military newspaper *Angkatan Bersenjata* there (Hendrawan 2016). This would have given Tito's father access to military and police circles—and made entry into the academy a natural choice. Furthermore, when Tito studied at the academy in the mid-1980s, Suharto's New Order was at the height of its power. Although the police were subordinated to the armed forces at that time, they were still a central element of the New Order's security infrastructure, and being among its leaders promised a chance to obtain a place at the table of the elite. His father later insisted that he would have preferred his son to study medicine (Inge 2019), but Tito's chosen pathway was at least as prestigious.

There is no doubt that Tito was exceptionally bright. He excelled at the academy and was sent to the United Kingdom in the early 1990s to get a master's degree in police studies. This was followed by a series of other study programs both in Indonesia and abroad, giving him good command of English and a wide network of contacts. In 2013, his educational career culminated with a PhD in security studies from the S. Rajaratnam School of International Studies at Nanyang Technological University in Singapore. Parallel to these educational achievements, he made a name for himself as a professional and straightforward police officer with a special interest in counter-terrorism. After the 2002 Bali bombings, he helped track down leading terrorists affiliated with Jemaah Islamiyah (JI), the organization responsible for the attacks. As an officer in the Special

Detachment 88 (Densus 88) for counter-terrorism from 2005, he helped arrest two of JI's key leaders, Azahari Husin and Noordin Mohammad Top. Partly because of these successes, he was made the head of Densus 88 in 2009, the deputy of the National Agency for the Management of Terrorism (BNPT) in 2011, and the police chief of Papua in 2012. Internationally and domestically, Tito now had the reputation of one of Indonesia's most outstanding police leaders (Della-Giacoma 2013).

But there was one additional feature in Tito's career that attracted Widodo's attention in 2015 when he was screening candidates for the future leadership of the police. Importantly, Tito was not part of Budi Gunawan's patronage network in the police, which had created many difficulties for Widodo at the start of his presidency. In the context of Widodo's coalition-building strategies, Tito's exclusion from the Gunawan clique made him highly qualified to assist the president in turning the police from a hostile actor into a reliable ally. Tito's close relationship with Luhut gave the president further confidence that the rising star would stay loyal if promoted to high office. Once Widodo and Luhut had made their choice, Tito's rise to the top was rapid. After the end of his stint in Papua in 2014 (just as the Yudhoyono presidency ended), Tito had initially been parked in a marginal post at police headquarters—an appointment some attributed to his lack of links to the Gunawan network. But under Widodo, Tito was made chief of the Jakarta police in June 2015—one of the most coveted two-star positions in the force. As Tito needed a third star before becoming police chief, he was moved up to BNPT chief in March 2016, before being nominated as head of police in July 2016. Within roughly a year, Widodo had maneuvered a loyalist into the top job at the police. To be sure, this appointment did not fully marginalize the Budi Gunawan network, but as its patron was handed the post of intelligence chief some months after Tito's installation, the clique felt better integrated into the president's regime as well (McBeth 2016). At the same time, Tito filled some other police posts with his allies.

The alliance between Widodo and Tito worked well for the president, the police, and Tito personally. We already noted that Tito stood up for Widodo as Islamist demonstrations threatened his presidency; helped mobilize voters to get to the ballot box in 2019; and built cases against Rizieq that encouraged the latter to leave the country. But Tito did significantly more than that. Under his watch, for example, the criminalization of critics of the president experienced a sharp increase, especially in the lead-up to the 2019 elections. Anti-government activists or ordinary citizens who criticized the president or other elite figures on social media were charged with violation of the 2008 Law on Information and Electronic Transactions. In Yudhoyono's second term (2009–2014), there had only been 74 such cases; in Widodo's first (2014–2019), this number shot up to

233, with 82 of them directly related to the alleged insult of the president (Mashabi 2020). In addition to entangling critics of the president in legal cases, the police's actions stifled the general willingness of citizens to state their view of the government openly. In a September 2020 opinion survey, 69.6 percent of respondents agreed that citizens were "increasingly" afraid of stating their opinion (Safitri 2020); interestingly, however, an equally large majority continued to approve of the president's performance. Thus, Tito's police had limited freedom of expression without undermining the president's standing in public opinion. If anything, the silencing of harsh criticism of the president contributed to the sense of Widodo's deepening entrenchment in the state and society.

For the police, the benefits they received from Tito's coalition with the president did not only include the budgetary increases mentioned above. More broadly, the police were able to cultivate their conservative socio-political agenda from a position of privileged access to the presidency. While initially viewed as a reformer, Tito increasingly propagated this police conservatism—which centered around the belief in a strong centralized state that imposes order on a chaotic citizenry—as he moved to the top of the organization. In June 2016, just one month before he was made police chief, he justified to this author the arrest of Papuan separatists on treason charges for simply raising pro-independence flags: "You [as a German] should understand that a state needs to protect itself against its enemies. In Germany, you also have rules against Nazi flags" (discussion with Tito Karnavian, Canberra, June 9, 2016). The parallelization of Papuan separatists with Nazis highlighted the widespread belief in the police force that state repression is acceptable against any opponent of the Indonesian national project and the majoritarian constituency in which it is embedded. As police chief, Tito also cemented the exclusion of LGBTI groups and citizens from this national consensus. Under his leadership, the police launched an unprecedented wave of raids on gay venues in 2016 and 2017, many operating as private clubs. To do so, he argued that homosexuals being naked in a private home violated the pornography law, as potentially anyone could walk into such a home (BBC Indonesia 2017). By way of explanation, he stated that "Indonesia is not Australia, England, or the United States. We have our own culture."

The alliance with the president also secured the material privileges of the officer class, including Tito. Like in the case of the armed forces, the president closed his eyes toward the signs of significant wealth among police leaders with nominally low salaries. When Tito was nominated as police chief, he disclosed to parliament that he owned an apartment in Singapore and that his children had gone to school there (Rini 2016)—all indications of remarkable affluence. Tito's wealth continued to grow proportionally to his professional advancement. Between 2014 and 2019, his officially reported net worth more than doubled from

Rp 7.7 billion to Rp 18 billion (US$1.3 million), with a 2018 salary and allowance of about Rp 49.6 million (US$3,500) per month, or Rp 595 million (US$42,500) per year. Among the five candidates for the chief of police position in 2021, four had a reported wealth of above Rp 5 billion, or US$350,000 (in a country where 82 percent of the population had a median wealth of less than US$10,000 in 2019). Thus, just as when Tito entered the academy in the mid-1980s, the career as a high-ranking police officer continued to promise lucrative income opportunities, despite the fall of authoritarianism and subsequent democratization. The police, through their coalitional arrangements with sitting presidents, have retained crucial socio-political weight in democratic Indonesia, which has translated into immense ideological influence and the successful defense of the officers' high social status.

Tito's promotion to minister of home affairs at the beginning of Widodo's second term in 2019 brought the police further opportunities to expand their socio-political influence. Tito quickly assumed the role of a leading skeptic of the democratic reforms that Indonesia had achieved since 1998. While illiberalism spread widely in the Indonesian elite and society in the late 2010s (Hadiz 2018), few key actors developed their conservative political ideas as systematically and eloquently as Tito. One of his main ideas was introducing the notion of "asymmetric local elections," by which poorer regions would not be given the right to vote for their governors, district heads, or mayors, while those with higher economic development levels would. "We have to look at [each region's] democratic maturity," Tito proclaimed in June 2020. "Are the people of a specific region really ready to elect a leader? Do they understand that they have to elect the right leader?" (CNN Indonesia 2020). Such a model, which in effect questioned the principle of universal suffrage, would throw Indonesia back behind the introduction of direct local elections in 2005. In terms of the ideas driving such a proposal, it would even question the one-person-one-vote paradigm that took hold in many older democracies after World War I and in the newly independent nations after World War II. But Tito was unimpressed by criticisms of his position. He was convinced that Indonesia's liberal post-Suharto reforms had created instability and that the state had to recapture some rights from its citizens that had been granted to them in a hurry after 1998. During the pandemic, he also styled himself as the representative of a strong-hand government, overseeing those public health measures that were the responsibility of local governments to enforce.[4]

Tito's rise, then, illustrated the growth of the police's power in the post–New Order era in general and under post-2004 coalitional presidentialism in particular. Through careful maneuvering and clever identification of the needs of incumbent presidents, Tito brought himself and the police into a position of great leverage vis-à-vis other actors. When Widodo needed a loyalist in the police to counterbalance the power of the Budi Gunawan network, Tito stepped up and carried out the job in exchange for rewards for him and his institution. By the time he moved into the Ministry of Home Affairs, the police were arguably at the zenith of their power in Indonesia's post-independence history. The president, for his part, benefitted from having a reliable coalition partner that he could mobilize in times of crisis. When Tito retired from the force in 2019, a temporary replacement was installed before the known Widodo loyalist Listyo was ready to take over. Although Listyo still faced the influence of the Gunawan clique, he ensured that the most senior police leadership positions were controlled by officers linked to the palace, and that the police were rewarded accordingly. Through their operations, Tito and Listyo embodied the relationship of mutual dependency between presidents and the police in post-2004 coalitional presidentialism. While presidents depend on the support of loyal police officers to protect their rule from security disturbances and disruptive dissent, police leaders appreciate that their material and ideological interests are best protected if the president is on their side.

The two preceding chapters have demonstrated how Indonesian presidents have integrated the country's two leading security agencies, the military and police, into their system of coalitional presidentialism. Both were given cabinet representation; both were rewarded with material favors; and both were targets of the president's appointment strategies, which made leaders of the two institutions part of the palace's inner circle but also tied them to the executive's interests. Indonesian presidents have, in times of heightened socio-political tensions, played the two actors off against each other. Widodo, trying to address the police's hostility at the beginning of his term, turned to the military for support. While this stabilized his rule, it also increased the president's dependence on both forces: once he had made Tito the chief of police, he found it hard to downgrade his ties to the military, and he also needed to hand more concessions to the police to reward Tito for his loyalty. Thus, the careful balancing of the military and the police—drawing from a decades-old rivalry between the two—has handed presidents short-term tactical wins. However, it has also forced them to consider the forces' vested interests when designing national policies. This pattern, in turn, has shielded both institutions from reform efforts that could threaten their privileges. In other words, the loyalty of both organizations to the sitting president is systematically purchased by their integration into the latter's broad coalition that protects the status quo and the distribution of resources underpinning the stability of its operations.

At the same time, it is important to note that Indonesian presidents are not puppets of the military or police.[5] Just as presidents rely on the two security agencies to prevent the destabilization of their governments, so do the military and police depend on the president's patronage. Senior military and police leaders can gain promotion to the next level in their career only with the approval or acquiescence of the president, and the way to more money for their institutions leads through the president's power of the purse. Security agency leaders may try to gain advancement with the support of other powerful allies and display hostility to the president—as Budi Gunawan initially did—and may succeed in retaining positions of significant influence. But as the Gunawan and Budi Waseso cases showed, presidents *can* remove opponents from posts that are most crucial to their interests. Hence, seeking a mutually beneficial relationship with the president has proven to be a more promising strategy for military and police leaders than aggressively trying to extort concessions from him or her. According to a senior Golkar politician, the police patrons Tito, Listyo, and Gunawan were all central figures in an (ultimately failed) attempt to allow Widodo to run for a third term, or at least extend his existing term by a few years. "We at Golkar received a lot of pressure from the president's inner circle to publicly call for a third term for [Widodo], or to extend his term. We first didn't pay much attention, but when the chief of police, the home minister and the intelligence chief conveyed that wish to us, we knew it was serious" (confidential interview, Jakarta, June 23, 2022). Evidently, the logic of exchanging loyalty for favors inherent in conventional coalitional presidentialism had deeply permeated the security forces.

This approach by both sides of the coalitional presidentialism equation—the head of state and the security agencies—has given Indonesia a less democracy-damaging outcome than experienced by some of its Southeast Asian neighbors. In Thailand and Myanmar, military and police forces have often eschewed compromise with executive leaders. Instead, they have aimed to coerce and—if that failed—replace them. The deep democratic crises of both countries, with coups occurring in the 2010s and 2020s, have been the direct result of the failure of civilian leaders and security agency officers to find a stable framework for cooperation. Indonesia, by contrast, has established such a framework by treating the security agencies in the same way that other socio-political actors with potential veto authority are treated. They are situated as recipients of presidential patronage as part of large executive coalitions as long as they pledge loyalty to the president. In return, presidents refrain from crossing the red lines drawn by the security agencies, both in the material and ideological realms. This allowed Indonesian democracy to endure overall but has also led to its quality declining whenever presidents needed to grant concessions to allied security actors to secure the survival of their coalitions. Within this framework of cooperation between presidents and security forces, the military revived its anti-communist scare campaign under Widodo, while the police pushed its conservative socio-political agenda and placed its leaders in influential positions outside of the police. Democracy suffered under these influences but did not collapse; with this, the narrative of the security agency's role in presidential coalitions fits neatly into the picture of Indonesian democracy in the 2010s and 2020s.

6
THE BUREAUCRACY

A thorough assessment of the relationship between the Indonesian presidency and the bureaucracy must begin by emphasizing a simple but important fact: they are separate, competing actors. While it is tempting to view the bureaucracy as an intrinsic part of government and thus not worthy of consideration as an actor that presidents need to lobby, punish, and domesticate, such an approach would mean ignoring the delicate power relations between the two institutions and omit a crucial arena of coalitional presidentialism. The Indonesian bureaucracy typically has a clear idea of what it wants from presidents in exchange for cooperation, and presidents know what they need to do to secure it.

A rich literature exists worldwide on the politically, empirically, and theoretically contested relationship between politicians and the bureaucracy (Aberbach, Putnam, and Rockman 1981). In the political realm, presidents try to ensure that bureaucracies act as nothing else than the implementing arm of the executive. Bureaucracies, by contrast, aim to protect their autonomy, arguing that they act as the servants of the state, not the government of the day. But hidden behind these protestations of autonomy are deep-seated vested interests of the bureaucracy itself and self-serving claims of embodying the state. Empirically, it is hard to ascertain the precise dynamics between the government and its bureaucracy. Is a government truly governing, or are its instructions ignored and re-interpreted by the bureaucracy? Even in Western democracies, the answer to this question is not self-evident, but it becomes even murkier in patronage-oriented, younger post-authoritarian states. And finally, in the theoretical arena, scholars have been unable to say what the ideal relationship between the executive and the bureaucracy should be. Some authors (e.g., Dasandi and Esteve 2017) have pointed to the dangers of bureaucracies becoming independent actors, while others insist (as many bureaucracies do) that a more autonomous bureaucracy produces better policy outcomes (Rasul and Rogger 2018). It is this contested field that presidents and bureaucracies step into when trying to establish their relationship.

In younger presidential democracies, we are more likely to find bureaucracies that are both the subject and object of politicization. On the one hand, presidents must find ways of enforcing the loyalty of the bureaucracy with a mix of threats and rewards. On the other hand, bureaucracies face the task of forming alliances with the president to protect as much as possible of their autonomy and vested interests (this is what Dasandi and Esteve call the "collusive" model of political-bureaucratic relations). Indonesia is no exception in this regard. Its bureaucracy has been widely viewed as one of the least reformed institutions to emerge from authoritarianism (Aswicahyono and Hill 2015), with many of its old practices (such as higher-ranking bureaucrats asking for fees from subordinates for promotions) surviving democratization. Throughout the process of democratic reform, senior bureaucratic leaders have tried, with significant success, to prevent fundamental change to the way they operate. They have stabilized and destabilized governments, depending on the situational goal they sought to achieve. Thus, this book situates the bureaucracy as an interested political actor, not as a neutral apparatus, as idealized in much of the literature on Western democracies (Aberbach, Putnam, and Rockman 1981). It operates neither as a group that dominates elected officials nor as an agent dominated by them. Rather, it thrives in an atmosphere of mutual interpenetration. In the Indonesian case, this interpenetration is achieved through coalitional presidentialism that stipulates the benefits and obligations of both sides.

To be sure, the Indonesian bureaucracy has a less centralized leadership structure than, for example, the military and police. As a result, articulating its interests vis-à-vis the president is more complex. But the bureaucracy united in times of crisis to defend collective interests that its leaders felt were threatened, using organizations such as the Indonesian Civil Servants Corps (Korpri) and the National Civil Service Agency (BKN). These organizations, which are institutionally entrenched in the government, can both lobby within the administration for changes to unfavorable policies and mobilize outside protests. The bureaucracy's representatives in cabinet can, at times, also be utilized to take up the case of bureaucratic interests. Accordingly, the bureaucracy has numerous mechanisms available to act as a coherent institution and make its voice heard in the all-important negotiations with the president.

This chapter discusses the bureaucracy's role in presidential coalitions, following the order of sections in previous chapters. The first section describes the powers the bureaucracy can use when negotiating with the president. These powers center around the threat of omission (that is, the possibility of the bureaucracy not carrying out the government's orders) and—conversely—the promise of passionate deliverance (that is, the prospect of the bureaucracy not only obeying orders but strongly working for the government's success). In addition to policy implementation, this can also imply assistance in elections, which is technically banned but practically widespread. As explored in the second section, presidents possess equally strong powers vis-à-vis the bureaucracy; they hold the supreme appointment authority for upper echelon administrators and can direct funds or withhold them. The display of their respective powers usually results in a settlement between presidents and the bureaucracy, detailed in the third section. Based on this settlement, the bureaucracy gets representation in cabinet, and its red line of vested interests—in its case, the practice of selling jobs and favors—is largely respected. Presidents, in return, obtain guarantees that their government will not be sabotaged. The fourth section offers a case study that focuses on the revision of the civil service law in 2013. The first draft of the law threatened key interests of the bureaucracy, leading it to mobilize against the bill. Fearful of the bureaucracy's insubordination, Yudhoyono agreed to address its concerns. Consequently, the coalitional relationship between the president and the bureaucracy was restored.

The Power of the Civil Service

The Indonesian civil service was the bureaucratic backbone of Suharto's New Order regime from the late 1960s to the late 1990s, complementing the repressive resources of the armed forces (Emmerson 1978). Suharto kept the size of the military limited because he feared a challenge to his rule from another general. But he aggressively pushed for the expansion of the civil service. In 1963, three years before the New Order came to power, there were 608,000 civil servants; this number grew to 1.6 million in 1974, 2.7 million in 1984, and around 3.5 million at the time of Suharto's fall (Bresnan 1993, 105; Tjiptoherijanto 2008, 42). The civil service enforced the regime's policy of bringing society into line with uniform administrative and political standards, leveling the significant cultural differences in the country's societal organization before 1966. For instance, from Aceh to Papua, villages were squeezed into the same administrative framework, regardless of their different traditions. This approach allowed for greater control of society, which the bureaucracy was in charge of executing. The bureaucracy also formed a key component of Golkar, Suharto's electoral machine, and mobilized its members for the party at election times. The civil service continued to grow after Suharto's resignation, ballooning to 4.5 million members before cuts were made to excess staff to bring the number down to 4.2 million by 2020 (Pratama 2020). While 23 percent of these were civil servants directly attached to the central government, 77 percent were formally under local administrations but remained answerable to the central government in Jakarta (BKN 2020).

Under democracy, attempts were made to depoliticize the bureaucracy (Pierskalla, Lauretig, Rosenberg, and Sacks 2021, 266). Civil servants could no longer be members of parties, and penalties were imposed on those found assisting candidates in elections. Similarly, the decentralization of the service made it harder for a national leader to monopolize it, with civil servants more tied to a governor, district head, or mayor than to a president. Despite these depoliticization campaigns, the civil service continued to face interventions by politicians—and it still sought to infiltrate the political sphere as well. Its unity, too, was only partially undermined by regional fragmentation; it sustained a significant level of central organization and corporate identity. One major reason for this is the survival of some of the New Order's institutions for managing the civil service. Chief among them is Korpri, which—despite several attempts at its dissolution—remains operational as a link between the government and the civil service *and* as a bureaucratic lobbying group vis-à-vis presidents and their agencies. Importantly, heads of the post-Suharto Korpri have typically been (as under the New Order) senior civil servants in the Ministry of Home Affairs, which retains oversight of the majority of Indonesia's bureaucracies attached to local administrations. Korpri, which continues to have representation offices in most government agencies nationwide, thus remains engrained in the politics of government and still commands an organizational structure that can be used for mobilization and communication purposes.

While Korpri is nominally an independent organization for civil servants, BKN is the state's official management body for civil service affairs (Tjiptoherijanto 2018). It is directly positioned under the president but is coordinated by the Ministry for the Utilization of the State Apparatus and Bureaucratic Reform. It sets the rules for civil service recruitment and determines the technicalities of salaries and hierarchical advancement. In reality, however, Korpri and BKN often coordinate their activities and viewpoints on matters affecting the status and privileges of the civil service. Hence, the heads of Korpri and BKN are powerful voices in defending the interests of the civil service against attacks from inside and outside of government.

With more than four million civil servants placed in key positions of the state, bureaucratic interest groups such as Korpri and BKN have considerable political leverage (Berenschot 2018). Presidents depend on citizen satisfaction with public service delivery if they want to sustain high approval ratings. Studies have shown that "the impact of a negative experience with a public agency is much more pronounced than the effect of a positive one" (Kampe, de Walle, and Buckaert 2006, 387). Thus, bureaucracies that—intentionally or unintentionally—do not professionally discharge their duties can massively damage citizens' trust in presidents and their government. Conversely, if public services are delivered satisfactorily, presidents stand a significantly better chance at the ballot box than in the case of civil service dysfunction. Beyond guaranteeing basic citizen satisfaction with the incumbent, bureaucracies also have—in some polities and contexts—the option of actively boosting the government's election chances. In mid-2008, for example, Yudhoyono rolled out a US$2 billion cash assistance program to compensate poor citizens for reduced fuel subsidies. For Yudhoyono, who was behind in the polls at that time, the handouts were a stunning success. Photographs of housewives happily waving banknotes into cameras were omnipresent in the media, and Yudhoyono quickly overturned his deficit in the polls (Mietzner 2009b). Arguably, any serious logistical problems with the cash delivery would have damaged Yudhoyono at a time when he could least afford it. But it did not come to that—the bureaucracy carried out its task without much disruption.

Many examples exist of Indonesian bureaucrats refusing to support—or of them directly sabotaging—their political superiors. During the Wahid presidency, some senior bureaucrats stopped taking commands from him once they had concluded that he was certain to be impeached. In the post-2004 presidential system, acts of open defiance are rarer (due to the integration of the bureaucracy into coalitional presidentialism mechanisms); however, cases at the local level routinely provide warnings to presidents of what could happen to them if they were to face a hostile bureaucracy. At the provincial and district level, the most senior bureaucrat is the regional secretary [*sekretaris daerah*], who heads the local apparatus of civil servants. Conflicts between the secretary and the governor or district head are common, often paralyzing local government and sometimes leading to legal proceedings. In January 2018, for instance, the secretary of the district of Cirebon refused to accept his removal, mobilizing the rest of the bureaucracy against the district head (Aryani 2018). The conflict was discussed widely in the news, distracting from the government's agenda and damaging its reputation. Similarly, the secretary of Bekasi city reported the mayor to the police in July 2018, accusing him of incompetence, lack of understanding of how the bureaucracy works, and smearing his (the secretary's) name (Niman 2018). Once again, the conflict fed weeks of unflattering reporting by news outlets. In both the Cirebon and Bekasi cases, political ambitions on the part of the bureaucratic chiefs played a role in the turmoil, driving home the point that their accommodation in a political settlement must be a high priority for executive leaders.

Senior bureaucrats hold a range of roles and powers that, in turn, tend to produce considerable patronage resources and personal wealth. High-level civil servants oversee the process of internal promotions; organize, and often chair, the panels for project tenders; and handle the details of budget formulation and implementation. All these powers can be monetized, making many top-level bureaucrats as affluent as their police or military counterparts. Kuntoro Mangkusubroto, then the head of Yudhoyono's monitoring agency UKP4, estimated in 2013 that the trade in bureaucratic positions was worth at least US$1 billion a year. "It's a big business," he explained. "Bureaucrats are victims and actors in this. They get squeezed by their political superiors for funds, so they recoup that money by extorting their own subordinates" (interview, Jakarta, December 5, 2013). Taufiq Effendi, the former minister for the utilization of the state apparatus, confirmed this pattern. "It's a vicious cycle," he said. "Politicians have to pay for their elections, so they turn to people below them [in the bureaucracy] for funds. The bureaucrats then turn to the level below them, and so forth" (interview, Depok, November 28, 2013). Getting specific, the head of the State Civil Service Commission (KASN), an oversight body, stated in 2017 that regional secretary posts are typically sold for Rp 1 billion (US$71,000), while lower-level leadership posts go for between Rp 200 to 400 million. "Not only higher-ranking positions are traded, but all civil service posts," he maintained, adding that the practice is most prevalent at the local level (Firmanto 2017).

The financial prowess of bureaucrats has increased their bargaining powers vis-à-vis elected officials and has furthered the interpenetration between the two spheres. While routinely subject to attempts by elected officials to politicize (and extort) them, bureaucrats have also entered politics and directly sought political power. In the 223 local executive elections held in December 2015, 26.8 percent of the candidates were active and retired civil servants (Aspinall and Berenschot 2019, 192). The Cirebon and Bekasi cases were entangled in such electoral competitions between civil servants and politicians who—in non-election times— rank above them. In addition to the material resources that allow them to launch strong campaigns, civil servants are often popular with voters because of their supposed non-partisanship and their experience in governance (both of which are normally cornerstones of their electoral branding). At 27.7 percent, the success rate of the civil servants running in 2015 was higher than that of business representatives, 17.7 percent of whom won their races. Thus, civil servants are powerful not only because of their formal prerogatives that can be used to support or destabilize elected officials (and collect significant resources) but also because they can emerge as potential challengers to professional politicians themselves. This includes the president, who needs to make constant judgments about who might challenge him or her for political authority, both in election times and outside of them.

Consequently, Indonesian presidents need to have the civil service on their list when assembling their coalitions. It is insufficient for them to simply entrust oversight over the bureaucracy to aides tasked with enforcing the professionalism of the state apparatus. As a political actor with a host of interests, the bureaucracy expects to be given a level of participation in governance and resource distribution that reflects its importance to sitting presidents. Seeing how the military and police obtained such status in presidential coalitions, the civil service has demanded equal treatment—which includes seats at the cabinet table, protection of material privileges, and respect toward red lines that should not be crossed. But presidents have not only accepted this proposition; they have also utilized their powers to discipline the civil service, limit its expectations, and ensure its loyalty as a coalition partner.

Presidential Powers over the Bureaucracy

As in the case of the military and the police, the president's most important instrument in controlling the civil service is his or her appointment powers. The 2014 Civil Service Law situates the president as the "holder of the highest authority in [determining] the policy, professional oversight, and management of the civil service." This means that the president is superior to each civil servant. While some of his or her powers are delegated to subordinates, the source of the latter's authority continues to rest in the presidency. A 2020 government regulation further strengthened the president's direct appointment powers. It stipulated that in cases of violations of appointment procedures in the civil service, the president can cancel the automatic delegations to subordinates and pull the appointment decision to the presidential level (Adyatama 2020). It also specified that the president can decide to do so even if no violation occurred; all the president has to do to justify an appointment without involving delegates is to certify that such a step is taken "in order to increase the effectiveness of governance" (Adyatama 2020). Thus, presidents can intervene in the appointment of civil servants to remove office holders they view as obstructing "the effectiveness of governance," or to place civil servants in these positions that are seen as supporting this effectiveness. In realpolitik language, the president can dismiss disloyal civil servants and replace them with loyalists if he or she wishes to do so.

Even without invoking these special powers, the president sits at the apex of the regular appointment process for high-level civil servants. These include the heads of ministerial bureaucracies, non-ministerial government agencies, and other state-controlled entities. In this process, the agencies involved first conduct their internal selection process through an appointment panel, and the three top-ranked candidates are subsequently submitted to the Final Assessors Team [*Tim Penilai Akhir*]. The team is chaired by the president, with the vice president as deputy chair. The president's cabinet secretary is the team's secretary who oversees the administrative aspects of the selection. The state secretary, minister for the utilization of the state apparatus and bureaucratic reform, and the head of BKN are permanent members of the team, while ministers from the departments affected by appointments can be named as non-permanent members. The state intelligence agency and other government bodies can, if asked, submit assessments of the candidates to the team. Although the team formally operates as a collective, it is self-evident that the president's vote carries the greatest weight. This is particularly the case if presidents take an active interest in the details of the appointment process, or have particular favorites they would like to advance. In such cases, the team endorses the president's call. In his two stints as vice president of both Yudhoyono and Widodo (2004–2009, 2014–2019), Jusuf Kalla was known to aggressively push for his nominees, successfully using occasional presidential disinterest in the process. However, presidents tend to strengthen their direct role in senior bureaucratic appointments during their second terms—both Yudhoyono and Widodo did so, profiting from greater familiarity with the process compared to their early presidential careers.

The 2020 decree on presidential special powers in bureaucratic appointments indicated Widodo's increasing interest and authority in this arena, but there were other signs of this trend, too. When Widodo replaced the minister for state-owned enterprises Rini Soemarno with Erick Thohir in 2019, he also pushed for a change in how the leaders of state-owned enterprises were selected. During her tenure, Rini made direct appointments and then had them endorsed by general shareholders meetings, using the dual status of state-owned enterprises as both businesses and state agencies (Situmorang 2019). Thohir, by contrast, announced after his appointment that he would transfer the selection process to the authority of the Final Assessors Team, effectively handing it to the president. "The president instructed that appointments in state enterprises have to go to the Final Assessors Team. All of them," Thohir said, making clear who had initiated the change (Kumparan 2019). Widodo, who increased the role of state-owned enterprises during his presidency as part of his development plans, made extensive use of his new role and directly chaired numerous sessions of the team that reshuffled senior positions in the enterprises. Only a week after the change in the procedure was announced, Widodo presided over a team meeting that appointed, among others, new leaders in key state banks. Thohir made no secret that Widodo had made several picks before the team had formally been in session. "The directors of [two large state banks] have already been decided by the president," Thohir told journalists in November 2019, "if you like to know the names, ask him" (Kumparan 2019).

The president's changes to bureaucratic procedures highlight the regulatory powers of the head of state vis-à-vis the civil service. On their initiative, presidents can introduce measures that either advance or run counter to the vested interests of the bureaucracy and its members. As most such steps can be taken in the form of presidential or government decrees, they do not require the legislature's approval (and much less of the bureaucracy itself). For instance, the president's 2020 consolidation of his appointment powers was done through Government Regulation 17 of 2020 that changed Government Regulation 11 of 2017—both signed by Widodo. For larger reforms to the bureaucracy, the president can initiate and co-promulgate laws in cooperation with the legislature. This was the case in 2013, when Yudhoyono's government deliberated a new civil service law with parliament. The draft threatened core interests of the bureaucracy (more on this below). In mobilizing opposition to the draft, the bureaucracy challenged but also implicitly acknowledged the president's powers over its institutional agenda. Accordingly, much of the opposition was directed toward the president and his representatives in the deliberation rather than the legislators that held an equal share of responsibility for the passing of the law. The outcome of the process—the 2014 Civil Service Law, a compromise between the president and the bureaucracy—highlighted the powers of both sides and re-calibrated their mutually accommodating relationship.

The president's budgetary authority is also of great importance to the bureaucracy—as is his or her influence over law enforcement agencies. The state budget approved jointly by the president and the legislature is the source of the bureaucracy's patronage opportunities. As in the case of the military and the police, the president can determine the size of those funds and make it easier or harder to access them in legal and illicit ways. If bureaucrats get caught up in corruption cases involving the misuse of state funds, presidents can offer protection—or choose not to. In June 2015, Widodo's then-chief of staff Luhut Pandjaitan told a meeting of law enforcers that the president was concerned about the many bureaucratic decision makers charged with corruption, as he feared this would slow down development. "We don't want people who take policy decisions to be brought to trial so that they become anxious to make decisions," Luhut insisted (Sholeh 2015). "That's why in this meeting [I explained] that those who make decisions shouldn't easily be accused of violating the law." This was music to the ears of bureaucrats who chaired project tender panels and got subsequently charged with siphoning off funds. Bureaucrats also benefitted from Widodo's later weakening of the KPK—civil servants made up one-fifth of all cases in the anti-corruption agency between 2004 and 2020, and they constituted the third-largest group of suspects (KPK 2021). After the 2019 changes to the KPK law, in 2020 the number of bureaucrats charged by the KPK dropped to its lowest level since 2016, and its proportion of overall cases to below 10 percent.

Finally, presidents have the power to shape the image, reputation, and standing of the bureaucracy in society, thus influencing its ability to continue its traditional operations. For many presidents, it is tempting to shift blame for their policy failures by accusing the bureaucracy of not accurately carrying out their orders. Presidents who choose this option prioritize their own political interests over that of the bureaucracy, leading to substantial damage to the latter. Widodo, for instance, demonstrated this presidential power during the early phase of the COVID-19 pandemic, when he routinely blamed unnamed officials on the ground for the continued spike in cases and deaths—while most experts agreed that the failures were a result of Widodo's policies rather than of incompetent grassroots actors. Widodo's campaign was successful for him but damaging for the bureaucracy: in an April 2021 survey, 67 percent of respondents expressed satisfaction with Widodo's management of the pandemic, while only 44 percent had confidence in the work of the health ministry's apparatus (Indikator 2021, 33–24). In July of the same year, Widodo warned civil servants that they are "not officials who should ask being served, who act like officials in the colonial era in times past. This can't happen again, the times have changed" (CNN Indonesia 2021b). He left unexplained who and what exactly he meant, but he had highlighted once again his capacity to either protect or attack the bureaucracy, depending on his political interests of the day. In turn, this capacity to make credible threats has been kept in store by presidents as one of the instruments of enforcing the bureaucracy's loyalty.

In consequence, while bureaucracies have significant powers to extract concessions from the president, and in many ways hold the key to the stability and success of an administration, the president can also put pressure on the civil service by granting or withholding benefits and protections. This means, on the one hand, that the president cannot feel assured of the automatic support or professional neutrality of the bureaucracy; on the other hand, the civil service cannot rely on the president generously rewarding it for its role in governance. The president's expectation of loyalty, and the bureaucracy's demand that its interests be shielded, hence become elements of intense and routine negotiation between the two sides. Coalitional presidentialism offers the institutional framework for these negotiations and their outcome. The next section analyzes how this outcome is achieved, and how it has helped Indonesian presidents to sustain their rule while accepting that it also limits their ability to initiate reform.

The Bureaucracy in Presidential Coalitions

As with other actors that presidents tie into their coalitions, using presidential appointment powers is one of the most frequently used strategies to contain opposition and incentivize cooperation in the bureaucracy. A central element of this strategy is the placement of loyalists in key posts. As noted, presidents can appoint the upper echelons of the bureaucracy through their role in the Final Assessors Team. One case in which the president made direct use of this authority was the appointment of Basuki Tjahaja Purnama as the chief commissioner of Pertamina, the state oil company, in November 2019. Purnama had been Widodo's deputy governor in Jakarta, and in 2014, became governor when Widodo took up the presidency. Recall that in 2016 Islamist opposition to the re-election campaign of Purnama, a Christian of ethnic Chinese descent, exploded on the streets of Jakarta. Widodo tried to protect Purnama, but the pressure became so strong that the president allowed the police to charge Purnama with blasphemy—this accusation had been the formal justification for the Islamist street mobilization (Peterson 2020a). Purnama eventually lost the election and was sentenced to two years in prison. Upon his release in January 2019, the president considered new positions for his former deputy. Purnama's reputation as a no-nonsense administrator with low levels of tolerance for bureaucratic dysfunction and office abuse (Hatherell and Welsh 2017) made him, in Widodo's eyes, an ideal candidate to be placed in one of the state's most important, but also most unruly, enterprises.

Purnama's appointment initially created much commotion in the giant state company. Even when his possible selection was only a rumor, the union of Pertamina employees expressed opposition. Arguing that Purnama lacked the necessary credentials for the post and that his appointment would violate bureaucratic protocol, the union threatened legal action should Purnama become chief commissioner (Ismoyo 2019). But for Widodo, the protest was a sign that Purnama was the right choice: as the president's direct representative in the company's bureaucracy, he could keep the latter in check, negotiate over its interests, and ultimately enforce its adherence to the goals formulated by the president. When Widodo met with Purnama officially after his appointment in December 2019, he asked him to turn Pertamina into a profitable company that could help Indonesia overcome its notoriously entrenched trade deficit—which was partly due to the large volume of oil imports (Ishanuddin 2019). Over time, resistance to Purnama in Pertamina's bureaucratic ranks declined, as he promised greater opportunities for lower-ranking staff. He set up a "team of transformers" whose task was to accelerate the careers of young, promising staff (Rosana 2020). At the same time, he cut the credit card limits of the most senior staff, which he claimed previously reached up to Rp 30 billion (US$2.1 million) (Bestari 2021). In short, he applied a carrot-and-stick approach that was in line with Widodo's overall strategy for the bureaucracy's role in his coalition: he wanted to provide sufficient incentives for the majority of civil servants to remain loyal, while demonstrating enough powers of punishment to disincentivize disloyalty and mismanagement.

Another aspect of the president's appointment powers as a strategy of coalition-building with the bureaucracy is the granting of cabinet representation. Bureaucrats have traditionally been given a share of the non-party contingent in cabinet, with two to three seats held by bureaucrats in Yudhoyono and Widodo cabinets. These bureaucratic ministers represent the president's interests in the bureaucracy but also voice the aspirations of the civil service to the head of state. One example of this pattern is Basuki Madimuljono, often described as Widodo's favorite minister (Ningrum 2019). As minister of public works and housing in both Widodo cabinets, he was responsible for the president's main policy initiative in his ten years in office: that is, the upgrading of Indonesia's infrastructure. Basuki had entered the ministry as a civil servant immediately after graduation from university and worked himself up the bureaucratic ladder. At the time of his ministerial appointment, he was a director general with three and a half decades of experience in the department. As minister, he became an active lobbyist for Korpri, perpetuating the civil service narrative as being at "the front line of the effort to cultivate the oneness and unity of the nation" (PUPR 2020). He was known to have exclusive access to the president, reflecting Widodo's interest in Basuki's portfolio (which included the planned relocation of the capital from Jakarta to Kalimantan, the president's idea) but also delivering ample opportunities for the minister to communicate the thinking of the bureaucracy on critical issues.

Some senior bureaucrats have entered cabinet through party channels, further strengthening the glue that holds presidents, parties, and non-party actors such as the civil service together in one coalition. Siti Nurbaya Bakar, for instance, joined the civil service at the age of twenty-three in 1979. She spent most of her early career in the development planning agency of the province of Lampung on Sumatra before becoming head of the planning bureau at the Ministry of Home Affairs in 1998 (Nurbaya 2021). In 2001, she was promoted to the post of secretary-general in the ministry—in many ways, the most important position in the bureaucracy as it has oversight over the millions of civil servants placed in local administrations. After four years on the job, she took up the position of secretary-general of Indonesia's senate, the DPD. The DPD turned out to be a weak body, but Siti used the time at its helm to mingle with the elite of its powerful sister body, the DPR. Upon retirement in 2013, she became a politician in the Nasdem party, headed by the media tycoon Surya Paloh. She entered the first Widodo cabinet in 2014 as minister for the environment and forestry, and continued to hold this post in the president's second term. In office, Widodo appreciated her willingness to defend the president's policy of prioritizing economic investment over environmental concerns; in 2020, she portrayed Widodo's pro-business Omnibus Bill, which dismantled many environmental protections, as a pro-environment measure, drawing criticism from activists (Agustina 2020). Her technocratic efficiency and loyalty, internalized in her decades as a civil servant, made her a presidential favorite.

Timely salary increases for the civil service are also a significant component of the coalition dynamics between the president and the bureaucracy. We already discussed how Widodo increased the salary for the police and the military just ahead of the 2019 elections. Separately, but relatedly, he also announced a salary increase for the civil service—plus a big bonus (a thirteenth and fourteenth monthly wage) that would be paid out in April 2019, the month of the election. Unlike police and military members, civil servants hold voting rights, but they are not allowed to visibly support a particular candidate or party. At the time of Widodo's salary announcement, opinion surveys showed that Widodo was behind in the civil service vote. In a survey published in February 2019, Widodo was trailing his opponent Prabowo 40 to 44 percent among bureaucrats (BBC Indonesia 2019). While this was an improvement over the 2014 election, when the gap between the two men had been around 30 percent in Prabowo's favor, it still created nervousness in the palace. Widodo's use of his budgetary powers for a last-minute salary increase was arguably designed to give him the edge over Prabowo, and it came packaged in some unusually sweet-mouthed praise for the civil service. "The speed of the services rendered by bureaucrats is improving by the day," the president flattered (Damanik 2019). The government later claimed it lost the 2019 elections among civil servants—it used this argument against Prabowo's accusations that the president had unduly mobilized the civil service (Asmara 2019).[1] Whatever the actual outcome, it is clear that the president used his fiscal authority to woe civil servants as they went to the ballot box.

As in the case of other actors, public events are important sites for demonstrating and negotiating the coalitional relationship between the president and the bureaucracy. As mentioned, Widodo frequently used these sites for both praise (close to an election) and reprimands (when he wished to underline his authority). While presidents appropriate public events with the civil service to re-calibrate the conditions that tie the bureaucracy to their government, the civil service utilizes them as arenas for voicing demands and pledging loyalty. In November 2018, for example, Widodo attended the forty-seventh anniversary of Korpri—an event most presidents put as a must-go commitment into their calendar. At the gathering, Zudan Arif Fakhruloh, the chairman of Korpri (and at the same time a senior bureaucrat at the Ministry of Home Affairs), confronted the president with an unexpected request. For Korpri's anniversary, he said, "we expect a present from you, Sir. One of the presents for which civil servants all over Indonesia have waited anxiously is a government regulation on the organization of Korpri" (Ihsanuddin 2018). The expression of this request was met with thunderous applause by the thousands of civil servants present at the ceremony. To soften the aggressiveness of the demand, the Korpri chief followed up with a pledge of increased loyalty and performance: "if this government regulation has been completed, you, Sir, can trust that we at Korpri will fly even higher, run even faster, and jump even longer."

The promulgation of a government regulation as a foundation of Korpri has been a goal of crucial importance for the civil service corps and its ambition to represent the bureaucracy's vested interests through a coherent organizational actor. At the time of the 2018 event, Korpri's institutional anchoring was shaky: its strongest claim to a permanent position in Indonesia's legal-political hierarchy was a 1971 presidential decision that was now widely seen as outdated. A 2004 government regulation signed by Megawati had stipulated a code of ethics for the corps without reaffirming its post-Suharto existence, while the 2014 Civil Service law referred to a civil service corps but did not mention Korpri. In fact, the Ministry of Home Affairs had announced in 2012 that Korpri would be dissolved, or at least renamed (*Liputan6* 2012); yet the organization continued to exist long after that, albeit with an unclear status. Hence, Fakhruloh's public confrontation of Widodo on the issue went to the heart of the bureaucracy's relationship with the president. A renewed government regulation would entrench Korpri as the president's sole negotiation partner over the interests of the civil service, while its continued absence was set to weaken its position in such high-level negotiations. Fully aware of this dynamic, Widodo was in no hurry to accelerate the drafting of the Korpri decree, and at the time of writing, it has yet to be issued. As a result, it remains a key bargaining chip that the president could use should the loyalty of the civil service come under more serious questioning than during the 2018 ceremony.

In the history of the alliance between presidents and the bureaucracy in post-2004 coalitional presidentialism, there has been only one instance in which the relationship was close to a breakdown. At that point, all the techniques of coalition-building and maintenance—the placement of presidential allies in the civil service; the inclusion of bureaucrats in cabinet; the use of the budget to incentivize loyalty; or the celebration of the alliance at public ceremonies—seemed to be insufficient to prevent a major crisis between the two sides. At the end, however, the principle of compromise that is so central to the concept of coalitional presidentialism prevailed, and the bureaucracy returned to the table of joint government. The case that carried such conflict potential was the deliberation of the 2014 Civil Service Law. Due to its importance, we turn to its detailed discussion in the next section.

The 2014 Civil Service Law

The passing of the 2014 Civil Service Law resulted from both President Yudhoyono's interest in creating a more professional civil service and his hesitancy to take potentially confrontational measures to actually achieve this goal. In his first term, he had remained passive on the issue, noting that the bureaucracy was often uncooperative. A legislator of his party recalled that "the president frequently complained to us in the party [during his first term] that he found it difficult to implement his policies because the bureaucratic apparatus blocked, delayed, or sabotaged them; he told us he would use his second term to address the problem and clean up the bureaucracy—he wanted it to be a professional and reliable partner for the incumbent president" (interview with Khatibul Umam Wiranu, Jakarta, February 24, 2014). In 2009, therefore, Yudhoyono added "Bureaucracy Reform" to the name of the Ministry for the Utilization of the State Apparatus, and in May 2010, he set up the Steering Committee for the Reform of the National Bureaucracy, chaired by Vice President Boediono. He also created the Independent Team for the Reform of the National Bureaucracy, which consisted of academics, business practitioners, and former bureaucrats. Moreover, Yudhoyono's post-2009 speeches repeatedly defined bureaucracy reform as a cornerstone of his government.[2] According to a bureaucracy expert advising the government, Yudhoyono sought to replicate the success of the National Performance Review in the United States, which had been mandated by President Bill Clinton and overseen by Vice President Al Gore in 1994 (discussion with Prijono Tjipto Herijanto, December 12, 2013).

Despite this rhetoric by the president, it was parliament that took the initiative to revise the existing civil service law (Law 43/1999 on the Principles of the Civil Service), which was seen as part of the reason for the stasis in bureaucratic reform. Concretely, it was Taufiq Effendi, the minister for the state apparatus in Yudhoyono's first term and a member of Yudhoyono's Democratic Party, who actively pushed the issue. Frustrated with his lack of success as minister in moving bureaucratic reform forward, he used his post-2009 position as deputy chair of the domestic affairs commission of parliament to revive his plans of rewriting Law 43/1999. In this, Taufiq received encouragement from senior academics concerned with bureaucracy reform. One of them, Sofian Effendi, told Taufiq, "now you have the big chance to do what you couldn't do as minister" (interview, Jakarta, November 28, 2013). Subsequently, Taufiq explored two avenues for a comprehensive revision of Law 43/1999: first, he used his contacts in the State Administration Institute (LAN)—a research and education body for the bureaucracy—to initiate a first draft for the revisions; second, through his parliamentary commission, he assigned four senior professors (Eko Prasojo, Prijono Tjipto Herijanto, Miftah Thoha, and Sofian Effendi) to come up with a draft. While the LAN draft never made it far, the team of four presented its draft—an entirely new bill—in late 2010.

At the heart of the concept developed by the four scholars was the creation of a new Civil Service Commission (KASN). Consisting of a mix of independent experts and government representatives, the KASN was supposed to have direct appointment authority for the most senior echelons of the bureaucracy. In addition, it was to oversee the recruitment mechanism for the lower ranks. With this, it was hoped, the cycle of selling positions in the civil service could be halted. Other proposals advanced by the team of four included a strict application of the merit principle in all bureaucratic appointments and a change in the professional status of civil servants. For decades, Indonesia's bureaucracy had been notorious for its inflexible appointment procedures, with positions only available to candidates who had reached a specific rank (McLeod 2005). Even ministers found it impossible to appoint the staff they wanted because of these rigorous regulations. The draft of the team of four would have loosened these restrictions and made the competence and prior performance of candidates the main criteria for filling vacancies. The professors also proposed changing the civil service status from an internal government service [*status kedinasan*] to a profession. This change, if implemented systematically, would have changed the civil service from a corps institutionally tied to the government apparatus to a vocation. As such, its representative body—Korpri—would no longer have been an intrinsic part of government but an association of service providers to central and local administrations. According to Taufiq, "many officials in the Home Ministry particularly objected to this suggestion—it threatened to rob them of their closeness to power and its holders" (interview, Depok, November 30, 2013).

Predictably, the bureaucracy expressed strong opposition to the draft. The opposition was led by three main actors: the secretary-general of the Ministry of Home Affairs, Korpri, and BKN. To begin with, the secretary-general of the

Ministry of Home Affairs, Diah Anggraeni, was exceptionally powerful. Concurrently head of Korpri and of the internal bureaucratic networks of the ministry, she could also rely on her family connections with Sudi Silalahi, Yudhoyono's state secretary and most trusted aide. Hence, she felt politically protected enough to attack her opponents in the deliberation process openly. This included confronting her superiors in the government hierarchy, such as Boediono. There was much at stake for Anggraeni: a KASN with full appointment powers would have taken away her authority in selecting senior bureaucrats at the national and local level, removing the ministry's most lucrative source of patronage. Similarly, a strict implementation of the merit principle would have made the traditionally closed class of career bureaucrats vulnerable to challenges by professionals. That Anggraeni was able to challenge these two initiatives was also due to her allies' numerical dominance: in the technical deliberation teams (which the government had set up to engage in discussions with parliament on the draft), representatives of Korpri, BKN, and the ministry's various offices far outnumbered the delegates from other government agencies and parliament.

Korpri, for its part, was especially opposed to the proposal of the team of four to turn Korpri from a governmental into a professional body. This would have drawn a clearer demarcation line between government and the civil service subordinated to the former, and it would have ended the practice of Korpri officials receiving handsome government salaries. As in other areas, Diah Anggraeni was the most vocal opponent of this idea, using her ex officio post as head of Korpri to justify her intensive lobbying and activism. Conversely, BKN was most concerned about a potentially powerful KASN. Under existing regulations, BKN oversaw most aspects of civil service management, including the recruitment system, dismissal procedures, and retirement schemes. Like the Ministry of Home Affairs, BKN had its roots in the Dutch colonial state. Then called the Dienst voor Algemene Personele Zaken (DAPZ), it transferred its bureaucratic apparatus to the newly independent state in 1949. Under Suharto, much of the patronage surrounding civil service appointments had been channeled through BKN and its affiliated offices. However, all of this was threatened by the team of four's proposal to hand over the management of civil service recruitment to KASN—essentially, BKN would have been made redundant. Thus, Diah Anggraeni, Korpri, and BKN formed a formidable alliance to fight against the proposed law, defending their respective sectoral interests but also the broader institutional privileges of the civil service as a whole.

The protest of the bureaucracy included both internal and external mobilization of resistance. Internally, Anggraeni obstructed the discussions within government and between the executive and parliament. Externally, she encouraged actors such as the Association of Indonesian Municipality Governments

(APEKSI) to express their opposition. Touring the regions, she told local bureaucrats that the Civil Service Bill would expose them to competition from professionals. As a result, the associations sent delegates to Jakarta to protest against the bill, even if Anggraeni took a softer line in the official negotiations. Said one official at the office of Boediono, who tried to mediate the conflict: "this made dealing with Anggraeni so difficult—even after she reluctantly agreed to something in a formal meeting with us, she often just turned around and mobilized her political allies against this very same agreement" (confidential interview, Jakarta, December 2, 2013). Clearly, Anggraeni combined her control of key sections in the state with an effective use of Indonesia's post-1998 protest culture. Anggraeni proved far savvier in mobilizing support groups than her reformist rivals. Although Eko Prasodjo, one of the authors of the reformist draft, was appointed deputy minister for the utilization of the state apparatus and bureaucratic reform in October 2011, he seemed powerless against Anggraeni's influence. I Made Suwandi, the Ministry of Home Affair's director general of general governance, noted at the time that "Eko and his group didn't court the regional associations, that was a big mistake; Anggraeni had by far the superior networks" (interview, Jakarta, December 4, 2013).

Boediono and other officials reported to Yudhoyono that the bureaucracy would "rebel" if the initial draft of the civil service law were to be passed (confidential interview, Jakarta, December 2, 2013). The notoriously risk-averse president feared for the stability of his government and coalition and moved to de-escalate the situation. Initially, he thought that his subordinates could handle the situation, but in May 2013 he took direct control of the deliberations. This was prompted by the news of an increasingly angry bureaucracy and a newspaper column written by Sofian Effendi, in which he had criticized the president for not taking action. Yudhoyono suddenly called for a cabinet meeting on the bill on May 14, the day after Effendi's piece was published. This was the first cabinet meeting on the bill after more than two years of discussions, and the president immediately demonstrated that he was determined to drop the reformist draft and settle for a compromise. After Eko gave a detailed presentation on the draft bill, Yudhoyono dragged the debate back to philosophical principles; he asked eleven questions, such as "What kind of civil service do we need for Indonesia?" Opening a web dictionary on his iPad, Yudhoyono read the definition of "bureaucracy" to his cabinet. In two further cabinet meetings, on May 23 and July 16, 2013, Eko tried to answer the president's questions. It became obvious in those meetings, however, that the bill's opponents had strongly influenced the president. Yudhoyono emphasized that he rejected the extensive powers given to the KASN and that the appointment of civil servants still had to be based on seniority.

Eko and his team accepted Yudhoyono's decisions without further debate, realizing that the president had endorsed many of the arguments put forward by the Ministry of Home Affairs. "Once I heard the president [in cabinet], I knew that it was pointless to push the issue further," Eko recalled (interview, Jakarta, December 3, 2013). As a result, when the government asked to resume deliberations with parliament in July 2013, Eko carried Yudhoyono's mandate to seek a significantly diluted version of the bill. The KASN, for instance, was no longer to be a civil service appointment body but an oversight agency. According to one parliamentarian, "the government amputated the legs, arms, and finally the entire body from the KASN, leaving only the eyes, for monitoring purposes; it's a disgrace" (interview with Gamari Sutrisno, Jakarta, November 29, 2013). Some of the strongest supporters of the initial draft in parliament, including Taufiq, had since left the legislature, making the deliberations much less contentious than at the beginning of the process. In a joint team of government and parliamentary staffers, the bill's technical details were debated. In this team, the power balance was obvious: in one session attended by the author in November 2013, around twenty government team members—all experienced bureaucrats—faced off with two representatives of parliament, who struggled to stay on top of the issues. After the first draft had been comprehensively watered down, the bill was passed in December 2013.

In sum, Yudhoyono had avoided a major conflict with the bureaucracy by giving in to its demands and, despite minor reforms, maintaining the overall status quo in the relationship between the president and the civil service. Nothing was more abhorrent to Yudhoyono than the notion of "chaos" that could undermine the harmony of the ruling coalition and, by implication, governance. In Yudhoyono's eyes, he had done what was necessary if a president wanted to ensure a smooth process of government. Superficially, the Civil Service Law of 2014 provided some evidence that reform was occurring, but it left the general infrastructure of bureaucratic power intact. The new system still allowed for extensive trading of positions—and while Korpri continued to fight for more formal recognition well into the Widodo presidency, its de facto role as the bureaucracy's lobbying group vis-à-vis the government continued. Most importantly, however, the conditions of the bureaucracy's membership in the presidential coalition had been renegotiated, ultimately satisfying both sides. Widodo was able to pick up from where Yudhoyono left this presidential-bureaucratic coalition in 2014, and through maneuverings and deals, he cemented the alliance further.

Much of the literature on the role of the bureaucracy in politics has focused on either the president's endeavors to firmly subordinate the civil service or the quest of the latter to maintain its autonomy. But in patronage democracies such as Indonesia, the relationship between the two is closer to what Dasandi and Esteve (2017) called a "collusive" alliance. Several aspects of the Indonesian case stand out in this regard. First, the bureaucracy is a political actor with a host of vested interests. At best, its claim of institutional neutrality constitutes an ideational pretext for rejecting the intervention of politicians into its affairs; at worst, it is a self-interested mechanism to protect the illicit funding channels that feed the patronage dynamics in the civil service. Second, interpreting the role of the bureaucracy within the framework of Indonesia's coalitional presidentialism offers a nuanced picture of the mutual interpenetration of politics and the bureaucracy. Presidents insert themselves into the bureaucracy by placing loyalists in its ranks, while bureaucrats exploit their role in administration to defend their interests—and many use their wealth to enter politics themselves. Hence, while the bureaucracy is politicized in many ways, politics is also bureaucratized (Berenschot 2018). Third, the bureaucracy—beyond its lobbying power through Korpri and other bodies—has a permanent seat at the cabinet table as part of a larger coalitional deal that presidents offer to the civil service to institutionalize their cooperation.

Consequently, just as the literature on bureaucracy and politics can inform us of the core interests of both sides, so can the coalitional presidentialism scholarship add to the studies on politicized civil services. If we understand the bureaucracy, as in the Indonesian case, as one of many members of presidential coalitions, the boundaries between the president and the civil service become less rigid. This, in turn, allows us to situate the relationship not as one in which the president controls the civil service, or the latter occasionally refuses to follow directives; instead, we can conceptualize it as one that involves complicated give-and-take arrangements and continuous renegotiation. It is worth noting again that most established democracies of the West would perceive such patterns as an appalling diversion from the Weberian notion of a state-serving bureaucracy, and much of the literature (not coincidentally originating in the West) would agree. But this is precisely where the Indonesian case can deliver a reality check on how many bureaucracies in younger democracies work; there, the model of a "collusive" coalition is more prevalent than even Dasandi and Esteve assumed. Somewhat optimistically, Yudhoyono modeled his bureaucratic reform effort along the lines of the Clinton initiative headed by Gore; however, that attempt fell apart as the power of civil service lobbyists confronted the president. As one of the authors of the reformist first draft of the civil service law remarked, Yudhoyono's fear of a potential bureaucracy backlash led him to refrain from giving his deputy "Boediono the full powers that Al Gore had—in fact, Boediono was granted none" (discussion with Prijono Tjipto Herijanto, December 12, 2013).

Integrating the bureaucracy into coalitional presidentialism studies also sheds new light on the difficulty of civil service reform in Indonesia and beyond. The slow pace of change in this arena is not just the result of the massive size of the apparatus and the archaic rules that have traditionally governed it. Rather, bureaucratic elites have succeeded in defending, and presidents have been reluctant in attacking, privileges that the civil service has set as red lines in political negotiations. The bureaucracy's self-funding, predatory appropriation of state budgets, and entrenched patronage practices are chief among them, but conservative views of what and who constitutes the state are also included. Presidents have accepted these red lines because they fear not doing so would posit the bureaucracy outside of their coalitions and thus threaten the stability of their rule. The civil service, for its part, has allowed just enough reform for the president to be able to credibly claim that some change has been achieved. Other than that, both sides have endorsed an arrangement that permits the government to operate effectively while providing guarantees for the continued supply of major benefits to civil servants. Drastic reform, in this equation, always carries the risk of creating instability, and therefore is inherently antithetic to coalitional presidentialism.

7

LOCAL GOVERNMENTS

As in the case of the bureaucracy, it might be considered counterintuitive to situate local governments as partners in presidential coalitions. After all, Indonesia is a unitary state; formally, local administrations are extensions of the national government. But Indonesia's post-2001 decentralization process has turned the country into a quasi-federal polity, in which districts (more so than provinces) hold much autonomy and, therefore, bargaining powers vis-à-vis the presidency (Aspinall and Fealy 2003; Pepinsky and Wihardja 2011; Hill 2014; Rakmawati, Hinchcliff, and Pardosi 2019). This has forced presidents to integrate local governments into their coalition-building calculations, as non-cooperative district (or provincial) administrations can be a major obstacle to stable governance. Like other actors, they are given financial incentives to support the incumbent's policies or election campaigns; they are subject to presidential appointment powers, especially when electoral disputes or other unforeseen circumstances prevent an orderly succession in local government leadership positions; and they do enter, rarely but regularly, cabinet as representatives of specific local government interests and ways of thinking. Thus, presidents treat local administrations similarly to other key coalition partners, intending to prevent disloyalty and ensuring smooth governance. And as with other actors, too, failed coalition negotiations can result in significant problems for the incumbent president's alliance. Local governments, for their part, are aware of their status as coalition partners. One province chief described governors eloquently as "the president's biggest party."

No president has been more aware of the powers of local government than Widodo. As a former mayor of Solo and governor of Jakarta, he rose to the presidency thanks to the political dynamics of Indonesia's decentralization project. He ran in the country's first direct local executive elections in 2005, using his image as a hands-on furniture businessman to attract voters who wanted equally hands-on grassroots government. After a near-record landslide re-election in 2010, he gained national prominence, which led to his successful candidacy for the Jakarta governorship in 2012. In both positions, Widodo studied the extensive authority of local administrations, and how they can be used for leverage vis-à-vis the national elite. Consequently, when he became president, he was concerned about the difficulties of synchronizing national with local policies, and spent much of his presidency trying to re-strengthen the center over the regions (Diprose, Kurniawan, Macdonald, and Winanti 2022). At that point, however, decentralization had become so entrenched that a fundamental revision was out of the question because it would have enraged local government leaders and thus undermined the stability of the presidential coalition they supported. As such, the centralist reforms that Widodo undertook were designed to renegotiate the conditions under which local administrations participated in this coalition—they did not question their participation per se. Before Widodo, Yudhoyono had come to similar conclusions (SBY 2014, 53). Indeed, his appointment of a popular governor as minister of home affairs in 2009 set the tone for the coalitional negotiations between the president and local chiefs in subsequent years.

Discussing local governments as part of presidential coalitions means bringing decentralization studies closer to coalitional presidentialism scholarship. An impressive body of literature exists on the relationship between central governments and local administrations (Campbell 2001; Diaz-Cayeros 2006; Channa and Faguet 2016; Faguet 2021). However, few works have positioned this relationship as one in which presidents and local actors operate as political coalition partners. This chapter aims to achieve the latter, beginning with an overview of local administrations' powers over the presidency. Increased post-2001 fiscal rights are a major component of these powers, but political grassroots mobilization capacity is equally important. The second section describes the authority presidents can bear to coerce or incentivize local government cooperation and support. Budget allocations, especially for local infrastructure, are key to presidential leverage, as are administrative oversight functions and formal appointment rights. The third section looks at how the two sides balance their powers in coalitional presidentialism negotiations. The fourth part, finally, traces the rise of Tri Rismaharini from a low-level local bureaucrat in Surabaya to the city's wildly popular mayor and, in 2020, to a position in Widodo's cabinet. Her career illustrates how identities of members of presidential coalitions often overlap and hence tie their various actors even closer together: Risma was successively a bureaucrat, a local government official, and a party cadre before assuming a cabinet post that charged her with stabilizing the president's popularity amid the COVID-19 pandemic.

Local Government Powers

Before the 2001 decentralization push, Indonesia was one of the most centralized polities in the world (Booth 1992). Partly, this was because of an engrained aversion against federalism. During the independence struggle between 1945 and 1949, the Dutch had set up federal states in areas that were more sympathetic toward their return. Once The Hague had agreed to transfer national sovereignty to Indonesia, it insisted that the new state be federally structured (van der Kroef 1950). Nationalist leaders temporarily agreed but overturned this arrangement in August 1950. Afterward, federalism became an anathema for politicians in both democratic and autocratic regimes (Ferrazzi 2000). Centralism reached its peak in Suharto's New Order, when local governance was standardized across the nation, and no governor, district head, or mayor was installed without the regime's approval. While officially these local government heads were "elected" by regional legislatures, the chambers could only pick from pre-selected candidates, and the composition of the parliaments (with vast majorities of Golkar and military seats) meant that the votes were foregone conclusions. In consequence, as president and overall head of the regime, Suharto could rely on governors, district heads, and mayors to be executors of national policy as determined by him. Indeed, so firm was Suharto's grip over local government heads that the single case in which a regional legislature "accidentally" voted for a candidate not endorsed by him (in the 1985 gubernatorial "elections" in Riau) made international headlines (Malley 1999, 90). The "mistake" was rapidly corrected by forcing the successful nominee to withdraw.

After democratization began in 1998, interim president B.J. Habibie emphasized decentralization as a core element of political reform (Ostwald, Tajima, and Samphantharak 2016). Originating from Sulawesi, Habibie had long resented the dominance of Java over the rest of Indonesia. During the New Order's three decades in power, 73 percent of provinces outside of Java experienced governors from Java for at least one term (Mietzner 2014b, 51). In West Nusa Tenggara, Javanese governors ruled continuously from 1958 to 1998. Habibie told aides that if he wanted to achieve one thing during his presidency, it was decentralization (interview with his spokesperson Dewi Fortuna Anwar, Jakarta, December 3, 2013); it is, in fact, unlikely that a president from Java would have initiated it.

Under Habibie's watch, the decentralization laws—passed in 1999 and implemented after 2001—were predominantly written by non-Javanese officials. Based on the 1999 decentralization framework, fiscal resources and licensing powers gradually shifted from the center to the regions. Following a later amendment to the laws, local government heads were directly elected by the people from 2005 on. Politically and financially, districts and municipalities were the biggest beneficiaries of decentralization, while the provinces were situated only as coordinators. This was a deliberate move to prevent provinces from emerging as hotspots of secessionism—such a risk was viewed as negligible in the much smaller districts and cities. Equipped with new authority, however, many districts saw the rise of "small kings" (or queens) who acquired immense resources and self-confidence.

The increased powers of subnational government heads are reflected in the shifting fiscal statistics. Between 2001 and 2018, the proportion of central government expenditure toward overall state expenditure decreased from about 75 percent to 57 percent (World Bank 2020, 27). At the same time, the share of subnational governments increased from about 25 percent to 43 percent (with 31.5 percent spent by districts and 11.5 percent by provinces). Key to this shift was a stipulation that made it obligatory for the central government to transfer each year 26 percent of total revenues, including from oil and gas, to subnational administrations as a block grant under the General Allocation Fund (DAU) scheme (Lewis and Oosterman 2009, 34). This meant that presidents temporarily lost control over the amount they wished to send to the regions as a general allocation—which is why Jakarta successfully pushed for removing the fixed quota through a law revision in 2022. But even after this revision, local governments retained much fiscal power. For instance, a formula that promises poorer regions more DAU funds than resource-rich territories was maintained. Although the formula appears to be definitive, local governments can pressure the central government and parliament into granting greater allocations for their regions. In addition, subnational entities are entitled to various funds from Jakarta, such as the DAK. Overall, if one wanted to quantify the post-decentralization power relations between the center and the periphery, the 57 to 43 split of the expenditure is a good indication of the new balance.

Through decentralization, local government heads also significantly increased their licensing powers. One of the licensing authorities handed to local administrations involved granting and overseeing logging concessions. Research has shown that local executives have made extensive use of these rights. In a 2011 study on the relationship between illegal logging, the issuing of logging permits, and election cycles, a group of researchers (Burgess, Hansen, Olken, Potapov, and Sieber 2011) found that "illegal logging . . . increases during the run-up to local elections, but falls sharply in the year after the election, replaced by a steep increase in logging in 'conversion' zones" (summarized in Butler 2011). This suggested that "the shift from illegal to legal logging may be a consequence of politicians' paying back favours—in the form of logging concessions—to interests that sponsor their campaigns" (Butler 2011). In a later study, researchers also tied forest fires to elections, highlighting "political cycles in forest fires, suggesting that electoral incentives influence how permissive district governments are toward firms engaging in this illegal activity" (Balboni, Burgess, Heil, Old, and Olken 2021, 418). More specifically, "we find a significant decline in fires in election years followed by a steep increase the following year. . . . Fires appear to be something that governments wish to suppress in periods when they might damage the [district head's] election prospects." Our concern here is not the exact relationship between deforestation and the licensing as well as oversight powers of local governments, but the strong indication that the latter have been used with great regularity and self-interested effect.

Decentralization also equipped local government with more extensive legislative powers (Butt 2010). Local government regulations or decisions by governors and district heads have become key legislative instruments that reflect the priorities of specific regions and their leaders rather than those of the president. The ability of the central government to annul local government regulations it views to conflict with national policy and law has fluctuated over time. Before 2017, the minister of home affairs could cancel local government regulations if they collided with superior laws. However, that year, the Constitutional Court published a ruling that no longer allowed the minister to declare district and city regulations invalid. In the first two years of Widodo's presidency, and before the Constitutional Court decision, the home ministry had canceled 3,143 local government regulations that it claimed were an obstacle to national development and investment objectives (Fadhil 2016). Hoping to regain this right, in 2019 Widodo tried to pull the power to cancel local government regulations up to the presidential level through the Omnibus Law, which—as we have noted—changed dozens of laws through one massive legislative package (Putri 2020). In the final version of the bill, however, this specific article was removed. The tug of war between the president and local governments over legislation in the regions highlights how much this subject has become an area of contestation between the two sides, and how irritated presidents have become by the increased powers of the regional heads.

Local government heads also formally preside over their region's bureaucracy, giving them substantial control over an implementing apparatus the president would like to claim as his own. As noted, 77 percent of Indonesia's civil servants are placed under the supervision of provincial, district, and city governments, putting their chiefs at the apex of a complex patronage system that feeds off the sale of positions in the grassroots bureaucracy (Berenschot 2018). Local government heads often extract fees for appointing senior bureaucrats, with the practice replicated throughout the lower ranks. As a result, for many regional civil servants, the primary focal point of patronage and hierarchical subordination are the local government heads, not the president, who is nominally the superior of all civil servants. The appointment powers of local government heads are most visible in mass civil service reshuffles, which are frequently reported to—and criticized by—the KASN as violating existing regulations. In April 2021, the mayor of Padang reshuffled 180 bureaucrats in one round, provoking a reprimand by the commission (Chandra 2021). In a sign of the commission's powerlessness and the mayor's self-confidence, the latter remarked that he did not care about the reprimand, adding that "if I can't appoint [people], what is my function as mayor?" This mocking rebuke of a Jakarta-based commission appointed by the president emphasized local government heads' expansive interpretation of their independent powers, setting up regular tensions with state commissions and the presidency.

Beyond their formal powers, local government chiefs are credited with important political mobilization capacities. The extent of such capacities is up for debate, but there is a widespread belief in the Indonesian elite—and much of society—that governors, district heads, and mayors can mobilize large amounts of votes for or against particular candidates. This belief is rooted in their hierarchical authority over a range of lower-ranking officials, such as subdistrict chiefs and village heads, who are often accused of making the delivery of services to citizens dependent on their support for that official's favored nominee.[1] But whatever the exact mobilization powers of local government chiefs are, there is no doubt that presidents respect and fear them. In the 2019 elections, Widodo's campaign team lobbied local chief executives to declare their support for the president, often with a mixture of threats and promises. Eventually, 359 district heads and mayors (out of 514) and 30 governors (out of 34) offered their support (Kurnia 2018). The election's result gave some hints at the effectiveness of that support: it proved low to non-existent in areas in which Widodo was traditionally weak, but it seemed capable of driving up the votes in territories where citizens were already sympathetic to the incumbent. In West Sumatra, for instance, where Widodo's opponent Prabowo was strong, the support of 12 out of 19 district heads and mayors had no effect—the president's vote share shrank compared to 2014; in Central Java, by contrast, where Widodo did well in 2014, the strong support by the governor and of 31 out of 35 district heads and mayors helped to lift his vote by 10 percent. Hence, while not a silver bullet, the support of local government chiefs remains a desirable asset in national elections.

In sum, local governments and their heads have turned themselves from loyal subordinates of the president under the New Order into powerful and self-assured political actors in the post-2001 decentralized polity. Their powers are now so entrenched that no president dares to fundamentally attack them. According to Ganjar Pranowo, the governor of Central Java, "there would be a rebellion in the regions if a president tried to really roll back decentralization. We have come too far for that. So every president has to work with us, and not just command us. Each side needs to respect the other" (interview, Denpasar, August 7, 2019). Therefore, presidents have to carefully use their powers to negotiate a place for local government actors in their coalitions. As a consequence of these negotiations, the details of the relationship between the two sides can change over time, but its foundation (the mutual acknowledgment of each other's significance) persists.

Presidential Powers over the Regions

While decentralization has reduced the power of presidents vis-à-vis the regions, their influence remains substantial. At the very least, post-2001 presidents still can make life complicated for local government heads if they choose to do so. Most importantly, despite decentralization and direct elections of local chiefs, presidents continue to be the nominal supervisors of governors, district heads, and mayors. The president's hierarchical superiority is particularly strong in the case of governors but also affects district heads and mayors. With the head of state constitutionally placed above local chiefs, there are significant financial, administrative, and cultural implications. Financially, presidents retain a significant role in determining the details of local fiscal transfers that regions depend on. Administratively, the president can intervene in various aspects of local governance; for instance, governors can only appoint their provincial secretaries after receiving the approval of the president's minister of home affairs, allowing the center to control who holds the most powerful regional bureaucratic post. District heads and mayors, in turn, must seek the endorsement of governors (as "representatives of the central government") for their picks of regional secretary. Culturally, too, the president is widely seen as the supreme symbol of the state, forcing local government heads to pay respect through ritualized political subordination—particularly during presidential visits to the regions, when this relationship is symbolically performed.

Presidents have a wide range of other powers over local elites as well. One relates to the president's control over the police and the attorney general's office. The nominally independent KPK typically handles large, national-level corruption cases, but the bulk of local cases fall under the responsibility of the police and regional branches of the attorney general's office—which are directly under the president. Given the ubiquity of financial transgressions, there are few things that local officials fear more than being indicted for corruption (Lewis and Hendrawan 2019). Thus, local government heads have a powerful incentive to build a good relationship with presidents, in the expectation that the latter can use their authority over law enforcement to prevent corruption investigations from being started or to make them stop if they already have. Under Yudhoyono, some incumbent governors, district heads, and mayors joined the president's PD, or even became local chairpersons of the party to smoothen their relationship with the center and to protect themselves from legal action (Tempo 2011). In Widodo's first term, a similar phenomenon occurred—many local government heads joined Nasdem because the attorney general belonged to the party (Sukoyo 2018). In 2018, the mayor of Manado, Vicky Lumentut, switched from PD to Nasdem, with his former party claiming that he did so because the attorney general was beginning to investigate a possible misuse of flood funds (Ibrahim 2018). The attorney general was forced to publicly deny any inappropriate intervention—but Lumentut was not charged.

Presidents and their aides are acutely aware of the power of the threat of corruption charges—regardless of whether they have the intention or authority to initiate or stop them. Luhut Pandjaitan, then Widodo's chief political and security minister, flew to Papua in July 2016 to deal with recalcitrant local government heads—and to demonstrate to international observers (including this author) that Jakarta was serious about improving the province's prosperity. Pointing to a box of documents in his private plane, he said, "these are documents on the sins committed by some Papuan local government leaders. I won't mention names. But my message to them is clear: 'if you want, we can open up a new chapter in our relations. Let's leave the past behind us, and look toward the future.' If not, well, then not" (interview, Jayapura, June 16, 2016). It was clear that one of these officials was Lukas Enembe, the province's governor. He had been an ally of Yudhoyono, and since Widodo's election, he had proven a difficult partner for the central government. Unsurprisingly, he left Papua during Luhut's visit, handing the task of hosting Widodo's most senior minister to his deputy.[2] But the pressure exerted on Enembe by Luhut and others paid off, at least in terms of the governor's political loyalties. Before the 2019 elections, Enembe declared that he had secured the support of all twenty-nine district heads and mayors in Papua for Widodo's re-election. Not coincidentally, he made this announcement to Nasdem chairman Surya Paloh in the latter's party office, hoping that Nasdem's attorney general might continue to treat him gently (Liputan6 2018). Ultimately, it was the KPK that charged him in 2022—at that time, Enembe was approaching the end of his term and thus his political usefulness for the center.

The president's traditional appointment powers also come in handy when negotiating with local government leaders. Presidents can appoint temporary governors, district heads, and mayors if the position becomes vacant for various reasons, ranging from arrest to the expiry of the term before an election can be held.[3] But the president's appointment authority is attractive to local chiefs in other ways, too. Their term is limited to two terms, which means they often retire in their fifties or early sixties. This leaves the opportunity for another step in their careers, and the president can offer promising prospects. A cabinet position is the most sought-after post for retiring local government leaders, but jobs in state-owned enterprises, ambassadorships, or other state agencies are also attractive options. For example, Sinyo Harry Sarundajang, two-term governor of North Sulawesi (2005–2015), was appointed ambassador to the Philippines in 2018. Sarundajang, a career bureaucrat, had been one of the initially non-partisan governors who joined PD during Yudhoyono's presidency. In 2014, however, as Yudhoyono retired and PD nominally supported Prabowo in the presidential elections, Sarundayang openly lobbied for Widodo's election. Widodo went on to win the tight race in North Sulawesi by a margin of 53 to 47 percent, and the ambassadorship for Sarundayang was seen as a late reward for his contribution to the new president's victory. Sarundayang, who died while ambassador in 2021, hence became the embodiment of the mechanisms through which coalitional presidentialism shapes the political behavior of those local government heads who master its internal logic: he first joined the party of a sitting president before supporting the campaign of the incoming successor, with payoffs guaranteed in both cases.

Another power that presidents can use to pressure local government heads into cooperation is their co-legislative authority. Theoretically, the president could—in a joint initiative with parliament—overturn decentralization and revive pre-1998 centralism. This is because decentralization is not constitutionally anchored; instead, it operates based on a web of laws and government regulations that can be changed quickly. As Ganjar Pranowo reminded us, such a large-scale revoking of decentralization principles would be politically unfeasible, but the decentralization laws have frequently changed since 1999. The 1999 law was amended in 2004 and again in 2014 and 2015, and the fiscal relationship between Jakarta and the regions was rearranged through a new harmonization law in 2022. Through these amendments, presidents have pushed for a retransfer of power from the regions back to the center—and in some cases, they succeeded. Through the 2014 revisions, for example, the power to issue licenses in the mining and energy sector was returned to the central government

(Pramudya 2015), although the exact interpretation of the new rules remains in dispute. The 2022 harmonization law gave the center more powers to withhold money from regions in case of non-compliance with national directives and, as noted, removed the fixed quota for DAU transfers. Thus, while presidents know they cannot touch the principle of decentralization, they have demonstrated their power to change how it operates. This power, in turn, has become a crucial asset in negotiations with local leaders.

Among the state policies presidents have the greatest influence over are the payments to the regions outside of the DAU transfers. Most important among them is the DAK, which the central government distributes to regions to advance national development priorities. The president's various ministries determine the recipients of these funds, and the money is transferred through a decree of the Ministry of Finance. In 2021, the DAK funds totaled Rp 196.4 trillion (US$14 billion), with one-third going to "physical" spending (i.e., infrastructure) and two-thirds to "non-physical" items (Kementrian Keuangan 2020). Further, there is the Revenue Sharing Fund (DBH), which in 2021 contained Rp 102 trillion (US$7.3 billion). Although the DBH is partially given to areas where revenues originated, the government can use a large portion to balance the gap between richer and poorer territories. Moreover, it can reduce the payment to the territories of revenue origin if they violate certain rules in the decentralization laws. This budgetary authority of presidents and their ministers makes them a constant target of lobbying efforts by local government heads. As Klemens Tikal, the deputy governor of Papua, complained in 2016, "ministers always say to us that we spend too much time in Jakarta; but if we're not there, we lose out on funds, and money gets transferred late or not at all. So we have to talk to central government officials all the time and make sure that we get our proper share" (interview, Jayapura, June 16, 2016).

Presidents have aggressively touted their budgetary authority to local government leaders and have been unsubtle about how it can benefit those who offer the head of state political support. Less than a fortnight after the 2019 presidential elections, Widodo rolled out the palace's red carpet for the governors of the three provinces—Bali, NTT, and North Sulawesi—that had achieved the highest vote shares for him.[4] In meeting these governors, Widodo was accompanied by the minister of finance and the minister for public works and housing, signaling that he was ready to talk business with the three top-ranking presidential vote getters. According to the governor of Bali, Widodo "of course" thanked them, after which the governors presented their respective wish lists: Bali wanted funds for a Cultural Centre and several infrastructure projects; NTT requested money for dams, roads, electricity lines, water facilities, and housing; and North Sulawesi asked for support for the Manado airport and the "revitalization" of

Lake Tondano (Egeham 2019). Widodo and his aides had no objections to media reports that framed the encounter as a publicly performed transaction between electoral support and government handouts to loyal regions. Indeed, such reports assisted in disseminating the palace's core message that local government heads who help the president can expect assistance in return.

The powers of presidents vis-à-vis local government heads constitute formidable instruments that can be quickly deployed from their coalitional presidentialism toolbox. Governors, district heads, and mayors who want to have their nominations for the regional secretary job confirmed; protect themselves from potential corruption investigations; be considered for post-retirement positions; prevent the president from changing the decentralization regime; and need to gain access to national government budgets are well advised not to antagonize the head of state. This is despite all the powers that local government heads can mobilize against the center in Jakarta and its president. As in the other cases we examined, rational cost-benefit calculations typically lead both sides to seek cooperation rather than confrontation, with regional bosses taking their place at the coalitional presidentialism table. At this table, both sides define the conditions under which they are satisfied enough with the other to allow the overall polity to operate without disruptions, and they draw the lines within which the membership of local chiefs in the coalition is sustained.

Presidents and Local Governments

Indonesian presidents have a wide range of channels to negotiate with local governments over the framework of their coalitional cooperation. These channels allow the president to deal with local government heads as a collective and as individuals, both formally and informally. The main formal connection between presidents and local chiefs is the minister of home affairs. Institutionally the administrative supervisor of governors—and, to a lesser extent, district heads and mayors—the minister issues regulations that govern the daily operations of regional governments (for instance, he or she has to approve foreign travels of local chiefs). Accordingly, presidents can use the minister as their main liaison to local governments' bosses, receiving feedback from the latter and conveying presidential expectations. Unlike the president, the minister is in daily and direct contact with local governments, and specific grievances from both sides can be discussed quickly. If unresolved, problems can be brought to the attention of the president and addressed in personal negotiations. This pattern was particularly visible during the COVID-19 pandemic, when home minister Tito Karnavian communicated critical instructions of the president to local governments but also relayed their complaints back to the president. Widodo would then discuss these complaints in online forums with the complainants or with a broader range of local government chiefs.

Although the minister of home affairs is the main contact point to collate concrete governance issues between the president and local governments, other official and direct forums exist between the president and local chiefs. These are called Coordinating Meetings of Local Government Heads and Deputy Heads and are chaired by the president. They are often scheduled after local elections, giving the president a chance to lay out the ground rules to new office holders. One such event occurred in April 2021 for the government heads and deputy heads elected under COVID-19 restrictions in December 2020. In his speech to the new local chiefs, Widodo asked them not to obstruct Indonesia's economic recovery from the pandemic by instituting complicated investment rules (Pemda Bengkulu 2021)—one of the president's recurring themes throughout this period. Recall that the president had pushed a deregulation package, formalized through the Omnibus Law, through parliament just a few months earlier. He had done so in the hope that the central government would be able to make investment processes easier and achieve better coordination with local administrations. For Widodo, then, the buy-in by local government into his agenda was a key element of the cooperation between the two sides, and the forum delivered him the opportunity to communicate his conditions for the smooth operation of the coalition.

While local government heads can also use these forums to submit their demands to the president, the representation of these vested interests is primarily the task of specific lobbying groups. The governors' interests are channeled through the Association of Indonesian Provincial Governments (APPSI), while mayors are organized in the APEKSI, and district heads in the Association of Indonesian District Governments (APKASI). These bodies are crucial in submitting the demands of local governments as a group, often related to the general defense of the decentralization regime and requests for more funds. Meetings between presidents and lobbying groups are especially important when presidents assume office or start second terms, as the conditions for the coalition need to be reaffirmed or readjusted. In November 2014, for instance, APPSI held a meeting with newly inaugurated president Widodo. Its chairman, South Sulawesi governor Syahrul Yasin Limpo, reminded Widodo to respect the principles of decentralization, and he asked for a special fund of Rp 1 trillion (US$71 million) for each province. Highlighting in clear-cut terms the status of local governments as a presidential coalition partner, he boasted that APPSI is "the biggest party of the president, and the governors are the chairpersons of this party in the regions" (Detik 2014). Coincidentally or not, Limpo was made a Widodo minister (for agriculture) in 2019, cementing the coalitional arrangement verbalized in 2014. While Limpo was also a party member (of Nasdem), his inclusion signaled that Widodo was willing to continue Yudhoyono's accommodation of local bosses in national politics.

Similar to their use of Coordinating Meetings, presidents also utilize lobby groups for communicating their demands vis-à-vis local governments. In a speech to an APKASI congress in March 2021, Widodo requested that local governments apply greater care when spending their budgets and consider national priorities in fund allocations. This reflected the traditional post-decentralization frustration of presidents over their limited influence on local budgets and the fragmented nature of policies at the grassroots. "Don't just spend the budget on as many items as you can," Widodo said in rare off-the-cuff remarks that indicated the extent of his indignation. "If you give to all offices, it means you don't set priorities. For the district level, in my opinion, setting two priorities is enough" (Yuniartha 2021). With reminders such as this, Widodo defined his expectations toward local governments if they wished to continue receiving benefits from their coalitional relationship with the president. In response, the APKASI chairman agreed with the president's direction but asked in return that Widodo ensure an equal distribution of COVID-19 vaccines across Indonesia—a sensitive topic for the president (Media Indonesia 2021). At that time, vaccinations had been concentrated in Jakarta and other urban centers, leaving rural districts uncovered. Like others before it, therefore, this APKASI meeting served as an institutionalized arena of negotiation between the president and district governments over their respective interests. Generally, such events succeeded in preventing major conflicts between the two sides.

Presidents also use their cabinet appointment powers to manage their coalition with local government heads. Yudhoyono, for example, appointed the governor of West Sumatra, Gamawan Fauzi, as minister of home affairs in 2009. Fauzi was a local government representative par excellence: from the private secretary of a previous West Sumatran governor, he had worked himself up to become the head of the provincial public relations unit, and from there to the post of district head of Solok. After holding this position for two terms (1995–2005), he became governor of the province in 2005, as part of the first wave of directly elected local government heads. His appointment as minister of home affairs four years later marked the first time since 1964 that a non-military figure held this post: Yudhoyono had previously filled the post with Mardiyanto, a former general and ex-governor of Central Java. In Fauzi, Yudhoyono had picked a local government lobbyist to head the ministry most important to local government, and thus could rest assured that their chiefs across the archipelago felt accommodated. Fauzi subsequently played a crucial role in conveying to Yudhoyono the rejection of local government heads toward the DPR's decision in September 2019 to return the election of local government heads to each region's legislature.[5] Yudhoyono had passively agreed to this change, but APKASI and APEKSI protested (Kemendagri 2014)—adding to massive popular, civil society, and media opposition. Facing this backlash, Yudhoyono reversed course and issued an emergency law that restored the direct election mechanism.

In some cases, presidential coalitions benefitted not only from local government heads in cabinet but also from the reverse constellation. That is, members of presidential cabinets have become local government heads, providing an equally strong platform maintaining the coalition between presidents and regional chiefs. In 2018, for example, Khofifah Indar Parawansa (Widodo's minister for social affairs) successfully ran for the governorship of East Java, the second-most populous province of Indonesia and thus a main electoral battleground. In 2014, she had campaigned for Widodo, using her position as a leader of NU's women's organization Muslimat to protect the then-candidate from accusations that he was not sufficiently devout. In that campaign, she worked in concert with Luhut, who credited her with turning the situation in East Java around for Widodo: "without her, it would have been difficult. She's an electoral juggernaut, and she's a good team player in our campaign, too" (interview, Jakarta, April 21, 2014). After winning the 2018 gubernatorial elections, she immediately began mobilizing voters for Widodo again. While reminding her followers that her post as governor limited her ability to campaign, she put a network of volunteers in place that did the lobbying in her name (Susetyo 2019). As a result, Widodo's vote share in the province increased by 12 percent to almost 66 percent, and given the size of the electorate, this proved decisive in securing his re-election. As noted, the result coincided with a 10 percent increase in Central Java, governed by Ganjar Pranowo—another Widodo loyalist who mobilized district heads below him for the president.

One of the most important sites for cultivating the relationship between the president and local chiefs is the presidential visit to the regions. Politically and culturally, the visiting president is expected to bring gifts for the hosting government and its chief, mostly in the form of national commitments to projects or additional budget allocations. Consequently, visits by the president are a much-contested prize, even by those government heads whose parties might not be formally members of the presidential coalition. Local chiefs, therefore, go to extreme lengths to secure such visits. In June 2021, the district head of Wakatobi in Southeast Sulawesi waited for hours in front of the office of the province's governor to submit a request for a visit by Widodo. "I waited for the right moment, and at about 2:30 pm the governor came out of his office and walked to his car," at which point the district head handed over the request (Surya 2021). He also harassed a cabinet minister for his mobile phone number to lobby for the Widodo visit. But as much as local chiefs hope for benefits, they also know that the president expects something in return. As Irianto MS Syafiuddin, the two-time district head of Indramayu (2000–2010) recalled, "we are not naive. We want something from the president, and he wants something from us. That's the game we all play, and you have to play it well" (interview, Karawang, June 12, 2012). As mentioned earlier, local chiefs who deliver for the president electorally can expect special benefits.

The alliance between presidents and local chiefs is managed and held together, then, through the supervising role of the Ministry of Home Affairs; direct Coordination Meetings; the mutual lobbying through APPSI, APKASI, and APEKSI; the presence of former local government heads in cabinet and of former ministers in local government; and all-important presidential visits to the regions. Through these channels, both sides communicate their respective demands to each other, based on which the coalition is consistently recalibrated. As is the case with other actors in the coalition, red lines are drawn and defended: for local governments, it is essential that no president moves to attack core decentralization principles; and for presidents, the minimum expectation is that local chiefs do not sabotage their government, while the maximum outcome is loyal support even during elections. We have seen how presidents can deal with uncooperative local government heads (i.e., through threats, as in the case of Lukas Enembe) and how regional chiefs can pressure heads of state to cancel decisions detrimental to their interests (i.e., through lobbying groups, as in the 2014 re-introduction of direct elections). This management of the relationship has generally produced stability, with no local government head seriously challenging Yudhoyono or Widodo, and the two presidents refraining from questioning the decentralization project. In the following section, we look in more detail at how this relationship has been stabilized: the case of Tri Rismaharini shows how presidents pulled local government figures into their cabinets, and by doing so accommodated not only regional chiefs, but other actors claiming an affiliation with them as well.

Risma, Local Government, and Presidentialism

Tri Rismaharini, popularly known as Risma, has become an embodiment of the patterns through which local government leaders are tied into national politics in general and coalitional presidentialism in particular. Widodo was politically socialized in this ecosystem, as was the governor of West Java, Ridwan Kamil. In this ecosystem, a particular class of politicians has emerged since the mid-2000s that traces its origins back to professional or bureaucratic roots at the local level (Hatherell 2019). Such politicians cultivate a brand centered on a no-nonsense, no-time-to-waste pragmatism that views politics as an unnecessary pastime for partisans. Pledging to stay out of the machinations of politicking, they style themselves as doers who solve the day-to-day problems of the people. Having successfully propagated this image and won elections by using it, the local governance pragmatists subsequently get drawn and insert themselves into broader mechanisms of national politics and the logic of coalitional presidentialism. In Widodo's case, this led him to the top, from where he—now sitting on the other side of the fence—began to perceive local government heads as actors that needed to be tamed. Risma, for her part, rose from the technocratic work of city planning to a cabinet position, in which she served as a crucial link between the president and the local government heads from whose ranks both had emerged.

Risma was born in 1961 in Kediri in East Java as the daughter of a civil servant in the tax office. Like Widodo himself, she has portrayed her upbringing as humble (VOI 2020), but as in the president's case, there are reasons to believe—given her father's occupation—that she was then part of the middle class rather than the poor. It is also true, however, that neither Risma nor Widodo belonged to the traditional elites of Indonesian politics: the military, big business, entrenched party networks, or influential Muslim organizations. As such, they had to work their way up—a fact they both exploited for their political campaigns in later years. Risma, like her father, became a civil servant, and she spent most of her life in the Surabaya bureaucracy in planning and urban design departments. Her highest post in the civil service was head of Surabaya's cleaning and park maintenance service, which she reached in 2010. She used the position to launch park beautification projects that attracted national attention. But 2010 was also the year in which she got recruited into politics. The mayor at the time, Bambang Dwi Hartono from PDI-P, had lost a legal challenge to be able to re-contest the post in the 2010 elections (he had, according to the court, already served two terms, while he argued that the half-term he had recorded between 2002 and 2005 should not count). Thus, Hartono was looking for a proxy to run as mayor, with him as deputy. Risma, then popular for her park and other development projects, was approached and agreed to run. The pair won the race, but with the mediocre result of 38.5 percent of the vote.

Once mayor of Surabaya, Risma began to quickly emancipate herself from her patron and entered national and presidential politics (Surabaya Pagi 2020). Several factors supported this process. First, Hartono—already frustrated with

Risma's increasing self-confidence—decided to run for the East Java governorship and resigned as deputy mayor in 2013. In the gubernatorial ballot, he only finished third with 13 percent of the votes, damaging him irreparably. In consequence, Hartono—who had challenged several of Risma's policies, including the development of light rail—was not only removed from Risma's surroundings but also politically unable to control her. Eventually, he settled for a seat in the provincial parliament and assumed a role in the national party office, leaving Surabaya fully to Risma. Second, Risma cemented her image as a capable local government leader with a populist touch. She made it a habit to stop her car on the way to the office to directly intervene in the public services offered by her subordinates—whether that involved putting out fires, regulating traffic, or cleaning up dirty sections of a park area (Amin 2014). She also made friends in the city's conservative Muslim community by closing a large prostitution area—a move criticized by public health experts because it caused prostitutes to move elsewhere but with less supervision through authorities. Whatever the effectiveness of her actions, they were immensely popular.

Riding this wave of popularity, Risma went on to win re-election in 2015 with 86 percent of the votes—a result that came close to Widodo's 2010 outcome in Solo. With that, Risma had arrived at the center of national attention (as Widodo had before her). PDI-P, her party, which initially had looked at her only as a proxy to cover for one of its leading functionaries, now presented her as a major asset.[6] Risma, who previously (again, similar to Widodo) viewed parties with disdain and bewilderment, now took a deeper interest in internal PDI-P affairs. In September 2016, her chairwoman Megawati asked her to speak at an induction meeting for the party's candidates in the upcoming 2017 local executive elections. She arrived at the event amid speculation that she would be named PDI-P's candidate for the Jakarta governorship. In front of Megawati, she gave a detailed PowerPoint presentation about her achievements, and while she asked not to be recruited as a candidate for Jakarta, it was clear that she was working toward a national profile. Asked about her most pressing concern at that time, she said, "I am currently assisting Papuan youth with their education; we really have to fix this problem, it's essential for the development of our nation" (discussion with Tri Rismaharini, Tapos, September 6, 2016). The frequency of her meetings with Widodo also increased, and during at least one of them the possibility of her running in Jakarta was discussed. In 2019, she was made a deputy chair of PDI-P, responsible for cultural affairs; this appointment secured her entry into the party's closest leadership circle, completing the remarkable rise of a woman who had only the feeblest of links with political parties a few years earlier.

While Risma climbed up the ladder to national politics, she also cemented her role as a representative of local government. She became a senior figure in

APEKSI, serving as its deputy chairperson. In numerous events, she enjoyed showcasing Surabaya as an example of success to other APKESI members, and her colleagues recognized her capacity to defend the interests of local administrations vis-à-vis the center and other political actors (Kota Ternate 2017). Risma also became known as a collector of national and international awards for her role in city government. The international City Mayors Foundation named her "mayor of the month" in 2014, an award followed by many others. Indeed, the frequency with which she received awards soon became a source of speculation, with 2014 press reports in local papers suggesting that at least one of the prizes had been paid for (Harsaputra 2014). The affair did not damage her reputation, however, and she continued to both receive awards and celebrate major political successes. When she reached the end of her second and final term in 2020, it was clear to everyone that more was to come. It was also obvious that she figured in the calculations of both Megawati and Widodo. As two of her options, namely running for either the governorship of East Java or Jakarta, were premature at the time (those elections were only scheduled for 2024), a position in cabinet was widely seen as the most logical solution. The only question was which position she would fill and who she could replace without disturbing the architecture of the presidential coalition.

As at other junctures of her career, external circumstances helped facilitate Risma's advancement—this time, her entry into cabinet in December 2020. Embarrassingly for both Megawati and Widodo, the PDI-P minister for social affairs, Juliari Batubara (also the party's deputy treasurer), was arrested in that month for siphoning off money from the COVID-19 social assistance budget. Batubara was not the first social minister to get caught up in corruption cases: PPP's Bachtiar Chamsyah, minister from 2001 to 2009, and Golkar's Idrus Marham, the office holder in 2018, were both imprisoned for corruption. Thus, Megawati and Widodo needed a popular figure known for relative cleanliness to restore the reputation of the party and the cabinet. Risma, just two months away from officially leaving her post in Surabaya, was the obvious choice. Her inclusion through the party channel did not create an imbalance in the coalition, but at the same time, Widodo had integrated Indonesia's most recognized mayor—and local government figure more broadly—into his alliance. In his mind, this ensured better coordination between the center and local government at a time when it was needed most. In the eyes of local government heads, it placed a representative of their interests in national cabinet who could feed the president and his staff input from the country's regional base.

Risma's appointment paid off for the president—and for Risma. The former Surabaya mayor replicated many of her local government approaches in her ministry. Among others, she continued the practice of hands-on interventions, stopping at various locations (such as the poor city quarters of Jakarta) on her way to the office. This gave Widodo's government a much-needed flair of grassroots authenticity and helped to distract from negative news associated with the pandemic (at the time of Risma's appointment, Indonesia's COVID-19 case and fatality numbers were the highest in Southeast Asia). Her connections in APEKSI also gave Widodo an additional channel to communicate informally with city governments. For Risma, the cabinet position further boosted her national standing. In a May 2021 survey, she placed second on a list of the most popular Widodo ministers, with 77.4 percent of respondents opining that she did a "very good" or "good" job (Purnamasari 2021). This, in turn, assisted Widodo in defending his own popularity during the pandemic, which remained stable at around 60 to 70 percent despite the spiraling case numbers (that was true even in July 2021, when Indonesia briefly became the world's epicenter of the Delta variant outbreak). In short, Risma's appointment to cabinet served the interests of the president, local government, her party, and Risma herself, stabilizing the presidential coalition in times of potential crisis.

Risma's rise, then, illustrates how local government actors have become integral elements of presidential politics and coalitions. Local government offers a pathway to national prominence and even the presidency (as Widodo demonstrated), but presidents also draw from local government to strengthen their national coalitions. By integrating local government figures into their alliances, presidents can accommodate the ambitions of grassroots leaders and benefit from their connections, lobbying capacity, and mobilization capabilities. At the same time, local government figures tied into the president's political circle provide further links to the parties they belong to and the bureaucracies actively or formerly under them. Risma—as a member of PDI-P, former bureaucrat, and ex-mayor—offered a cross-sectoral appeal that served the president's interest in not only forming an alliance with local government heads, but with two other key actors of coalitional presidentialism as well. Widodo's Risma, even more so than Yudhoyono's Gamawan Fauzi, became a symbol of the interpenetration that characterizes the coalitional relationship between presidents and local bosses—rather than the confrontational dynamics one might expect when considering their respective institutional powers.

Limpo's portrayal of governors as the provincial "chairpersons" of the "president's biggest party," presented in front of Widodo in November 2014, perfectly encapsulates the membership of local government heads in Indonesian presidential coalitions. Naturally, there are diverse political and ideological factions in this "party," but most local government heads—regardless of geographical background and party affiliation—seek access to central government resources by aligning to varying degrees with the president's alliance. Opposing the president delivers few benefits, and while local bosses might occasionally do so rhetorically to appease other interests (some regional chiefs affiliated with PDI-P were publicly critical of Yudhoyono because their chairwoman, Megawati, held a grudge against him), the behind-the-scenes negotiations are invariably marked by the give-and-take spirit of coalitional presidentialism. Similarly, presidents have few incentives for open conflict with local government heads. They are too important for the delivery of government outcomes at the grassroots and the political mobilization of the masses to be antagonized. This does not mean that presidents do not try to claim back centralist powers when the opportunity arises, or that they refrain from blaming local governments for policy failures (as both Yudhoyono and Widodo routinely did). But these frictions are part of the broader negotiations over the rules that govern the alliance of the two sides. In deals, the red lines of both remain respected: presidents accept the principle of local autonomy empowering regional chiefs, while the latter respect the mandate of a president to rule without being sabotaged.

Yudhoyono, for his part, has cited this arrangement as a main reason for what he thought was a significant stabilization of center-periphery relations during his presidency. He claimed that the overall attitude of local government heads at the beginning of his term in 2004 was confrontational or even dismissive. "It was like: 'say good bye to Jakarta,'" he recalled (interview, Cikeas, December 2, 2014). "But now, we have renegotiated and rearranged [the authority of the various actors]: this is the power of Jakarta, this is the power of the provinces, and this is the power of the districts," Yudhoyono said proudly. With this mutual acceptance of each actor's powers and interests, the compromises reached between the center and local chiefs reflected Yudhoyono's general philosophy of presidential governance. Recall that he viewed it as the main task of presidents to prevent "chaos" and thus the destabilization of government—which made it mandatory to accommodate actors rather than insisting on a president's electoral and constitutional mandate to rule. For all of Widodo's criticism of Yudhoyono during the 2014 campaign, he, too, did not touch this principle, especially in relation to local governments. If anything, he further deepened the notion that it was politically inevitable to integrate local government heads into presidential coalitions, with considerable rewards offered to purchase their loyalty. After all, he knew their potential powers from his own experience—and he knew what they wanted in exchange for their cooperation.

There is little doubt that avoiding center-periphery tension through alliance-building has helped sustain Indonesia's decentralization project. Unlike in other countries, where decentralization is unpopular and considered a failure—South

Africa being one example (Koelble and Siddle 2013)—regional autonomy in Indonesia continues to enjoy strong elite and mass support. (In a 2019 poll, for instance, 93 percent of respondents demanded to retain their right to directly vote for local government heads [Ahmad 2020].) But the transactional and political nature of the coalition dynamics between the president and local government heads not only protected decentralization—it also entrenched the predatory and corruptive practices of both sides. There are no indications that budget wastage has decreased under decentralization; if anything, it has become more complex and involves more actors. As noted, presidents have used corruption allegations to pressure local government heads into cooperation but are happy to turn a blind eye once that cooperation has been achieved. Conversely, local government bosses are aware of the shady channels through which many decentralization funds are distributed but prefer to succeed in working through these channels rather than challenging them. Consequently, both sides are tied into a pact in which one side tolerates the rent-seeking and budget-scalping projects of the other. Yudhoyono's famous principle of preventing "chaos", then, has come at the cost of more credible attempts to modernize the foundations upon which Indonesia's central and local governance rest.

8

THE OLIGARCHS

Thus far, this book has analyzed members of presidential coalitions with legal-institutional powers as their main political leverage. Like presidents, they have strong rights and privileges anchored in law or the constitution that allow them to negotiate their place in coalitional presidentialism. Parties, for instance, hold the nomination rights for presidential candidacies; legislators approve budgets and laws, and are involved in key appointments; the military and police control the monopoly of violence; bureaucrats have the exclusive right of policy implementation; and local government heads are legally charged with delivering public services on the ground and spending a significant percentage of the state budget in the process. To entice these state-anchored actors to use their powers in a way that does not collide with the president's interests, heads of state see the need to integrate them into their coalitions through a combination of concessions and threats. There are also actors, however, that are not equipped with legal-institutional authority but exercise immense power. Indeed, some of them are not even mentioned in laws and much less given any specific privileges by them. In the two remaining core chapters, we turn to two such actors that have figured prominently in presidential coalitions: first, the oligarchs, who are accommodated by presidents because of their wealth and their role in managing the economy; and second, influential Muslim mass organizations, which are essential sources of religio-political legitimacy for incumbent presidents and those who aspire to occupy this post.

When assessing the role of oligarchs in presidential coalitions, it is important to begin by defining who an oligarch is—and who is not. This book defines oligarchs as *actors whose primary instrument of exercising political influence is their directly controlled, personal wealth.* Thus, it does not share the broad, classic definition (derived from its Greek origins) of oligarchs as an exclusive clique of people governing a polity. Such a definition has been used to describe, for instance, the men ruling Meiji Japan, although wealth was not their main source of power (Beckmann 1957). Subsequently, the discussion of oligarchy shifted gradually to focus on wealth, but the exact definitional boundaries have often remained blurred. This also applies to the use of the terms "oligarchy" and "oligarchs" in the context of post-Suharto Indonesia. Hadiz and Robison (2004), for example, defined oligarchy as a system and shied away from defining what exactly an oligarch is—presumably because, in Marxist tradition, they view this system as affecting everyone who operates within it. Winters (2011), by contrast, delivered a precise definition of oligarchs, but he included figures who have access to, as opposed to direct control of, wealth. This opens the door to the inclusion of political leaders who can call on favors from rich entrepreneurs, or who have obtained some wealth as a result of, rather than as a condition for, getting involved in politics. Instead, the definition used by this book focuses on actors who would not have the political influence they possess if it were not for their wealth. It excludes those who have other primary resources of political power, even if they become affluent through them.

To illustrate what the application of this definition means in practice, it is useful to explain it with the help of examples. Based on this book's definition, a figure such as Akbar Tandjung, the former head of Golkar and chairman of the DPR (1999–2004), is not considered an oligarch. That is despite the affluence he acquired in his political career, which began under Suharto's regime. According to Winters, Tandjung was an oligarch who eventually lost out to an oligarch with larger resources (Jusuf Kalla)—the latter, as vice president, replaced the former as Golkar leader in December 2004. But in deploying his definition, Winter appears doubtful about whether Tandjung truly was an oligarch. At the beginning of Winters's discussion, Akbar is called a full "*pribumi* [indigenous Indonesian] oligarch" (Winters 2011, 182). Later, Akbar is first downgraded to a "middle oligarch" (187) and ultimately to a "minor oligarch" (189). But if oligarchs are defined as actors whose primary source of power is direct, personal wealth, Tandjung is not an oligarch at all. Rather, he is best understood as a politician who used his primary political resource (connections in politics and mass organizations) to exert influence and add to his private wealth. Figures such as Megawati and Yudhoyono are also in this category. As tempting as it may be to subsume most Indonesian leaders into a "broader array of oligarchic elites" (Fukuoka and Djani 2016, 213), this approach obstructs the analytical view of those who weaponize their wealth for political purposes. We already encountered members of this oligarchic class in this book: Surya Paloh, for instance, or Hari Tanoesoedibjo, both chairpersons of parties in Widodo's coalition.

Although this book uses a narrower definition of the term "oligarch" than others, this does not mean that its application is easy and unproblematic. For instance, it is impossible to quantify the wealth threshold after which an actor is classified as an oligarch; wealth reports and estimates in Indonesia are notoriously unreliable and can only hint at the true wealth possessed. In consequence, although this book uses available quantitative data to assess an actor's oligarchic status, data alone are not definitive in this regard—a person's background and career are also evaluated. Furthermore, classifying an actor as an oligarch does not preclude that this person has talents, knowledge, and expertise that qualify him or her for a position of political power and responsibility. However, in a patronage-driven society like Indonesia's, it is unfeasible to withhold the categorization of "oligarch" from persons of extraordinary wealth who claim that the latter played no role in their appointment to a post of political influence. Many such oligarchs have obtained positions that allowed them to make policy in the business areas in which they concurrently have had private commercial interests. In such a constellation, even allegedly good intentions do not change the fact that a person who possesses large amounts of private capital and obtains public office as a result is part of a group that is more likely than not to reproduce the socio-economic conditions under which this wealth is increased or at least protected.

With these definitions and qualifications in mind, this chapter discusses how oligarchs have become members of presidential coalitions. This has occurred through direct membership of cabinet; the chairing of political parties; leadership positions in lobby groups; the financing of politics in general and presidential expenditures in particular; and more subtle forms of indirect influencing. The first section highlights the powers of oligarchs vis-à-vis the presidency. It focuses on the wealth of oligarchs and presidents' dependence on it but also examines how oligarchs—through their role in the economy—are key to macroeconomic stability. In the second section, we look at the authority of presidents that oligarchs fear and would like to draw from. This includes the president's control of state contracts and regulatory frameworks that are crucial for the existence of oligarchs and their enterprises. The third section explores the mechanisms of cooperation between the two sides, with coalitional presidentialism offering an effective framework for their interdependence. In the final section, a case study of Aburizal Bakrie, the former Golkar chair and minister, offers valuable insights into the extent and limitations of oligarchic power when dealing with presidents. On the one hand, Bakrie's wealth allowed him, an unpopular and uncharismatic politician, to penetrate the most exclusive circles of political power. On the other hand, his wealth did not protect him from being excluded from this circle once he had decided to confront the president. Accordingly, Bakrie's case tells the story of how oligarchs become members of presidential coalitions—and how presidents can withdraw this membership.

Oligarchic Power

In any political system, wealthy actors enjoy privileged access to the political infrastructure (Winters and Page 2009). Dictators and democratic leaders alike need money to fund their operations and must grant significant concessions in return. Arguably, the power of the wealthy is even more consequential in democratic systems, as the costs associated with electoral campaigning put a premium on the provision of funds to parties and candidates, and hence on those who can deliver them. In democracies, oligarchs can exert influence by becoming donors to state leaders, both legally and illicitly; turning into political actors themselves by shouldering the cost of creating new parties; establishing lobby groups; paying for advertising campaigns, or even buying media outlets that run such campaigns; entrenching large patronage networks that influence politicians dependent on funds; and funding activities that can assist some power holders or oppose others. Not coincidentally, some populist leaders running campaigns in democratic systems since the beginning of the twenty-first century have been oligarchs—Thaksin Shinawatra in Thailand, Donald Trump in the United States, and Andrej Babiš in the Czech Republic are prominent examples of this trend. Moreover, oligarchs have made it to the top even without becoming populists, such as in the case of Sebastián Piñera of Chile. In Indonesia, the populist Prabowo Subianto established a party with the wealth of his tycoon brother and ran expensive presidential campaigns paid for by oligarchic running mates (Aspinall 2015). Although unsuccessful in 2014 and 2019, his political career is far from over.

For many reasons, Indonesia's political system remains especially vulnerable to oligarchic power (Fukuoka 2013). Despite a quarter of a century of democratization, Indonesia is still a patronage-oriented polity and society in which few institutions work without extra money being paid to persons of authority to deliver a service. Related to this, Indonesia has also done little to build correctives against oligarchic influence into its party and electoral system. Unlike other democratic systems that introduced public party and campaign funding to reduce the influence of external sponsors, Indonesia provides little state funding to its political actors (Mietzner 2015). Presidential candidates receive no assistance, and parties get only a fraction of the real expenditure covered. Indeed, the amount national parties receive annually per vote obtained in the last election was reduced from US 10 cents to 1 cent in 2005, before being raised again to 10 cents in 2017. Additional funding is available for regional chapters, but far from enough to significantly contribute to the management of complex party chapters in a nation of 275 million people. A 2016 study by the KPK estimated that only around 4 percent of parties' operational costs (not including campaign expenses) were covered by state subsidies (Amalia 2016). In this context, oligarchs often appear as the only option for cash-strapped parties and candidates, who turn to them for one-time support or long-term involvement (the latter can even lead to an oligarch taking over the party). In return, parties and candidates promise to defend the sponsor's interest when in power.

Presidents or presidential candidates are particularly reliant on oligarchic support as the size of the Indonesian archipelago makes effective campaigning prohibitively expensive. The magnitude of national campaigns forces presidential aspirants to rely on party networks—but it also requires accessing large funds only top oligarchs can deliver. This is because the absence of a functioning public financing system is aggravated by a lacking tradition of small-scale donations. Few Indonesians donate to parties and candidates; on the contrary, many expect material compensation for their votes (Muhtadi 2019). Even during the exceptional election of 2014, when Widodo appeared to symbolize the rise of an ordinary man fighting the vested interests of the rich elite, only 59,000 citizens donated Rp 43 billion (US$3 million) to his campaign (Anwar 2014). By comparison, small donors gave Joe Biden US$368 million in 2020, or 38 percent of the donations received (Gratzinger 2020). Widodo's 2019 campaign suspended any systematic attempt to raise money from small donors: only Rp 21 billion was raised from a mere 252 donors (Jawa Pos 2019). In total, the Widodo campaign reported donations of Rp 606 billion (US$43 million), which is likely to be only a small part of the actual amount received and spent. In such campaigns, the bulk of the funds is typically provided by oligarchs who prefer to give off-the-books donations. In doing so, they wish to avoid inquiries by the tax office about the true extent of their wealth and to obscure the circumstance that they not only donated to the winner but to all sides.

Indonesia's political system hands extraordinary power to the wealthy by limiting the ability of non-oligarchic actors to form new parties. Some oligarchs have taken over existing parties (Golkar, for instance, has seen a succession of oligarchic chairmen since 2004). Although numerous parties led by non-oligarchic chairpersons still exist, new entries to the party system have been almost exclusively oligarchic. This is because the establishment requirements for political parties have been raised over time. In 1999, parties had to have branches in half of the provinces and half of the districts of those provinces.[1] By the 2014 elections, this requirement had increased to 100 percent in provinces, 75 percent in districts, and 50 percent in sub-districts. Concretely, this meant a massive increase in the costs needed to establish a new party. At the same time, the elite reduced the chances of a new party succeeding by raising the parliamentary threshold from 2.5 percent in 2009 to 3.5 percent in 2014 and 4 percent in 2019. This presented a cost-benefit calculus that only oligarchs could take on. Consequently, all four new parties running in the 2019 elections had oligarchic chairmen or backers: media tycoon Hary Tanoesoedibyo's Perindo; Berkarya, the party chaired by Suharto's son Tommy; PSI, a quasi-liberal party sponsored by a reformist oligarch; and an obscure party also believed to have been funded by Suharto-linked interests. Tellingly, none of these parties made it into national parliament, further highlighting the near-impenetrability of the existing party system.

Hence, oligarchs have made significant inroads into Indonesia's electoral landscape as donors, party sponsors, and direct political actors. But the power of oligarchs extends well beyond the electoral arena. When in office, Indonesian presidents invariably need funds for political operations: paying for events involving supporters, handing out favors, topping up salaries for their staff, and so forth. Presidents can access state funds for some of these costs, but others need to be paid for by non-state sources. This is when oligarchs offer their services by making payments at the direction of their patrons. They also provide in-kind services, such as private planes, that only the wealthy can afford. Said one politician, "experienced political leaders don't collect cash from oligarchs and hide it in some bank account. That's very antiquated. What really counts is the ability to make a call to an oligarch and ask them whether they can pay for a congress of party A, give a scholarship to the kid of minister B, or lend a plane to delegation C. Of course, once the leader does that, he or she becomes entangled in the web of financial power possessed by those who provide the services" (confidential interview, Jakarta, December 5, 2019). As another politician put it, "oligarchs are the credit cards of presidents and other leaders. Some may feel sorry for the oligarchs. But in reality, they love fulfilling this function because the use of their money is what gives them power over who uses it" (confidential interview, Jakarta, September 10, 2018).

Oligarchs have also amassed much power in the political arena by controlling large media empires (Tapsell 2017). Hari Tanoesoedibjo, for instance, heads a conglomerate that in 2017 included "three free-to-air national television networks that command some 40 percent of prime-time audience share" (Suzuki 2017). These media companies not only greatly influence election outcomes but are also decisive in sustaining a president's popularity in between ballots. Accordingly, presidents and other politicians who wish to gain access to the media instruments owned by oligarchs need to find ways to entice them to grant this access. As will be shown in more detail later, presidents have successfully done so by pulling media-owning oligarchs into their coalitions through threats and offers of political, material, and policy-related privileges.

Outside of active politics, oligarchs play an important role as business practitioners. Business decisions made by oligarchs can support or weaken the stability of the national economy; this stability, in turn, is essential for presidents if they want to avoid social upheaval. Suharto, for instance, saw both domestic oligarchs and international investors abandoning him in 1998, which destabilized the polity so much that it became unsalvageable (Pepinsky 2009). Suharto and his aides openly blamed ethnic Indonesian Chinese oligarchs—whose money he had previously accepted to distribute patronage—for the country's trouble (Cohen 1998). Similarly, under democratic rule, successive presidents have appealed to oligarchs to repatriate their overseas funds, parked there for security and commercial reasons. Widodo tried to achieve repatriation through a tax amnesty in 2015, but the subsequent inflow of funds was widely viewed as disappointing (only some Rp. 136 trillion, or US$9.7 billion, were repatriated).[2] Oligarchs are also some of Indonesia's largest employers, responsible for workers' welfare and productivity. How they pay, treat, and train their workers has strong implications for the political satisfaction of the citizenry. Polling experts have long pointed to the close relationship between a citizen's assessment of the condition of the economy and their economic well-being, on the one hand, and satisfaction with the president, on the other (Mujani, Liddle, and Ambardi 2018). Oligarchs, then, are major determinants of politico-economic outcomes.

Oligarchs have powerful lobby groups to channel their interests as a collective. The Indonesian Chamber of Industry and Trade (Kadin) is chief among them. The Chamber represents the views of the business sector and its actors vis-à-vis the government and often deals directly with the president. Its power is so substantial that presidents have sought to place loyalists at its helm to mitigate its potential to damage the government. In July 2021, Widodo engineered the election of a pro-government entrepreneur as Kadin chairman (Taher 2021), mostly to thwart the candidacy of Anindya Bakrie, the son of Aburizal. In addition to Kadin, there is the Indonesian Association of Young Entrepreneurs (HIPMI), whose members often go on to hold key positions in Kadin, the government, or parties. Airlangga Hartarto, a businessman and HIPMI functionary, became chairman of Golkar in 2018, and Sandiago Uno, a HIPMI chairman between 2005 and 2008, ran for the vice presidency in 2019 and then joined cabinet. While ethnically indigenous Indonesians dominate Kadin and HIPMI, this is not the case with the Indonesian Association of Entrepreneurs (Apindo). A cross-ethnic lobby group for oligarchs, it has significant ethnic Chinese representation. Between 2003 and 2014, its chair was Sofjan Wanandi, an ethnic Chinese oligarch with wide connections in the political arena. In short, whereas oligarchs as individuals seek to maneuver themselves into advantageous positions by aligning with (and funding) the right political protégés, they also exercise a level of power as a group that no president can ignore.

In brief, although oligarchs have no official position in Indonesia's constitutional framework, they can mobilize powers that put them on par with some of Indonesia's primary political protagonists. They function as the main generator of patronage resources that fuel the operations of the polity, ranging from elections, political mobilization, media coverage, and organizational activities. Substituting more formal means of funding politics, oligarchs make themselves indispensable to various actors, the president among them. Moreover, the oligarchs' lobby groups have a political clout similar to that of parties, and thus expect the same attention from the president when power is distributed. It would be wrong to assume, however, that oligarchs are the all-powerful rulers of the post-1998 democracy, as some of the proponents of the oligarchy theory in Indonesia appear to suggest. Despite their influence, oligarchs have to accept, manage, and accommodate the interests and powers of leading political institutions, including the presidency. Presidents, therefore, are not mere instruments of oligarchs, and as the next section demonstrates, have an arsenal of tools available to them to counter oligarchic influence.

Presidential Power and Oligarchs

Presidents possess regulatory, constitutional, and political powers over oligarchs. To begin with, the regulatory arena is of great importance in this regard. Most oligarchs in Indonesia lead business conglomerates reaching into numerous commercial fields, at least some of which are highly dependent on government regulation (the term *konglomerat* in Indonesian is a synonym for oligarch). For instance, many oligarchs are heavily invested in the natural resource sector, which the national government regulates through the issuing of licenses, export quotas, revenue sharing stipulations, and environmental rules. Many of the country's oligarchs have become wealthy by receiving licenses for coal, gold, oil, gas, and other minerals, and used this wealth to branch out into other business sectors. Luhut Pandjaitan, who launched his post-military business career in 2004 by establishing the Toba Sejahtera Group, started with coal mining, oil, gas, and palm oil projects before becoming active in the power plant business. (As noted, Luhut later turned into Widodo's closest aide, highlighting the interest that oligarchs have in being close to presidential power.) Similarly, tycoons whose key business is in the media sector depend on government regulations that determine where TV stations can be located, who gets a license and who does not, and so forth (Tapsell 2017). For example, after the television and newspaper oligarch Surya Paloh joined government with his Nasdem party, he had direct access to the president and his institutional authority to regulate the media sector.

Traditionally, the Indonesian state has been a leading actor in the economy, giving presidents crucial powers vis-à-vis those who wish to gain advantages from government-driven projects. The economic primacy of the state is anchored in the constitution, with Article 33 mandating leaders to control natural resources and key "production branches". Different presidents have interpreted this mandate differently, but Widodo decided to give state-owned enterprises (SOEs) a prominent role in his infrastructure plans. Between 2013 (the year before Widodo took office) and 2017, the assets of nine major infrastructure-oriented SOEs—airport operators Angkasa Pura I & II, the state's five largest construction companies, toll road operator Jasa Marga, and railway company Kereta Api Indonesia—increased by 262 percent, from Rp 119 trillion (US$8.5 billion) to Rp 432.5 trillion (US$30.8 billion) (Guild 2019). These companies, which function as the main channels of state funds into the market, are encouraged to work with private investors, often through suppliers and contractors (Ramalan 2021). During the pandemic, the state's role in the economy expanded further. The government exceeded the traditional budget deficit ceiling of 3 percent to pump money into the suffering economy (in 2020, the budget deficit was 6 percent). Thus, oligarchs have strong incentives to gain the ear of the president when the state plans large-scale infrastructure projects managed through SOEs or when it flushes the market with emergency liquidity.

Presidents have also used their power to offer protection to non-indigenous oligarchs in exchange for support and donations. In 2016, the Forbes list of the fifty richest Indonesians featured forty-four ethnic Chinese, holding 87.4 percent of the combined wealth of these top fifty tycoons (US$86.42 billion out of US$98.825 billion) (Forbes 2016). One ethnic Indian is also on the list—with his wealth added, non-indigenous oligarchs hold 92.5 percent of the total wealth owned by the fifty richest entrepreneurs. In a country with a long history of anti-Chinese and other ethnic violence, these oligarchs are used to paying political patrons for protection (Chong 2015). Suharto had masterfully used this paradigm to exploit the wealth of his ethnic Chinese backers while perpetuating the social discrimination that forced them to offer funds to him (Borsuk and Chng 2014). But even after democratization began and some of the formal discriminations of ethnic Chinese were lifted (especially by President Wahid between 1999 and 2001), non-indigenous oligarchs remain aware of their vulnerability. The mass demonstrations against Purnama, the ethnic Chinese governor of

Jakarta, in 2016 and 2017 saw persistent ethnic stereotyping of wealthier Chinese Indonesians. Purnama, it was alleged, was the proxy of Jakarta's ethnic Chinese oligarchs (the so-called nine dragons), who were—in turn—seen as Beijing's agents (Rezkisari 2016). Opinion surveys confirmed the existence of these sentiments in society at large (Mietzner and Muhtadi 2019), cementing the anxieties of non-indigenous oligarchs and their urgently felt need to turn to the president for protection.

At the same time, presidents have not hesitated to use their oversight of law enforcement agencies to exert pressure on oligarchs, both indigenous and non-indigenous. As in the case of local government heads, threats of legal investigations have been weaponized to bring politically hostile oligarchs into line. One of the most blatant cases in this regard has been that of Hary Tanoesoedibjo, an ethnic Chinese, the head of the Perindo party, and the country's leading media tycoon. In the 2014 elections, Tanoesoedibjo's stations supported Prabowo, giving the latter an advantage (Tapsell 2017). But in early 2017, investigators opened a case against Tanoesoedibjo for threatening a prosecutor through text messages. Shortly afterwards, Tanoesoedibjo announced that he would abandon Prabowo and support Widodo's re-election, which was widely interpreted as his attempt to stop the investigations (Retaduari 2017). Whatever his intentions, the case did not make it to court—and in Widodo's second term, Tanoesoedibjo's daughter was made deputy minister for tourism and the creative economy (because her father's party did not pass the parliamentary threshold, it was not given a full cabinet seat). Through maneuvering by the legal apparatus, then, Widodo's government had turned an oligarchic foe into an ally and gained access to his massively influential television network. As discussed below, similar tactics were used in the case of Bakrie, whose marginalization helped Widodo to transform his initial minority position in parliament into a supermajority.

The president's appointment powers, as applied in the case of Tanoesoedibjo's daughter, are of great interest to other oligarchs, too. Presidents have routinely filled some of the non-party (and party-affiliated) cabinet seats with oligarchs, incentivizing those who want to be considered for an appointment to demonstrate support for the president. While oligarchs in cabinet must formally relinquish control over their businesses, there are often reasonable doubts about whether they did. In most cases, the chairpersonship of the conglomerate in question is handed to a family member or a close business associate, with the oligarchs transitioning into a position of power that allows them to shape a beneficial environment for their businesses.[3] It has been common for oligarchs to be directly put in charge of the business sector in which their businesses operate. Luhut, for instance, controlled the Coordinating Ministry for Maritime Affairs and Resources after 2016—an institution with the Ministry of Energy and Minerals under it.

Moreover, Luhut held the latter ministry for some time in 2016. Similarly, Chairul Tanjung, head of a vast conglomerate, and worth an estimated US$4 billion, was appointed coordinating minister for the economy by Yudhoyono in 2014 (his predecessor, Hatta Radjasa, had interests in the oil business, which was also under his coordination at that time). Thus, ministries are an important avenue for oligarchs to secure both their interests and those of big business as a collective, giving much value to the cabinet seats that the president can distribute.

When earlier discussing the president's power over parties, we emphasized that in Indonesia's post-2004 regime of direct elections, presidents possess decisive capital that party leaders lack: that is, electoral popularity. The same is true for the president's advantage over oligarchs. There has been no shortage of oligarchs who have sought the presidency for themselves but have failed because of their poor standing with voters. Surya Paloh, Tanoesoedibjo, Bakrie, Jusuf Kalla, and others openly declared their presidential ambitions, but few were nominated to run, let alone had a chance in the actual election (Hadi 2011). For all the funds oligarchs have invested in electoral machines, they found that nationwide popularity in presidential races is not purchasable. Facing the same dilemma as unpopular party leaders, the only option for oligarchs who wish to participate in frontline politics is to attach themselves to a popular non-oligarchic politician, such as Yudhoyono and Widodo. Even for oligarchs who prefer to remain in the background, the popularity of presidents and presidential candidates is the key motivation to support them. Said one leading opinion pollster, "oligarchs are some of our best customers. They want to know who is going to win, because that determines how much they give to each candidate" (confidential interview, online, December 1, 2021). In short, presidents' electoral attractiveness is a form of social capital that some oligarchs wish they had and others seek to align with for strategic business purposes.

It is therefore misleading to portray Indonesian presidents as weaklings under the control of oligarchic paymasters. Winters (2013, 15), for instance, described Widodo's rise as an "oligarchic move in which the power of wealth placed [Widodo] before the voters." While there is no doubt that some oligarchs supported Widodo's candidacy, it is equally self-evident that many other tycoons wanted that slot for themselves. However, they eventually had to accept Widodo's electoral superiority, which tells us much about the relationship between oligarchs and presidents in Indonesia. Of comparable importance are the other powers presidents can mobilize in their negotiations with oligarchs, ranging from their regulatory authority to their role in the state economy and influence over law enforcement apparatuses. Consequently, the interaction between oligarchs and presidents is a more complex affair than oligarchy theorists often imply. Hadiz and Robison (2014) partly conceded this point by stating that

Widodo "has displayed considerable acumen in negotiating within established elite structures." But for them, this was just further evidence that he was "embedded in the system of oligarchy." By contrast, the following section demonstrates how Indonesian presidents have managed oligarchs with the same instruments of coalitional presidentialism through which other actors have been integrated into broad presidential alliances.

Presidents and Oligarchs

To assess how post-2004 presidents have managed oligarchs as part of their coalitions, we begin by analyzing how Suharto dealt with them. Significant differences and similarities emerge from this analysis. One of Suharto's main mechanisms to discipline oligarchs and extract resources from them was holding group meetings, sometimes publicly. In March 1990, for instance, he famously assembled the country's leading tycoons, almost all ethnic Chinese, to his ranch in Tapos and called on them to "share their wealth" with cooperatives. (In practice, this meant sharing their wealth with him so that he could redistribute it.) Such meetings would also occur before every election, with Suharto telling tycoons that "We must make sure that Golkar wins. For that I will ask Lim Sioe Liong [Suharto's chief crony] to ask donations from you" (Borsuk and Chng 215, 5).[4] Liong was then in charge of deciding who should donate how much (because he knew how much they were worth) and collected the money, too. Aside from these gatherings with oligarchs as a collective, Suharto would also meet separately with them in private. Liong's visits to the palace or Suharto's home at Cendana Street in Jakarta, often in sandals and shorts, were legendary. Suharto did not mind the occasional publicity of the meetings in Tapos and elsewhere because it conveyed to the citizenry that he forced the oligarchs to share their riches, and because it increased the sense of vulnerability among the oligarchs, especially those of non-indigenous backgrounds. This sense of vulnerability—in turn—drove the donations up.

But Suharto drew a clear line between his milking of the oligarchs and their formal participation in politics. Oligarchs paid Suharto so that they could operate in his polity and obtain commercial advantages, not to become ministers or political leaders themselves. This reflected the narrow politico-economic power structures in the fully Suharto-centric New Order. Thus, the incentives for oligarchs to seek direct political participation were lower under Suharto than in today's competitive, multi-layered system. Indeed, Suharto's cabinets created oligarchs rather than accommodating them. In putting together his ministry, Suharto tended to hand economic ministries to Western-educated technocrats, who used their offices to build connections that helped them and their offspring launch business careers. The economist Sumitro Djojohadikusumo, for instance, was a Suharto minister from 1968 and 1978, establishing networks that allowed one of his sons, Prabowo, to marry Suharto's daughter and another, Hashim, to become a successful businessman. Hartarto Sastrosoenarto, minister between 1983 and 1999, saw his son Airlangga become a medium-level oligarch and, under Widodo, chairman of Golkar. Similarly, Ginandjar Kartasasmita collected considerable wealth during his time as minister between 1978 and 1988, with his son Agus Gumiwang subsequently entering both business and politics to eventually emerge as a Widodo minister. Only once did Suharto put an established oligarch into his cabinet: Bob Hasan, also a member of his family, became a minister in Suharto's last ministry, which was widely seen as a sign of his desperation and distrust of anyone outside of his inner circle.

By contrast, the oligarchs' involvement in post-2004 presidential coalitions is more direct, formal, and institutionalized. Private meetings between presidents and oligarchs continue, both to extract donations and to ensure their support for government policies. But oligarchs are now visible and even prominent actors in public politics, demonstrating their increased ambition to be both sponsors and active drivers of policymaking. Presidents, too, have dropped any attempt to hide the influence of oligarchs on their governments. Quite to the contrary, oligarchs have been proudly displayed in cabinet. Inclusion in the ministry line-up, then, has been a key instrument of coalitional presidentialism through which heads of state have tied oligarchs to their government. As noted in chapter 1, oligarchs (party-affiliated and independent) have seen the most consistent gradual increase in their cabinet participation of all surveyed groups. In fact, because table 1.1 only captures the situation at the beginning of each president's term, it misses the even stronger increase in oligarchic cabinet participation in the second Widodo administration achieved through the reshuffle of December 2020. Of the six new appointments, three were multi-millionaires: Sandiaga Uno, with a wealth of about half a billion dollars; banker Budi Gunadi Sadikin, with about US$15 million; and Sakti Wahyu Trenggono, with about US$190 million. One newspaper even calculated that Uno's net worth increased by about US$19 million on the day of his appointment through an increase in the value of his stock (Citradi 2020).

The 2020 additions to Widodo's cabinet joined an impressive concentration of minister-cum-oligarchs. Partly this was because Widodo, as a small-scale businessman, believed that wealth was an indicator of success and competence. Of course, Widodo's 2014 campaign presented him as a man of the people, and he portrayed the elite as unable to understand the social realities that he could grasp. However, Widodo believed that "we need to appreciate the entrepreneurs;

they know how to do things. They don't just talk. They have success, so we need to allow them to contribute to government" (interview, Jakarta, September 15, 2014). Based on this principle, Widodo recruited Erick Thohir into government in 2019. While Thohir reported a net worth of "only" US$200 million, his stock investments seem to go much further than that (at one point, he bought Italian soccer club Inter Milan).[5] Widodo, after using Thohir as head of his 2019 campaign team, made him minister of state-owned enterprises—a portfolio in which the SOEs under his coordination both competed and interacted with his firms (and those of his brother Garibaldi, whom Forbes estimated to be worth US$1.65 billion in 2020). Similarly, Widodo made Nadiem Makarim, the founder of the ride application Gojek, minister of education in 2019. Makarim reported a wealth of about US$100 million, while his company was estimated to be worth US$5 billion. As a symbol of innovation, Makarim was expected to break through the antiquated education bureaucracy. Yet, he was soon embroiled in accusations of a conflict of interest because his ministry's schools used Gojek's digital payment arm to collect contributions from parents (Saeno 2020).

In addition to direct ministerial appointments, presidents have used party channels to integrate oligarchs into their coalitions without them sitting at the cabinet table. Some oligarchs want to avoid the trouble of having to nominally transfer their companies to others and submit a state officials' wealth report, and thus prefer to participate in coalition politics through their parties. Surya Paloh, for instance, the chair of Nasdem and a media tycoon, opted to give the allocated cabinet seats for his party to other cadres he could control. Paloh began his political career in Golkar, unsuccessfully contesting its presidential nomination in 2004 and the party chairmanship in 2009. He subsequently established Nasdem, still hoping to win the presidency one day. But he recognized the rise of Widodo in 2013 and 2014, and was one of the first party leaders to throw his support behind him. Exercising influence through his membership in the informal council of party chairs in the coalition, he focused on expanding his businesses beyond his media empire, which owns the television station Metro TV and the daily newspaper *Media Indonesia*. In the oil sector, he cooperated with China Sonangol, a joint venture between Angola's state-owned oil company, Sonangol E.P., and Hong Kong-based company New Bright International. Once Widodo became president, Paloh invited China Sonangol officials to meet with Widodo to negotiate a deal to import oil from Angola. The import went ahead, although Widodo later complained to aides about "how pushy" Paloh was (confidential interview, Jakarta, October 25, 2019). In the 2020 Forbes list of the 100 richest Indonesians, Paloh was estimated to be worth US$440 million (VOI 2021).

Apart from cabinet and party forums, oligarchs have also entered presidential coalitions through other institutions. One important body in this regard is the Council of Advisers to the President (DPP). While not possessing strong formal powers, membership on the council gives its holder proximity to the president and significant prestige with which to open doors in the state bureaucracy. Of the nine DPP members appointed in 2019, five could be categorized as oligarchs: Tahir, worth US$3.3 billion; Arifin Panigoro, with assets of US$550 million; Wiranto, valued at about US$50 million; Putri Kuswisnuwardhani, the heir to a cosmetics empire, estimated to be worth about US$30 million; and Muhamad Mardiono, who reported a wealth of around US$100 million. At least two other members were millionaires. The absence of ordinary citizens on the council—who could give the president advice from the perspective of workers, farmers, or other professionals from lower social strata—is striking and highlights the importance presidents have given to accommodating oligarchs into their government infrastructure. The lack of public protest toward this overrepresentation of oligarchs in state institutions also demonstrates how normalized the role of the wealthy in presidential coalitions has become.

Other institutional mechanisms designed to involve oligarchs in government and policymaking have focused on Kadin, HIPMI, and Apindo. Individually and through these organizations, oligarchs have been asked to participate formally in critical legislative initiatives. One example was the drafting of the Omnibus Bill, which deregulated important sectors of the economy and reduced workers' benefits as well as environmental protections. For the drafting process, the government established a Task Force in December 2019, which was jointly headed by Kadin chair Rosan Roeslani, worth US$450 million, and Airlangga Hartarto as coordinating minister of the economy (himself worth at least US$8 million but also the owner of several companies before taking up the ministry). As members, the Task Force included James Riady, the son of one of the country's wealthiest oligarchs with assets of US$1.4 billion, and Erwin Aksa, a former HIPMI chairman and associated with the Bosawa Group run by Jusuf Kalla's family (Aziz 2019). Airlangga and major oligarchs, then, oversaw the drafting of legislation that cut labor costs for their companies and watered down environmental regulations that they had long viewed as a nuisance. It would be inaccurate to assume, however, that the oligarchs had imposed this agenda on Widodo. By all accounts, he was a passionate defender of the initiative, believing that it would generate the money necessary to pay for his infrastructure projects (and help recover from COVID-19). As noted, he viewed oligarchs as experts in the field of economic policy, as evidenced by their wealth, and thus their wealth accumulation strategies deserved adoption by the state.

Finally, presidents have built ties to oligarchs through private and family business links. Suharto was the master in this field, but this practice has continued under the democratic polity. The benefits of such ties are compelling: they directly merge the interests of the oligarchs with those of the president and generate income for members of the presidential family. Widodo had already formed ties to oligarchs as mayor of Solo, when he entered into a furniture joint venture with Luhut in 2007. But under his presidency his two sons, Gibran and Kaesang, established businesses that leading oligarchs found advantageous to support. In 2019, Gibran and Kaesang helped founding GK Hebat, a company primarily operating in the food business. Also involved in the company were Theodore Permadi Rachmat, an oligarch worth US$1.6 billion, and Gandi Sulistiyanto, a major official of the multi-billion dollar Sinar Mas Group (Salam 2020). In 2021, Erick Thohir, the SOE minister, also developed a business with Kaesang (at that point, Gibran, the president's oldest son, had already become mayor of Solo and thus had to be more careful about overt business activities). Together, they bought shares in a Solo soccer club, with Erick holding 20 percent and Kaesang 40 percent (Sholikah 2021). It was not reported who paid for the shares, and how much they were worth. But for Erick, the business connection consolidated his relationship with the president, and for Widodo, it tied a key oligarch even more strongly to his administration. For Kaesang, it was part of a rapid increase in his wealth: in late 2021, the then twenty-six-year-old paid US$7 million for a share in another company, leading to public speculations about the source of his funding and affluence (Muhardianto 2021).

But business opportunities for their families is not the only thing presidents receive in exchange for integrating oligarchs into their coalitions. More importantly, oligarchs provide essential campaign donations and other funding. While much of Indonesia's political funding is off the books, even the official reports give us some clues. In 2019, two golfing clubs donated about Rp 40 billion (or US$2.9 million) to Widodo. However, research by the Indonesian Corruption Watch (ICW) showed that the likely donor behind these clubs was Wahyu Sakti Trenggono, then the treasurer of the president's campaign (who was later rewarded with a ministry) (Widowati 2019). Similarly, Prabowo's campaign aides protested that Widodo had donated Rp 19.5 billion to his own campaign, when the president's wealth report only acknowledged possession of Rp 6 billion in cash reserves (Paat 2019). It is not implausible to assume, therefore, that the self-donation was raised through other sources. It is also likely that Erick Thohir, the head of the campaign, covered his own expenses and that of his campaign team. A second benefit presidents receive from oligarchs in return for granting them privileges is positive TV coverage of the government. In 2019, most of Indonesia's private television stations and other media outlets sided with the president (much in contrast to 2014, when the majority backed Prabowo). In the 2019 campaign, stations owned by Paloh, Tanoesoedibjo, Bakrie, Thohir, and others offered Widodo largely uncritical and officious coverage, contributing to the fact that the president was able to secure re-election comfortably (Souisa 2019).

More generally, the accommodation of oligarchs by presidents as part of their coalition purchases them the tycoons' support of, or at least acquiescence toward, the government's operations. Whenever Indonesian presidents face public demonstrations, for instance, speculation is rife that particular oligarchs sponsored these protests. While proof is often sketchy, and such an approach overlooks the agency of many of the protesters involved, there is little doubt that oligarchic sponsorship of demonstrations exists and that presidents and their aides firmly believe in its possibility. In October 2020, for instance, Airlangga claimed that protests by labor unions against his Omnibus Bill had been sponsored. "Actually, we know who paid for and was a sponsor of these actions," the coordinating minister said then, without elaborating (Ainurrahman 2020). In this context, integrating members of the oligarchic class into the government offers the prospect of limiting the number of actors who have the resources and will to sabotage presidential administrations, promising greater stability.

Overall, the oligarchs' participation in presidential coalitions is a transactional arrangement in which presidents gain personal financial security, political funds, positive media coverage, and acceptance of their rule, while oligarchs obtain cabinet positions, policy influence, and privileged access to business projects. This arrangement is managed formally and informally, with presidents engaging oligarchs privately and through organizations such as Kadin, HIPMI, and Apindo. We already noted, in the case of Tanoesoedibjo, that the president possesses various instruments to punish and reward oligarchs in order to secure the functionality of their coalition membership as a mutually beneficial proposition. When Tanoesoedibjo opposed the government, he was first punished by the legal apparatus under the president's authority, and subsequently rewarded with a post of deputy minister for his daughter when the oligarch changed course. In the next section, we look in more detail at another case that illustrates how exactly presidents manage oligarchs, and what can happen to some of them when they try, for whatever reason, to stand outside of the president's coalition.

Oligarchic Inclusion and Exclusion: Bakrie

The case of Aburizal Bakrie illustrates both the political opportunities and limitations of Indonesian oligarchs. While Bakrie's wealth allowed him to mingle with state elites and protect his businesses, his biggest dream—the presidency—

remained unfulfilled. Ultimately, he even found himself at the margins of elite politics. In the early 1970s, Bakrie had joined his father's company, helping to turn it into a large conglomerate (Robison 1986, 332). In his business career, he leaned on New Order ministers such as Ginandjar Kartasasmita, who privileged Muslim entrepreneurs over their ethnic Chinese rivals (Winters 1996; Robison and Hadiz 2004, 85). When Bakrie's businesses suffered large losses in 1998 (Robison and Rosser, 2000), they only survived thanks to a generous debt restructuring deal. Reportedly, Bakrie had to settle only 20 percent of his US$1.1 billion debt (Asia Sentinel 2008). Under the new democratic regime, Bakrie used his continued government connections—he was chairman of Kadin between 1994 and 2004—to gain access to lucrative coal mining licenses. With the price of coal quintupling between 2000 and 2008, Bakrie's business flourished, and he decided to enter frontline politics. In 2004, he unsuccessfully sought Golkar's presidential nomination, but then supported Yudhoyono's bid (against the wishes of his party) and was rewarded with a ministry. Initially coordinating minister for the economy and then coordinating minister for people's welfare, Bakrie's businesses continued to prosper; in 2008, Globe Asia declared him Southeast Asia's wealthiest oligarch, with a net worth of US$9.2 billion (Globe Asia 2008).

Among many other advantages, Bakrie's inclusion in Yudhoyono's cabinet protected him from major crises threatening his business interests. After one of Bakrie's drilling companies was accused of causing a mud volcano in Sidoardjo (East Java) to erupt and flood more than 700 hectares of land in May 2006, the government did not make Bakrie fully liable for the damage. While Yudhoyono required Bakrie to buy the destroyed land for US$700 million, the government shouldered all other long-term costs. Furthermore, after global commodity prices dropped sharply in October 2008, Bakrie benefitted from the Jakarta stock exchange temporarily suspending the share trade of his company Bumi Resources. However, Finance Minister Sri Mulyani Indrawati overturned the decision, leading Bakrie's shares to collapse (Kompas 2009). According to an economist who spoke to Bakrie then, "he was furious, and said Sri Mulyani had to go, that was non-negotiable" (confidential interview, Jakarta, May 6, 2010). After incessant attacks by Bakrie's Golkar party—he became its leader in October 2009—Sri Mulyani resigned in May 2010. By then, Bakrie had been rescued by foreign banks, including a $1.9 billion loan from a Chinese sovereign wealth fund (Montlake 2011). Undoubtedly, Bakrie's influence in government and party circles played a role in securing these loans. After another financial rescue in 2011, Bakrie—who gave up his ministries in 2009—decided it was time to begin another presidential campaign.

In his renewed bid for the presidency, Bakrie enjoyed the support of other oligarchs who wanted to prevent the political rise of Prabowo Subianto. As

Yudhoyono was barred from running again in 2014, Indonesia's oligarchs were looking for a new patron to back. For a variety of reasons, Prabowo seemed to be an unsafe bet—especially for ethnic Chinese tycoons (Prabowo had blamed them for the 1998 crisis) and military-affiliated oligarchs who had had conflicts with Prabowo in the past. Among the latter was Luhut, who established a unit in his business office to help Bakrie with his presidential campaign. "Bakrie isn't perfect, but we can work with him," Luhut said. "The most important thing is that he can challenge Prabowo" (interview, Jakarta, April 12, 2013). But Bakrie's campaign struggled to take off. In 2012, his aides organized a safari for him, in which the Golkar chair toured parts of Indonesia in a luxurious bus to introduce himself to the electorate. The privileged candidate failed to connect with grassroots voters, however. In a speech at a West Java school in June 2012, Bakrie tried to convey that he had weathered many crises, saying that "when my businesses were down, I even had to fly economy class" (notes by the author, Karawang, June 13, 2012). Students and teachers, many of whom had never been on a plane, remained unimpressed; they only showed signs of satisfaction when Bakrie distributed computers to them. Other audiences were not enthusiastic either. As a result, Bakrie's electability ratings remained stuck in the single digits: a month after his West Java tour, he polled at 4 percent (Dewi 2012).

Widodo's emergence as the presidential frontrunner for 2014 killed off whatever chances Bakrie may have had. As Widodo took the lead in the polls by early 2013, many oligarchs shifted their support to the most likely winner. Luhut, too, despite having invested significantly in Bakrie's campaign, abandoned Bakrie and began to back Widodo as the best alternative to Prabowo. "I like Bakrie, but this is politics. We need to get behind the nominee with the greatest chance against Prabowo, and that's [Widodo]," Luhut explained (interview, Jakarta, November 9, 2013). Luhut felt that his furniture joint venture with Widodo gave him a special connection with the president-in-waiting, and he happily turned his pro-Bakrie campaign operation into a pro-Widodo machine. As for Bakrie, he found no parties other than his own to nominate him (Golkar needed partners to meet the nomination requirements). Watching Widodo and Prabowo firming as the only credible contenders, Bakrie overplayed his hand in negotiations with both candidates; he first asked Widodo to run as his (Bakrie's) deputy, and then offered to Prabowo that he would settle for the latter's vice presidential nomination (Asril 2014). Neither nominee showed interest, and after Widodo rejected a Bakrie request for a concrete promise of cabinet seats, the Golkar chairman ultimately aligned with Prabowo, even though he was not on the ticket. Bakrie's television station TV One switched to heavily anti-Widodo coverage, and on election day, it published a manipulated count that falsely declared

Prabowo the winner. In short, Bakrie had managed to maneuver himself out of the race and into a position of hostility to the incoming president.

Initially, Bakrie believed that he could take on Widodo. The coalition of parties that Prabowo had put together for his nomination held a majority in both the outgoing and incoming parliament, leading Bakrie to assume that Widodo would be a weak president. Before Widodo's inauguration, the Prabowo coalition in the DPR demonstrated its power by abolishing direct elections for local government heads (as noted, Yudhoyono later reversed that move). Triumphantly, Bakrie said at the time that the coalition would go on to change "122 laws" that he deemed to be in violation of "Pancasila Democracy" (the term Suharto had used for his polity) (Wardi 2014). The first on his list were the mining, telecommunications, and banking laws—all directly related to his oligarchic interests. But Bakrie's sense of superiority did not last long. When Bakrie was re-elected as Golkar chairman in December 2014, a pro-Widodo faction in the party split off, challenged the result of the party congress, held its own, and installed a new chairman, Agung Laksono. Recall that the Indonesian government has the authority to recognize the legality of each party's leadership, and the Widodo administration used this power to endorse the pro-government Golkar board and reject Bakrie's. Behind the scenes, the government also pressured Bakrie, exploiting his precarious financial position to threaten him with sanctions or reward him if he gave up his claim on the Golkar leadership. After trying to cling to his position throughout 2015, Bakrie surrendered by early 2016 and agreed to be replaced by a new chairman.

In return for making way for a pro-government Golkar leader, Bakrie was allowed to move into the party's advisory board chairman position. This post held no executive authority but signaled to Bakrie that while he had been expelled from the inner circle of power, he was still considered part of the elite as long as he did not openly challenge the president. But this could not distract from the fact that by the second half of the 2010s, Bakrie was a shadow of his former self. He disappeared from the list of the 100 richest Indonesians—a list he once topped; many of the headlines he made related to protracted debt restructuring deals his company had to enter into (Hermansyah 2018); and he no longer mattered in the negotiations between party leaders over the big issues, whether in regards to coalition-building or policymaking. As mentioned, Widodo also cut short a brief attempt of the Bakrie family to stage a comeback in 2021: when Bakrie's son Anindya ran for the chairmanship of Kadin, government agencies reportedly advised delegates not to vote for him. An ally of Widodo was elected instead. Replicating the approach used to marginalize his father, the government tolerated the inclusion of Anindya in Kadin's advisory board. This ensured that the Bakrie family had no access to concrete instruments of power—but also kept it within the broader parameters of the regime.

Bakrie's rise and fall demonstrate the limitations both oligarchs and presidents face when trying to contain each other. Oligarchs have immense powers that help them launch political careers, even if they are unpopular. But money alone is insufficient to lift them into the presidency—that, as Yudhoyono and Widodo showed, requires a genuine connection with the electorate. Similarly, oligarchs can create significant troubles for incumbent presidents, but the latter have strong instruments to respond to such challenges. Once Bakrie had openly positioned himself against Widodo, the president succeeded in politically neutralizing him. Yet Widodo's victory over Bakrie—and how he achieved it—also highlight the constraints of presidents' counter-oligarchic measures. Widodo battled Bakrie not because he was an oligarch, or because he had tried to defend his vested interests in politics. Rather, Widodo decided to sideline Bakrie because he was an opponent of the government. Other oligarchs in Widodo's circle were treated with none of the hostility that Bakrie was confronted with; on the contrary, their share of cabinet positions increased under Widodo. Consequently, while presidents have the means to contain and remove individual oligarchs who have chosen to oppose them, they have been reluctant to use these weapons to challenge oligarchy as a whole. For presidents, oligarchs who support them are not only tolerable but also useful. By the same token, "bad" oligarchs are not defined by their potentially corrupt insertion of business interests into state affairs—but rather by their stance vis-à-vis the president. Put differently, the checks presidents have placed on oligarchs have been partisan and fragmentary.

Discussing the state of political funding in Indonesia, Yudhoyono told this author that "Prabowo has trillions of Rupiah, [Bakrie] has trillions of Rupiah, Mrs Mega[wati] has many entrepreneurs as friends, . . . but where can I get money from?" (interview, Cikeas, December 2, 2014). Yudhoyono's complaint gives a telling insight into the mindset of Indonesian presidents when justifying their interaction with oligarchs. They see themselves surrounded by competitors with a lot of money, and the only way to create a level playing field with politicians-cum-oligarchs is to access oligarchic funds themselves. To some extent, that is an accurate perception. But it is also true that neither Yudhoyono nor Widodo took action during their presidencies to reform the political arena they were operating in. Asked why during his rule the amount of state subsidies to political parties was reduced by almost 90 percent, Yudhoyono said that he could not remember, but that he now favored higher subsidies. Widodo, as incoming president, said he would raise the state subsidies to their pre-2005 levels—which he did in 2017 (interview, Jakarta, September 15, 2014). However, it was clear to everyone that after twelve years of general inflation and rising political expenditures, such a re-adjustment to the old level would not be enough to significantly alter Indonesia's system of funding politics. At the same time, presidents possess crucial legislative and executive powers to shape political institutions, and have used them to advance issues they considered important. Apparently, the reform of the political financing system was not among those issues. Instead, both Yudhoyono and Widodo perpetuated, and even expanded, the regime they complained about.

The reason for the presidents' perpetuation of the status quo was that situating oligarchs as members of their coalitions, even if they lacked party connections or any other institutional power, was a matter of political convenience. It is obvious that any president, regardless of the country or system he or she operates in, has to decide how to handle oligarchic actors and their vested interests. Politicians need money to operate, and a certain degree of dependence on donors is thus a logical consequence. But Yudhoyono and Widodo institutionalized this dependence and viewed it as a normal element of political coalition-building rather than as a defect to overcome. Taking on the oligarchic class as a collective would have, in Yudhoyono's political thinking, created "chaos" and damaged the polity. Widodo initially campaigned against this approach in 2014, but quickly learned to appreciate it after taking office. Accordingly, both picked loyalist oligarchs to support them and pre-empt any oligarchic destabilization attempt. When they moved to punish an oligarch, it was almost invariably for disloyalty toward them, not corruptive behavior. We noted earlier how pleased Widodo was with Setya Novanto as chairman of the DPR, in the full knowledge of the latter's track record that stretched back deep into the New Order. In Novanto's case, what mattered was that he delivered useful services and therefore contributed to the stability of the Widodo presidency. Similarly, when the much-praised Finance Minister Sri Mulyani offered her resignation in 2010 to escape the continuous confrontation with Bakrie, Yudhoyono accepted it immediately. For him, the resignation helped to reduce the "chaos" he so dreaded.

The damage this pre-emptive accommodation of the oligarchs in Indonesia's coalitional presidentialism has done to the polity's democratic posture is self-evident. While oligarchs have largely refrained from sabotaging presidents and therefore helped to avoid the impeachments and presidential resignations so common in Latin America and other regions, their acquiescence has been bought with concessions that eat away at Indonesia's democratic quality. Oligarchic ministers pursue their business interests while in office; sponsors to parties and candidates can expect projects and policy favors; and ordinary Indonesians have increasingly been excluded from an electoral system fueled by oligarchic resources. The most disillusioning aspect of these trends is that Yudhoyono and Widodo accepted them as normal. Their acceptance, moreover, did not come after a long battle with oligarchic interests that they eventually lost, resulting in a truce with their opponents. Rather, Yudhoyono—despite his protestations of being victimized by oligarchs around him—saw the inclusion of oligarchs in his alliance as a part of his overall political strategy of keeping the polity calm, and Widodo gave up on his early anti-oligarchic promises only a few weeks into his presidency. Consequently, both presidents used their presidential powers for other purposes than to contain the influence of oligarchic actors on them and politics more broadly. Primarily, they deployed their instruments of power to enforce discipline among participating members of their coalitions, including the oligarchs, and control those actors trying to oppose them.

9
MUSLIM ORGANIZATIONS

In the last half-century, the political role of religious organizations worldwide has taken divergent paths, depending on the polity they operate in. In the parliamentary systems of Western Europe and Oceania, as well as in some Latin American countries, the power of churches and other religious groups has declined, in line with what much of the modernization literature predicted (Molteni and Biolcati 2018; Somma, Bargsted, and Valenzuela 2017). But in the United States, Africa, and some Asian polities, the opposite trend has occurred. Republican presidents George W. Bush and Donald Trump relied heavily on evangelicals to win elections and maintain public support while in office, rewarding them with policy influence in return (Martí 2019). In Africa, many presidents have used and fueled conservative religious activism that gave them access to a fanatic support base (McClendon and Riedl 2019). In Asia, the record has been mixed. Buddhist actors have gained influence in Thailand and Myanmar (Walton and Hayward 2014), and conservative forms of Islam have increasingly shaped Malaysian politics. In the Philippines, by contrast, populist president Rodrigo Duterte took on the powerful Catholic church in his 2016 campaign (Abellanosa 2018). He was only able to do this, however, because of two supportive factors: first, he rallied the country's minority religions (Islam and Protestantism) behind him; and second, in the Philippines' electoral system, he did not have to win an absolute majority of the votes to become president. Thus, he could afford to alienate the nation's most influential religious actor by courting others.

Indonesia fits into the group of countries that has seen an increasing role of religious groups in politics. Several factors have framed this trend. First, with

87 percent of the population being Muslim, appealing to the country's overwhelming religious majority has been the most promising strategy in post-1998 democratic politics. Second, Indonesia's electoral system—which, unlike in the Philippines, requires presidential candidates to gain an absolute majority in a possible run-off—further disincentivizes exclusive appeals to smaller constituencies and forces candidates to conform to majority understandings of piety. And third, private religiosity has intensified significantly in recent decades. Traditionally viewed as a country with a moderate version of Islam, religious conservatism has grown slowly but steadily since the 1970s (van Bruinessen 2013). By the mid-2010s, religious piety had become an important marker of societal acceptability for Muslims and hence for politicians, especially the president. Presidents—and presidential candidates—are under immense pressure to portray themselves as pious; even the slightest impression of secularism or disregard for Muslim practices and beliefs could prove electorally fatal (Bourchier 2019). This, in turn, drives presidents to enter into alliances with Muslim groups that can bestow the necessary religious legitimacy upon them. In exchange, as is the case with other actors of coalitional presidentialism, Muslim groups obtain cabinet representation, policy favors, and material benefits, both institutionally and for their leaders.

This chapter analyzes the importance of Muslim organizations for presidential coalitions in Indonesia by first sketching the growth of religious piety in society as the main power resource Islamic groups can leverage in political negotiations. Ironically or otherwise, this growth began at the height of the New Order's rule, despite Suharto's well-established preference for limiting the role of religion. By the 1980s, he had to respond to this societal trend, creating a more Islamic image for himself and inviting Muslim groups to play a bigger role in his regime. After 1998, conservative forms of Islam spread further, and faith became a key component of political competition. The second section highlights the powers that presidents can mobilize to win over Muslim groups and limit their ambitions. NU, for instance, is based primarily in poorer, rural areas and is thus dependent on government funds for its religious boarding schools and other educational institutions. The promise of such funds is consequently a main tool for presidents to integrate NU and other groups into their regimes. In the third section, we look at how the interaction between presidents and Muslim groups functions in the daily operations of coalitional presidentialism, with cabinet allocations at the center of the negotiations. Finally, the fourth section discusses the banning of two radical Islamic groups by Widodo, and how this inter-related with the vested interests of NU. An example of how presidents and Muslim groups mutually exploit each other, the incident highlights broader patterns of Indonesia's coalitional presidentialism.

Muslim Groups and Their Powers

While the overall narrative of Islam's influence on post-1998 politics has been one of gradual intensification, the details of its longer-term development have been far from linear and consistent. Indeed, its history has been full of contradictions. On the one hand, the largest Islamic organizations have dropped demands for the implementation of Islamic law. In the 1950s, the country's two biggest Muslim groups, the traditionalist NU and the more modernist Muhammadiyah, had called for the obligation to observe Islamic law for all Muslims to be featured in the constitution (Nasution 1994). However, Suharto forced both groups to formally abandon any notions of an Islamic state and to endorse the country's pluralist Pancasila ideology. Such endorsements also became the standard for the Muslim-based parties of the post-Suharto era, with only a few of them still pushing for Islamic law to be formalized in the constitution. But this trend of increasing religious moderation among mainstream Muslim groups and parties was, as we noted above, accompanied by counteracting patterns in society. From the 1970s, Muslims began to display increasing devoutness, with many women wearing a hijab and prayer groups mushrooming. Suharto recognized this development and performed an Islamic turn in the late 1980s: he went on the hajj pilgrimage for the first time and made more room for Islamic interests in his regime. By the time of his fall in 1998, therefore, Islamic groups of various orientations were well-positioned to play a stronger role in politics. In fact, their prospects were better than ever before as the controls Suharto had imposed on them were largely lifted.

As part of this trend, numerous smaller and more conservative Islamic groups were established outside the Muslim mass organizations and parties that some in the Islamic community viewed as too centrist. These smaller groups did not attract the massive following that their mainstream opponents did, but were well organized, connected, and vocal (Hasan 2006; Wilson 2008). They did not shy away from intimidation of other Muslims deemed not pious enough and were often openly hostile toward religious minorities. One such group was FPI, led by Rizieq Shihab. Recall that Rizieq led the Islamist mobilizations of 2016 and 2017, bringing him into conflict with the Widodo government. But even in the decade before that, Rizieq had been a prominent advocate of reopening the ideological debates of the 1950s; most importantly, he asked for Islamic interests to be more formally enshrined in Indonesia's constitution and laws. Surveys showed that about 20 percent of Indonesian Muslims sympathized with FPI and its agenda (Mietzner and Muhtadi 2018). While sympathy for FPI often overlapped with concurrent support for NU and Muhammadiyah, Indonesian politicians felt that they could not ignore the conservative fringes of Islam. This constellation left presidents with two broad choices of how to manage the country's religious right: they could try to accommodate some of its conservative ideas in the hope that this might convince the groups not to sabotage the government; or they could attempt to mobilize the large mainstream groups against their more radical rivals, opening the opportunity to repress the latter.

Under the first scenario, conservative fringe groups gain an amount of influence on presidents that is disproportionate to their size. Yudhoyono tried this approach with some success—but also with damaging consequences for Indonesia's minority protections (more about this later). In applying the second strategy, by contrast, the role of NU and Muhammadiyah becomes crucial, and it gives them much leverage over incumbent presidents. This was the option chosen by Widodo in his post-2016 dealings with Islamic politics. A look at the size of both groups indicates why this choice was appealing. In surveys, roughly 45 percent of Indonesian Muslims profess to be part of the broader "NU family" (Mietzner and Muhtadi 2020, 71). This means that they might not be card-holding members but that someone in their family is; that they married an NU supporter; or that they live near one of NU's boarding schools (which, in turn, form NU's organizational backbone). Thus, about 100 million Indonesians have some ties with NU, giving it—in theory at least—a great influence on society at large. Muhammadiyah, for its part, is much smaller—about 5 percent of Muslims say that they belong to its constituency (Mietzner and Muhtadi 2020, 71). But while NU's community is mostly rural, Muhammadiyah is more urban-based and therefore has better educated, more affluent, and politically connected cadres. Consequently, both groups can grant presidents access to large yet socially diverse Muslim communities to counterbalance more militant religious activists' actions and demands.

Their large followership also gives the two groups immense electoral power. While an electoral recommendation by the organizations' leaderships typically does not produce united voting blocs among their members, presidents and presidential candidates would be ill-advised to antagonize the two movements. As noted, NU had pressured Widodo to pick one of its leaders as his 2019 running mate, and as he was under simultaneous pressure from his party coalition, Widodo obliged. In the election campaign that followed, NU warned its grassroots members that a vote for the president's opponent, Prabowo, would strengthen Islamic hard-liners—that is, NU's adversaries (Aspinall 2019). It is not surprising, then, that significant increases in the president's vote shares in NU's strongholds in Central and East Java secured his re-election (Shofiah and Pepinsky 2019). This pattern in presidential elections is often replicated at the grassroots, where legislative candidates and nominees for the position of governor, district head, or mayor lobby the main Muslim groups for support, especially in the areas in which they are particularly strong. Moreover, many of the groups' cadres have run in elections themselves—mostly through their affiliated parties (PKB and PAN, respectively) but also as candidates of broader party coalitions or more nationalist parties, such as Golkar. The election of the senior NU cadre Khofifah Indar Parawansa in 2018 as governor of East Java was one such example, and her subsequent activism for Widodo's re-election showed her victory's national relevance.

Beyond direct vote mobilization, Islamic groups can provide something at least as valuable: that is, the bestowal of religious legitimacy on presidents and those who want the office. In terms of their faith, Indonesian presidents have predominantly been pragmatic Muslims rather than strict practitioners of Islam (there has never been a non-Muslim president or vice president). While the vast majority of Indonesians are Muslim, their views on what role Islam should play in state organization differ widely, placing candidates with moderate views on the issue in a better electoral spot than those with an exclusivist Islamist agenda. But there is much agreement that the president should be pious, which is seen as an indicator of moral cleanliness (Taufan 2019). Attacks on presidential candidates' religious credentials have been customary in Indonesian elections. During the 1999 and 2004 elections, pictures of Megawati seemingly praying at a Balinese Hindu temple were used to depict her as lacking commitment to the Islamic faith (her father, Sukarno, was half-Balinese). In 2014 and 2019, Widodo had to fight smear campaigns that questioned his devoutness and even suggested that he was the son of a Christian Singaporean Chinese. Religious organizations can offer protection from such attacks (of course, in return for rewards); Megawati and Widodo adopted NU figures as their running mates, with the former failing in 2004 and the latter succeeding in 2019. After having done his job as Widodo's protective shield in all matters of faith, the elderly Ma'ruf Amin was mostly sidelined in the president's second-term government (Peterson 2020b).

Widodo's struggle with the issue of his alleged religious deficiencies had a deep impact on him, and it drove him to lean closer to religious groups than he had intended. When the smear campaign began in the 2014 campaign, he felt the need to appear in the company of Islamic leaders and to display his devoutness publicly. Accompanying Widodo on a campaign trip to Lampung on Sumatra in March 2014, the author asked his staff for permission to photograph the candidate during a stop to pray at a mosque. The staff replied, "we not only give you permission, we *want* you to photograph him. The more pictures of him praying the better. That's the whole point" (interview, Bandar Lampung, March 22, 2014). During another trip to a mosque in Bogor (a town in West Java seen as particularly devout), he mingled with local Islamic leaders, and promised that he would help them to develop their communities. In return, the clerics praised Widodo for his commitment to Islamic causes and certified that, in their view, he was a pious and moral man (notes by the author, Bogor, June 7, 2014). While he initially thought that his 2014 election had settled the issue, the anti-Purnama demonstrations of 2016 and 2017 implicitly re-litigated Widodo's devoutness; once again he felt vulnerable on the religious front. In response, he moved ever closer to NU, culminating in his acceptance of Ma'ruf's 2019 vice presidential nomination and a much more aggressive approach to opponents who attacked him on religious grounds.

For sitting presidents, Islamic groups also hold crucial importance as providers of mass education. NU alone has 16,000 schools and 32,000 *madrasah* (religious schools, often affiliated with a mosque), in which 900,000 teachers instruct about 11 million students (Rohmat and Fahtoni 2017). Similarly, Muhammadiyah runs 4,623 preschools, 2,604 elementary schools, 1,772 junior high schools, 1,143 high schools, and 172 universities (Marnati 2015). With these vast educational networks, the two largest Muslim groups are key pillars of the national education machinery. In organizing national education plans, budgets, and delivery, any government needs to accommodate the expectations of NU and Muhammadiyah. Even slight mistakes by ministers of education in their relationship with the two groups can lead to major political upheaval. In April 2021, Minister of Education Nadiem Makarim was forced to apologize to NU because a historical dictionary edited by his department had not mentioned the founder of NU, Hasyim Asy'ari (Chaterine 2021). Similarly, Muhammadiyah protested in March of the same year that the term "religion" had disappeared from one of the ministry's education planning documents. The background to these attacks was that the young tycoon Nadiem had, unlike many of his predecessors, no ties with NU or Muhammadiyah, and thus attracted regular attacks on his policies from the two groups. As we will discuss in detail below, granting or denying the education ministry to one of the large Islamic groups has been a main instrument for the president to manage them as members of government coalitions.

Consequently, Islamic groups—whether small and radical or large and mainstream—can exercise an immense influence on Indonesian presidents. Fringe groups can develop an amount of power disproportionate to their size by vocally taking center stage in political activism, forcing presidents to respond. They run the risk, however, that presidents may decide to repress or otherwise sideline them by forming alliances with larger organizations that view their smaller rivals as a nuisance. In the longer term, therefore, the two large Muslim mass groups have had a stronger and more durable influence over presidents than their marginal counterparts. Big actors, not the fringe groups, have found themselves regularly represented in cabinet and showered with other material and policy favors. But in order to limit their expectations and impose discipline on them as parts of their alliances, presidents can bring their own powers into the equation, and they usually have done so effectively.

Presidential Power over Muslim Groups

As powerful as Islamic groups are through their societal entrenchment and ability to bestow religious legitimacy, they are attracted to, and feel dependent on, the office of the president as a distributor of resources and policy favors. As mass organizations and educational institutions, NU, Muhammadiyah, and other groups require significant funds to keep their operations running, pay compensation to their staff, and provide economic development opportunities to their members. Thus, the mainstream groups are keen to place their cadres in critical positions of the state, which they can then use to access resources, hire lower-ranking members to fill staff positions and protect their group's policy interests. This tradition began long before Indonesia developed full presidentialism. In the 1950s, under Indonesia's parliamentary democracy, NU (which formed its own political party in 1952) was known in political circles as being primarily interested in the Ministry of Religion as its main reward for participating in government (Fealy 1997). As Wasisto Raharjo Jati formulated, "this [perception] has cult status in a cultural sense—that NU as the largest Muslim organization has the right to occupy the office of minister of religion in a majority Muslim country" (Utomo 2019). Indeed, NU split from a larger Islamic party, Masyumi, in 1952 because in that year, a Muhammadiyah cadre had been appointed minister of religion, outraging the NU community. The post returned to NU a year later. After the end of parliamentary democracy, the authority to appoint ministers of religion shifted from the prime minister to the president, giving the latter a crucial patronage instrument.

But NU has learned to respect (and fear) Indonesian presidents not only as the key to acquiring the Ministry of Religion but also as more general dispensers of rewards and punishment. Under his autocracy, Sukarno gave seats to NU in cabinet and the appointed parliament in return for its recognition of his unconstitutional power grab in 1959 (Fealy 1997). Suharto, for his part, offered a deal to the group in 1984 by which NU would endorse Pancasila as its only organizational foundation, with the state in exchange promising to lift previous restrictions on NU members entering the civil service and on the disbursement of development funds to its boarding schools (Bresnan 1993, 240). This experience had a long-term impact on Wahid, who was NU chairman at the time and the one who arranged the Pancasila deal with Suharto. Reflecting on why he sought the presidency in 1999, Wahid told the author, "the reality is that if you want to shape things, and if you want to do good for NU, you must control the presidency. Those who say otherwise tell you non-sense. Yes, we could just go for the Ministry of Religion as we have done for decades, but what has that brought us? Most NU members are still poor, many are even illiterate. No, to protect NU from what Suharto has done to us (remember all the threats!), and to control where development funds go, we must gain the presidency for ourselves" (interview, Jakarta, August 25, 1999). As noted, Wahid's presidency ended in utter chaos, and his goals for NU remained unfulfilled. But the idea that NU needed to be at least close to the sitting president, and benefit from his or her powers of resource distribution, survived the Wahid presidency.

What the Ministry of Religion has been to NU, the Ministry of Education has been to Muhammadiyah. While far from claiming a monopoly on the post to the same extent as NU has done for the Ministry of Religion, Muhammadiyah has taken great interest in the education portfolio. It first obtained the position in 1948, but post-Suharto presidents in particular have frequently handed the ministry to Muhammadiyah to gain the group's support. With Muhammadiyah's wide network of schools and universities, holding the Ministry of Education allows it to set policies for its institutions and direct funds to them. How important the post is to Muhammadiyah in contemporary Indonesia showed on the rare occasions when it was denied to the group. This was the case in 2019, when Nadiem was appointed minister of education (replacing a Muhammadiyah cadre), and again in 2020, when Widodo offered the post of vice minister to Muhammadiyah's secretary-general, Abdul Mu'ti. Within Muhammadiyah, this offer was seen as an insult and thus declined (Detik 2020). The affront was considered especially hurtful because in the same 2020 cabinet reshuffle, the Ministry of Religion returned to NU after a brief hiatus. Muhammadiyah's disappointment was only slightly moderated by the fact that its previous minister of education, Muhajir Effendi, was made coordinating minister of human development and culture in 2019. While the coordinating ministry technically oversees the Ministry of Education, in reality, the power to move budgets and personnel lies in the core ministry. Hence, as for NU, the power of the president to give or withhold a key ministry is of existential importance to Muhammadiyah.

Outside the ministries of religion and education, NU and Muhammadiyah hope for additional appointments from the president. This may relate to other cabinet posts and senior bureaucratic appointments or lucrative positions in state-owned enterprises. As Nusron Wahid, an NU and Golkar cadre appointed in 2014 by Widodo as chief of the National Agency for the Placement and Protection of Indonesian Migrant Workers (BNP2TKI) explained, "many keep staring at the cabinet posts, but real governance is often happening at the level below them. This is where NU should play" (interview, Canberra, September 19, 2017). Such positions keep leading NU and Muhammadiyah cadres salaried and allow them to address constituency-specific issues. BNP2TKI, for instance, oversees the mechanisms through which mostly lowly educated migrant workers are sent abroad. Many of these workers are women from the rural areas of Central and East Java, NU's strongholds, who take up positions as domestic helpers in the Middle East, Singapore, Hong Kong, or Taiwan (Chan 2018). From Nusron's perspective, the BNP2TKI office (which he held until 2019, when he returned to the DPR) gave him an instrument to protect a major NU constituency and establish himself as a patronage distributor in his community. Unlike his NU colleagues in cabinet, he attracted little public controversy, highlighting below-cabinet-level positions as both important and convenient for Islamic groups interested in exerting quiet influence.

The co-legislative powers of presidents are also highly attractive to Islamic organizations. As the constitution-makers decided in 1945 not to privilege Islam over other religions, and after that decision was confirmed during amendment initiatives in the late 1950s and early 2000s, Islamic groups have to focus on laws and regulations to achieve policy advantages for the Muslim community. There have been many such stipulations, especially since the 1970s. Specific regulations for Muslims exist in marriage and inheritance rules, and laws governing the education sector have increasingly been written with an eye to the interests of Islamic groups. At the end of Widodo's first term, the government and parliament debated a law that would regulate religious education. To uphold religious pluralism, the draft initially aimed to regulate all religions and their educational activities. But Christian churches rejected the draft as an attempt of government intervention into their internal affairs, fearing that their autonomy would be watered down through a law primarily pushed by Islamic groups. Ultimately, the law—passed in September 2019—only regulated Islamic boarding schools, most of which belong to NU. Coming just a few months after Widodo's re-election, the law was widely interpreted as a reward to NU. To be sure, some NU leaders feared, like the churches, that the government might use it to justify increased government intervention in religion. But as the law also promised more government funding for the boarding schools, excitement prevailed in NU (Nurcahyadi 2021).

As in their relations with parties and oligarchs, presidents can leverage their electoral standing in negotiations with Muslim organizations. We noted that most Indonesian presidents have been Muslim pragmatists who can appeal to all religious constituencies. In other words, while Muslim organizations are instrumental in organizing votes for presidents, in Indonesia's post-2004 system of direct elections, they would find it hard to win the presidency for themselves. This is because the Muslim community is politically divided, and because the voting bloc of religious minorities (which makes up 13 percent of the electorate) is a crucial swing vote that can decide the outcome of tight races. Widodo's 2019 campaign, for instance, not only attracted the support of NU followers but also secured almost the entire religious minority vote. By contrast, NU's Wahid was only able to win the presidency in 1999 through backroom machinations in the MPR; he would not have been competitive in a direct election as he was deeply unpopular in non-NU segments of the Muslim community. Similarly, former Muhammadiyah chair Amien Rais, who was detested in NU, finished fourth in the 2004 elections. As a result of these vulnerabilities, Islamic groups have since settled on associating with the candidate they think is most likely to win—and on joining the latter's coalition once in office. In the post-2004 polity, then, the lack of personal electoral popularity is the greatest weakness of Islamic leaders, and its abundance is the biggest strength of pragmatists who can bridge constituency divides. Both Yudhoyono and Widodo exploited this constellation masterfully.

Smaller, more radical Islamic groups are even more dependent on presidents to give them access to state resources and positions than their mainstream rivals. Groups such as the FPI successfully made their voices heard in societal discourses; however, they found it difficult to penetrate political institutions monopolized by the established elite. We discussed the various thresholds that make it hard for non-mainstream groups to establish parties, enter parliament, or nominate one of theirs for the presidency. As a result, for all the attention Rizieq Shihab received for his advocacy of a greater role for Islam in state affairs, and as much as he flirted with the idea of his presidential candidacy (Damarjati 2018), he and his group are highly unlikely to ever make it into the palace. Other groups, such as HTI, even declined to turn themselves into political parties or to participate in presidential elections (Ward 2009)—largely for ideological reasons but also in recognition of their marginal chances. For them, attaching themselves to a mainstream candidate in exchange for policy concessions is the only way of having an impact in a political system favoring the catch-all establishment. Hence, the vast majority of hard-line Islamic groups associated with Prabowo in the 2014 and 2019 elections, hoping his victory would open the door to state privileges. While Prabowo came close to winning twice, eventually his affiliation with FPI and other radical Muslim groups scared away mainstream voters and sealed his defeat on both ballots. Without protection from the president they opposed, and having triggered his hostility, both FPI and HTI found themselves banned after Widodo's re-election.

In sum, presidents can use their appointment powers, legislative and budgetary authority, and electoral popularity to induce (or coerce) mainstream Islamic groups into their coalitions. The debacle of the Wahid presidency, in which an NU leader briefly held the presidency, further consolidated the view within large Muslim groups that forming an alliance with a cross-constituency president is the best way for them to exert influence. As Cholil Bisri, a senior NU and PKB leader, expressed in despair after Wahid's fall, "[Wahid] was a disappointment as president, for NU and Indonesia; we should have voted for Megawati [in 1999]" (interview, Jakarta, August 11, 2002). The selection of Ma'ruf Amin as Widodo's running mate in 2019 reflected this approach, giving NU access to state powers without exposing it to the political upheaval that presidents have to manage. In the case of radical groups, presidents can bring similar powers to bear, but tensions between the two sides can have even more existential consequences for small actors than for big groups. In addition to threatening radical groups with exclusion from state power, presidents can use their repressive authority to disband them, as HTI and FPI experienced. With Muslim groups (of both moderate or radical orientations) and presidents possessing significant powers vis-à-vis each other, the management of this relationship becomes essential. Its integration into the architecture of coalitional presidentialism has been the logical result of this necessity.

Presidents and Muslim Groups

Holding ministries of crucial importance to them is arguably the primary lens through which NU and Muhammadiyah view their relationship with presidents. For presidents, therefore, offering or denying ministries is a key instrument in managing the involvement of these Muslim groups in their coalitions. In this regard, calculating how many ministers in cabinet belong to which group is a matter of constant contestation. The president tends to use a broad definition of who is a member of a specific Muslim group to signal that its representation in cabinet is high. Conversely, the organization in question likes to apply a narrow understanding of membership to downplay its representation and ask for more. Several factors complicate this calculation. In addition to how to define "membership" (presidents normally consider family backgrounds, while organizations not only insist on formal card-holding membership but also on an endorsement by the group to represent it in cabinet), there is also the overlap between NU and Muhammadiyah, on the one side, and their respective parties, on the other. As noted, NU has a close relationship with PKB, and the latter's cadres are typically members of the former. Similarly, Muhammadiyah played a leading role in creating PAN, and this historic connection remains strong today. Accordingly, at the center of Islamic groups' role in coalitional presidentialism in Indonesia is the question of how many, and who specifically, among their leaders get invited to share power with the president in cabinet.

Some of these debates over cabinet representation are held behind closed doors, but they are occasionally displayed publicly. This is because both sides want to communicate their interpretation of the current coalition arrangement to voters and, in the case of Islamic groups, their followers. In June 2016, Widodo claimed at a public event that at least six cabinet members represented NU. "I want to clarify the issue of NU ministers," Widodo said, addressing indications of NU dissatisfaction with its level of cabinet representation. "A few moments ago, I quietly counted, there are six. So there is [a lot of] NU (Toriq 2016a)." But speaking to the media, NU deputy chair Marsudi Syuhud offered a vastly different calculation. He insisted that four PKB ministers not be counted as NU representatives, and he described the then-minister of social affairs, Khofifah Indar Parawansa, as a member of Widodo's 2014 campaign team, not of NU. This was despite the fact that Khofifah headed NU's women's organization Muslimat. "There is nobody from NU headquarters," Syuhud concluded, using the narrowest definition to claim low NU representation in cabinet. In the same event, Widodo stated, "since the Muhammadiyah chair didn't ask, I didn't count" (Toriq 2016b). In a later public commentary, Muhammadiyah turned this remark into an advantage: unlike the greedy NU, it implied, Muhammadiyah left the appointment of ministries to the president. While not entirely accurate (Muhammadiyah has clear expectations toward its representation, too), Muhammadiyah's reaction pointed to cabinet representation not only as an issue of contestation between the two large Muslim groups, on the one hand, and the president, on the other, but also between the organizations.

Presidents often opt to adjust the cabinet representation of Islamic groups to their changing strategic challenges. In Widodo's case, for instance, his dependence on the two Islamic groups increased significantly following the anti-Purnama mobilization in late 2016. After the first big protest, he immediately visited NU and Muhamadiyah to seek protection but was told in both cases that he had neglected them. According to palace assistants, Widodo was particularly taken aback by NU chair Said Aqil Siraj's remark that the president had failed to deliver "*barokah*" to NU—which broadly means "blessings," but is often understood to have a material meaning (confidential interview, Jakarta, November 24, 2016). The president's aides conceded, however, that during his first two years in office, Widodo had viewed courting the two groups in non-election times as not essential, believing that his task was to focus on day-to-day governance. "We dropped the ball on this, to be honest. And now we have to make up for that," they promised (confidential interview, Jakarta, February 8, 2017). This constellation eventually led to Widodo accepting an NU leader as his 2019 running mate. We already noted that his first choice was Mahfud MD, who had been nominated as presidential candidate of the NU-affiliated PKB in 2014. Widodo told polling advisers that Mahfud, in his view, had it all: "he's popular, decent, a professor and part of the NU crowd" (confidential interview, online, August 7, 2018). But he failed to coordinate this selection with NU headquarters, which then forced Ma'ruf Amin on him, with the help of anti-Mahfud parties in Widodo's coalition. Despite these irritations, the appointment of NU's spiritual head to the ticket formalized Widodo's alliance with NU, and the latter fought for him accordingly.

But just as presidents use the offer of important cabinet posts to purchase the support of Muslim groups, chief executives also weaponize the withholding of such posts to enforce discipline. After Widodo's re-election in 2019, which was partly due to NU's involvement in the campaign, there were expectations in the organization that the next cabinet would reflect NU's contribution to the president's victory. At an NU event in East Java in June 2019, one senior NU figure shouted into the crowd: "There is no political support that comes free of charge!," while another openly asked for "strategic cabinet posts" (Andriansyah 2019). In the same vein, one NU group explicitly demanded the Ministry of Religion, once again reminding the president how much he owed NU (Muhyiddin 2019). But faced with this pressure, Widodo feared that if he gave in to all demands, he would give NU a disproportionate amount of power and thus see his own authority reduced. No doubt, he was also still angered by NU's manipulative intimidation of him over Ma'ruf's nomination in 2018. In consequence, to remind NU of who was in charge, he broke with post-2004 tradition and gave the post of minister of religion to a retired military officer, Fachrul Razi. In a classic example of how presidents balance the various groups to sustain the architecture of coalitional presidentialism, Widodo had decided to show NU its limits and fill the slot with a representative of another group instead. NU's reaction was swift. One senior leader said that Widodo could be "cursed" for not picking an NU cadre as minister of religion, as that position was "non-negotiable" for the group (Indana 2019). After one year, Widodo returned the position to NU, and thus both sides had made their point: the president reconfirmed his authority, and NU the influence of its pressure.

Presidents have also exploited their budgetary and co-legislative powers at politically opportune times to attract or reward Islamic groups as partners in their coalition. Before the 2019 elections, the Widodo government launched financial initiatives benefitting NU. Aziz Anwar Fachrudin (2019) listed these projects with great precision. First, funds from the National Zakat Agency

(Baznas) were directed between 2017 and 2019 to forty-one Institutes for Syariah Micro-Finance (LKMS) attached to NU boarding schools. Second, Widodo told the Ministry of Manpower and Transmigration to create Vocational Training Centres (BLK) in Islamic boarding schools; there were 500 such centers as of March 2019. With the elections approaching, Widodo promised to build 1,000 more in 2019. Third, NU's central board was made a partner in a corn production program run by the Ministry for Agriculture. Fourth, NU received Rupiah 1.5 trillion (US$107 million) in credit from the Ministry of Finance for various micro-credit programs. Finally, in 2018, the Ministry of Finance's Agency for Education Fund Management (LPDP) launched the "Santri Scholarship" scheme, providing scholarships for students affiliated with NU and other Islamic groups.[1] After the elections, as noted, the law on Islamic boarding schools was passed. It included a stipulation on an eternal endowment, which is why NU had been attracted to the law in the first place. When Widodo signed the relevant implementing regulation in September 2021, NU welcomed the decree but complained that it did not include a concrete number (Syakir 2021). NU wanted this number to be 20 percent of the government's total education fund, or about Rp 14 trillion (US$1 billion).

While presidents manage the coalition membership of large Islamic groups through appointments, budgetary favors, and legislative benefits, they find the handling of smaller and more radical organizations to be more complex and fluctuating. At various points of his presidency, Yudhoyono believed that such groups needed to be accommodated to prevent "chaos." To the author, he explained his approach by citing how he dealt with the demand by radical Islamic groups to disband Ahmadiyah, a small Muslim sect that views its India-born founder Mirza Ghulām Ahmad as a prophet who appeared as the promised Messiah. In the late 2000s, FPI and affiliated groups attacked several Ahmadiyah mosques, putting pressure on the government to respond. Yudhoyono said that "if you have one mosque with 5,000 followers, and then next to it an Ahmadiyah mosque with 100 followers, and the first says Muhammad is the [Prophet] but the other one says he's not, then it's almost certain that there will be a clash" (interview, Cikeas, December 2, 2014). Although Indonesia's constitution guarantees freedom of religion, for Yudhoyono the need to avoid "chaos" is supreme. Thus, he suggested, if the radical Islamist groups want a ban on Ahmadiyah and "human rights groups" demand that it be allowed to operate freely, the president's task is to find a middle way. In 2008, therefore, Yudhoyono's government issued a decree that effectively forced Ahmadiyah to cease open operations without banning it. Most radical groups were pleased with this result, cementing their belief that Yudhoyono was not an ideal but acceptable president for them.

Widodo, by contrast, took first a passive and then primarily repressive approach to radical Islamic groups—while absorbing some of their conservatism to bolster his religious credentials. In the 2014 campaign, radical Islamic groups had decried Widodo as a "troublemaker and bringer of disasters" (Dunia Muallaf 2014)—because, for them, he embodied advocacy for secularism and liberalism (the latter being a particularly wrong perception). When Widodo took office, he initially ignored his adversaries; he did not try to accommodate them as Yudhoyono had done but did not see the need to actively repress them either. This all changed with the anti-Purnama mobilization of 2016 and 2017. To take a harder line vis-à-vis radical Islamists, he sought a closer alliance with NU and Muhammadiyah, knowing that repressing FPI and others would lead to more accusations of him being anti-Islamic. In other words, he strengthened the Muslim mainstream flank of his presidential coalition to move against radical groups that had previously operated within the parameters of coalitional presidentialism but that now, in Widodo's view, needed to be excluded. The bans of HTI in 2017 and of FPI in 2020 constituted the climax of this exclusionary and repressive strategy, but many other actions also fed into what Fealy (2020) called Widodo's "repressive pluralism." Universities and the civil service were asked to remove staff deemed to be close to conservative Islamic groups, and even the KPK sacked investigators who failed a nationalism test in 2021. At the same time, Widodo pointed to his conservative but still mainstream vice president Ma'ruf Amin as evidence of his continued piety.

Hence, the day-to-day management of Islamic groups as presidential coalition partners depends on their importance to the head of state at specific political junctures. When presidents feel that Islamic organizations can increase their electoral chances or consolidate their political legitimacy, funds and positions are promised or directly delivered to secure their loyalty. If, by contrast, presidents sense a greater level of stability in their position and want to warn Islamic groups not to become overly ambitious, these funds and positions are reduced, temporarily withheld, or adjusted. With this, the presidents' approach to Islamic groups is similar to that used to keep other coalition partners in line, but the political sensitivity of Islam in Indonesia gives this relationship a distinct flavor. The fact that Widodo integrated the large Muslim groups into his coalition but repressed the radical fringe that Yudhoyono still courted is an additional feature making the management of Islamic actors more multi-layered than other groups. In order to analyze in more detail how presidents and Muslim actors negotiate their vested interests within the context of coalitional presidentialism, the next section focuses on the abovementioned bans of HTI and FPI. Of particular interest here are the mechanisms through which both the president and NU pursued their various agendas, and exploited each other in the process.

Widodo, NU, and the Fight against Islamism

Recall that at the beginning of the anti-Purnama demonstrations in late 2016, NU was dissatisfied with the extent of its participation in Widodo's coalition. It felt that it did not have enough cabinet seats (which Widodo denied); it complained about not receiving sufficient material benefits (which Widodo acknowledged); and it sensed that its role as Indonesia's largest Muslim organization was overlooked. But the president's acute awareness of his vulnerability as a result of the anti-Purnama movement (at one point, an Islamist mob threatened to storm the palace) led to a significant recalibration of the relationship between NU and the head of state (Faturokhman (2016). Widodo recognized that he needed to engage NU to address the impression that he was ignorant of the ambitions of Muslim activists. He knew that asking NU for assistance would benefit him *and* come at a high cost. NU, for its part, viewed the new constellation as an opportunity to not only demand more positions and funds for its constituency from the president but also to settle bills with some of its old rivals in the struggle for hegemony over Indonesia's fragmented Muslim community. It was clear to NU leaders that Widodo now owed them for their support, and that he shared their interest in moving against groups at the fringe of the Islamic spectrum that NU had long perceived as a disturbance. In short, the post-2016 political landscape aligned in a way that increased NU's strategic value to the president and produced an overlap in the interests of both actors.

On the top of NU's list of organizational adversaries in the Muslim community was the Indonesian branch of Hizbut Tahrir (HTI). HTI believed that Islamic scripture demanded the establishment of a caliphate, and that participating in secular political arrangements such as democracy was in violation of God's will (Ward 2009). Thus, HTI possessed a truly revolutionary agenda, but at the same time, it did not condone violence to achieve its goals. Instead, it asked its cadres to infiltrate universities, mosques, state institutions, and other societal structures to trigger a religious movement both from below and the top. NU felt especially vulnerable to HTI's infiltration attempts. This was partly because NU, too, had long struggled to conceptually reconcile the pluralist Indonesian polity with the idealist idea of an Islamic state. It was only able to do so by referring to those parts of the scripture that allow for pragmatism benefitting the Muslim community. In this context, some NU cadres on the more conservative end of the Islamic spectrum were attracted to HTI's message, which appeared to them purer and less calculating than NU's centrism developed through decades of nationalist activism. NU leaders also suspected that HTI targeted NU for its recruitment because of the mass organization's influence in the state and society, which offered HTI an entry point for rapid expansion (Mustaqim 2019).

Consequently, even before the anti-Purnama mobilization began, segments in NU had aggressively moved against HTI and asked the state to ban it. In April 2016, local NU leaders disbanded an HTI event promoting the caliphate in Tangerang, a city close to Jakarta. The spiritual leader of Tangerang's NU branch gave a fierce speech during NU's protest, requesting that the state withdraw HTI's operating license: "we ask the state to take action on this. The local office for political affairs and the police must be pro-active in this regard. We are loyal to the state, and therefore we are giving our blood and soul to the state. Organizations such as HTI should not be given a license of any kind, as it has clearly offended the dignity of the nation and the state. They have already insulted the founding fathers of this nation, and that is the same as insulting us, the NU community" (Arrahmah News 2016). Another NU speaker called the HTI ideology "treason" [*makar*], an accusation that in Indonesia would attract heavy-handed penalties and cause the organization involved to be dissolved. The orator, a deputy chair in one of NU's educational institutions, promised to protect "mosques from being infiltrated by treasonous ideology." Similar demands for HTI's ban were made in Jombang, East Java, in May 2016 (NU Online 2016). Accordingly, well before Widodo thought about banning any Islamic organization (knowing that this would add to accusations that he was anti-Islamic), the discourse of banning HTI was already underway in NU and its affiliates.

As the anti-Purnama demonstrations unfolded (they stretched from November 2016 to mid-2017), the issue of HTI's ban became part of the negotiations between the palace and NU over their recalibrated relationship. While Widodo's assistants developed a package of new material concessions to NU—which was rolled out between 2017 and the elections of 2019—NU leaders kept proposing that the president take firm action against HTI. Initially skeptical, Widodo warmed up to the idea. As the president could be certain of NU's strong support, disbanding HTI would not carry a large risk of damaging his Islamic credentials. Furthermore, although HTI was vocal, it was less popular than FPI, for instance. In a 2017 opinion poll (LSI 2017), only 32 percent of Muslim respondents declared that they had heard of HTI, and of those, a mere 14 percent supported its agenda. Overall, only 4 percent of Indonesian Muslims sympathized with HTI. In FPI's case, 69 percent of Muslim respondents stated that they had heard of it, and 39 percent of those held sympathies for it—meaning that 27 percent of Muslims had a positive view of FPI. Against this background, banning HTI promised to a) send a signal of the president's political toughness to the Islamist fringe, b) satisfy NU's demands and thus tie it even closer to the government, and

c) not pose a serious risk to Widodo personally as HTI had few friends among its fellow Muslim groups or in society at large.

From April 2017, then, it was evident that "NU leaders collaborated with the palace to create conditions that enabled the government to act against HTI" (Fealy 2018). From NU's side, its youth organization staged more events of the kind already seen in 2016: it appeared at HTI events, protested, and asked the police to disband them. The police, in most cases, happily obliged. Meanwhile, Widodo asked his chief security minister, Wiranto, to prepare the mechanism to ban HTI. Eventually, it was decided to issue a government regulation in lieu of law (Perpu) that would allow the government to ban any societal organization without a court order—which previously had been required by a relevant 2013 law on mass organizations. Teten Masduki, Widodo's then-chief of staff, insisted that this was done because "we just can't trust the courts. You've seen how corrupt they are. We needed to do this quickly" (interview, Jakarta, July 20, 2017). In May, Wiranto announced that the Perpu would be used to disband HTI because its teachings violated the constitution and Pancasila, and because its activities provoked public unrest. As expected, NU immediately came out in support of the government's ban, with its chairman Said Aqil Siradj saying that HTI could create disunity, conflict, and even civil war in Indonesia (Gual 2017). At last, NU's long-standing campaign against HTI had succeeded, and while in the past it had feared that HTI might recruit its members, it now openly invited former HTI members to join NU (Kumparan 2018).

Three and a half years later, Widodo again moved to ban a radical fringe group, the FPI. This time, however, it appeared that the president and his aides, rather than NU, drove the initiative to outlaw FPI. To be sure, NU had suggested banning FPI several times, but there had been signs of reconciliation with its chairman Rizieq after the 2019 elections (Detik 2019a). Widodo, by contrast, continued to view Rizieq as a substantial threat to his presidency. Rizieq had led the anti-Purnama demonstrations, and even from exile, he had mobilized conservative Islamic voters for Prabowo in 2019. Indeed, Prabowo's biggest campaign event in Jakarta was largely organized by FPI networks and featured a video appearance by Rizieq himself (Aspinall 2019). Hence, when Rizieq returned to Jakarta to an enthusiastic airport welcome by his supporters in November 2020 (after rejecting government conditions that he refrain from politics), Widodo was alarmed. We already noted that the police began to systematically pursue Rizieq for violations of social mobility restrictions during the COVID-19 pandemic. Gradually increasing the repression, the police killed six of Rizieq's bodyguards in December before arresting him and banning FPI later in the month. The government accused FPI of violating the principles of Pancasila but also, controversially, of being involved in terrorism (the evidence for this was sketchy at best). With Rizieq's later imprisonment on pandemic-related charges and FPI outlawed, Widodo's most prominent opponent—after Prabowo's entry into government—was removed from the political scene.[2] The president was visibly relieved.

NU dutifully supported FPI's ban, but unlike in the case of HTI, it did not seem as if it was included in its planning. As a result, its expressions of loyalty sounded less powerful than in 2017. One NU spokesman said that the government could not be accused of Islamophobia because "more than eighty" other Muslim organizations were still allowed to exist (Kurniawan 2021). He also suggested that FPI only had to submit more paperwork to the government to have its legal status re-instated (Yusuf 2020)—a massive misreading of Widodo's determination to permanently paralyze the organization. Nevertheless, NU's backing of the ban helped Widodo to make it palatable to society. Surveys showed that about 60 percent of citizens who were aware of FPI's ban approved of it, and that FPI's favorability ratings were dropping considerably (Fealy and White 2021). In brief, while the president had helped NU get rid of HTI as part of his initiative to integrate NU more firmly into his coalition, NU leaders returned the favor in 2020 when Widodo was keen to neutralize his strongest adversary. The two incidents highlighted how coalitional presidentialism allows presidents and their allies to exploit each other to protect their respective realms of power. As long as both parties view this constellation as beneficial to them, the presidential coalition is preserved. In the Indonesian case, dissatisfaction on either side typically does not lead to the dissolution of the alliance but rather to its recalibration. Unhappy with its coalition privileges in 2016, NU was given a better deal but had to offer stronger support in return. With both sides satisfied, Indonesia's regime of coalitional presidentialism marched on.

As the world's largest Muslim-majority country, it is not surprising that Indonesia has seen high levels of involvement by Islamic actors in politics. Unlike in many countries of Europe or Latin America, the role of religion in politics in Indonesia has not decreased but increased, partly due to rising piety in public life. This constellation has pressured Indonesian presidents to accommodate Islamic interests in their coalitions to win elections and sustain their postelection alliances. Some of this accommodation has occurred through the channels suggested by the traditional coalitional presidentialism school: that is, through political parties. PKB, PAN, and, to a lesser extent, PPP have played a key role in facilitating the coalition arrangements between presidents on the one side and NU and Muhammadiyah on the other. But as the 2016 dispute over the level of NU representation in cabinet showed, such party avenues are insufficient to satisfy the expectations of the large Islamic organizations. Their relationship with their respective parties has fluctuated over time—under the NU chairmanship of Hasyim Muzadi (1999–2010), for instance, NU and PKB were estranged. As a result, the Muslim groups want their own cabinet representation, funds, and benefits. Put differently, they wish to be treated as coalition partners outside of the party arena. Demonstrably, this is exactly what post-2004 presidents have done, and Widodo's strong relationship with NU after 2016 embodied the kind of coalition arrangement sought by Islamic actors. As NU was showered with material favors, and its spiritual leader became vice president in 2019, NU felt sufficiently appreciated to support the president's causes.

We have also ascertained that the expanded framework of coalitional presidentialism gives presidents strong tools to keep Islamic groups in check and to punish them for disloyalty or excessive expectations. Just when NU thought after the 2019 elections that Widodo had become dependent on its protection, the president took away its most prized possession: the Ministry of Religion. At the same time, he removed the Ministry of Education from Muhammadiyah's control. With these moves, the president reaffirmed his status as the primary actor in the coalition, demonstrating that Islamic groups were only one among many coalition partners. Tellingly, the Ministry of Religion went to the military and the Ministry of Education to an oligarch. Subsequent events then showed how the contractual details underpinning coalitional presidentialism are constantly renegotiated: the Ministry of Religion returned to NU after a year, and Muhammadiyah rejected the offer to occupy the position of vice minister of education. With rotations and offers such as this, presidents fuel the inter-actor rivalry that is so important to maintain the architecture of coalitional presidentialism. There is little that a president fears more than a situation in which all coalition partners unite against him or her. Such occurrences are rare, but Widodo got a taste of this when all political parties in the coalition, plus NU and some oligarchs, rebelled against his initial choice of vice president in 2018. As in many other political arenas, divide et impera is a core principle of coalitional presidentialism, keeping presidential allies on their toes and the president in the center of power.

The fragmented nature of Indonesian Islam has given presidents ample opportunities to use intra-Islamic and inter-religious rivalries to their advantage. Faced with a challenge by small but influential hard-line Islamic groups, Widodo turned to the larger organizations (and, in elections, to non-Muslim groups) for help. With this move, Widodo overturned Yudhoyono's long-standing approach of trying to have everyone, from Islamic radicals to mainstream Muslims and non-Muslims, in his presidential tent. This difference in approaches explains why Widodo never reached the 60 percent vote share that Yudhoyono won in 2004 and 2009 (Widodo won 53 percent in 2014 and 55 percent in 2019), and why his margins of victory were significantly smaller. It also explains why radical groups, excluded from presidential favors after Yudhoyono, rose against Widodo in 2016, and why they were subsequently repressed. Hence, while Widodo and Yudhoyono used similar patterns of coalitional presidentialism, their specific balancing of the various groups differed, and nowhere more so than in the management of Islamist fringe groups. Coalitional presidentialism, therefore, is not a static concept in which every actor is assured of his or her privileges. On the contrary, it is a dynamic system of distributing power in which all sides must continually reassess their position and lobby for adjustments if necessary. In Indonesia, the absence of impeachment proceedings or incumbency losses since 2004 suggests that this system has worked well for sitting presidents and most of their allies. Whether it has worked for the quality of Indonesian democracy, however, is an entirely different matter.

Conclusion

DRIVERS AND CONTEXTS

Having analyzed how Indonesian presidents use coalitional presidentialism strategies to integrate a wide variety of actors into their alliances, we now need to reflect on the key findings of this book and what they mean for our understanding of presidential politics, both in Indonesia and globally. The main puzzle that led us to investigate post-2004 presidentialism in Indonesia was its remarkable transformation from a previously feeble polity that conformed to Linz's prediction of unworkability into one of the most stable presidential systems in the world. This transformation was not accompanied by increasing democratic stability, however; instead, it produced growing illiberalism. Thus, in a first concluding reflection, we need to summarize the steps that post-2004 Indonesian presidents took to stabilize their rule. The book found that many of the tools the coalitional presidentialism school had described in other cases were used with great effect in the Indonesian context, while other instruments were also added. This condensed portrayal of how Indonesian presidents have secured their longevity in government (and their untouchability after leaving it) builds the foundations for a more penetrating analysis of its deeper layers and contexts.

One of these contexts relates to the question of Indonesian exceptionalism in coalitional presidentialism studies. This book has established that Indonesian presidents have gone beyond the traditional parameters of coalitional presidentialism (that is, the party and legislative arenas) to situate non-party actors as members of their coalition in the same way they deal with parties. The strategies used to accomplish this are similar to those applied to parties. But to what extent can the Indonesian case serve as a generalizable example? There is no doubt that the Indonesian case is an extraordinary example of a broad-based system of coalitional presidentialism, both in terms of the number of actors included and the stability it created. Other polities, especially in Latin America, have used narrower approaches and have seen more instability (mostly in the form of impeachments) as a result (Pérez-Liñán and Polga-Hecimovich 2017). But it is also clear that, similar to Indonesia, many other countries have a significant percentage of non-party coalition representation by key actors that have thus far been understudied in coalitional presidentialism scholarship. The military is one such actor, especially in Latin America and parts of Asia, but others are equally important. Separating Indonesian exceptionalism from more commonly found patterns will therefore be a major task of this concluding chapter.

We also need to ask why Indonesian presidentialism has developed the way it did after 2004. It is worth re-emphasizing that between 1998 and 2004, one president stepped down (Suharto), one was effectively removed by the MPR (Habibie), one was impeached (Wahid), and yet another lost re-election (Megawati). Therefore, the pattern of impeachment-free rule and big-margin re-election victories is a post-2004 narrative, with all the advantages and drawbacks this entails. But what explains this change? The enactment of constitutional amendments in 2002 and their coming into full operation in 2004 are primary candidates to explain the stability of post-transition coalitional presidentialism. However, there are strong reasons to be skeptical of a purely institutionalist explanation. Indonesian presidents, it seems, were more fearful of impeachment than the institutional framework for such removals would allow for; in other words, they did not need to accommodate their partners so strongly, and did not have to target so many, as the barriers for impeachment are extraordinarily high. Accordingly, we need to consider other explanations. For instance, we have to look at how the presidents' governance approach was shaped by the experiences of their predecessors. Yudhoyono was influenced by Wahid's fall, while Widodo adopted Yudhoyono's strategies once his promise of ignoring them had become difficult to fulfill. There are also deep-seated ideational justifications for the coalitional presidentialism approach that should not be dismissed outright despite their self-serving nature.

Finally, and returning to the damaging effects of the stability coalitional presidentialism has guaranteed, we need to appraise the link between coalitional presidentialism and the degree of democratic quality. For the Indonesian case, this requires unpacking the concurrence of strengthening coalitional presidentialism, on the one hand, and democratic decline, on the other (Power and Warburton 2020). This does not mean that coalitional presidentialism is inherently bad for democracy, however. Indonesia's all-time peak of democratic quality occurred in the early Yudhoyono period between 2004 and 2008. It was in subsequent years that democracy first experienced signs of stagnation and, eventually, recession. This suggests that the *degree* of coalitional presidentialism (that is, the broadness of coalitions and the level of determination of presidents to hold them together) is key to identifying the tipping point after which it turns from an asset of democracy into a liability. At its most intense in Indonesia, during Widodo's second term, coalitional presidentialism suffocated the previously more competitive political society, producing illiberalism both at the top and at the grassroots. At the same time, it is important to distinguish Indonesia's coalitional presidentialism from presidential autocracies—there remain crucial elements of democratic openness not seen in the latter. While Indonesia is slowly moving away from the (never particularly realistic) Western ideal of a liberal democracy, it is also far away from transforming into an authoritarian polity of the kind found in Russia, for example.

This concluding chapter discusses these points in four sections. The first summarizes the book's findings, emphasizing the strategies both presidents and their partners use to sustain their coalition. The treatment of the various actors differs somewhat based on their respective powers vis-à-vis the president, but it is possible to identify a set of common approaches. The second section offers a comparative perspective, revisiting the question of how the Indonesian case fits into the larger framework of global coalitional presidentialism studies. In the third section, we analyze the drivers behind the specific format of Indonesia's coalitional presidentialism, while the fourth assesses its impact on the quality of democracy in the country. Overall, the discussion finds that coalitional presidentialism is behind Indonesia's remarkable political stability since 2004 as well as its later illiberal tendencies. The fact that most citizens appear to approve of these trends is further testimony of coalitional presidentialism's deep entrenchment in post-Suharto Indonesia.

Key Findings

This book has found that within a decade, Indonesia moved from one extreme of the "stability of presidentialism spectrum" to the other. In the transitional period following Suharto's fall in 1998, Indonesia seemed to conform to all the instability features Linz had ascribed to multi-party presidentialism. Parties in the MPR effectively ended Habibie's presidency in 1999; put in place a president (Wahid) whose party had only won 12 percent of the vote; and impeached him in 2001 when he fell out with his coalition. Subsequently, key parties deserted Wahid's successor, Megawati, in the 2004 direct presidential elections, contributing to her defeat and Indonesia recording five presidents in six years (McIntyre

2005). After 2004, however, the picture changed dramatically, and Indonesia experienced a level of formal stability in its presidential system that Mainwaring had predicted was possible and that Chaisty, Cheeseman, and Power had declared a new trend. Yudhoyono and Widodo ruled without any impeachment proceedings; served two terms after winning re-election with significant margins; and oversaw periods of stable economic growth—only interrupted by the pandemic—and low levels of communal upheaval. And most Indonesians seem to approve not only of their presidents' performance but also of the system overall. In August 2019, before the COVID-19 pandemic, 69 percent of Indonesians were satisfied with the way democracy was practiced (Ariyanti 2019), and while this level declined somewhat in the middle of the pandemic, consistently more than half of the citizenry remained satisfied.[1]

When putting together and sustaining their coalitions, Indonesian presidents have used the five tools of coalitional presidentialism identified by Chaisty, Cheeseman, and Power (2017), but they have also added other instruments and important nuances. Most significantly, they have directed these tools not only at parties in the legislature—as Chaisty and colleagues suggest—but also at a variety of other socio-political actors. We established that these actors are not veto powers in the traditional Tsebelian sense, but hold powers that presidents *believe* could be used against them. This book has demonstrated, for instance, how Indonesian presidents have used their co-legislative powers (the first tool of coalitional presidentialism listed by Chaisty, Cheeseman, and Power) to entice political actors, party-based and otherwise, into their coalitions. While parties and parliaments are most directly concerned with legislation as the president's co-legislative partners, the products of this process concern other actors as well. The military has been anxious about legislation that could take away more of its traditional authorities; the police would like to gain some of the latter; bureaucrats wish to prevent legislative reforms to their standing; local government heads have a fundamental interest in upholding existing decentralization legislation; the oligarchs want laws that meet their interests in achieving lower labor costs and obtaining licensing privileges; and Islamic groups rely on legislation to defend the role of Islam in politics and to receive financial support from the state. This web of interests gives presidents ample opportunities to use their legislative influence as coalition-sustaining leverage.

The second instrument in the traditional toolbox of coalitional presidentialism, namely that of partisan powers, is less prominent in the Indonesian context. This power normally describes a president's authority over his or her own party, which is then used as an asset in political negotiations. In Indonesia, by contrast, presidents benefitted most when parties other than their own became close allies—and the latter often did so not because of the *strength* of the president's partisan powers but because of their *weakness*. Yudhoyono, for example, exercised strong control over his party, but as it only had won 7 percent of the votes in 2004, this mattered little in terms of establishing a dominating position in the political system. His coalition only stabilized after Golkar, the largest party, entered the coalition via a friendly takeover by Yudhoyono's vice president. Widodo, for his part, was a member of the largest party (that is, PDI-P) but had marginal influence over it. He, too, relied on other parties to bring stability to his alliance. Indeed, he used these parties to contain the influence of PDI-P, and he ultimately emerged as the controlling figure atop a pyramid of competing political parties, all vying for his attention. Keeping inter-party rivalry alive, then, was critical to Widodo's dominance over the party-based side of coalitional presidentialism. As noted, he feared nothing more than a scenario in which all parties, including his own, united against him, as in the 2018 vice presidential nomination. Such cases remained scarce, with Widodo successfully fending off one party's specific demands by pointing to contravening interests of others.

The president's appointment powers are also crucial in the Indonesian case, but go well beyond the cabinet. Indonesia's tradition of reserving around half of the cabinet seats for non-party figures, developed under authoritarianism and sustained after 1998, has given presidents room to make concessions to non-party members of their coalition. Military and police figures, bureaucrats, local government heads, oligarchs, and members of Islamic organizations have all been invited to join cabinet, tying their institutions to the presidential alliance. Below the cabinet level, presidents have used their authority over many other positions to reward loyalists and punish defectors. Presidents can appoint military and police leaders close to them and ask them to ensure the loyalty of their subordinates; presidents possess, and have gradually expanded, the right to intervene in bureaucratic appointment processes, allowing them to install loyal civil servants; presidents can appoint acting local government heads in specific situations, and pull others into cabinet; presidents can give big oligarchs ministries and smaller ones side jobs in the administration; and presidents have satisfied Islamic groups with cabinet posts and lower-level appointments alike. Presidents' juggling of these positions, both as an inducement and as a threat to their partners, has been a major element in the dynamic negotiation between heads of state and their coalitional allies. As illustrated in the case of NU, the number and importance of positions are constantly re-calibrated—as is the definition of who counts as a representative of which political organization.

The budgetary powers of the president are an essential element of Indonesia's coalitional presidentialism practices as well. In a polity still embedded in patronage as a socio-political glue, Indonesian elites remain dependent on the financial benefits provided by the state. Although the president shares budgetary powers with the legislature, we found that there is much room for him or her to move funds to politically interested beneficiaries. Presidents have used this constellation to increase salaries for military and police personnel around election times; pump money into the bureaucracy, which feeds off state budgets to fund its patronage system; promise or withhold local transfers to local government heads in exchange for political support; allocate projects benefitting allied oligarchs; and shower NU with a range of lucrative initiatives before elections. The parties and the legislature get a particularly generous share as well, given that their consent is needed to design the budget. Chaisty, Cheeseman, and Power have situated the exchange of favors as a fifth element of coalitional presidentialism; however, in the Indonesian context it is possible to think of this item as a practice in which the president draws from his or her co-legislative, appointment, and budgetary powers to hand out inducements to actual and potential partners. In some instances, the president may ask oligarchs in their coalition to dish out favors to other alliance partners, but the tycoons typically do so only if they are regular recipients of presidential patronage themselves.

In post-2004 Indonesia, these presidential tools have been applied so effectively to counterbalance the powers of the various coalition actors that none of the latter have seriously turned against the president. When dissatisfaction occurred, coalition deals between the president and key forces in the coalition were renegotiated—sometimes collectively but more often on an individual basis. An additional appointment here and more funds there have rectified disgruntlement among such actors. The stability of Indonesia's political order after 2004 flows from this ability of coalitional presidentialism to dynamically accommodate actors that hold potential veto powers. It is not surprising, then, that the only case of significant instability in the two decades of the Yudhoyono and Widodo presidencies was the Islamist mass mobilization of 2016 and 2017. Recall that this oppositional movement arose from Widodo's exclusion of the Islamist fringe from the parameters of coalitional presidentialism, into which Yudhoyono had invited them. Widodo opted, in this case, not to solve the problem by simply reintegrating the troublemaker into the presidential coalition. Instead, he used repression and asked another member of his coalition, NU, to do the groundwork for him in terms of delegitimizing the Islamist fringe and protecting the president from a backlash in the Muslim community. The gamble paid off, and stability was restored within about a year of the outbreak of the protest.

Widodo's handling of Islamist protest points to an important additional presidential tool that Chaisty, Cheeseman, and Power did not sufficiently consider: that is, the instrument of coercion. Such coercion is not the prerogative of autocrats; it is a standard practice of presidents in unconsolidated democracies (and, as the Trump presidency has shown, in some consolidated polities, too). Presidents in Indonesia have both enticed and coerced actors to join their coalitions. For example, Widodo exploited his power to determine the legality of party leadership boards to remove oppositional figures and install pro-government politicians—who then took their previously reluctant parties into the coalition. Widodo also allowed his law enforcers to flip an oppositional tycoon into a pro-government oligarch, who subsequently shifted the party under him into the presidential camp. Consequently, while it is true that most of Indonesia's political forces and leaders have a natural interest in being involved in coalitional presidentialism and consuming its spoils, there have also been cases in which groups or individuals were unwilling to join the alliance but were forced to do so. In fact, this coercive element of coalitional presidentialism played a large role in further consolidating the system as it transitioned from Yudhoyono to Widodo. While Yudhoyono was reluctant to use coercion, Widodo seemed to enjoy it (Power 2020). His bans of HTI and FPI, and the arrest of opponents, caused him no moral conflicts, and their shock effect added to his reputation as a president determined to punish disloyalty.

But while the effectiveness of the president's use of coalitional presidentialism tools goes a long way to explain the stability of Indonesia's post-2004 regimes, it does not tell the full story. This is because even pre-2004 presidents used elements of coalitional presidentialism but evidently with much less success. Wahid built a large coalition only to watch it impeach him. Megawati presided over a broad alliance that included non-party actors such as the military, but she failed to mobilize these resources to stay in office. Hence, we need to dig deeper to understand why the post-2004 system produced more stability (but also more democratic calcification) than its predecessor polity between 1998 and 2004. But before we do that, we have to reflect further on Indonesia's place in the comparative spectrum of coalitional presidentialism studies. This will assist us in making judgments about the applicability of the Indonesian case to other parts of the world and explore in a more systematic fashion the structural reasons why it evolved the way it did after 2004.

The Comparative Context

At the beginning of this book, we briefly assessed how Indonesia compared to other presidential systems in the world regarding key indicators such as stability and coalition size. Four main characteristics stood out. First, post-2004 Indonesia has been significantly more stable than other presidential systems, experiencing no impeachment attempts at all for two decades. This contrasts sharply with countries such as Peru, where presidential impeachments and resignations are routine affairs. Second, the president's party is comparatively small, with neither Yudhoyono's nor Widodo's party holding more than one-fourth of the seats in the legislatures between 2004 and 2024. In countries such as Kenya, Chile, Bolivia, and South Korea, the size of the president's party in parliament has traditionally been much larger. Third, the size of the presidential coalition has been significantly larger in Indonesia than in other presidential systems. In his second term, Widodo's coalition controlled 82 percent of parliamentary seats, and the size of Yudhoyono's coalitions was not much smaller. Except for the Philippines, all other cases we analyzed in the introduction had smaller coalitions. And fourth, while Indonesian presidents give more than half of their cabinet seats to non-party actors, and this allocation is a crucial element of the coalitional presidentialism architecture, other presidential systems have exhibited similar patterns. This is a surprising finding, given that non-party cabinet representation has been given marginal attention at best by conventional coalitional presidentialism studies.

Let us revisit each of these patterns and their significance for Indonesia's place in coalitional presidentialism studies. In many ways, post-2004 Indonesia is the ultimate example of successfully practiced coalitional presidentialism, given its stability. Like no other presidential regime, post-2004 Indonesia provides evidence, disproving Linz, that presidents can navigate the perils of minority status in parliament to establish stable governance and avoid impeachment if they use the tools offered by coalitional presidentialism effectively. But while this makes Indonesia exceptional—given the incidence of impeachments in other countries practicing coalitional presidentialism, such as South Korea, Brazil, or the Philippines—it does not remove it from comparability with other cases. This is because the stability of Indonesia's presidential system is not a quasi-cultural long-term product but the result of institutional design and the post-2004 agency of leaders. Indeed, Indonesia's pre-2004 instability offers important insights into the conditions under which coalitional presidentialism, albeit attempted, can be ineffective and break down. As Slater (2004) showed, the Wahid and Megawati cabinets were intended to operate as coalitional presidentialism vehicles, but they failed because of the institutional framework in which they were placed and because of miscalculations by their leaders. Their successors learned from these mistakes. In this context, studying Indonesia delivers lessons not only in how coalitional presidentialism is *practiced* but in how it is *created*.

With regard to the size of presidential parties, Indonesia is at the low end of the spectrum but generally follows a global trend, too. Many party systems worldwide have splintered, with voters moving from large catch-all parties to narrower constituency or issue-based parties (Lupu 2015). This pattern has been particularly pronounced in Latin America, the heartland of presidentialism (Mainwaring 2018). In Southeast and East Asia, traditionally weak parties have faced further challenges from social modernization and populists (Kenny 2018). In some areas, there have even been tendencies toward "hyperfragmentation" (Zucco and Power 2021)—Brazil being one such example. This trend toward shrinking and more parties has also affected the size of the president's party. In Indonesia's 2014 election, for the first time in the country's history no party reached more than 20 percent of the votes, and that result was replicated five years later. In the 2019 elections, only three parties achieved more than 10 percent of the votes, with the president's party emerging as the largest, but still a far cry away from holding majority status. However, contrary to Linz's warnings, this multi-partyism—even in its more extreme forms—has not undermined the stability of presidentialism. If anything, as the increasing examples of solid coalitional presidentialism arrangements have demonstrated, party proliferation has strengthened presidential control. The reason for this has been illustrated in this book: the existence of smaller and more parties can increase the presidents' leverage through clever divide et impera strategies, allowing them to avoid being domesticated by their own parties.

While Indonesia is part of the global party system fragmentation story, it also fits into the trend of party outsiders emerging as the most popular presidential candidates. This may take the form of marginal party figures becoming more popular than their party leaders or of independent politicians establishing parties purely for the functional purpose of their candidacy. In the Philippines, popular figures often co-opt a fringe party or parties as a base for their candidacy. Brazil's Bolsonaro used a similar strategy by joining the Social Liberal Party in 2018, and Kenyatta established the Jubilee Party in Kenya to facilitate his presidential ambitions. In Indonesia, as shown, Widodo became the candidate of PDI-P only because its leaders saw no alternative to the popular politician, and both Yudhoyono and Prabowo Subianto founded personalist parties. At first glance, this trend might lead us to conclude that presidents who are not the central figures of their parties or only preside over their own but poorly rooted groups might face difficulties ruling. Linz openly decried this risk, and even Chaisty, Cheeseman, and Power implied that such a constellation was disadvantageous to incumbents. But as this book highlighted, presidents who do not control their parties or only dominate their shell parties can still establish stable rule as long as they possess something that the parties desperately lack: electoral popularity. This popularity has emerged as the core political asset of presidents with which to control parties, regardless of their formal position within the latter. In demonstrating this pattern, post-2004 Indonesia joined the ranks of many other countries with outsider presidencies.

If the size of the presidential party in Indonesia is small by comparison, its coalitions tend to be bigger than in other countries. This correlation is not coincidental—a similar relationship exists in the Philippines (Bongbong Marcos's party alliance UniTeam won only 22 percent of the House seats in 2022 elections, but quickly built an 85 percent majority after taking office). While there are Indonesia-specific reasons why Widodo and Yudhoyono opted for large coalitions to overcompensate for their relatively small presidential parties, there appear to be generalizable patterns that relate to the inner logic of coalitional presidentialism. First, being able to rely only on a small home base in parliament seems to create more anxieties in a president than is the case in those heads of state who can draw from the support of a larger partisan caucus. These anxieties, in turn, drive the push to build oversized coalitions. Second, presidents with smaller support bases in parliament are more likely to explore the benefits of divide et impera strategies. Widodo has been particularly skilled in playing a variety of party and non-party actors against each other, increasing his political leverage enormously. Presidents whose parties are larger do not have the same incentive structure to engage in such effective (but also risky) experiments in balancing, and are therefore less likely to reap their benefits. In fact, the need to observe the vested interests of all actors involved in large coalitions (identified in this book as both a guarantor of stability and a hindrance to reform) might turn off incumbents with ambitious political agendas.

Finally, the tendency in Indonesia toward appointing non-party ministers echoes, despite its apparent country-related context, the situation in many other presidential systems. As our initial assessment in the introduction showed, presidents allocate significant proportions of cabinet seats to non-party actors. Despite that fact, the appointment of such actors remains understudied, including in the work of Chaisty, Cheeseman, and Power. One exception has been the study by Lee (2018, 345) on South Korea, which discovered that "the posts wherein ministers can influence the government's overall reputation typically go to nonpartisan professionals ideologically aligned with presidents, while the posts wherein ministers can exert legislators' influence generally go to senior copartisans." Such findings suggest that comparative presidentialism studies need to reconsider their traditional over-concentration on the parliamentary arena as the most decisive factor in determining the character of presidential rule. The data from South Korea also indicate that the nature of, and the motivations for, the allocation of cabinet seats to non-party actors are diverse. In the Indonesian case, non-party appointees are not only "professionals ideologically aligned with presidents" (Lee 2018, 345). They are representatives of important groups whose exclusion from cabinet would expose presidents to the risk of being politically and socially sabotaged by them. Thus, this book's focus on Indonesia not only deepened comparative studies of coalitional presidentialism but also broadened their perspective by paying more attention to non-party politics.

Where, then, does Indonesia sit exactly in the comparative spectrum of coalitional presidentialism? It ranks highest in overall regime stability, suggesting that Indonesian presidents have been more successful than others in using the instruments of the coalitional presidentialism toolbox. Furthermore, Indonesia has smaller presidential parties and bigger coalitions than many of its counterparts, making it an ideal case to study the interrelationship between these two factors. This relationship, in which the presidents' sense of exposure to risks of instability breeds initiatives to include all relevant actors in their coalitions, also led Indonesia into a specific format of non-party participation in political alliances. Such non-party engagement appears to be more institutionalized in Indonesia than in South Korea, for example, but points to modifications in the traditionally party-centered behavior of presidents around the world. In other words, the investigation of Indonesia in this book has firmly anchored the country in the study of coalitional presidentialism, and where Indonesia has slightly diverted from comparative norms, this has not underlined its exceptionalism but the need to expand the concept's initial boundaries.

Drivers of Stability

Thus far, we noted how Indonesian presidents have effectively used traditional tools of coalitional presidentialism, plus other ones, to stabilize their rule. Moreover, our comparative analysis has pointed to their weak position in the party system (that is, as heads of small parties or marginal figures in larger ones) as a possible motivation for their behavior. But we need to ask more systematically why Indonesian presidents have acted the way they did, and—by the same token—why party and non-party actors alike have refrained from even trying to remove them from office when such attempts are common in other presidential systems. This means that we have to reflect more deeply on the specific circumstances under which presidents and their allies operated after 2004, as well as on broader social structures that may have contributed to their actions. In this section, therefore, we look at four dimensions: first, the institutional set-up of the post-2004 polity that strengthened both the president and other actors, making the search for a compromise more desirable than conflict; second, the individual experience of Yudhoyono with Wahid's fall, which informed both his presidency and Widodo's; third, deeply rooted images of the power of leading actors, whether the president's or that of their allies, that convinced both sides that challenging the other would be disadvantageous; and fourth, strong ideational traditions of cooperation in Indonesian political culture that incentivized the inclusion of a maximum amount of actors into presidential coalitions.

To begin with, the sharp break between the instability of the political order in place between 1998 and 2004, on the one hand, and the solidity of the post-2004 polity, on the other, suggests that the constitutional amendments of 2002 had a major role in causing the shift of political practices (Horowitz 2013). Indeed, the amendments had an important impact on both the president and his or her institutional counterparts as, rather unusually, both were strengthened by the new arrangements. Presidents were protected more effectively from impeachment—so much so that removal of the president through the DPR and MPR became almost impossible. This circumstance created a compelling incentive for political actors to work with presidents rather than attempting to launch impeachment procedures with little chance of success. Other actors, however, also saw their powers expanded: parliament, for instance, gained additional appointment authorities, forcing the president to accommodate legislators even if he or she had reasons to feel secure from the threat of impeachment. Similarly, the shift to direct presidential elections increased the powers of non-state actors, such as oligarchs and religious organizations. The former paid the bills for the increased campaign efforts, while the latter mobilized voters and offered religious legitimacy to candidates. Hence, the post-2004 order left the president and other actors dependent on each other, with presidents fearing the effects of alienation from potential veto forces and these forces becoming more inclined to benefit from presidential patronage than to forego it through opposition.

It is hard to overstate the significance of this institutionalist approach to explaining coalitional presidentialism behavior and its stability in the post-2004 regime. To put it simply, the experience of Yudhoyono and Widodo—that is, sailing through their presidencies with no serious attempt to remove them from office—would not have been thinkable under the pre-2004 arrangements. On the day Wahid was elected president by the MPR in October 1999, the author asked a Golkar politician why he had voted in a figure with such a long record of unreliability and erratic behavior. "That's easy to answer," the politician said, "he serves our interests now, and if he stops doing that, we'll just impeach him" (interview with Achmad Arnold Baramuli, Jakarta, October 20, 1999). And so they did. No such easy avenue is available to post-2004 politicians, who have to accept that a just-elected president is likely going to be around for at least one term (more likely two), and that therefore making deals with him or her promises more benefits than trying to score points through self-exclusion from presidential favors. Similarly, Wahid's false notion that a president can do whatever he or she likes (recall that he issued decrees to freeze parliament and ban Golkar) was put to rest by the 2002 constitutional amendments, disciplining presidents and driving home the point that more was to be gained by cooperation than hostile acts against mainstream opponents.

Yet the institutionalist explanation only goes so far. For instance, it does not capture the continued fear of Indonesian presidents of impeachment despite its bar being set so high by the 2002 amendments. This incessant anxiety is also not fully explicable by pointing to the minority status of Yudhoyono's and Widodo's parties in parliament and the weak control of the latter over PDI-P. Rather, we must take seriously what Indonesian presidents have told us about why they chose broad coalitional presidentialism over narrow simple-majority rule. As mentioned, Yudhoyono was explicit about his fears. Despite the 2002 amendments, he continued to call Indonesia's system "semi-presidential" or "semi-parliamentary," implying that removal by parliament was an ever-present threat. In addition, he thought that unhappy political actors would create instability in society, and that their integration into government served a wider purpose of protecting socio-political harmony. For Yudhoyono, the trauma of being a senior minister during the days of Wahid's impeachment was undeletable (Kurdi and Wahid 2003). What he saw at that time shaped his views of what could happen to a president who aggressively confronted his foes. As Yudhoyono recalled much later, "for five months I was able to convince [Wahid] not to [disband parliament] because it is against the constitution, I was saying that, but I lost, I left (or he threw me out), and then he fell" (interview, Cikeas, December 2, 2014). For Yudhoyono, presidents fall if they make enemies instead of allies, and Wahid was toppled because he ignored that advice. Coalitional presidentialism in Indonesia cannot be understood without this historical context shaping the views of presidents, beyond the institutional framework that operated after 2004.

Widodo, for his part, adopted Yudhoyono's approach despite having actively campaigned against it in 2014. Initially, he viewed Yudhoyono's inclusion of so many actors in his coalition as akin to the president being taken hostage by his allies. But his determination to pursue a different path crumbled within weeks of his inauguration, and he became convinced of the political convenience and benefits of inclusive coalition-building. He quickly dropped the rhetoric of opposing broad coalitions and started building his own, now explaining that Indonesian democracy differed from its Western counterparts. He began to use the term *demokrasi gotong royong*—that is, a democracy in which all actors help each other (BBC Indonesia 2020). According to one of his assistants, Widodo would not acknowledge copying Yudhoyono's approach, given the rivalry between the two. "But every president learns from his or her predecessor, and it is clear that at the beginning we were a bit naïve about the challenges ahead of us," the aide said. "And yes, it has become more understandable to us why Yudhoyono had done things the way he did. It is a lot easier to have many actors supporting us inside the presidential tent than facing their sabotaging actions launched from outside" (confidential interview, Jakarta, February 8, 2017).

The presidents' fear of impeachment by the MPR highlights broader historical threat assessments that presidents make vis-à-vis a range of actors. It is worth pointing out that in 2014 Yudhoyono was the first president or prime minister—after sixty-nine years of post-independence history—to leave office without being dismissed by the DPR or MPR, overthrown by the military, or removed by voters at the ballot box. Thus, the trauma of Wahid's impeachment was embedded in a larger history of presidential downfalls and the actors who caused them. In the 1950s, prime ministers were typically replaced in the DPR as a result of shifting party loyalties; Sukarno was removed by the military; Suharto fell because of a popular uprising and because most elites deserted him; Habibie lost a decisive confidence vote in the MPR; the same body impeached Wahid; and Megawati lost the 2004 elections, which she mostly blamed on Yudhoyono who had challenged her despite serving in her cabinet. In short, Indonesia's coalitional presidentialism was born out of a desire to end a long streak of presidential misfortunes that the various incumbents believed resulted from allies not offering sufficient support. At the same time, history had shown that coercion alone was not enough to keep presidents in office. Both Sukarno and Suharto went down despite (or even because of) their repressive rules, and Wahid's last-minute attempt to govern as an autocrat was also unsuccessful. For incumbents, therefore, the need to accommodate potentially disloyal partners seemed to be the most compelling lesson from fallen ex-presidents.

This sense of Indonesia's presidential history has led heads of state to adopt often-exaggerated threat assessments of specific actors. As noted, the various members of presidential coalitions have significant powers, which encouraged presidents to tie them into their regimes. But it is unclear whether any of these groups would have the strength to remove a sitting president, especially if acting on their own. In many cases, it is the imagined *potential* of an actor to cause trouble, rather than the certainty that it can successfully challenge the president, that has persuaded incumbents to pre-emptively accommodate a particular player. In the case of the military, for instance, it is questionable whether it would have the power to launch a coup if the political and economic conditions are otherwise stable. Nevertheless, Indonesian presidents and large segments of the public remain married to the idea that the military constitutes the indispensable power behind the throne. (In a December 2021 poll, 92 percent of Indonesians trusted the military, leaving the president in second place at 82 percent) (LSI 2022, 43). Similarly, the oligarchs are immensely powerful but other than withholding funds and sponsoring opponents, their options for successfully removing a president are limited. Presidents, for their part, have chosen not to try to find out what would happen if they aggressively took on the oligarchs or any other major actor. Avoidance of conflict, rather than experimental challenges to see how far they can go, has been the premise of Indonesian presidents since 2004.

A maverick bound to challenge the foundations of coalitional presidentialism has yet to emerge. Widodo campaigned as such a maverick in 2014, but once in office, perpetuated the system he found. Even Prabowo, the most aggressive self-styled populist in modern Indonesia, was unlikely to follow through with his "burn the system" rhetoric if elected. At a campaign event in June 2014, Prabowo addressed a stadium full of supporters in Jakarta by delivering one of his standard speeches on the corruption of the existing system and why only he could dismantle it. Meanwhile, the representatives of that system had lined up at the stage behind him: among them were Bakrie, one of the most blatantly self-interested political oligarchs; Amien Rais, representing politicized religious groups; and Suryadharma Ali, the PPP chair and minister of religion who had just been declared a corruption suspect. Recognizing the tension between his anti-system speech and his pro-system supporters, Prabowo briefly turned to them and said, "by the way, when I attack the corrupt system, I don't mean them. They are very fine people" (notes by the author, Jakarta, June 22, 2014). Later, of course, Prabowo joined the system as well by becoming a minister. Partly, the absence of committed political mavericks is due to the presidential nomination monopoly held by political parties; however, it is also due to the obvious expediency of aligning with powerful actors rather than trying to destroy them and getting burnt in the process.

While Indonesian presidents have sought cooperation over conflict by preempting real and imagined threats, their coalition partners have adopted the same approach. In doing so, they have been motivated by an image of the Indonesian presidency that reflects not only its current powers but is an amalgamation of past experiences. The memories of Sukarno's and Suharto's autocracies are still fresh, with most of today's politicians having been socialized during the latter. Suharto's presidency appeared all-powerful and long-lasting to them, instilling a sense that cooperation with sitting presidents is more promising than waiting for a more favorable one. The quick succession of short-term presidents Habibie, Wahid, and Megawati, as well as the reduction of presidential powers compared to the New Order, did little to change the long-term impression that the presidency remains the center of power and needs to be both respected and exploited. To be sure, the post-Suharto changes increased the self-confidence of actors to position themselves vis-à-vis the presidency, giving them a clear awareness of which rewards they could demand in exchange for their cooperation. Nonetheless, in the background still looms the fear of exclusion and punishment—a fear that Widodo revived by applying some of the coercive strategies that Suharto had used.

Finally, however easily dismissed as pure rhetoric, there is an ideational element to the preference for broad coalition-building in democratic Indonesia. We already noted Widodo's mentioning of *gotong royong* democracy, which referenced Sukarno's concept of mutual assistance. Megawati, for her part, has often voiced her surprise at the practice of deciding policy issues by majority vote, given that Indonesia traditionally celebrates the principle of *musyawarah mufakat*, or discussion until a consensus is reached (the term is reflected in the name of the MPR). In 2015, she told a PDI-P congress that "actually we can use *musyawarah mufakat*, not voting [to decide any issue]. Voting is not our culture, it's the culture of Western people imported to us" (notes by the author, Sanur, April 8, 2015). Implicit in this concept of *musyawarah mufakat*, a household term in Indonesia, is the idea of accommodating everyone, regardless of their strength, electorally or otherwise. Yudhoyono, too, expressed his belief in the principle: "I love check and balances, but if it leads to a president being overthrown midterm, I don't agree. [*Musyawarah mufakat*] can soften our politics, and that makes me happy" (interview, Cikeas, December 2, 2014). Hence, whether the notion of *musyawarah mufakat* breeds inclusivist coalition-building behavior, or whether it just cloaks pragmatic interests in a cultural vocabulary, Indonesian politicians use it to explain their approach. Ultimately, it combines with other historical experiences to form a lens through which presidents view power-sharing as the most effective path to power maintenance.

In sum, the process through which Indonesia's coalitional presidentialism developed and stabilized involved several domestic drivers: institutional changes coming into effect in 2004 that gave both presidents and other actors more power; Yudhoyono's experience with Wahid that motivated him to pursue an accommodative path (one then continued by Widodo); historically grounded but often exaggerated perceptions both on the part of presidents and their partners of what the other side could do to them in case of non-cooperation; and a cultural affinity toward ideas of cooperation. These factors created an equilibrium in which both sides accepted each other's red lines of vested interests, and in which stability became the political premise for most actors involved. This stability, while setting Indonesia apart from many other presidential systems around the world, has come at a high cost, however. In the last section, we assess this price Indonesia paid for stability in more detail: effectively, coalitional presidentialism—as practiced in its post-2004 form in Indonesia—produced democratic erosion.

Democratic Decline

In the introduction to this book, we noted that the concurrence of stabilizing presidentialism and democratic backsliding that presented itself in the post-Suharto polity does not seem to be unique to Indonesia—democratic quality in Indonesia has declined in concert with that in Latin America, the world's stronghold of post-authoritarian presidentialism. The various chapters of this book highlighted that this interrelationship is indeed not coincidental, but a logical linkage in which the stabilization of presidential rule has been fed by the absorption of, and thus a reduction in, democratic substance. In each chapter, we investigated the damaging effects of a president purchasing the accommodation or acquiescence of an actor by making concessions to their vested interests. In combination, these acts of accommodation guaranteed the endurance of the post-Suharto order *and* its colonization by patronage-driven players. Indonesia's stability and democratic decline, then, are two sides of the same coin (Aspinall 2010).

These dynamics, already visible in pre-2004 governments, were institutionalized during the Yudhoyono and Widodo presidencies. Yudhoyono's inclusion of the radical Islamist fringe into his broader coalitional presidentialism parameters set the tone for systematic compromises on democratic quality in the name of political stability. The same approach was used for other actors, with ever-increasing straightforwardness. With the protection of each coalition partner's red lines emerging as the core organizing principle of coalitional presidentialism, areas of critical importance to democratic quality became taboo zones. Subsequently, these zones turned into arenas of democratic decline as actors clawed back privileges lost in earlier periods of democratization. Whether the military reclaimed civilian roles; the oligarchs overturned the soft labor laws of the early 2000s; bureaucrats fended off attempts to dry up their patronage resources; or parties paralyzed the anti-corruption commission that had arrested many of their leaders—coalitional presidentialism offered the framework in which actors could exploit the president's real or exaggerated sense of vulnerability to restore old privileges or demand new ones. Presidents, believing that they guaranteed stability by giving in to these demands, were satisfied as long as they could defend and expand their own powers. Coalitional presidentialism in Indonesia, therefore, works so well for presidents and the accommodated elites because it is a win-win proposition—both sides gain, but at democracy's expense.

The specific mechanism through which presidents and their allies feed on democracy's substance also explains the *pace* and *extent* of democratic decline in Indonesia. While this decline has been serious, it has been slow and gradual—and stopped short of overturning democracy per se. This is because democracy is both an obstacle and an enabling necessity for presidents, elites, and their power-sharing under coalitional presidentialism. Although democracy can expose the predatory behavior of leaders and their machines, it also equips them with all-important legitimacy. In this regard, the elite's wish to diminish the effects of democratic transparency is balanced by their interest in maintaining democracy as the system that justifies their rule. Post-1998 democracy, for all the upheaval and changes it has brought for socio-economic elites, has served most of the country's leaders well, and its replacement by a new autocratic system might offer more uncertainties than benefits for them. Accordingly, the characteristics of Indonesia's democratic decline under coalitional presidentialism—slow-paced and regime-preserving—is not an accident but in line with the elite's strategic priorities.

One of the most consequential impacts of this gradual democratic decline under coalitional presidentialism has been the undermining of the principle of checks and balances. In his analytical description of Indonesian party coalitions in Indonesia as cartels, Slater (2004, 2018) found that Indonesia is caught in an "accountability trap"; that is, neither do the various actors hold each other to account, nor can voters fulfill that task due to everyone being in government. While the cartel model overlooks crucial aspects of coalitional presidentialism—for instance, it underestimates the level of competition in the coalition and dismisses the role of the president as negligible—it accurately captures the illiberal pitfalls linked to coalitions that try to accommodate too many actors. Although the intense inter-actor rivalry in the coalition sustains a degree of competitiveness that has allowed Indonesia to remain an electoral democracy, it is no substitute for effective mechanisms of control and accountability in which oppositions scrutinize governments through the legislature and societal oversight. Building up the latter is near-impossible if the government coalition controls four-fifths of parliamentary seats; most media outlets are in the hands of presidential allies; and other non-party actors with the potential to counterbalance the ruling alliance have joined it. The bigger these coalitions grow, the more the media becomes a soft companion of government rather than its controller—and the more non-party institutions trade their accountability powers for benefits, the more democratic quality erodes.

But the risk that coalitional presidentialism can pose to democratic substance is not related only to its *inclusion* of too many actors. Equally important is its *exclusion* of actors deemed too hostile or not influential enough to be invited into the coalition. At best, this exclusion leads to the denial of access to democratic processes and the distribution of societal resources. At worst, it takes the shape of outright repression. Under Indonesia's coalitional presidentialism regime, both trends have been witnessed, with the first slowly but steadily combining with the second. Early in presidential terms, reformist civil society groups, labor unions, social and political minorities, and other marginal actors often enjoy the president's attention as they can bestow democratic credibility. In his first term, Yudhoyono liked to move in such circles, and Widodo integrated them into his 2014 campaign platform. But as they began to demand more than just rhetorical praise, and as they asked for reforms that threatened the interests of important actors in the coalition, presidents moved away from such marginal groups. In later phases of Widodo's rule, human rights and environmental activists who supported him in 2014 became increasingly criminalized and otherwise repressed (Jong 2018). We also noted what occurs to actors who once were important enough to be invited into the outer rings of presidential coalitions but then thrown out from them: the Islamist fringe, courted by Yudhoyono but excluded by Widodo, became the target of systematic and arguably disproportionate government repression after 2017.

The development of coalitional presidentialism in Indonesia, and the country's concurrent democratic decline, thus point to important sequential dynamics in both. It is crucial to acknowledge that coalitional presidentialism is not per se disadvantageous for democracy. Indeed, it can help to avoid a democratic breakdown in some cases and provide the necessary stability for democracy to consolidate in others. Democracy indexes identified much of Yudhoyono's first term as Indonesia's democratic peak—that is, in a period in which coalitional presidentialism was still experimented with, and most actors (including the president) were unsure about the limits of their powers. But as the system gradually expanded to include more actors, its players became more brazen in demanding what they perceived to be their rightful privileges. Newcomers to the coalition oriented themselves at what others had received and requested the same. In hindsight, the tipping point of coalitional presidentialism turning from being an asset for democracy into a liability was Yudhoyono's re-election in 2009. With an ever-growing coalition, and a bigger winning margin in a shrinking field of candidates, Yudhoyono had demonstrated the concept's success and, therefore, its desirability. His second term, consequently, was described as one of stagnation, in which he simply administered the coalition and gave up on any attempts at broader reform (Aspinall, Mietzner, and Tomsa 2015). Widodo, who only briefly flirted with abandoning coalitional presidentialism, quickly reversed course, broadened the coalition, and further narrowed Indonesia's democratic space.

The transformation of Indonesia's coalitional presidentialism from a potentially democracy-stabilizing into a democracy-damaging force was particularly visible in the *kind* of actors who saw their influence in the coalition increasing. As noted, the two actors who recorded the biggest increase in their cabinet representation over time were the police and the oligarchs. This increase fittingly reflected the growing reliance of the Widodo government on security agencies and on the wealthy to survive challenges to its stability and fundraising needs. That democracy suffered under such a visible shift in power distribution and priorities is obvious.

Hence, post-2009 coalitional presidentialism in Indonesia lost the balance between the rival concerns of stability and democratic contestation. The way coalitional presidentialism has been practiced solved the problem of instability that haunted Indonesia between 1998 and 2004 but created a new, opposite deficiency: that is, excessive stability equivalent to stagnation. In this "irony of success" (Aspinall 2010), the stabilizing effects achieved by appeasing Indonesia's veto powers have caused its failure to further advance the quality of democracy. A web of red lines drawn up by vested interests became the foundation of coalitional presidentialism, while the red lines set by democracy were increasingly made subject to negotiation. As coalitional presidentialism was entrenched beyond its point of healthy saturation, democracy receded. Given that Indonesia's adoption of coalitional presidentialism and its concurrent democratic recession are both parts of a global pattern, its experience can tell us much about other cases around the world. As recognized earlier, the level of stability in coalitional presidentialism regimes has varied but one thing is clear: the problem described by Linz, namely that presidential systems are inherently unstable, is no longer the main issue confronting them. Neither is it the main challenge to explain why presidential systems can orderly co-exist with multi-party systems. Indonesia has impressively shown that it can, with a frightening level of political orderliness. The more pressing challenge is to explore how coalitional presidentialism can work without sucking the oxygen out of democratic societies—and without stability becoming a source of political calcification.

Finally, it is worth noting how little the COVID-19 pandemic has changed the political architecture of coalitional presidentialism regimes in Indonesia or elsewhere. While the pandemic was a period of socio-economic upheaval, it left almost no dent in the political order through which power is distributed. In Indonesia, Widodo's coalition not only persisted but consolidated during the crisis. Oligarchic interests pushed through legislation that they had pursued unsuccessfully before 2020, and Widodo relied on the police—a member of his coalition—to stifle dissent that could have destabilized his rule. The crisis did not create cracks in Indonesia's elite coalition, but instead nurtured a sense that it needed to hold together even more firmly to survive. Similar trends were apparent in the Philippines, where President Duterte rode out the COVID-19 crisis on the back of his oversized coalition. He subsequently handed over power to an even larger alliance of elite forces under Marcos. In Brazil, the pandemic led to a rotation of power that brought a previous coalition back into government, but it did not transplant the system of coalitional presidentialism itself. Democratic quality continued to decline during the pandemic in all of these countries, as it did in Indonesia. But for better or worse, the system of power-sharing institutionalized in coalitional presidentialism survived the storm—and is set to continue its existence as the dominant form of presidential rule in the younger democracies of the twenty-first century.

Notes

INTRODUCTION

1. Widodo is often referred to by his nickname "Jokowi," an amalgamation of Joko and Widodo. This book consistently uses his family name, which has been the standard in much of the international press reporting.

2. See the various country reports of Freedom House's annual Freedom in the World surveys, https://freedomhouse.org/report/freedom-world.

CHAPTER 1. THE PRESIDENT

1. The constitution was passed by the BPUPKI's successor body, the Preparatory Committee for Indonesian Independence (PPKI).

2. From 2017, the head of the secretariat was Heru Budi Hartono, whom Widodo knew from his time as governor of Jakarta. When Widodo had to fill a two-year vacancy in the position of Jakarta governor in 2022 due to changes in the electoral schedule, Widodo opted for Hartono. This gave the president de facto control over the capital for the two years of the interregnum.

3. The circumstance that the military secretary also handles the appointment of presidential adjutants who are members of the police has its origins in the pre-1999 period, when the police was still part of the armed forces.

4. The only presidents who lived in the Jakarta palace were Sukarno and Wahid. Suharto famously lived in a large family complex on Cendana Street in the elite inner-city suburb of Menteng; Habibie resided in a house in Kuningan, also an elite suburb; and Megawati used a state-owned house in Menteng, the ownership of which was transferred to her after her presidency.

CHAPTER 2. THE PARTIES

1. Widodo was aware of the dominance of Megawati and her family over the party and thus knew he would not be able to play a leading role. Ideologically, PDI-P broadly reflected his preferences, but he was not a passionate Sukarno admirer, as most party cadres are. He recalled some Sukarno books being in his family home when he grew up but dodged the question of whether he had ever read them (interview, Jakarta, September 15, 2014).

2. At the PDI-P congress in August 2019, deputy treasurer Juliari Batubara (who was appointed social affairs minister about two months later) received the task from the party leadership to help raising an election fund of Rp 1 trillion (US$71.4 million) for the 2024 elections (interview with a party leader at the congress, Denpasar, August 9, 2019).

3. In 2022, PAN joined the Widodo ministry and was given only one cabinet seat.

4. In 2016, Widodo conducted a cabinet reshuffle that reduced Hanura's number of ministries from two to one but, in return, the party received a coordinating ministry for its chairman, Wiranto. Hanura officials commented that one coordinating ministry had the same value as two ordinary ministries.

5. This flurry of speculation and self-campaigning led one seasoned Western journalist to report in early July 2018 that "barring any last minute changes, Indonesian President Joko Widodo is close to naming Golkar Party chairman and Industry Minister

Airlangga Hartarto as his running mate in next April's simultaneous presidential and legislative elections" (McBeth 2018).

CHAPTER 3. THE LEGISLATURE

1. In most cases, the chair of the DPR asks the plenary session, "Can we agree that the budget becomes law?," which—in the absence of explicit expressions of opposition—is followed by a confirming strike of the gavel (CNN Indonesia 2022). This approach creates a disincentive against legislators voicing or otherwise indicating opposition to the collectively bargained outcome unless they are prepared to stand up and delay proceedings.

2. Significant funds for legislators are hidden behind descriptions such as "recess money." Celebrity singer Krisdayanti, who became a legislator for PDI-P in 2019, disclosed in a 2021 interview just how much money she received (she mentioned, for instance, that she received Rp 450 million (US$32,140) "five times a year" as "aspiration fund"). Her colleagues were horrified and corrected her use of the term "aspiration fund" (which was the discretionary fund rejected several times) but confirmed the overall amounts that were paid (Rizal 2020).

3. This equilibrium between the two former presidents continued to be tested over time. In March 2021, Widodo's chief of staff Moeldoko launched a renewed attempt at taking over the PD leadership. Widodo claimed to have no knowledge of this operation. After some deliberation, the government refused to endorse Moeldoko's leadership, which Widodo supporters showcased as evidence that the president had no hand in the affair. Many within the party were enthusiastic about the failure of Moeldoko, believing that it would give PD a much-welcome electoral boost (discussion with Tomi Satryatomo, chair of PD's research agency, online, April 5, 2021).

4. In 2019, the regulation on selecting the DPR speaker changed again, with the largest caucus given the position automatically.

CHAPTER 4. THE MILITARY

1. Chaisty, Cheeseman, and Power (2017, 39) only feature the military as the ruler of pre-democratic regimes whose downfall paved the way to coalitional presidentialism.

2. Numbers provided by a military officer in the Armed Forces Information Section (confidential interview, Jakarta, March 7, 2019). The same applies to the budget numbers cited in the following sentence.

3. The decree served as the basis for the later promulgation of Law 34 of 2004 on the National Indonesian Military.

4. After the appointment of the new TNI commander Andi Perkasa in November 2021, for instance, the key post of Strategic Reserve commander needed to be filled. Asked about who would get the job, Andika told the press that "I want to report to the president first . . . Later, there will be a proposal from us that the president then decides upon" (Michella 2021). This procedure suggests that military commanders collect input from the president before starting their selection process.

5. When appointed as defense minister in 2021, Prabowo Subianto challenged this arrangement and became the most powerful defense minister in the post-1998 era. However, his power was primarily based on his military connections and his special deal with Widodo over his joining the government rather than a result of the institutional role of the ministry (Mietzner 2023).

6. In June 2016, Widodo felt compelled to issue an explicit statement on his determination to defend the territorial command structure. The army subsequently put this statement on its website (TNI AD 2016).

7. In 2021, an investigative report produced by several NGOs claimed that numerous active and retired military officers had significant business interests in Papua (Rakhman, Ma'rufah, Kausan, and Ardi 2021).

8. Hendropriyono was accused of overseeing a 1989 massacre and had been accused of involvement—without concrete proof—in the fatal poisoning of prominent human rights activist Munir in 2004, when he was Megawati's intelligence chief.

9. In January 2023, Widodo "acknowledged" that past human rights violations had occurred in twelve cases in the past, and the "1965/66 events" were one of them. He did not say specifically, however, who was at fault, and no meaningful action followed from this acknowledgement.

CHAPTER 5. THE POLICE

1. One such demonstration occurred in May 2021, when an apparently paid crowd appeared at the KPK to defend its chairman Firli Bahuri, a police officer widely seen as having been placed in this position to weaken the commission (CNN Indonesia 2021a).

2. Ardi was later sentenced to one year in prison (against the prosecution's recommendation), but that verdict was overturned on appeal.

3. In 2023, however, tensions emerged between Bahuri and the police, with some police investigators seconded to the KPK protesting against Bahuri's leadership.

4. As in the case of elections, Tito believed that Indonesia's lower-class citizens were a problem as they were more vulnerable to COVID-19 conspiracy theories than the middle class (Waluya 2020). Thus, he suggested that effective pandemic management was easier for "oligarchic" countries such as China or Vietnam, which could enforce policies with more authority (Gunadha and Sari 2020).

5. According to Supriatma (2019), Widodo treated the military the way he did because he "knows full well that the armed forces are still the most important political player in Indonesia." While such statements capture the military's importance, they also overstate it.

CHAPTER 6. THE BUREAUCRACY

1. Widodo's chief of staff told the media that 72 percent of civil servants had voted for Prabowo.

2. In August 2011, Yudhonoyo defined eleven national priorities for his government, with bureaucracy reform topping the list.

CHAPTER 7. LOCAL GOVERNMENTS

1. During local elections in Central Java in 2018, nineteen village heads were accused by the Election Supervision Board (Bawaslu) of having supported or obstructed specific candidates (Aris 2018).

2. Enembe's deputy confirmed that the governor had most likely left Papua because he "was afraid" (interview with Klemen Timal, Jayapura, June 16, 2016).

3. Because of a change in the electoral schedule, the terms of many local government chiefs expired in 2022 and 2023, while the first nationwide local government head elections were scheduled for November 2024. This allowed the president to appoint 271 temporary local government chiefs during 2022–2023. As noted, this included appointing the head of his Presidential Secretariat as temporary governor of Jakarta.

4. Papua and West Papua also recorded good results for Widodo, but these two provinces are special autonomy regions and thus have a particular relationship with the president.

5. Although many local government heads have complained about the costs of direct, popular elections, they generally view elections by local legislatures as a defective and unpredictable mechanism that favors unpopular candidates.

6. After Hartono's departure, Risma faced opposition from her local PDI-P branch and had to accept its chair as the new deputy mayor against her wishes. But her eventual quiet acceptance of this outcome further endeared her to the national party leadership.

CHAPTER 8. THE OLIGARCHS

1. The rationale for this stipulation was to motivate parties to operate as national entities rather than as parties based on ethnic or regional constituencies, as was the case in the fragmented party landscape of the 1950s.

2. See Wanandi 2016. While Jusuf Wanandi, the brother of an oligarch, lauded other aspects of the amnesty, he acknowledged that the "not so rosy outcome seemingly showed in the amount of repatriated assets, which hovered at only Rp 136 trillion, a far cry from the Rp 1 quadrillion targeted."

3. For example, Luhut confirmed in a 2023 court case that he still owned shares in Toba Sejahtera, while he had handed over the management to a CEO.

4. Borsuk and Chng quoted Jusuf Wanandi, who recounted what Suharto had told the oligarchs.

5. Bromley (2014) concluded that while "Thohir has never been listed on any of Forbes' lists of billionaires, either worldwide or in the Indonesia-specific article, . . . the truth is something more confusing, and somewhere that cannot be found through traditional stock listings."

CHAPTER 9. MUSLIM ORGANIZATIONS

1. *Santri* is the Indonesian term for a devout Muslim.

2. Rizieq was released from prison in July 2022 but was put under strict conditions to keep a low profile.

CONCLUSION

1. In early 2022, as the pandemic came to an end, Indikator measured the highest satisfaction with democracy ever recorded in its surveys since 2004, at 77.3 percent (Indikator 2022).

References

Abellanosa, Rhoderick John. 2018. "Setback in Secularization: Church and State Relations under the Duterte Administration." *Journal of Applied Philosophy* 4 (5): 55–80.

Aberbach, Joel D., Robert D. Putnam, and Bert A. Rockman. 1981. *Bureaucrats and Politicians in Western Democracies*. Cambridge: Harvard University Press.

Adinda Putri, Cantika. 2020. "Jokowi Lebih Disukai Rakyat dari Sukarno, Tapi Soeharto No.1." *CNBC Indonesia*, February 24.

Adyatama, Egi. 2020. "Teken PP Manajemen PNS, Jokowi Punya Wewenang Angkat-Mutasi ASN." *Tempo*, May 15.

Agastia, Dharma IGB. 2016. "A Case against the Military's Newfound 'Proxy War' Obsession." *Jakarta Post*, December 22.

Agustina, Dewi. 2020. "Menteri Siti Nurbaya: UU Cipta Kerja Penting untuk Sederhanakan Prosedur Perizinan." *Tribun News*, October 17.

Ahmad, Saidiman. 2020. "Menjaga Pilkada Langsung." SMRC, January 15.

Aini, Aulia Nur Wihdlatil, Abdul Muntholib, and Andy Suryadi. 2019. "Dinamika Integrasi dan Pemisah POLRI dari ABRI Tahun 1961-2002." *Journal of Indonesian History* 8 (2): 105–112.

Ainurrahman. 2020. "Tudingan Aksi Demontrasi Tolak UU Ciptaker Didanai Pihak Tertentu Harus Dibuktikan." *Akurat*, October 9.

Albala, Adrián. 2021. "When Do Coalitions Form under Presidentialism, and Why Does It Matter? A Configurational Analysis." *Latin America Politics* 41 (3): 351–370.

Alemán, Eduardo, and Thomas Schwartz. 2006. "Presidential Vetoes in Latin American Constitutions." *Journal of Theoretical Politics* 18 (1): 98–120.

Almendares, Nicholas. 2011. "Politicization of Bureaucracy." In *SAGE International Encyclopedia of Political Science*, edited by Bertrand Badie et al., 1–4. London: SAGE.

Amalia, Yunita. 2016. "KPK Usulkan Dana Partai Politik dari APBN sebesar Rp 9,3 triliun." *Merdeka*, November 21.

Ambardi, Kuskridho. 2009. *Mengungkap Politik Kartel: Studi Tentang Sistem Kepartaian di Indonesia Era Reformasi*. Jakarta: Kepustakaan Populer Gramedia.

Amelia, Rizky. 2013. "Busyro Akui Adanya Praktik Suap untuk Lolos Seleksi di DPR." *Berita Satu*, September 19.

Ames, Barry. 2001. *The Deadlock of Democracy in Brazil*. Ann Arbor: University of Michigan Press.

Amin, Al. 2014. "4 Aksi Heroik Risma Turun ke Jalan." *Merdeka*, September 28.

Aminuddin, M. Faishal. 2017. "The Purnawirawan and Party Development in Post—Authoritarian Indonesia, 1998-2014." *Journal of Current Southeast Asian Affairs* 36 (2): 3–30.

Amorim Neto, Octavio. 1998. "Of Presidents, Parties, and Ministers: Cabinet formation and Legislative Decision-making under Separation of Powers." PhD diss., University of California, San Diego.

———. 2006. "The Presidential Calculus: Executive Policy Making and Cabinet Formation in the Americas." *Comparative Political Studies* 39 (4): 415–440.

Amorim Neto, Octavio, Gary Cox, and Matthew McCubbins. 2003. "Agenda Power in Brazil's Camara dos Deputados, 1989-1998." *World Politics* 55 (4): 550–578.

Anderson, Benedict R. O'G. 1972. *Java in a Time of Revolution: Occupation and Resistance, 1944–1946*. Ithaca: Cornell University Press.
Andriansyah, Moch. 2019. "NU Blak-blakan Minta Jatah Menteri: Dukungan Nahdliyin ke Jokowi Tidak Gratis." *Merdeka*, June 20.
Antara. 2021. "Tampil Perdana di Raker DPR, ini Permintaan Menteri KP." *Antara*, January 27.
Anwar, Akhirul. 2014. "Pilpres 2014: Dana Kampanye Jokowi Lebih Besar dari Prabowo." *Kabar24*, July 18.
Aris, Budi. 2018. "Bawaslu: Ada 19 Kades Yang Terancam Pidana Karena Diduga Tak Netral." Idola, March 1.
Aritenang, Adiwan F. 2020. "The Effect of Intergovernmental Transfers on Infrastructure Spending in Indonesia." *Journal of the Asia Pacific Economy* 25 (3): 571–590.
Aritonang, Margareth S. 2016. "FPI Threatens to Impeach Jokowi over 1965 Apology." *Jakarta Post*, June 1.
Arnaz, Farouk. "Budi Waseso: Pimpinan KPK Kurang Kredibel." *Berita Satu*, February 5.
Arnold, Christian, David Doyle, and Nina Wiesehomeier. 2017. "Presidents, Policy Compromise, and Legislative Success." *Journal of Politics* 79 (2): 380–395.
Arrahmah News. 2016. "Kongres Khilafah (HTI) di Tangerang, Dibubarkan Warga NU." *Arrahmah News*, April 25.
Aryani, Ani Nunung. 2018. "Konflik Sekda dan Bupati Cirebon Berujung di Jalur Hukum?" *Pikiran Rakyat*, January 3.
Asia Sentinel. 2008. "The Bakrie Group and Economic Meltdown in Indonesia." *Asia Sentinel*, October.
Asmara, Chandra Gian. 2019. "72% Anggota PNS Ternyata Pilih Prabowo-Sandiaga, Percaya?" *CNBC Indonesia*, May 28.
Aspinall, Edward. 2005. *Opposing Suharto: Compromise, Resistance, and Regime Change in Indonesia*. Stanford: Stanford University Press.
——. 2010. "Indonesia: The Irony of Success." *Journal of Democracy* 21 (2): 20–34.
——. 2015. "Oligarchic Populism: Prabowo Subianto's Challenge to Indonesian Democracy." *Indonesia* 99: 1–28.
——. 2019. "Indonesia's Election and the Return of Ideological Competition." *New Mandala*, April 22.
Aspinall, Edward, and Gerry van Klinken, eds. 2011. *The State and Illegality in Indonesia*. Leiden: KITLV.
Aspinall, Edward, and Greg Fealy, eds. 2003. *Local Power & Politics in Indonesia: Decentralisation & Democratisation*. Singapore: ISEAS.
Aspinall, Edward, and Ward Berenschot. 2019. Democracy for Sale: Elections, Clientelism, and the State in Indonesia. Ithaca: Cornell University Press.
Asril, Sabrina. 2014. "Bertemu Jokowi, Aburizal Bakrie Minta Kejelasan Koalisi." *Kompas*, May 14.
Aswicahyono, Haryo H., and Hal Hill. 2015. "Is Indonesia Trapped in the Middle?" Discussion Paper Series 31, University of Freiburg.
Aziz, Abdul. 2019. "Daftar Anggota Satgas Omnibus Law: James Riady hingga Erwin Aksa." *Tirto*, December 16.
Aziz, Rizky Amalia. 2020. "Kiai dan Politik Elektoral: Peran Kiai Yusuf Chudlori dalam Pemenangan Kandidat Jokowi-Ma'ruf Amin pada Pilpres 2019 di Kecamatan Tegalrejo." *Jurnal PolGov* 2 (2): 223–276.
Badan Kepagaiwan Negara. 2020. *Buku Statistik Pegawai Negeri Sipil Desember 2020*. Jakarta: BKN. https://www.bkn.go.id/wp-content/uploads/2021/03/STATISTIK-PNS-Desember-2020.pdf.

Baker, Jacqui. 2012. "The Rise of Polri: Democratisation and the Political Economy of Security in Indonesia." PhD diss., London School of Economics.
———. 2013. "The Parman Economy: Post-Authoritarian Shifts in the Off-Budget Economy of Indonesia's Security Institutions." *Indonesia* 96: 123–150.
Balboni, Clare, Robin Burgess, Anton Heil, Jonathan Old, and Benjamin A. Olken. 2021. "Cycles of Fire? Politics and Forest Burning in Indonesia." *AEA Papers and Proceedings* 111: 415–419.
Bareksa. 2014. "Faisal Basri: 'Keterlibatan Riza Chalid di Impor Minyak Bermula dari Purnomo.'" *Bareksa*, November 26.
Barrett, Luke. 2011. "Something to Believe In: Ideology and Parties in Indonesian Politics." *Review of Indonesian and Malaysian Affairs* 45 (1–2): 69–94.
Barton, Greg. 2006. *Gus Dur: The Authorized Biography of Abdurrahman Wahid*. Jakarta: Equinox.
Batubara, Puteranegara. 2019. "HUT Ke-73, Kapolri Minta Presiden Jokowi Tingkatkan Tunjangan Kinerja TNI-Polri." *Okezone*, July 10.
BBC Indonesia. 2015. "Presdir Freeport: Ketua DPR Meminta Saham Proyek Pembangkit Listrik di Timika." *BBC Indonesia*, December 3.
———. 2017. "Tito Karnavian: Korban Perkosaan Bisa Ditanya oleh Penyidik 'Apakah Nyaman' Selama Perkosaan?" *BBC Indonesia*, October 19.
———. 2019. "Dukungan ASN ke Jokowi 'Naik', tapi 'Masih Kalah Populer' dari Prabowo." *BBC Indonesia*, February 4.
———. 2020. "Presiden Jokowi dalam Wawancara Eksklusif dengan BBC: 'Prioritas Saya ekonomi, tapi Bukan Saya tidak Senang HAM dan Lingkungan.'" *BBC Indonesia*, February 13.
Beckmann, George M. 1957. *The Making of the Meiji Constitution. The Oligarchs and the Constitutional Development of Japan, 1868–1891*. Lawrence: University of Kansas Press.
Berenschot, Ward. 2018. "Incumbent Bureaucrats: Why Elections Undermine Civil Service Reform in Indonesia." *Public Administration and Development* 38 (4): 135–143.
Bertrand, Jacques. 2002. "Legacies of the Authoritarian Past: Religious Violence in Indonesia's Moluccan Islands." *Pacific Affairs* 75 (1): 57–85.
Beschloss, Michael. 2007. *Presidential Courage: Brave Leaders and How They Changed America, 1789–1989*. New York: Simon & Schuster.
Bestari, Novina Putri. 2021. "Respons Eks Bos Pertamina soal Kartu Kredit, Ahok: Buka Semua." *CNBC Indonesia*, June 26.
Blakkarly, Jarni. 2015. "Defending Indonesia's Anti-Corruption Fighters." *New Mandala*, January 29.
Blöndal, Jón R., Ian Hawkesworth, and Hyun-Deok Choi. 2009. "Budgeting in Indonesia." *OECD Journal on Budgeting* 9 (2): 1–32.
Bolton, Alexander. 2021. "Senate GOP Poised to Give Biden Huge Political Victory." *The Hill*, August 5.
Booth, Anne. 1992. "Can Indonesia Survive as a Unitary State?" *Indonesia Circle* 20 (58): 32–47.
Borges, André, and Mathieu Turgeon. 2019. "Presidential Coattails in Coalitional Presidentialism." *Party Politics* 25 (2): 192–202.
Borsuk, Richard, and Nancy Chng. 2014. *Liem Sioe Liong's Salim Group: The Business Pillar of Suharto's Indonesia*. Singapore: ISEAS.
Bourchier, David M. 2019. "Two Decades of Ideological Contestation in Indonesia: From Democratic Cosmopolitanism to Religious Nationalism." *Journal of Contemporary Asia* 49 (5): 713–733.

Bourchier, David, and John Legge. 1994. *Democracy in Indonesia: 1950s and 1990s*. Melbourne: Monash Centre of Southeast Asian Studies.

Bradley, Curtis A., and Trevor W. Morrison. 2013. "Presidential Power, Historical Practice, and Legal Constraint." *Columbia Law Review* 113 (4): 1097–1161.

Bresnan, John. 1993. *Managing Indonesia: The Modern Political Economy*. New York: Columbia University Press.

Bromley, Ben. 2014. "Is Erick Thohir a Billionaire? A Look at What We Know about Hs Finances and His Ownership of D.C. United." D.C. United, May 19.

Budi, Arya. 2016. "Golkar Party and the Survival of Oligarchy. *Jakarta Post*, May 19.

Burgess, Robin, Matthew Hansen, Benjamin A. Olken, Peter Potapov, and Stefanie Sieber. 2011. "The Political Economy of Deforestation in the Tropics." NBER Working Paper 17417.

Bush, Robin. 2015. "Religious Politics and Minority Rights during the Yudhoyono Presidency." In *The Yudhoyono Presidency: Indonesia's Decade of Stability and Stagnation*, edited by Edward Aspinall, Marcus Mietzner, and Dirk Tomsa, 239–257. Singapore: ISEAS.

Butler, Rhett A. 2011. "Election Cycle Linked to Deforestation Rate in Indonesia." *Mongabay*, April 14.

Butt, Simon. 2010. "Regional Autonomy and Legal Disorder: The Proliferation of Local Laws in Indonesia." *Sydney Law Review* 32 (2): 177–197.

Butt, Simon, and Tim Lindsey. 2012. *The Constitution of Indonesia: A Contextual Analysis*. Oxford: Hart.

Cammack, Mark. 2015. "Crimes against Humanity in East Timor: The Indonesian Ad Hoc Human Rights Court Hearings." In *Trials for International Crimes in Asia*, edited by Kirsten Sellars, 191–225. Cambridge: Cambridge University Press.

Campbell, T. 2001. *The Quiet Revolution: The Rise of Political Participation and Leading Cities with Decentralization in Latin America and the Caribbean*. Pittsburgh: University of Pittsburgh Press.

Carreras, Miguel. 2012. "The Rise of Outsiders in Latin America, 1980–2010: An Institutionalist Perspective." *Comparative Political Studies* 45 (12): 1451–1482.

Carroll, Jacinta. 2016. "A Powerful Partnership to Counter Terrorism: Australia and Indonesia." *The Strategist*, June 14.

Chaisty, Paul, Nic Cheeseman, and Timothy J. Power. 2017. *Coalitional Presidentialism in Comparative Perspective: Minority Presidents in Multiparty Systems*. Oxford: Oxford University Press.

Chambers, Paul. 2021. "Khaki Capital and Coups in Thailand and Myanmar." *Current History* 120 (827): 221–226.

Chan, Carol. *In Sickness and in Wealth: Migration, Gendered Morality, and Central Java*. Indianapolis: Indiana University Press.

Chandra, Riki. 2021. "Mutasi Pejabat Pemkot Padang Ditegur KASN, Hendri Septa: Saya Cuma Melantik." *Suara Sumbar*, April 21.

Channa, Anila, and Jean-Paul Faguet. 2016. "Decentralization of Health and Education in Developing Countries: A Quality-adjusted Review of the Empirical Literature." *World Bank Research Observer* 31 (2): 199–241.

Char, James. 2016. "Reclaiming the Party's Control of the Gun: Bringing Civilian Authority Back in China's Civil-Military Relations." *Journal of Strategic Studies* 39 (5–6): 608–636.

Chaterine, Rahel Narda. 2021. "Nadiem Makarim Minta Maaf ke PBNU." *Kompas*, April 22.

Cheibub, José Antonio. 2007. *Presidentialism, Parliamentarism, and Democracy*. Cambridge: Cambridge University Press.

Cheibub, José Antonio, Adam Przeworski, and Sebastian M. Saiegh. 2004. "Government Coalitions and Legislative Success under Presidentialism and Parliamentarism." *British Journal of Political Science* 34 (4): 565–87.
Chong, Wu-Ling. 2015. "Local Politics and Chinese Indonesian Business in Post-Suharto Era." *Southeast Asian Studies* 4 (3): 487–532.
Citradi, Tirta. 2020. "Ditunjuk Jadi Menparekraf, Kekayaan Sandi Nambah Rp 267 M!" *CNBC Indonesia*, December 23.
CNN Indonesia. 2019. "Jokowi Naikkan Gaji Anggota Polri Jelang Pilpres." *CNN Indonesia*, March 17.
———. 2020. "Tito Usul Opsi Pilkada Tak Langsung untuk Daerah IPM Rendah." *CNN Indonesia*, June 20.
———. 2021a. "Massa Demo Dukung Firli Akui Tak Paham Alasan Demonstrasi." *CNN Indonesia*, May 28.
———. 2021b. "Jokowi: ASN Melayani, Bukan Dilayani Seperti Pejabat Kolonial." *CNN Indonesia*, July 27.
Cohen, Margot. 1998. "'Us' vs 'Them.'" *Far Eastern Economic Review*, February 12.
Conley, Richard S. 2007. "Presidential Republics and Divided Government: Lawmaking and Executive Politics in the United States and France." *Political Science Quarterly* 122 (2): 257–285.
Croissant, Aurel. 2013. "Coups and Post-Coup Politics in South-East Asia and the Pacific: Conceptual and Comparative Perspectives." *Australian Journal of International Affairs* 67 (3): 264–280.
Croissant, Aurel, and David Kuehn, eds. 2017. *Reforming Civil-Military Relations in New Democracies: Democratic Control and Military Effectiveness in Comparative Perspectives*. Singapore: Springer.
Croissant, Aurel, David Kuehn, and Tanja Eschenauer. 2018. "The "Dictator's Endgame": Explaining Military Behavior in Nonviolent Anti-incumbent Mass Protests." *Democracy and Security* 14 (2): 174–199.
Croissant, Aurel, and Philip Völkel. 2012. "Party System Types and Party System Institutionalization: Comparing New Democracies in East and Southeast Asia." *Party Politics* 18 (2): 235–265.
Crouch, Harold. 1978. *The Army and Politics in Indonesia*. Ithaca: Cornell University Press.
———. 2003. "Political Update 2002: Megawati's Holding Operation." In *Local Power & Politics in Indonesia: Decentralisation & Democratisation*, edited by Edward Aspinall and Greg Fealy, 15–34. Singapore: ISEAS.
———. 2010. *Political Reform in Indonesia after Soeharto*. Singapore: ISEAS.
Daly, Tom Gerald. 2019. "Democratic Decay: Conceptualising an Emerging Research Field." *Hague Journal on the Rule of Law* 11: 9–36.
Damanik, Caroline. "Presiden Jokowi: Gaji PNS Naik Awal April, Sekaligus Gaji Ke-13 dan Ke-14." *Kompas*, March 8.
Damarjati, Danu. 2018. "Wacana Habib Rizieq Nyapres Sudah Muncul di 3 Pilpres." *Detik*, March 25.
Danendra, Ida Bagus Kade. 2012. "Kedudukan dan Fungsi Kepolisian dalam Struktur Organisasi Negara Republik Indonesia." *Lex Crimen* 1 (4): 41–59.
Dasandi, Niheer, and Marc Esteve. 2017. "The Politics–Bureaucracy Interface in Developing Countries." *Public Administration and Development* 37 (4): 231–245.
Della-Giacoma, Jim. 2013. "Indonesia's Police: The Problem of Deadly Force." *Interpreter*, June 18.
Derfler, Leslie. 1983. *President and Parliament: A Short History of the French Presidency*. Boca Raton: University Presses of Florida.

Detik. 2014. "Asosiasi Gubernur Minta Jokowi Gelontorkan Rp 1 Triliun untuk Provinsi." *Detik*, November 24.
——. 2018. "NU Bicara Opsi 'Tinggalkan' Jokowi bila Mahfud Md Jadi Cawapres." *Detik*, August 8.
——. 2019a. "PBNU yang Kini Hangat ke FPI." *Detik*, November 1.
——. 2019b. "Survei LSI: Kepercayaan Publik terhadap DPR Paling Rendah." *Detik*, October 6.
——. 2020. "Ketika Din Anggap Tawaran Wamendikbud Rendahkan Muhammadiyah." *Detik*, December 25.
——. 2021. "Isu Nia Ramadhani-Ardi Bakrie Makan di Restoran, Balai Rehab Bersuara Tim." *Detik*, November 3.
DeWalt, Kathleen M., and Billie R. DeWalt. 2011. *Participant Observation: A Guide for Fieldworkers*. Plymouth: AltaMira Press.
Diamond, Larry. 2009. "Is a 'Rainbow Coalition' a Good Way to Govern?" *Bulletin of Indonesian Economic Studies* 45 (3): 337–340.
——. 2021. Democratic Regression in Comparative Perspective: Scope, Methods, and Causes." *Democratization* 28 (1): 22–42.
Diprose, Rachael, and Muhammad Najib Azca. 2019. "Past Communal Conflict and Contemporary Security Debates in Indonesia." *Journal of Contemporary Asia* 49 (5): 780–805.
Diprose, Rachael, Nanang Kurniawan, Kate Macdonald, and Poppy Winanti. 2022. "Regulating Sustainable Minerals in Electronics Supply Chains: Local Power Struggles and the 'Hidden Costs' of Global Tin Supply Chain Governance." *Review of International Political Economy* 29 (3): 792–817.
DPR. 2015. "Transkrip Rekaman Diputar dalam Didang MKD 2 December 2015." https://bem.cs.ui.ac.id/isi-lengkap-rekaman-papa-minta-saham/.
Dunia Muallaf. 2014. "Habib Rizieq Syihab: 'Jokowi Pembawa Masalah dan Pengundang Musibah Bagi Umat Islam!'" *Dunia Muallaf*, November.
Eggert, Nina, Ruud Wouters, Pauline Ketelaars, and Stefaan Walgrave. 2018. "Preparing for Action: Police Deployment Decisions for Demonstrations." *Policing and Society* 28 (2): 137–148.
Elgie, Robert, and Sophia Moestrup, eds. 2008. *Semi-Presidentialism in Central and Eastern Europe*. Manchester: Manchester University Press.
Elson, Robert E. 2001. *Suharto: A Political Biography*. Cambridge: Cambridge University Press.
——. 2013 "Engineering from Within: Habibie the Man and Indonesia's Reformasi." In *Democracy Take-off? The B.J. Habibie Period*, edited by Dewi Fortuna Anwar and Bridget Welsh, 27–47. Jakarta: Sinar Harapan.
Emmerson, Donald K. 1978. "The Bureaucracy in Political Context: Weakness in Strength." In *Political Power and Communications in Indonesia*, edited by Karl D. Jackson And Lucian W. Pye, 82–136. Berkeley: University of California Press.
Esen, Berk, and Sebnem Gumuscu. 2018. "The Perils of 'Turkish Presidentialism.'" *Review of Middle East Studies* 52(1): 43–53.
Fachrudin, Azis Anwar. 2019. "Jokowi and NU: The view from the Pesantren." *New Mandala*, April 11.
Fadhil, Haris. 2016. "Mendagri Batalkan Ribuan Perda Penghambat Investasi." *Detik*, October 19.
Faguet, Jean-Paul. 2021. "Understanding Decentralization: Theory, Evidence and Method, with a Focus on Least-Developed Countries." Working Paper 21-203, International Development, London School of Economics.

Fajri, Rahmatul. 2019. "LSI Prediksi Nama Pejabat Publik yang Masuk Bursa Capres 2024." *Media Indonesia*, July 2.
Farhan, Yuna. 2018. "The Politics of Budgeting in Indonesia." PhD diss., University of Sydney.
Faturokhman, Toni. 2016. "Jelang Demo 4 November 2016, Jokowi 'Ngacir' ke Bandara?" *Rancah Post*, November 4.
Fealy, Greg. 1997. "Ulama and Politics in Indonesia: A History of Nahdlatul Ulama, 1952–1967." PhD diss., Monash University.
——. 2018a. "Ma'ruf Amin: Jokowi's Islamic Defender or Deadweight?" *New Mandala*, August 28.
——. 2018b. "Nahdlatul Ulama and the Politics Trap." *New Mandala*, July 11.
——. 2020. "Jokowi in the Covid-19 Era: Repressive Pluralism, Dynasticism and the Overbearing State." *Bulletin of Indonesian Economic Studies* 56 (3): 301–323.
Fealy, Greg, and Sally White. 2021. "The Politics of Banning FPI." *New Mandala*, June 18.
Feith, Herbert. 1962. *The Decline of Constitutional Democracy in Indonesia*. Ithaca: Cornell University Press.
——. 1963. "Dynamics of Guided Democracy." In *Indonesia*, edited by Ruth T. McVey, 309–409. New Haven: HRAF.
Ferrazzi, Gabriele. 2000. "Using the 'F' Word: Federalism in Indonesia's Decentralization Discourse." *Publius: The Journal of Federalism* 30 (2): 63–85.
Firmansyah, Bima. 2015. "Alasan Jokowi Betah di Istana Bogor." *Liputan6*, February 16.
Firmanto, Danang. 2017. "KASN: Jual-Beli Jabatan Sekretaris Daerah Capai Angka Rp 1 M." *Tempo*, January 30.
Forbes. 2016. "Rise in Fortunes for More Than Half of 50 Richest on Forbes Indonesia Rich List." *Forbes*, December 1.
Fossati, Diego, and Mietzner, Marcus. 2019. "Analyzing Indonesia's Populist Electorate: Demographic, Ideological, and Attitudinal Trends." *Asian Survey* 59 (5): 769–794.
Freudenreich, Johannes. 2016. "The Formation of Cabinet Coalitions in Presidential Systems." *Latin American Politics and Society* 58 (4): 80–102.
Fukuoka, Yuki. 2013. "Oligarchy and Democracy in Post-Suharto Indonesia." *Political Studies Review* 11(1): 52–64.
Fukuoka, Yuki, and Luky Djani. 2016. "Revisiting the Rise of Jokowi: The Triumph of Reformasi or an Oligarchic Adaptation of Post-Clientelist Initiatives?" *South East Asia Research* 24(2): 204–221.
Fukuyama, Francis, Björn Dressel, and Boo-Seung Chang. 2005. "Challenge and Change in East Asia: Facing the Perils of Presidentialism?" *Journal of Democracy* 16 (2): 102–116.
Gabrillin, Abba. 2017. "Dakwaan Kasus Korupsi E-KTP, Setya Novanto Diberi Jatah Rp 574 Miliar." *Kompas*, March 9.
Galih, Bayu. 2019. "Wakil Ketua DPR Taufik Kurniawan Divonis 6 Tahun Penjara." *Kompas*, July 15.
Gera, Iris. 2015. "Presiden Jokowi, Pimpinan DPR RI Sepakati Calon Kapolri, APBNP 2015." *VOA*, April 6.
Globe Asia. 2008. "Aburizal Bakrie Richest Man in Southeast Asia." *Globe Asia*, May.
Gobel, Rahmat Teguh Santoso. 2019. "Rekonseptualisasi Ambang Batas Pencalonan Presiden dan Wakil Presiden (Presidential Threshold) Dalam Pemilu Serentak." *Jambura Law Review* 1 (1): 94–119.
Gratzinger, Ollie. 2020. "Small Donors Give Big Money in 2020 Election Cycle." *Open Secrets*, October 30.

Gual, Marselinus. 2017. "PBNU Dukung Pembubaran HTI yang Merongrong Pancasila." *CNN Indonesia*, May 12.

Guild, James. 2019. "Is Indonesia's State-led Development Working?" *East Asia Forum*, August 28.

Gumilang, Prima. 2016. "TNI Klaim Tak Pernah Kudeta Pemerintah." *CNN Indonesia*, December 8.

Gumilang, Prima, and Suriyanto. 2016. "Agus Widjojo: Masyarakat Bersikap Masih Seperti 1965." *CNN Indonesia*, October 1.

Gunadha, Reza, and Ria Rizki Nirmala Sari. 2020. "Mendagri Tito: Negara Oligarki Lebih Mudah Tangani Pandemi Covid-19." *Suara*, September 3.

Hadi, Syamsul. 2011. "Last Chapter of an Uneasy Partnership: The Loss of Jusuf Kalla in the 2009 Presidential Election." In *Political Parties, Party Systems and Democratization in East Asia*, edited by Liang Fook Lye and Wilhelm Hofmeister, 189–209. Singapore: World Scientific.

Hadiz, Vedi R. 2018. "Imagine All the People? Mobilising Islamic Populism for Right-Wing Politics in Indonesia." *Journal of Contemporary Asia* 48 (4): 566–583.

Hadiz, Vedi R., and Richard Robison. 2004. *Reorganising Power in Indonesia: The Politics of Oligarchy in an Age of Markets*. London: Routledge.

——. 2014. "President Jokowi vs Oligarchy." *New Mandala*, July 10.

Hari, Ariyanti. 2019. "Survei LSI: 68,7 Persen Warga Puas dengan Demokrasi di Indonesia." *Merdeka*, August 2019.

Haripin, Muhamad. 2019. "Remnants of Authoritarianism: The Military in Indonesia." In *The Spectra of Authoritarianism in Southeast Asia*, edited by Azmi Sharom and Magdalen Spooner, 105–122. Bangkok: SHAPE-SEA.

Harsaputra, Indra. 2014. "Surabaya Mayor's Award Sparks Controversy." *Jakarta Post*, May 10.

Harsono, Yuli. 2010. "Polemik Penolakan Perpu JPSK." *Hukum Online*, January 19.

Hatherell, Michael. 2019. *Political Representation in Indonesia: The Emergence of the Innovative Technocrats*. London: Routledge.

Hatherell, Michael, and Alistair Welsh. 2017. "Rebel with a Cause: Ahok and Charismatic Leadership in Indonesia." *Asian Studies Review* 41 (2): 174–190.

Helmke, Gretchen, YeonKyung Jeong, and Seda Ozturk. 2019. "Upending Impunity: Prosecuting Presidents in Contemporary Latin America." Duke University, April 17.

Hendrawan, Parliza. 2016. "Ayah Tito Karnavian Wartawan Senior di Palembang." *Tempo*, June 17.

Hermansyah, Anton. 2018. "Bakrie & Brothers to Convert Trillions of Debt into Equity." *Jakarta Post*, June 27.

Hill, Hal, ed. 2014. *Regional Dynamics in a Decentralized Indonesia*. Singapore: ISEAS.

Hoff, Samuel B. 1991. "Saying No: Presidential Support and Veto Use, 1889–1989." *American Politics Quarterly* 19 (3): 310–323.

Honna, Jun. 2003. *Military Politics and Democratization in Indonesia*. London: Routledge.

——. 2012. "Inside the Democrat Party: Power, Politics and Conflict in Indonesia's Presidential Party." *South East Asia Research* 20 (4): 473–489.

——. 2019. "Civil-Military Relations in an Emerging State: A Perspective from Indonesia's Democratic Consolidation." In *Emerging States at Crossroads*, edited by Keiichi Tsunekawa and Yasuyuki Todo, 255–270. Singapore: Springer.

Horowitz, Donald L. 2013. *Constitutional Change and Democracy in Indonesia*. Cambridge: Cambridge University Press.

Huxley, Tim. 2002. "Disintegrating Indonesia? Implications for Regional Security." London: International Institute for Strategic Studies, 2002.

Iaryczowera, Matias, and Santiago Oliveros. 2016. "Power Brokers: Middlemen in Legislative Bargaining." *Journal of Economic Theory* 162: 209–236.
Ibrahim, Gibran Maulana. 2018. "Kader Pindah Partai, PD Tuduh Jaksa Agung Jadi Alat Politik NasDem." *Detik*, September 28.
Ihsanuddin. 2018. "HUT Ke-47, Korpri Tagih Hadiah dari Presiden Jokowi." *Kompas*, November 29.
——. 2019. "Bertemu Ahok dan Dirut Pertamina, Ini Instruksi Jokowi." *Kompas*, December 10.
Indana, Wanda. 2019. "Kecewa Kader Tak Masuk Kabinet, PBNU Sumpahi Jokowi Kualat? Ini Faktanya." *Medcom*, October 29.
Indikator. 2021. "Survei Nasional Persepsi Ekonomi dan Politik Jelang Lebaran: Temuan Survei 13–17 April 2021." Jakarta: Indikator Politik Indonesia.
——. 2022. "Pemulihan Ekonomi Pasca COVID-19, Pandemic Fatigue, dan Dinamika Elektoral Jelang Pemilu 2024: Temuan Survei Nasional 6–11 Desember 2021." Jakarta: Indikator Politik Indonesia.
Inge, Nefri. 2019. "Mengenang Mendiang Ayah Tito Karnavian yang Bangga Anaknya Jadi Kapolri." *Liputan6*, October 24.
IPAC (Institute for Policy Analysis of Conflict). 2016. "Update on the Indonesian Military's Influence." *IPAC Report* 26, March 11.
Iskandar, Jean Daryn Hendar. 2018. "Kedudukan Kepolisian Negara Republik Indonesia dalam Sistem Ketatanegaraan." *Lex Administratum* 6 (4): 46–55.
Ismoyo, Bambang. 2019. "Karyawan Pertamina Nilai Ahok Cacat Persyaratan Bila Jadi Bos BUMN." *Warta Ekonomi*, November 18.
Jaffrey, Sana. 2020. "Coronavirus Blunders in Indonesia Turn Crisis into Catastrophe." *Carnegie Commentary*, April 29.
Jakarta Post. 2012. "Mega, Prabowo, Bakrie All Bottom Out in New Survey." *Jakarta Post*, July 9.
Jawa Pos. 2019. "TKN Jokowi Laporkan Sumbangan Rp 606,7 M, Ada Rp 253,9 M dari Perusahaan." *Jawa Pos*, May 2.
Jones, Sidney, 2012. "TNI and Counter-Terrorism: Not a Good Mix." *Strategic Review* 2 (1): 14–18.
Jong, Hans Nicholas. 2018. "Indonesian Ruling Rings Alarms over Criminalization of Environmental Defenders." *Mongabay*, January 26.
Julcarima Alvarez, Gerson Francisco. 2020. "Types of Semi-Presidentialism and Party Competition Structures in Democracies: The Cases of Portugal and Peru." PhD diss., University of Lethbridge.
Kahin, George McTurnan. 1952. *Nationalism and Revolution in Indonesia*. Ithaca: Cornell University Press.
Kamarck, Elaine C. 2020. *Picking the Vice President*. Washington, DC: Brookings Institution Press.
Kampen, Jarl K., Steven Van De Walle, and Greet Bouckaert. 2006. "Assessing the Relation between Satisfaction with Public Service Delivery and Trust in Government: The Impact of the Predisposition of Citizens toward Government on Evaluations of Its Performance." *Public Performance & Management Review* 29 (4): 387–404.
Kasuya, Yuko, and Julio C. Teehankee. 2020. "Duterte Presidency and the 2019 Midterm Election: An Anarchy of Parties?" *Philippine Political Science Journal* 41: 106–126.
Katz, Richard S., and Peter Mair. 1995. "Changing Models of Party Organization and Party Democracy: The Emergence of the Cartel Party." *Party Politics* 1 (1): 5–28.
Kellam, Marisa. 2017. "Why Pre-Electoral Coalitions in Presidential Systems?" *British Journal of Political Science* 47 (2): 391–411.

Kemendagri. 2014. "Mendagri Pertimbangkan Aspirasi Kepala Daerah yang Tolak Pilkada via DPRD." Kemendagri, September 12.

Kemenhan. 2015. "Panggil Saksi, KPK Minta Restu Jokowi Gandeng TNI." Kementerian Pertahanan, January 30.

———. 2021. "Tugas dan Fungsi." Kementerian Pertahanan.

Kementerian Keuangan. 2020. "Rincian Alokasi Transfer ke Daerah dan Dana Desa (TKDD) dalam APBN Tahun Anggaran 2021." Kementerian Keuangan, September 29.

Kenny, Paul. 2018. *Populism in Southeast Asia*. Cambridge Elements. New York: Cambridge University Press.

Klaus, Kathleen. 2020. *Political Violence in Kenya: Land, Elections, and Claim-Making*. Cambridge: Cambridge University Press.

Koelble, Thomas A., Andrew Siddle. 2013. "Why Decentralization in South Africa Has Failed." *Governance* 26 (3): 343–346.

Kompas. 2009. "Sri Mulyani: 'Aburizal Bakrie Is Not Happy with Me.'" *Kompas*, December 11.

Kontan. 2021. "Buka Munas Apkasi, Jokowi Ingatkan Bupati Lakukan Konsolidasi Anggaran." *Kontan*, March 26.

Kosandi, Meidi, and Subur Wahono. 2020. "Military Reform in the Post-New Order Indonesia: A Transitional or a New Subtle Role in Indonesian Democracy?" *Asian Politics & Policy* 12 (2): 224–241.

Kota Ternate. 2017. "Walikota Surabaya Pastikan Hadiri Muskomwil VI APEKSI Di Ternate." Kota Ternate, July 19.

Kovalevskyi, Ihor. 2022. "Civil-Military Relations in Putin's Russia." In *The Routledge Handbook of Civil-Military Relations*, edited by Florina Cristiana Matei, Carolyn Halladay, and Thomas C. Bruneau, 13–25. London: Routledge.

KPK. 2021. "Graph TPK Berdasarkan Profesi/Jabatan." KPK, August 15. https://www.kpk.go.id/id/statistik/penindakan/tpk-berdasarkan-profesi-jabatan.

Kramer, Elisabeth. 2014. "A Fall from Grace? 'Beef-Gate' and the Case of Indonesia's Prosperous Justice Party." *Asian Politics & Policy* 6 (4): 555–576.

Kuhlmann, Jürgen, and Jean Callaghan, eds. 2017. *Military and Society in 21st Century Europe: A Comparative Analysis*. London: Routledge.

Kumparan. 2018. "Sekjen PBNU Ajak Eks Anggota HTI Gabung NU." *Kumparan*, May 7.

———. 2019. "Erick Thohir Libatkan Lagi Tim Penilai Akhir untuk Tunjuk Direksi BUMN." *Kumparan*, November 12.

Kurdi, Mustafa, and A. Yani Wahid. *Susilo Bambang Yudhoyono dalam 5 Hari Mandat Maklumat*. Jakarta: Aksara Kurnia, 2003.

Kurnia, Endah. 2018. "Didukung 30 Gubernur dan 359 Bupati/Walikota, Pasangan Jokowi-Ma'ruf Diunggulkan akan Menang di Pilpres 2019. *Kompasiana*, October 3.

Kurniawan, Rudy Cahya. 2021. *Pengaturan Kewenangan KPK Dan Polri Dalam Penyidikan Tindak Pidana Korupsi Di Indonesia*. Yogyakarta: Deepublish.

———. 2021. "PB NU: Pemerintah Tidak Anti-Ormas Islam dengan Bubarkan FPI." *Jawa Pos*, January 3.

Kuwado, Fabian Januarius. 2016. "Jokowi Perintahkan Luhut Cari Kuburan Massal Korban 1965." *Kompas*, April 25.

———. 2017. "Pidato Hari Lahir Pancasila, Jokowi Singgung Komunisme." *Kompas*, June 1.

Laisila, Laban, and Agung Sandy Lesmana. 2015. "Jaksa Agung Janji Cari Cara Tuntaskan Kasus Pelanggaran HAM Berat." *Suara*, April 21.

Laksmana, Evan A. 2019. "Reshuffling the Deck? Military Corporatism, Promotional Logjams and Post-authoritarian Civil-military Relations in Indonesia." *Journal of Contemporary Asia* 49 (5): 806–836.

Lappin, Kate. 2020. "A Neoliberal Pandemic in Asia." *International Union Rights* 27 (4): 3–5.
Lee, Don S. 2018. "Portfolio Allocation as the President's Calculations: Loyalty, Copartisanship, and Political Context in South Korea." *Journal of East Asian Studies* 18 (3): 345–365.
Legge, John D. 1972. *Sukarno: A Political Biography*. London: Allen Lane.
Lev, Daniel S. 1966. *The Transition to Guided Democracy: Indonesian Politics, 1957–1959*. Ithaca: Cornell Southeast Asia Program.
Lewis, Blane D., and Adrianus Hendrawan. 2019. "The Impact of Majority Coalitions on Local Government Spending, Service Delivery, and Corruption in Indonesia." *European Journal of Political Economy* 58: 178–191
Lewis, Blane D., and Andre Oosterman. 2009. "Public Budgeting and Finance: The Impact of Decentralization on Subnational Government Fiscal Slack in Indonesia." *Journal of Public Budgeting and Finance* 29 (2): 27–47.
Lex Rieffel, and Jaleswari Pramodhawardani. 2007. *Out of Business and on Budget: The Challenge of Military Financing in Indonesia*. Washington, DC: Brookings Institution Press.
Linz, Juan J. 1990. "The Perils of Presidentialism." *Journal of Democracy* 1 (1): 51–69.
Liputan6. 2018. "Lukas Enembe: 29 Kepala Daerah di Papua Dukung Jokowi-Ma'ruf." *Liputan6*, September 27.
Lowry, Robert. 1996. *The Armed Forces of Indonesia*. St Leonards: Allen & Unwin.
———. 2017. "Political Nous Checks Military Might in Indonesia." *Australian Institute of International Affairs*, December 18.
LSI. 2017. "Potensi Radikalisme dan Intoleransi Sosial-Keagamaan di Kalangan Muslim Indonesia. Temuan Survei: Agustus 2017." Jakarta: Lembaga Survei Indonesia.
Lupu, Noam. 2015. *Party Brands in Crisis: Partisanship, Brand Dilution, and the Breakdown of Political Parties in Latin America*. New York: Cambridge University Press.
Maharani, Esthi. 2015. "Luhut: Presiden tak Pernah Perintah dan Restui Sudirman Lapor ke MKD." *Republika*, December 2.
Mainwaring, Scott. 1993. "Presidentialism, Multipartism, and Democracy: The Difficult Combination." *Comparative Political Studies* 26 (2): 198–228.
———, ed. 2018. *Party Systems in Latin America: Institutionalization, Decay, and Collapse*. New York: Cambridge University Press.
Malley, Michael. 1999. "Regions: Centralization and Resistance." In *Indonesia Beyond Suharto*, edited by Donald K. Emmerson, 71–108. London: Imprint Routledge.
Mardiansyah, Whisnu. 2019. "Golkar Yakin Dapat Efek Elektoral Jokowi." *Medcom*, April 1.
Marnati. 2015. "Jumlah Lembaga Pendidikan Muhammadiyah Lebih dari 10 Ribu." *Republika*, August 2.
Martahan Sohuturon. 2017. "Tito Sebut Anggaran Polri Naik Dua Kali Lipat di Era Jokowi." *CNN Indonesia*, July 10.
Martí, Gerardo. 2019. "The Unexpected Orthodoxy of Donald J. Trump: White Evangelical Support for the 45th President of the United States." *Sociology of Religion* 80 (1): 1–8.
Martin van Bruinessen, ed. 2013. *Contemporary Developments in Indonesian Islam: Explaining the "Conservative Turn."* Singapore: ISEAS.
Martínez-Gallardo, Cecilia, and Petra Schleiter. 2015. "Choosing Whom to Trust: Agency Risks and Cabinet Partisanship in Presidential Democracies." *Comparative Political Studies* 48 (2): 231–264.
Mashabi, Sania. 2020. "Amnesty: Kasus Penjeratan UU ITE Saat Kepemimpinan Jokowi Meningkat Tajam." *Kompas*, October 28.

Maulia, Erwida. 2020. "Jokowi's Bid to Centralize Power Stirs Suharto Memories." *Nikkei Asia*, February 27.
McBeth, John. 2016. "A Win for Widodo: Indonesia's New Police Chief." *Strategist*, July 18.
——. 2018. "Widodo's Re-election Strategy Comes into View." *Asia Times*, July 2.
McClendon, Gwyneth H., and Rachel Beatty Riedl. 2019. *From Pews to Politics: Religious Sermons and Political Participation in Africa*. Cambridge: Cambridge University Press.
McIntyre, Angus. 2005. *The Indonesian Presidency: The Shift from Personal toward Constitutional Rule*. New York: Roman and Littlefield.
McLeod, Ross, 2005. "The Struggle to Regain Effective Government under Democracy in Indonesia." *Bulletin of Indonesian Economic Studies* 41 (3): 367–386.
Media Indonesia. 2021. "Munas Dibuka Presiden, Apkasi Laporkan Refocusing APBD." *Media Indonesia*, March 26.
Melvin, Jess. 2018. *The Army and the Indonesian Genocide: Mechanics of Mass Murder*. London: Routledge.
Merdeka. 2019. "Panggil Gubernur Bali, Sulut dan NTT, Jokowi Ucapkan Terima Kasih Serta Bahas Proyek." *Merdeka*, April 22.
Metcalf, Lee Kendall. 2000. "Measuring Presidential Power." *Comparative Political Studies* 33 (5): 660–685.
Mezey, Michael L. 2013. *Presidentialism: Power in Comparative Perspective*. Boulder: Lynne Rienner.
Michella, Widya. 2021. "Teka-teki Pangkostrad Baru, Panglima TNI: Ini Baru Mau Lapor Presiden." *Sindo News*, November 22.
Mietzner, Marcus. 2000. "The 1999 General Session: Wahid, Megawati and the Fight for the Presidency." In *Indonesia in Transition: Social Dimensions of Reformasi and Crisis*, edited by Chris Manning and Peter van Diermen, 39–57. Singapore: ISEAS.
——. 2001. "Abdurrahman's Indonesia: Political Conflict and Institutional Crisis." In *Indonesia Today: Challenges of History*, edited by Shannon L. Smith and Grayson J. Lloyd, 29–44. Singapore: ISEAS.
——. 2009a. *Military Politics, Islam, and the State in Indonesia: From Turbulent Transition to Democratic Consolidation*. Singapore: ISEAS.
——. 2009b. "Indonesia's 2009 Elections: Populism, Dynasties and the Consolidation of the Party System." Sydney: Lowy Institute for International Policy.
——. 2013. *Money, Power, and Ideology: Political Parties in Post-authoritarian Indonesia*. Honolulu: Hawai'i University Press.
——. 2014a. "Jokowi: Rise of a Polite Populist." *Inside Indonesia*, April 27.
——. 2014b. "Indonesia's Decentralization: The Rise of Local Identities and the Survival of the Nation-State." In *Regional Dynamics in a Decentralized Indonesia*, edited by Hal Hill, 45–67. Singapore: ISEAS.
——. 2015. "Dysfunction by Design: Political Finance and Corruption in Indonesia." *Critical Asian Studies* 47 (4): 587–610.
——. 2016. "Coercing Loyalty: Coalitional Presidentialism and Party Politics in Jokowi's Indonesia." *Contemporary Southeast Asia* 38 (2): 209–232.
——. 2019. "Indonesia's Elections in the Periphery: A view from Maluku." *New Mandala*, April 2.
——. 2020. "Indonesian Parties Revisited: Systemic Exclusivism, Electoral Personalisation and Declining Intraparty Democracy." In *Democracy in Indonesia: From Stagnation to Regression?*, edited by Thomas Power and Eve Warburton, 191–209. Singapore: ISEAS—Yusof Ishak Institute.

———. 2023. "Democracy and Military Oversight in Crisis: The Failed Civilianization of Indonesia's Ministry of Defence." *Journal of Asian Security and International Affairs* 10 (1): 7–23.

Mietzner, Marcus, and Lisa Misol. 2013. "Military Businesses in Post-Suharto Indonesia: Decline, Reform and Persistence." In *The Politics of Military Reform: Experiences from Indonesia and Nigeria*, edited by Jurgen Ruland, Maria-Gabriela Manea, and Hans Born, 101–120. Heidelberg: Springer.

Mietzner, Marcus, and Burhanuddin Muhtadi. 2018. "Explaining the 2016 Islamist Mobilisation in Indonesia: Religious Intolerance, Militant Groups and the Politics of Accommodation." *Asian Studies Review* 42 (3): 479–497.

———. 2019. "The Mobilisation of Intolerance and Its Trajectories: Indonesian Muslims' View of Religious Minorities and Ethnic Chinese." In *Contentious Belonging: The Place of Minorities in Indonesia*, edited by Greg Fealy and Ronit Ricci, 155–174. Singapore: ISEAS—Yusuf Ishak Institute.

———. 2020. "The Myth of Pluralism: Nahdlatul Ulama and the Politics of Religious Tolerance in Indonesia." *Contemporary Southeast Asia* 42 (1): 58–84.

Mietzner, Marcus, Burhanuddin Muhtadi, and Rizka Halida. 2018. "Entrepreneurs of Grievance: Drivers and Effects of Indonesia's Islamist Mobilization." *Bijdragen tot de Taal-, Land- en Volkenkunde* 174: 159–187.

Molteni, Francesco, and Ferruccio Biolcati. 2018. "Shifts in Religiosity across Cohorts in Europe: A Multilevel and Multidimensional Analysis based on the European Values Study." *Social Compass* 65(3): 413–432.

Montlake, Simon. 2011. "Bailing Out Indonesia's Bakrie: Commodity Brokers to the Rescue?" *Forbes*, October 14.

Morgenstern, Scott, Juan Javier Negri, and Aníbal Pérez-Liñán. 2008. "Parliamentary Opposition in Non-Parliamentary Regimes: Latin America." *Journal of Legislative Studies* 14 (1–2): 160–189.

Mrázek, Rudolf. 1994. *Sjahrir: Politics and Exile in Indonesia*. Ithaca: Cornell Southeast Asia Program.

Muchlishon, Rochmat, and Fathoni. 2017. "ATM NU, Langkah PBNU Permudah Santri Bertransaksi." *NU Online*, July 24.

Muhardianto, Bayu. 2021. "Harta Kekayaan Kaesang Buat Publik Bertanya-tanya, Jokowi Harus Bersuara? Pengamat: Secara Etis . . ." *Warta Ekonomi*, December 18.

Muhtadi, Burhanuddin. 2015. "Jokowi's First Year: A Weak President Caught between Reform and Oligarchic Politics." *Bulletin of Indonesian Economic Studies* 51 (3): 349–368.

———. 2019. *Vote Buying in Indonesia: The Mechanics of Electoral Bribery*. London: Palgrave.

Muhyiddin. 2019. "IPNU Ingatkan Jokowi Pilih Menteri Agama dari NU." *Republika*, October 22.

Mujani, Saiful, and R. William Liddle. 2021. "Indonesia: Jokowi Sidelines Democracy." *Journal of Democracy* 32 (4): 72–86.

Mujani, Saiful, William R. Liddle, and Kuskridho Ambardi. 2018. *Voting Behavior in Indonesia since Democratization: Critical Democrats*. Cambridge: Cambridge University Press.

Muradi. 2019. *Politics and Governance in Indonesia: The Police in the Era of Reformasi*. London: Routledge.

Mustafa, Şen. 2010. "Transformation of Turkish Islamism and the Rise of the Justice and Development Party." *Turkish Studies* 11 (1): 59–84.

Mustaqim, Syaiful. 2019. "Warga NU Jadi Sasaran Empuk Dakwah HTI." *NU Online*, October 28.
Nasrudin, Achmad. 2020. "Setahun Firli Bahuri Pimpin KPK: OTT Terendah Dalam 5 Tahun Terakhir." *Kompas*, December 31.
Nasution, Adnan Buyung. 1992. *The Aspiration for Constitutional Government in Indonesia: A Socio-legal Study of the Indonesian Konstituante 1956–1959*. Jakarta: Pustaka Sinar Harapan.
Niman, Mikael. 2018. "Konflik Memuncak, Sekda Kota Bekasi Lapor ke Gubernur Jabar." *Berita Satu*, July 31.
Ningrum, Desi Aditia. "Ke Mana Langkah Jokowi Pergi Selalu Ada Menteri Basuki." *Merdeka*, October 10.
Noorhaidi Hasan. 2006. *Laskar Jihad: Islam, Militancy, and the Quest for Identity in Post-New Order Indonesia*. Ithaca: Cornell Southeast Asia Program.
NU Online. "Ngotot Dirikan Khilafah, Puluhan Ormas di Jombang Minta HTI Dibubarkan." *NU Online*, April 30.
Nugroho, Tri, Arry Bainus, and Wawan Budi Darmawan. 2018. "TNI Involvement Strategy on Determination of Defense Budget Policy in Legislative Institutions." *Central European Journal of International and Security Studies* 12 (4): 165–179.
Nurbaya. 2021. "Profil Siti Nurbaya Bakar." https://www.sitinurbaya.com/profilku.
Nurcahyadi, Ghani. 2021. "Kalangan Santri Sambut Baik Perhatian Pemerintah Pada Pesantren." *Media Indonesia*, October 22.
Nurtjahyo, Hendra. 1997. "Posisi Otoritas Legislatif Presiden dan DPR." *Jurnal Hukum & Pembangunan* 27 (2): 94–101.
Octaviyani, Putri Rosmalia. 2019. "Survei: 69% Masyarakat Percaya Pemilu 2019 Berlangsung Jurdil." *Media Indonesia*, June 6.
Ostwald, Kai, Yuhki Tajima, and Krislert Samphantharak. 2016. "Indonesia's Decentralization Experiment: Motivations, Successes, and Unintended Consequences." *Journal of Southeast Asian Economies* 33 (2): 139–156.
Paat, Yustinus. 2019. "Prabowo-Sandi Pertanyakan Sumbangan Dana Kampanye Jokowi-Ma'ruf." *Berita Satu*, June 13.
Pangaribuan, Robinson. 1995. *The Indonesian State Secretariat, 1945–1993*. Translated by Vedi Hadiz. Perth: Asia Research Centre, Murdoch University.
Patterson, Bradley H., and James P. Pfiffner. 2001. "The White House Office of Presidential Personnel." *Presidential Studies Quarterly* 31 (3): 415–438.
PDI-P. 2019. "Pidato Pengantar Laporan Pertanggungjawaban DPP PDI Perjuangan Masa Bakti 2015–2020." Sanur, August 9.
Pebrianto, Fajar. 2020. "Jumlah Halaman UU Cipta Kerja Dinilai Masih Bisa Berubah." *Tempo*, October 17.
Pemda Bengkulu. "Presiden Jokowi Minta Kepala Daerah Permudah Izin Investasi untuk Buka Lapangan Pekerjaan." Pemda Bengkulu, April 14.
Pepinsky, Thomas B. 2009. *Economic Crises and the Breakdown of Authoritarian Regimes: Indonesia and Malaysia in Comparative Perspective*. Cambridge: Cambridge University Press.
Pepinsky, Thomas B., and Maria M. Wihardja. 2011. "Decentralization and Economic Performance in Indonesia." *Journal of East Asian Studies* 11 (3): 337–371.
Pérez-Liñán, Aníbal, and John Polga-Hecimovich. 2017. "Explaining Military Coups and Impeachments in Latin America." *Democratization* 24 (5): 839–858.
Peterson, Daniel. 2020a. *Islam, Blasphemy, and Human Rights in Indonesia: The Trial of Ahok*. New York: Routledge.
———. 2020b. "What Is Ma'ruf Amin Doing?" *Indonesia at Melbourne*, July 15.

Pierskalla, Jan H., Adam Lauretig, Andrew S. Rosenberg, and Audrey Sacks. 2021. "Democratization and Representative Bureaucracy: An Analysis of Promotion Patterns in Indonesia's Civil Service, 1980–2015." *American Journal of Political Science* 65 (2): 261–277.

Pion-Berlin, David, and Rafael Martínez. 2017. *Soldiers, Politicians, and Civilians: Reforming Civil-Military Relations in Democratic Latin America*. Cambridge: Cambridge University Press.

Polsek Karang Bintang. 2019. "Polsek Karang Bintang Pasang Spanduk Sinergitas TNI-Polri 'Nyoblos Itu Keren.'" *Tribata News*, March 8.

Power, Thomas. 2014. "Ideology Resurgent in Indonesia's Presidential Coalitions." *East Asia Forum*, June 9.

———. 2018. "Jokowi's Authoritarian Turn and Indonesia's Democratic Decline." *Bulletin of Indonesian Economic Studies* 54 (3): 307–338.

———. 2020. "Assailing Accountability: Law Enforcement Politicisation, Partisan Coercion and Executive Aggrandisement under the Jokowi Administration." In *Democracy in Indonesia: From Stagnation to Regression?*, edited by Thomas Power and Eve Warburton, 277–302. Singapore: ISEAS—Yusof Ishak Institute.

Power, Thomas, and Eve Warburton, eds. 2020. *Democracy in Indonesia: From Stagnation to Regression?* Singapore: ISEAS—Yusuf Ishak Institute.

Pradewo, Bintang. 2020. "Listyo Pernah Ditolak MUI, Kata Pakar Intelijen Soal Calon Kapolri."*Jawa Pos*, November 24.

Pramudya, Rorry. 2015. "Implikasi UU No 23 Tahun 2014 Tentang Pemerintahan Daerah Terhadap Peraturan Daerah Kabupaten/Kota Yang Mengatur Tentang Kewenangan Perizinan Bidang Energi Dan Sumber Daya Mineral." Biro Hukum Sekretariat Daerah Provinsi Kalimantan Tengah.

Pratama, Aditya. "Jumlah PNS di Indonesia 4,2 Juta, Didominasi Tenaga Administrasi." *iNews*, January 27.

Pratama, Andrian Peran. 2021. "Jokowi di Balik Suksesi Ketum Kadin & Pemilihan Arsjad Rasjid." *Tirto*, June 30.

Priamarizki, Adhi. 2021."Indonesia's Military still Preoccupied with Internal Security." *East Asia Forum*, June 4.

Prihandoko. 2015. "Di DPR, Jokowi Sebut Tak Akan 'Golkar-kan' Demokrat." *Tempo*, April 6.

PUPR. 2020. "HUT Korpri Ke-49, Menteri Basuki: ASN Tetap Harus Produktif dan Inovatif." PUPR, November 27.

Purnama Putra, Erik. 2020. "Eks Ajudan Jokowi Jadi Kepala Staf Kodam Diponegoro." *Republika*, April 15.

Purnamasari, Deti Mega. 2021. "3 Menteri dengan Kinerja Terbaik Versi Survei Puspoll: Sandiaga, Risma, Erick." *Kompas*, May 23.

Putratama, Abyan Faisal. 2019. "DPR Belum Terima Surpres Jokowi soal Revisi UU KPK." *Kumparan*, September 11.

Quigley, John. 2020. "Impeached, Jailed, Wanted: In Peru, President Is a Dangerous Job." *Bloomberg*, November 11.

Rachman, M. Anwar. 2016. "Penyelesaian Perselisihan Internal Partai Politik." *Yuridika* 31 (2): 189–219.

Rakhman, Ode, Umi Ma'rufah, Bagas Yusuf Kausan, and Ardi. 2021. *Ekonomi-Politik Penempatan TNI di Papua: Kasus Intan Jaya*. Jakarta: Kontras, Walhi et al.

Rakmawati, Trisya, Reece Hinchcliff, and Jerico Franciscus Pardosi. 2019. "District-level Impacts of Health System Decentralization in Indonesia: A Systematic Review." *International Journal of Health Planning and Management* 34 (2): 1026–1053.

Ramalan, Suparjo. 2021. "Erick Thohir Sebut Tiga Syarat Utama Swasta Bisa Kerja Sama dengan BUMN." *IDX Channel*, October 1.
Rastika, Icha. 2015. "Politisi PDI-P: Yang Punya Peluang, Sekarang Saatnya Makzulkan Jokowi!" *Kompas*, January 26.
Rasul, Imran, and Daniel Rogger. 2018. "Management of Bureaucrats and Public Service Delivery: Evidence from the Nigerian Civil Service." *Economic Journal* 128 (608): 413–446.
Rattinger, Alexandra. 2017. "The Impeachment Process of Brazil: A Comparative Look at Impeachment in Brazil and the United States." *University of Miami Inter-American Law Review* 49 (1): 129–166.
Repucci, Sarah, and Amy Slipowitz. 2021. "Democracy in a Year of Crisis." *Journal of Democracy* 32 (2): 45–60.
Retaduari, Elza Astari. 2017. "Tanda Tanya di Balik Hary Tanoe Dukung Jokowi Capres 2019." *Detik*, August 3.
Rezkisari, Indira. 2016. "Punya Kedekatan dengan 9 Naga, Tambah Modal Kekuatan Ahok." *Republika*, September 25.
Rini, Citra Listya. 2016. "Tito Cerita Soal Keluarganya di Hadapan Anggota Dewan." *Republika*, June 22.
Ritzky, Awali. 2019. "Wow, Anggaran Polri Meroket Karena Kebutuhan Mendesak. Pikiran Bebas, September 25. https://www.watyutink.com/topik/pikiran-bebas/Wow-Anggaran-Polri-Meroket-Karena-Kebutuhan-Mendesak.
Rizal, Jawahir Gustav. 2021. "Ramai Dibicarakan gara-gara Krisdayanti, Ini Besaran Gaji dan Tunjangan Anggota DPR." *Kompas*, September 16.
Robison, Richard. 1986. *Indonesia: The Rise of Capital*. Sydney: Allen & Unwin.
Robison, Richard, and Andrew Rosser. 2000. "Surviving the Meltdown: Liberal Reform and Political Oligarchy in Indonesia." In *Politics and Markets in the Wake of the Asian Crisis*, edited by Mark Beeson, Kanishka Jayasuriya, Hyuk-Rae Kim, and Richard Robison, 171–191. London: Routledge.
Roosa, John. 2006. *Pretext for Mass Murder: The September 30th Movement and Suharto's Coup d'État in Indonesia*. Wisconsin: University of Wisconsin Press.
Rosana, Francisca Christy. 2020. "Cerita Ahok Bentuk Tim Transformer di Pertamina." *Tempo*, June 28.
Saeno. 2020. "Viral Bayar SPP Lewat Gopay, Nadiem Bantah Kemendikbud Terkait." *Kabar24*, February 20.
Safitri, Eva. 2020. "Survei Indikator: Mayoritas Responden Takut Nyatakan Pendapat Saat Ini." *Detik*, October 25.
Salam, Fahri. 2020. "Keluarga Pebisnis & Konglomerat di Balik Bisnis Gibran dan Kaesang." *Tirto*, December 7.
Santika, I Gusti Ngurah. 2019. "Presidensialisme Dan Problematika Mekanisme Impeachment Presiden Dan/Atau Wakil Presiden Berdasarkan UUD 1945 Pasca Perubahan (Perspektif Pergulatan Hukum Dan Politik)." *Jurnal Ilmiah Ilmu Sosial* 5 (1): 23–34.
Saputra, Andi. 2021. "Jejak Kasus Dugaan Korupsi Heli AW-101: 'Mangkrak' di KPK, Digugat ke PM Jaksel." *Detik*, March 30.
Saragih, Sadariah. 2021. "Konstelasi Golkar dan Elite dalam Politik Indonesia Pasca Pemerintahan Orde Baru." *Jurnal Ilmu Sosial dan Ilmu Politik* 18 (1): 14–25.
Schwarz, Adam. 2004. *A Nation in Waiting: Indonesia's Search for Stability*. Singapore: Talisman.
Sekretariat Negara. 1995. *Risalah Sidang Badan Penyelidik Usaha-usaha Persiapan Kemerdekaan Indonesia (BPUPKI), Panitia Persiapan Kemerdekaan Indonesia (PPKI), 28 Mei 1945–22 Agustus 1945*. Jakarta: Sekretariat Negara.

Seo, Yohanes. 2014. "Gurita Bisnis Setya Novanto di NTT." *Tempo*, October 3.
Setijadi, Charlotte. 2021. "The Pandemic as Political Opportunity: Jokowi's Indonesia in the Time of Covid-19." *Bulletin of Indonesian Economic Studies* 57 (3): 297–320.
Sherlock, Stephen. 2009. "Parties and Decision-Making in the Indonesian Parliament: A Case Study of RUU APP, the Anti-Pornography Bill." *Australian Journal of Asian Law* 10 (2): 159–183.
———. 2012. "Made by Committee and Consensus: Parties and Policy in the Indonesian Parliament." *South East Asia Research* 20 (4): 551–568.
Shimazu, Naoko. 2014. "Diplomacy as Theatre: Staging the Bandung Conference of 1955." *Modern Asian Studies* 48 (1): 225–252.
Shofia, Naila, and Thomas B. Pepinsky. 2019. "Measuring the 'NU effect' in Indonesia's Election." *New Mandala*, July 1.
Sholeh, Muhammad. 2015. "Jokowi Minta Pejabat Ambil Keputusan tak Mudah dituduh Langgar UU." *Merdeka*, June 19.
Sholikah, Binti. 2021. "Kaesang, Kevin, Erick Thohir Pegang Saham Mayoritas Persis." *Republika*, March 21.
Shugart, Matthew Soberg, and John M. Carey. 1992. *Presidents and Assemblies: Constitutional Design and Electoral Dynamics*. Cambridge: Cambridge University Press.
Situmorang, Anggun P. 2019. "Berbeda dari Rini, Erick Thohir Pakai Tim Penilai Akhir Pilih Pimpinan BUMN." *Merdeka*, November 5.
Skowronek, Stephen. 1993. *The Politics Presidents Make: Leadership from John Adams to Bill Clinton*. Cambridge: Harvard University Press.
Slater, Dan. 2004. "Indonesia's Accountability Trap: Party Cartels and Presidential Power after Democratic Transition." *Indonesia* 78: 61–92.
———. 2018. "Party Cartelization, Indonesian-style: Presidential Power-sharing and the Contingency of Democratic Opposition." *Journal of East Asian Studies* 18 (1): 23–46.
Slater, Dan, and Erica Simmons. 2012. "Coping by Colluding: Political Uncertainty and Promiscuous Powersharing in Indonesia and Bolivia." *Comparative Political Studies* 46 (11): 1366–1393.
Soedirgo, Jessica. 2018. "Informal Networks and Religious Intolerance: How Clientelism Incentivizes the Discrimination of the Ahmadiyah in Indonesia." *Citizenship Studies* 22 (2): 191–207.
Somma, Nicolás M., Matías A. Bargsted, and Eduardo Valenzuela. "Mapping Religious Change in Latin America." *Latin American Politics and Society* 59 (1): 119–142.
Sorik, Sutan, and Dian Aulia. 2020. "Menata Ulang Relasi Majelis Permusyawaratan Rakyat dan Presiden Melalui Politik Hukum Haluan Negara." *Jurnal Konstitusi* 17 (2): 372–387.
Souisa, Hellena. 2019. "Partisan Players: Television and the Elections." *Indonesia at Melbourne*, April 8.
Sukoyo, Yeremia. 2018. "Gubernur Papua Barat Jadi Ketua DPW Partai Nasdem." *Berita Satu*, May 9.
Suliyanto, Erwin. 2021. "Tindakan Represif Aparat Kepolisian Republik Indonesia dalam Menghadapi Aksi Demonstrasi Ditinjau dari Undang-Undang Nomor 9 Tahun 1998 Tentang Kemerdekaan Menyampaikan Pendapat Dimuka Umum." *Jurnal Ilmiah Ilmu Hukum* 27 (15): 2277–2296.
Sundhaussen, Ulf. 1972. "The Military in Research on Indonesian Politics." *Journal of Asian Studies* 31 (2): 355–365.
Supomo. 1964. *The Provisional Constitution of the Republic of Indonesia: With Annotations and Explanations on Each Article*. Ithaca: Cornell Southeast Asia Program.
Supriatma, Antonius Made Tony. 2019. "Jokowi and His Generals: Appeasement and Personal Relations." *ISEAS Perspective* 238, April.

Surabaya Pagi. 2020. "Risma, Pernah Dimakzulkan dan 2 Kali Konflik dengan Wawalinya." *Surabaya Pagi*, December 8.

Surya, Nova Ely. 2021. "Bupati Haliana Minta Presiden Jokowi Berkunjung ke Wakatobi." *Zona Sultra*, June 30.

Suryadinata, Leo Military. 1989. *Ascendancy and Political Culture: A Study of Indonesia's Golkar*. Athens: Ohio University, Center for International Studies.

Susetyo, Heri. 2019. "Khofifah dan Relawan Semaksimal Mungkin Menangkan Jokowi-Amin." *Media Indonesia*, January 31.

Suyadi, Asip. 2018. "Pembentukan dan Kewenangan Kantor Staf Presiden (KSP) dalam Struktur Lembaga Kepresidenan Republik Indonesia." *Jurnal Surya Kencana* Satu 10 (2): 91–102.

Suzuki, Wataru. 2017. "Legal Woes Mount for Indonesian Media Mogul." *Nikkei Asia*, July 7.

Syahrul, Yura. 2019. "Jokowi Isyaratkan Tak Setuju Amendemen UUD 1945 dan GBHN." *Katadata*, August 15.

Syakir, Muhammad. "Perpres Dana Abadi Pesantren Diteken, RMI PBNU: Besarannya Tidak Dinyatakan Jelas." *NU Online*, September 14.

Tapsell, Ross. 2017. *Media Power in Indonesia: Oligarchs, Citizens and the Digital Revolution*. London: Rowman and Littlefield.

Taufan, Sabik Aji. 2019. "Survei Cyrus: Jokowi Lebih Taat Beribadah Ketimbang Prabowo." *Jawa Pos*, March 1.

Tempo, 2011. "Bupati Seluma Jadi Ketua Demokrat Bengkulu." *Tempo*, January 17.

———. 2012. "Seperti Apa Renovasi WC DPR Senilai Rp 1,4 Miliar?" *Tempo*, November 7.

Teresia, Ananda. 2015. "Jokowi Jadi Warga Kehormatan Kopassus, Marinir, dan Paskhas." *Tempo*, April 16.

Tjiptoherijanto, Prijono. 2008. "Civil Service Reform in Indonesia." In *Comparative Governance Reform in Asia: Democracy, Corruption, and Government Trust*, edited by Bidya Bowornwathana and Clay G. Wescott, 39–53. Bingley: Emerald Group Publishing.

———. 2018. "Reform of the Indonesian Civil Service: Looking for Quality." *Economics World* 6 (6): 433–443.

TNI AD 2016. "Jokowi: Komando Teritorial Tetap Dipertahankan." *TNI AD*, June 28.

Tomsa, Dirk. 2006. "The Defeat of Centralized Paternalism: Factionalism, Assertive Regional Cadres, and the Long Fall of Golkar Chairman Akbar Tandjung." *Indonesia* 81: 1–22.

———. 2008. *Party Politics and Democratization in Indonesia: Golkar in the post-Suharto Era*. London: Routledge.

———. 2010. "Indonesian Politics in 2010: The Perils of Stagnation." *Bulletin of Indonesian Economic Studies* 46 (3): 309–328.

———. 2018. "Regime Resilience and Presidential Politics in Indonesia." *Contemporary Politics* 24 (3): 266–285.

Toriq, Ahmad. 2016a. "Siapa 6 Menteri NU yang Dimaksud Jokowi?" *Detik*, June 10.

———. 2016b. "Jokowi Singgung Kursi Menteri, Muhammadiyah: Kami Biasa-biasa Saja." *Detik*, June 9.

Utami Putri, Budiarti. "Omnibus Law RUU Cipta Kerja Sebut Presiden Bisa Batalkan Perda." *Tempo*, February 17.

Utomo, Budi. 2019. "Menteri Agama Era Soekarno Hingga Jokowi, Selalu dari NU?" *Tagar*, July 20.

van der Kroef, Justus M. 1950. Indonesia: Federalism and Centralism." *Current History* 19 (108): 88–94.

van Klinken, Gerry. 2007. *Communal Violence and Democratization in Indonesia: Small Town Wars*. London: Routledge.
VOI. 2020. "Siapa Tri Rismaharini Sebenarnya." *VOI*, December 16.
——. 2021. "Forbes Version of the Latest 100 Richest Indonesians: The Hartono Brothers Remain in the Top Position." *VOI*, March 9.
Walton, Matthew J., and Susan Hayward. 2014. "Contesting Buddhist Narratives: Democratization, Nationalism, and Communal Violence in Myanmar." *Policy Studies* 71, East West Center.
Waluya, Ramadhan Dwi. 2020. "Tito Karnavian: Masyarakat di Negara Majority Low Class Anggap Covid-19 sebagai Hoaks dan Konspirasi." *Pikiran Rakyat*, September 22.
Wanandi, Jusuf. 2016. "President Jokowi's Tax Amnesty Policy a Success Story." *Jakarta Post* October 17.
Warburton, Eve. 2016. "Jokowi and the New Developmentalism." *Bulletin of Indonesian Economic Studies* 52 (3): 297–320.
——. 2019. "Indonesia's Pro-Democracy Protests Cut across Deep Political Cleavages." *New Mandala*, October 3.
Ward, Ken. 2009. "Non-violent Extremists? Hizbut Tahrir Indonesia." *Australian Journal of International Affairs* 63 (2): 149–164.
Wardi, Robertus. "Aburizal Bakrie Nilai 122 UU Harus Ditinjau Ulang." *Berita Satu*, September 26.
Wicaksono, Dian Agung. 2013. "Implikasi Re-Eksistensi Tap MPR dalam Hierarki Peraturan Perundang-Undangan terhadap Jaminan atas Kepastian Hukum yang adil di Indonesia." *Jurnal Konstitusi* 10 (1): 143–178.
Wicaksono, Ronny. 2016. "Istana Bantah Isu Jokowi Berusaha Redam Kudeta." *Times Indonesia*, November 14
Widdowson, H.G. 2004. *Text, Context, Pretext: Critical Issues in Discourse Analysis*. Oxford: Blackwell.
Widowati, Hari. 2019. "Wahyu Trenggono, Raja Menara & Heboh Dana Kampanye dengan Tim Prabowo." *Katadata*, October 25.
Wilson, Ian Douglas. 2008. "'As Long as It's Halal': Islamic Preman in Jakarta." In *Expressing Islam: Religious Life and Politics in Indonesia*, edited by Greg Fealy and Sally White, 192–210. Singapore: ISEAS.
Winters, Jeffrey A. 1996. *Power in Motion: Capital Mobility and the Indonesian State*. Ithaca: Cornell University Press.
——. 2011. *Oligarchy*. Cambridge: Cambridge University Press.
——. 2013. "Oligarchy and Democracy in Indonesia." *Indonesia* 96: 11–33.
Winters, Jeffrey A., and Benjamin I. Page. 2009. "Oligarchy in the United States?" *Perspectives on Politics* 7 (4): 731–751.
World Bank. 2020. "Indonesia Public Expenditure Review: Spending for Better Results." World Bank.
Yamin, Muhamad. 2021. "Presiden Berharap Kehadiran TV dan Radio Polri Memberikan Edukasi Masyarakat." *Sindo News*, April 12.
Yusuf, Ali. 2020. "Ini Saran PBNU Setelah FPI Dibubarkan." *Republika*, December 30.
Yusuf, Slamet Effendi, and Umar Basalim. 2000. *Reformasi Konstitusi Indonesia: Perubahan Pertama UUD 1945*. Jakarta: Pustaka Indonesia Satu.
Zedner, Lucia. 2006. "Policing before and after the Police: The Historical Antecedents of Contemporary Crime Control." *British Journal of Criminology* 46 (1): 78–96.
Zucco, Cesar, and Timothy J Power. 2021. "Fragmentation Without Cleavages? Endogenous Fractionalization in the Brazilian Party System." *Comparative Politics* 53 (3): 477–500.

Index

accommodation of coalition actors
  of the bureaucracy, 144–45, 148
  in coalitional presidentialism, 15–16, 26, 237
  in democratic decline, 242, 243
  in Indonesian presidentialism, 38
  of legislators, 81–82, 237
  of local government leadership, 172–75, 179
  of the military, 23–24, 118–19
  of Muslim organizations, 207–8, 210, 218–19, 223–24
  of non-party actors, 180
  of oligarchs, 195–96, 198, 203–4
  of oppositional parties, 66–67
  of the police, 129
  in stability, 237, 239–41
accountability, 88, 100–101, 243
Aceh peace deal, 110–11
activism/activists
  anti-corruption, in KSP, 47–48
  anti-presidential, in the history of the presidency, 34
  against civil service reform, 156–57
  Muslim, 208–9, 210–11, 220–21
  oligarchic sponsorship of, 198
  and the police, 122, 134–35
  repression of, and democratic decline, 243–44
  See also mobilization
adjutants, military, 109
administrative operations of the presidency, 32–33, 43–48, 53–54, 109, 187, 189, 198
Africa, 20–21, 205, 234
agencies, security, 137–39, 244–45
  See also military/civil-military relations; police
Ahmadiyah, 218
Airlangga Hartarto, 72, 188–89, 193–94, 196, 198
ambassadorial appointments, 85–86, 169
amendments, constitutional
  in DPR power, 79
  in limiting impeachments, 2, 12–13
  in political parties' power, 57
  in presidential elections, 12–13
  in presidential power, 40, 104, 213
  in stability, 18, 227, 236–38
Amin, Ma'ruf, 56–57, 73–75, 209–10, 215, 216–17
Anggraeni, Diah, 155–57
anti-communism, 99–100, 114–17, 138–39
Anung, Pramono, 45–46
APEKSI (Association of Indonesian Municipality Governments), 156–57, 172–74, 177–79
Apindo (Indonesian Association of Entrepreneurs), 188–89
APKASI (Association of Indonesian District Governments), 172–74
appeasement, 24–25, 98–99, 100–101, 103–4, 118
appointments/appointment authority
  in the 1945 constitution, 33–34
  in building and sustaining coalitions, 230
  and the bureaucracy, 142, 146–52, 155, 165–66
  and the DPR, 82, 85–86
  in hybrid transitional presidentialism, 12–13
  and local governments, 162–63, 165–66, 167, 169, 173–74, 249n3
  and the military, 99–100, 104–5, 111, 112–13, 114–15, 117–18, 248n5
  and Muslim groups, 206, 212–13
  and oligarchs, 191–92
  and the police, 125, 126–28, 129, 132–33
  in the powers of the president, 42–43
  See also cabinets/cabinet appointments
APPSI (Association of Indonesian Provincial Governments), 172–73
Arismunandar, Wismoyo, 91
Asia
  Asian Financial Crisis, 37
  in comparative context, 233–34
  impeachments in, 39–40
  Indonesia as model of stability in, 2
  presidentialism in, 8, 10–11
  religion in politics of, 205
attorney general's office, 167–69
authoritarianism, 6–7, 32–33, 117–18, 121, 122

271

autocracy and autocratic presidentialism
  in the history of the presidency, 35–38
  legacies of, in the constitution, 53
  lessons from, in drive for stability, 239, 240–41
  military in, 98, 100, 121
  police in, 121
  presidential centrality in potential of, 6–7
  under Sukarno and Suharto, 11–12
  See also illiberalism
autonomy
  of the bureaucracy, 140–41, 158–59
  of the legislature, 12–13, 78, 86
  of local governments and regions, 161, 180–81
  of the military, 98
  of the police, 128
  of the president, in the 1945 constitution, 33–34
  of religious organizations, 213

Bakrie, Aburizal, 94–95, 184–85, 191, 198–202
Bakrie, Anindya, 188–89, 201–2
Bakrie, Ardi, 123
Bali, 170–71
Bali Bank scandal, 91–92
Bamus (Consultative Agency), 88–89
Bareskrim (Criminal Investigation Agency), 126–27, 130
Barton, Greg, 1
Basuki Madimuljono, 151
Batubara, Juliari, 178, 247n2
Bekasi, civil service conflict in, 144–46
BKN (National Civil Service Agency), 141, 143–44, 147, 155–56
  See also bureaucracy/bureaucrats
BNP2TKI (National Agency for the Placement and Protection of Indonesian Migrant Workers), 212–13
boarding schools, Islamic, 59, 206, 211–12, 213, 217–18
Boediono, 71–73, 156–57, 159
Bolivia, 22
  See also Latin America
BPUPKI (Investigating Committee for Preparatory Work for Indonesian Independence), 33, 34
Brazil, 21–22, 245–46
  See also Latin America
breadth of coalition actors
  in coalition-building, 49, 50–51, 53–54
  in comparative context, 21–22, 24
  in democratic decline, 227–28, 242, 244

  in Indonesian coalitional presidentialism, 4–5, 13–14, 18
  legislators in, 78, 88, 90–91
  military in, 99
  oligarchs in, 192–93
  post-2004 constitution in, 42–43
  range of parties in, 59–60, 65–66, 69–70, 74–75
  in stability, 226–28, 238–39, 241
  See also coalition size
brokers, 58, 79, 88–96
Budget Agency (DPR), 80–81
budgets/fiscal power
  in building and sustaining coalitions, 230–31
  and the civil service, 148–49, 152, 160
  and the legislature, 79–81, 87–89, 91, 94
  and local governments, 162–64, 167, 169–71, 172, 180–81
  military, 100–101, 107–8, 111–12, 117–18
  and Muslim groups, 206, 211–12, 213, 217–18, 219
  police, 122–23, 128–29, 132–33
  presidential power over, 42–43, 64, 84–85, 170–71
  in the presidential toolbox, 3–4
  See also funding
bureaucracy/bureaucrats
  and the 2014 Civil Service Law, 154–58
  in administrative structure, 43–48
  autonomy of, 140–41, 158–59
  in the cabinet, 141, 142, 151–52, 158–59
  as implementing arm of the executive, 140–41
  and local governments, 142–43, 144–45, 151–52, 155, 165–66
  power of, 142–46
  in presidential coalitions, 4, 25, 150–54
  presidential isolation from, 53–54
  presidential power over, 146–50
  reform of, 25, 141, 147–48, 149–50, 154–58, 159–60
bureaucratization of politics, 158–59
business sector, 188–90, 191–92, 196–97
  See also oligarchs

cabinets/cabinet appointments
  and the bureaucracy, 141, 142, 151–52, 158–59
  in coalitional presidentialism, 10–11
  in democratic decline, 244–45
  and local governments, 161, 169, 173–74, 178–79

INDEX

and the military, 24–25, 105–7, 109, 111, 117–18, 244–45
Muslim groups in, 212–13, 215–17, 223–24
non-party members of, 9–10, 21–22, 23–24, 50–52, 232–33
oligarchs in, 191–92, 194–95
police in, 121, 125, 127–28, 131, 132–33, 244–45
political parties in, 52, 56, 58–59, 64, 65–68
as presidential asset, 64, 85–86
in the presidential toolbox, 3–4
religious actors in, 26
reshuffling of, 1, 67–68
as reward or punishment, 230
technocrats in, 151–52, 193–94
See also appointments/appointment authority
Cabinet Secretariat, 45–46
campaigns, presidential
and democratic decline, 243–44
legislators in, 78
local governments in, 166, 174
military in, 115
Muslim groups in, 208–10, 213–14, 216, 219, 222–23
in mutual dependence, 237
oligarchs in, 185–86, 194–95, 197–200, 203
police in, 124, 128–29
political parties in, 55, 58–59, 61–62, 63, 71
Castillo, Pedro, 1–2, 21–22
center-periphery relations, 164, 180–81
See also centralization/decentralization; local governments and leaders
centrality
of the president, 6–7, 14–15, 32, 36–37, 38, 52–53
of presidential-party relations, 74
centralization/decentralization
of the civil service, 141, 143
and local governments, 161–62, 163–65, 167, 169–70, 171, 172–73, 174–75, 180–81
ceremonies/ceremonial events, 131–32
Chalid, Reza, 93–94
chaos prevention
in accommodation of radical Muslim groups, 218
bureaucracy in, 158
coalition-building in, 49–50
DPR in, 88, 94
local governments in, 180–81
military inclusion in, 99, 101

oligarchs in, 203
party inclusion in, 59–60
checks and balances, 241, 243
Chile, 20–21, 56
See also Latin America
Cirebon, civil service conflict in, 144–46
civil emergencies, 101–2
civil service. *See* bureaucracy/bureaucrats
Civil Service Law of 2014, 146, 148, 153–58, 159
clientelism, 88–89, 90, 91–92, 129
See also patronage
coalitional presidentialism
in comparative global context, 232–36
defined, 9–11, 24–27
in Indonesia, 11–18
and post-2004 presidents, 49–53
coalition size, 21, 49, 50, 232–33, 235–36
See also breadth of coalition actors
coattail effect, 63
See also popularity
coercion
of local governments, 162–63
of the military, 98–99
of Muslim groups, 215, 231–32
of oligarchs, 190–91
police powers of, 120, 122–25
as presidential tool, 231–32
of presidents by security forces, 138–39
in stability, 240–41
co-legislative power
in building and sustaining coalitions, 229
constitutional, 40–41, 42–43
and the DPR, 77, 79, 85
in interactions with Muslim groups, 213, 217–18
in power over local governments, 169–70
Commission XI (Budget Agency), 80–81
committees, DPR, 81–82, 88
communists/Communist Party. *See* anti-communism; PKI (Indonesian Communist Party)
compromises
in avoiding impeachment, 13–14
with the bureaucracy, 148, 153–54, 157
in democratic decline, 242
with the DPR, 42, 77, 86–87, 95–96
with local governments, 180
in local-presidential relations, 180
with the military, 113–14, 117, 138–39
with police, 138–39
in stability, 236–37

INDEX

concessions
　in coalitional presidentialism, 9–10
　in coalition-building, 50
　in democratic decline, 138–39, 242
　to the DPR, 78, 82–83, 87–88, 95–96
　for logging, in local power, 164–65
　to the military, 24–25, 98, 99–100, 106–7, 112–13, 114–15, 117–19
　to Muslim groups, 214, 221–22
　to non-party coalition members, 230
　to oligarchs, 25–26, 182, 185, 203–4
　to the police, 122–23, 129, 137
　to political parties, 58–59, 60–61
confidants of the president, 43–44, 46, 48, 109
conflict
　2014 Civil Service Law in, 153–58
　avoidance of, in coalitional presidentialism, 239–40
　ethno-religious, and the military, 100–101
　inter-institutional, 8–9, 70–74, 75, 144–45
　intra-elite in coalitional presidentialism, 14–16
　intra-party, presidents in outcome of, 56–57, 63–64
　with local governments, 144–45, 179–80
　military-police, 113–14
　with Muslim groups, 207–8
　with oligarchs, 194–95, 199–200
　with police, 112–14, 116, 121–22
　with political parties, 70–74, 75
　regional, in military command structure, 102–3
　religious, in integration of religious actors, 26
consensus, 6–7, 33–34, 64–65, 76–77, 241, 248n1
conservatism/conservative ideology
　in the bureaucracy, 160
　Islamic, 26, 205–6, 207–8, 219, 220–21, 222–23
　in the military, 105, 110–11, 114–16
　and the police, 121–22, 132–33, 135, 136, 138–39
　religious, 205–6, 207–9, 219
constitution
　of 1950 (UUDS 1950), 35–36
　in coalitional presidentialism, 11–14, 27
　DPR in, 33–34, 39–42, 79–83
　in the history of the presidency, 33–38
　and impeachments, 2, 39–40, 42–43, 227
　local government in, 163–64, 167–71
　the military in, 27, 98, 99–100, 104–8

　and Muslim groups, 207–8, 213
　political party powers in, 57, 59–60
　in power over oligarchs, 189–93
　in presidentialism, 6–7
　presidential power in, 9, 32–33, 38–43, 104, 213
　in stability, 18, 227, 236–38
Constitutional Court, 39–40, 82, 165
consultation forum, DPR, 87–88
cooperation
　with the bureaucracy, 148, 150, 154, 158–59
　with the legislature, 79, 83, 86–87, 93, 94–97
　with local governments, 161, 162–63, 169–72, 180–81
　with the military, 98–99, 100–101, 103–8, 111
　with oligarchs, 184–85
　with the police, 120, 126–27, 129, 138–39
　in political culture and stability, 236–38, 240–41
corruption
　in the civil service, 148–49
　in the DPR, 90–95, 96
　of DPR speaker Novanto, 91–95, 96
　and legislative budgetary powers, 79–80
　local-presidential relations in, 180–81
　in military budgeting, 107
　party coalitions in policy on, 74–75
　in police power, 123–24
　in in presidential power over local government, 167–69
　in Widodo's policy platform, 113–14
coups, 12, 36, 103–4, 118–19, 239–40
COVID-19 pandemic, 101–2, 149, 171–72, 173, 178–79, 222–23, 245–46, 249n4

DAK (Special Allocation Funds), 90, 170
DAU (General Allocation Fund), 164, 169–70
DBH (Revenue Sharing Fund), 170
decrees
　emergency, 40–42
　financial, and local governments, 170
　MPR, 36–37, 40, 104, 105–6
　on Muslim groups, 217–18
　in power over the military, 104, 105–6
　in power over the police, 127
　rule by, 9–10, 41–42, 105–6, 148
　on special powers in bureaucratic appointments, 147–48
democracies/democratization
　bureaucracies in, 141
　civil service under, 143
　indexes of, 16–17, 23, 244

in local government power, 163–64
military in, 100–101
police in, 125
police skepticism of, 136
post-authoritarian, in the history of the presidency, 37–38
presidentialism in instability of, 1–2
public satisfaction with, 228–29
democratic decline
  coalitional presidentialism in, 13–15, 16–18, 27, 227–28
  in comparative context, 23–24
  global, 245
  local-presidential relations in, 180–81
  military in, 99–100, 118–19, 244–45
  oligarchs in, 203–4
  police in, 244–45
  security agencies in, 138–39
  stabilizing of presidentialism in, 2–3, 5, 242–46
  Tito and police politics in, 136
democratic presidentialism, 13, 52–53
dependence/interdependence
  of the DPR, 33–34, 85
  of local governments, 166
  of the military, 107–8
  of Muslim groups, 206, 211, 214, 216–17, 224
  of oligarchs, 184–85, 189–90, 193–98, 202–3
  of police, 122–23, 136–37
  of political parties, 70, 74–75
  in stability, 237
  on state budgets, 230–31
disciplining
  of the bureaucracy, 146, 150–51
  of cabinets, 9
  of the legislature, 81, 86
  of the military, 104, 110, 117–18
  of Muslim groups, 211–15, 217, 224
  of oligarchs, 193, 200–202, 203–4
  of parties, 67–69
  of police, 127
  See also punishment
dissent
  by the DPR, 81–82, 83
  police in preventing, 122, 134–35, 245–46
  stifling of, in democratic decline, 245–46
divide-and-rule approach, 69, 224, 233–34, 235
Djojohadikusumo, Sumitro, 194
donations, political, 25–26, 186, 190–91, 193, 197–98, 203

DPD (Region's Representative Council), 151–52
DPP (Council of Advisers to the President), 195–96
DPR (People's Representative Council). *See* legislature
Dutch colonialism, 34–35, 52–53, 156, 163
Duterte, Rodrigo, 20–21, 205, 245–46
Dwipayana, Ari, 46

economy/economic stability
  DPR budgetary power in, 79–80
  and oligarchs, 182, 184–85, 188, 190, 192–93, 196
education, 206, 210, 211–12, 213, 217–18
Education, Ministry of, 212, 224
Effendi, Djohan, 1
Effendi, Sofian, 157
Effendi, Taufiq, 145, 154–55
Eko Prasodjo, 156–58
electability
  of Bakrie, 199–200
  in choice of running mate, 72–73
  of civil servants, 145–46
  Muslim groups in, 72–73, 219
  in political party support, 234
  in presidential power over Muslim groups, 213–14
  in presidential power over oligarchs, 192
  See also popularity
elections
  bureaucracy in, 142–44, 145–46, 152
  in constitutional power, 39, 40–41
  in the history of the presidency, 33–34, 37–38
  indicators of stability in, 19–21
  legislative, personalization of, 82–83
  local government, 163–64, 167, 173–74
  local government support in, 170–71
  in local power, 164–65
  MPR in, 12–13, 39
  Muslim groups in, 207–9
  non-state actors in, 237
  oligarchs in, 185–86, 192, 197–98, 202–4
  political party power in, 56–57, 58–59, 60–63
  in power over Muslim groups, 213–14
  in power over oligarchs, 192–93
  for the presidency, post-2004, 39
  in presidentialism, 7–8
  religion in, 205–6
  vote buying in, and democratic decline, 17
  See also re-election of presidents

elections, direct
   in constitutional power, 39, 40–41
   in the history of the presidency, 37–38
   and local government, 163–64, 167, 173–74
   and Muslim groups, 213–14
   and oligarchs, 192
   in presidentialism, 7–8
   in stability, 237
Enembe, Lukas, 168–69
equilibrium, 52–53, 70–71, 74, 75, 86–87, 117, 241, 248n3
ethnic Chinese oligarchs, 188–89, 190–91
events, public, 88, 152–53
exceptionalism, Indonesian, 226–27
executive presidentialism, 11–12, 52–53

Fakhruloh, Zudan Arif, 153
Fauzi, Gamawan, 173–74
favors
   in coalitional presidentialism, 3–4, 230–31
   in coalition-building by police, 125, 128–29
   in exchange for loyalty of security agencies, 138
   in Indonesian coalitional presidentialism, 15–16
   in local government power, 164–65
   for Muslim organizations, 210–11, 223–24
   as presidential asset, in party relations, 64
   See also patronage; rewards
federalism, 34–35, 163
   See also local governments and leaders
Final Assessors Team, 147–48, 150
Finance, Ministry of, 80–81, 170, 218
Firli Bahuri, 123–24, 132, 249n1
fiscal power. *See* budgets/fiscal power
floor-based coalitions, 10–11
Forkopimda (police local leadership forum), 124
FPI, 207–8, 214–15, 218, 219, 221–23, 231–32
   See also Muslims/Muslim groups
France, 31
Freedom House index, 16
Freeport Indonesia, 93–94
funding
   of the bureaucracy, 148–49, 158–59, 160
   for development, in the case of Setya Novanto, 92–93
   development funds, 92–93, 111–12, 206, 211–12
   discretionary, for legislators, 84–85, 248n2
   of local governments, 164, 170–71, 172–73
   of Muslim schools, 206, 211–12, 213, 217–18
   off-budget, by the military, 107–8, 111–12, 117–18

   by oligarchs, 185–87, 197–98, 202–3, 239–40
   of the police, 128–29
   of political parties, 62–63, 64
   of security agencies, in democratic decline, 244–45
   See also budgets/fiscal power

Gatot Nurmantyo, 114–15, 116–17
GBHN (Broad Outlines of State Policy), 40
generals
   appointment of, 104–5, 117–18, 248n4
   leverage of, 100–101, 103–4
   in managing the military, 106–8, 111, 112–13
   and Widodo, 113–17
   See also military/civil-military relations
Gerindra (Great Indonesia Movement Party), 60–61, 63, 66–67
Gibran Rakabuming Raka, 196–97
Golkar (Functional Group Party)
   and Bakrie, 199–201
   DPR speakers from, 89–90
   in the history of the presidency, 37
   ministers of, in coalition-building, 52
   New Order civil service in, 142–43
   in presidential leverage in the DPR, 85–86
   and Setya Novanto, 91–95
   in stabilizing Yudhoyono's coalition, 229–30
   in Widodo's coalition, 63–64
gotong royong (mutual assistance), 241
Government Regulation in Lieu of Law (Perpu), 41–42, 79, 222
Government Regulations (PP), 41–42
governors
   and bureaucrats, 144–45
   management of coalitions with, 172–75
   as "party," 161, 172–73, 179–80
   powers of, 163–64, 165, 166–67
   presidential powers over, 167–69, 170–71
   See also local governments and leaders
grassroots networks, 58, 162–63, 173, 178–79, 208–9
Guided Democracy regime, 36–37
Gunawan, Budi, 113–14, 121–22, 125, 126–28, 132, 138

Habibie, B. J., 13, 101, 104
Hadi Utomo, 110
Haiti, Badrodin, 114
Hanura (People's Conscience Party), 61, 247n4
harmonization law of 2022, 169–70

INDEX

Hartono, Bambang Dwi, 176–77
Hartono, Heru Budi, 247n2
Hasan, Bob, 194
Hatta, Mohammad, 35
Hatta Radjasa, 123
Hendrayudha, Dadang, 112
Hendropriyono, A. M., 113, 249n8
hierarchy, political and administrative, 45–46, 125, 126, 131, 165–66, 167
HIPMI (Indonesian Association of Young Entrepreneurs), 188–89, 196
Home Affairs, Ministry of, 131, 136–37, 143, 155–56, 165, 171–72, 173–74
HTI (Hizbut Tahrir), 214–15, 219, 220–22, 223
  See also Muslims/Muslim groups
human rights abuses, 100–101, 111–12, 114–17

identity card scandal, 92–93, 95, 96–97
ideology, 14–15, 65–67, 117–18, 121–22, 132–33, 207
illiberalism, 16–17, 136, 226, 227–28, 243
  See also autocracy and autocratic presidentialism; democratic decline
impeachments
  compromises in avoiding, 13–14
  danger of, in coalition-building, 49, 50, 227
  in the history of the presidency, 37–38, 53–54
  as indicator of stability, 19–21
  and the legislature, 83, 89–91
  military acquiescence to, 101
  political parties in, 69, 70–71, 75
  post-2004, 2, 39–40, 42–43, 227, 228–29, 232–33, 236–39
  in presidential systems, 1–2
incentives
  and the bureaucracy, 150–51, 153–54
  constitutional, for broad coalitions, 42–43
  financial, for Muslim groups, 217–18
  and the legislature, 33–34, 78, 81, 95–96
  and local governments, 161, 162–63, 164–65, 167–68
  for military loyalty, 103–4, 106–8
  for oligarchs, 190, 191–92, 193–94
  for police support, 122, 129
  size of party in, 235
  for stability, 236–37
independence
  of the bureaucracy, 140–41
  in the history of the presidency, 33–35, 38
  in Indonesian coalitional presidentialism, 11–12
  of legislators, 82–83, 95–96

  of local governments, 163, 165–66 (See also centralization/decentralization)
  military in, 99–100
  of the police, 127, 128
  of the president, in coalition-building, 50
  struggles for, in presidential centrality, 6–7
Independent Team for the Reform of the National Bureaucracy, 154
infrastructure
  government-driven projects in, and oligarchs, 190
  local, 162–63, 170–71
  political, access of oligarchs to, 185–88, 195–96
  political, militaries in, 98
interpenetration
  of bureaucracy and politics, 141, 145–46, 158–59
  of local and national government, 179
Isir, Jhonny Eidizon, 45
Iskandar, Muhaimin, 72
Islam. See Muslims/Muslim groups
Isman, Hayono, 91

Japan/Japanese military administration, 33–34
Java, 163–64
Jokowi. See Widodo, Joko
Justice and Human Rights, Ministry of, 63–64
Juwaini, Jazuli, 83

Kadin (Indonesian Chamber of Industry and Trade), 188–89, 196, 201–2
Kaesang Pangarep, 197
Kalla, Jusuf, 49–50, 71, 147
Kartasasmita, Agus Gumiwang, 95
Kartasasmita, Ginandjar, 194
Kasim, Ifdhal, 47–48
KASN (Civil Service Commission), 145, 155–56, 157–58, 165–66
Kenya, 20–21, 234
Khofifah Indar Parawansa, 174, 209, 216
KNPI (Indonesian Central National Committee), 34
Komarudin, Ade, 94–95
Korpri (Indonesian Civil Servants Corps), 25, 141, 143–44, 152–53, 155–56, 157
KPK (Corruption Eradication Agency)
  and the bureaucracy, 148–49
  and the DPR, 85, 95
  and local governments, 167–69
  and the police, 113–14, 123–24, 126–27, 132
  and political parties, 74–75

Krisdayanti, 248n2
Kristiyanto, Hasto, 69–70
KSP (Office of the Staff of the President), 43, 46–48
Kurniawan, Taufik, 90

LAN (State Administration Institute), 154–55
Latin America, 8, 19–20, 21–22, 23, 56, 78, 232–34, 242
Law on Information and Electronic Transactions of 2008, 134–35
Law on the Responsibility for Budget Execution, 81
legislation/legislative process
  inclusion of oligarchs in, 196
  on Islamic boarding schools, 217–18
  local government power in, 165
  non-budgetary, DPR powers in, 81–82
  party powers in, and presidential concessions, 58–59
  in the post-2004 constitution, 40–43
  as presidential tool over police, 127
  in president-party relations, 64–65
  See also co-legislative power
Legislative Agency of the DPR, 81–82
legislature
  brokers in, 91–95
  budgetary powers of, 79–81, 87–89, 91, 94
  and cabinet appointments, 85–86, 95–96
  in civil service reform, 154–55
  in coalitional presidentialism, 10–11, 74–75
  consensus building in functioning of, 77
  and democratic decline, 243
  discretionary funds for, 84–85, 248n2
  in the history of the presidency, 36–38
  in hybrid and transitional presidentialism, 12–13
  independence of, 82–83, 95–96
  individualization of, 78, 82–83
  management of coalition with, 87–91
  in military appointments, 105
  and police, 125, 126–27
  political weight of, in coalitions, 75–76
  in the post-2004 constitution, 39–42
  powers of, 79–83
  in presidential elections, 33–34
  in presidentialism, 6
  presidential leverage over, 83–87
  relations with, in the presidential toolbox, 3–4
  strength of presidential party in, 21–22, 23–24
  See also MPs (members of parliament); political parties

legitimacy
  and democratic decline, 242–43
  military support in, 103–4
  and political parties, 59, 63–64
  presidential, post-2004 constitution in, 39
  religious, 182, 205–6, 209–10, 219, 237
leverage in coalitional relationships
  with the bureaucracy, 142–50
  constitutional powers as, 38–39, 40–41
  with the DPR, 79–87, 229
  with local governments, 162–71
  with the military, 99–108, 117
  with Muslim groups, 206, 207–15
  with oligarchs, 185–93
  with the police, 120, 122–29, 136–37
  with political parties, 57–65, 233–34, 235
  size of party in, 233–34, 235
LGBTI groups and citizens, 135
Liberal Democracy Index (V-Dem), 16–17, 23
licensing powers, 164–65, 169–70, 198–99, 221
Limpo, Syahrul Yasin, 172–73
Linz, Juan: "Perils of Presidentialism," 1–2, 7–9
Liong, Lim Sioe, 193
Listyo Sigit Prabowo, 130, 136–37
lobbying/lobby groups, 55, 57, 143, 159, 172–73, 188–89
local governments and leaders
  and the bureaucracy, 142–43, 144–45, 151–52, 155
  in coalitional presidentialism, 161–62
  in coalition-building, 50–52, 179–80
  Coordinating Meetings of Local Government Heads and Deputy Heads, 172
  and decentralization, 161–62, 163–65, 167, 169–70, 171, 172–73, 174–75, 180–81
  military units in, 102–3
  power of and over, 162–75, 249n3
  presidential appointment authority over, 162–63, 165–66, 167, 169, 173–74, 249n3
  Tri Rismaharini, 175–79
Luhut Pandjaitan, 46–47, 67–68, 111, 113, 116, 134–35, 148–49, 199–201
Lumentut, Vicky, 168

Mahfud MD, 72–74, 216–17
Mainwaring, Scott, 8
majorities, legislative, 6, 7–8, 9–10, 21–22, 49–50, 53–54, 96
Mallarangeng, Andi, 68
Mangkusubroto, Kuntoro, 47, 145
Masduki, Teten, 47, 222
mayors, 165–66, 167–69, 176–79
  See also local governments and leaders

media sector, 84–85, 187–88, 189–90, 191, 197–98, 200–201, 243
Megawati Sukarnoputri
　on consensus in political culture, 241
　legislative obstruction by, 85
　military appointments by, 105
　and Muslim groups, 209
　in the rise of Risma, 177–78
　and Widodo, 50, 57–58, 69, 113–14
meta-cleavages, 10
military/civil-military relations
　and the 1965 communist massacres, 113–17
　anti-communist scares of, 138–39
　and the cabinet, 24–25, 105–7, 109, 111, 117–18, 244–45
　in coalitional presidentialism, 24–25, 27, 99, 239
　in democracies, 98
　in democratic decline, 99–100, 118–19, 244–45
　in the history of the presidency, 36, 37, 53
　management of, 108–13, 118–19, 129–30
　as members of the legislature, 14–15
　military-affiliated oligarchs and Bakrie, 199–200
　off-budget funding of, 107–8, 111–12, 117–18
　police subordination to, 121
　power of, 99–104, 105, 108, 112–13, 114–15, 117–18
　in presidential administration, 45
　presidents as supreme commanders over, 99–100, 104–9, 114–15, 117
　ties with Novanto, 92
　toolbox in oversight of, 27
Military Secretariat, 45, 53–54, 105–6, 109–10, 129–30
minorities, religious, 207–8, 213–14, 218
minority presidents
　in coalitional presidentialism, 3–4
　coalition-building by, 9, 11, 49–50, 63–64, 233
　in comparative context, 21–22
　majority-building by, 95–96, 191
　in presidentialism, 7–9
mobilization
　anti-Purnama, 216–17, 219, 220, 221
　of the bureaucracy, 141, 142–43, 144–45, 148, 152, 156–57
　Islamist, 59, 73, 130–31, 231–32
　against Islamists, 207–8
　by local government, 162–63, 166
　by nominating parties, 63

　by oligarchs, 189
　of police, 122–23, 136–37
　of voters, 128–29, 166, 174, 208–9, 222–23
　See also activism/activists
Moeldoko, 47–48, 106, 108–9, 248n3
Morales, Evo, 22
MPR (People's Consultative Assembly), 12–13, 33–34, 36–38, 39–40, 101–2, 104, 105–6, 228–29
MPs (members of parliament), 77–78, 82–83, 84–85, 87–91
　See also legislature
mud volcano, 199
Muhammadiyah, 207–9, 210, 211, 212–14, 215–17, 219, 223–24
　See also PAN (National Mandate Party)
multi-party systems
　coalitional presidentialism in, 3–5, 9–11, 24
　in comparative context, 233–34
　post-election coalitions in, 95–96
　presidentialism in, 7–8, 245
　stability of, 1–2, 3–5, 228–29
Muslims/Muslim groups
　accommodation of, 207–8, 210, 218–19, 223–24
　in anti-communist human rights abuses, 115
　cabinet representation of, 212–13, 215–17, 223–24
　in coalitional presidentialism, 26
　and democratic decline, 17
　demonstrations by, in dangers of a military coup, 103
　in the fight against Islamism, 220–23
　in the history of the presidency, 53
　increasing role of, 205–6
　in interactions with presidents, 215–19
　Islamic conservative fringe, 207–8, 210–11, 214, 215, 218–23, 224–25, 231, 242, 243–44
　Islamic political parties, 59
　piety in power of, 206
　police in repression of radicalism, 130–31, 222–23
　political role of, 207, 223–24
　in post-2004 coalition-building, 50–52
　power of, 207–11
　presidential power over, 211–15
　repression of, 26, 207–8, 215, 219, 222–23, 224–25, 231–32
　See also NU (Nahdlatul Ulama); PKB (National Awakening Party); PPP (Unity Development Party); religion/religious groups
Muzadi, Hasyim, 224

INDEX

Nadiem Makarim, 195, 210, 212
Nasdem (National Democrats Party), 61, 63, 167–69
National Development Planning Agency (Bappenas), 80–81
nationalists, 34, 37, 105, 115
  See also Golkar (Functional Group Party); PDI (Indonesian Democracy Party)
National Resilience Institute (Lemhannas), 116
natural resources sector, 189–90
negotiation/renegotiation with coalition partners
  appointment powers in, 230
  on the ban of HTI, 221–22
  with the bureaucracy, 142–46, 149–58, 159–60
  in coalition stability, 231
  constitutional powers in, 9, 39
  with the DPR, 78, 79–81, 84–91, 95–96
  with Islamic groups, 224
  with local governments, 161–62, 167, 169–70, 171–75
  with the military, 108, 117–18
  with Muslim groups, 206, 213–14, 219–20, 221–22, 224
  with oligarchs, 182, 192–93, 200–202
  with the police, 120, 129–33
  with political parties, 57–65, 68–69, 70–74, 229–30
  in stability, 231
  of vested interests, in democratic decline, 245
new developmentalism, 17
New Order
  bureaucracy in, 142–43
  local governance in, 163–64
  military in, 100, 111–12
  oligarchs in, 193–94, 198–99
  police in, 128, 133, 136–37
  in rise of piety in Islamic power, 206
nominations/nomination powers
  of the legislature, 85–86
  of military commanders, 42–43, 99–100, 105–6, 110–11, 113–14
  of police commanders, 42–43, 121–22, 125, 126–27, 130–31
  of political parties, 55, 56–59, 61–62, 63, 65, 69–75
  for vice-presidential candidates, 70–75, 200–201
non-party actors
  in the cabinet, 9–10, 50–52, 111, 151–52, 191–92, 230, 232–33, 235–36
  in coalitional presidentialism, 4–5, 13–15, 24–26, 27, 75–76, 226–27

  in coalition-building, 49–50, 52, 53–54, 229
  in democratic decline, 243
  inclusion of, in comparative context, 18, 21–22, 23–24
  and political parties, 55, 75–76
  in presidential administration, 43–46
  in stability, 236–37
  See also bureaucracy/bureaucrats; military/civil-military relations; Muslims/Muslim groups; oligarchs; police
North Sulawesi, 170–71
Novanto, Setya, 79, 87–88, 91–95, 96, 203
NTT (East Nusa Tenggara), 170–71
NU (Nahdlatul Ulama)
  cabinet representation of, 53, 215–17, 223–24
  in the fight against Islamism, 220–23
  financial incentives for cooperation of, 217–18
  in the history of the presidency, 53
  power of, 207–10
  presidential power over, 211–15
  and Widodo, 220–24
  in Widodo's choice of 2018 running mate, 72–73
  See also Muslims/Muslim groups; PKB (National Awakening Party)
Nusron Wahid, 212–13

oligarchs
  and the cabinet, 191–92, 194–95
  defined, 182–84
  in delivering favors, 230–31
  in democratic decline, 203–4
  as driver of coalitional presidentialism, 239–40
  inclusion and limitations of, 196, 198–202
  influence of, 25–26, 185–88, 194
  management of coalitions with, 193–98
  military officers' relationships with, 107–8
  political donations by, 25–26, 186, 190–91, 193, 197–98, 203
  power of, 185–89
  presidential tools in power over, 189–93
Omnibus Bill Task Force, 196
opinion surveys (LSI), 29
outsiders, political, 60–62, 234
  See also non-party actors

Paloh, Surya, 195
PAN (National Mandate Party), 51–52, 56, 67–68, 215–16
  See also Muhammadiyah; Muslims/Muslim groups

INDEX   281

Pancasila ideology, 207, 211–12, 222–23
Papuan local government, 168–69
Paspampres (Presidential Guard), 109–10, 129–30
patronage
  in budgets, 42, 79–81, 84, 87–88, 230–31
  and the civil service, 145, 148–49, 155–56, 158–59, 160
  in coalitional presidentialism, 9–10, 15–16
  in democratic decline, 242
  and the DPR, 79–81, 82, 87–92, 95–97
  local government powers in, 164–65
  in loyalty of security agencies, 138–39
  and the military, 106, 107–8, 111–12, 117–18
  and oligarchs, 185–86, 189
  and police, 120, 127–28
  and political parties, 64, 66–67
  See also clientelism
Paulus, Lodewijk Freidrich, 63
PD (Democratic Party), 57–58, 60–61, 66, 86–87, 167–68, 169
PDI (Indonesian Democracy Party), 37
PDI-P (Indonesian Democracy Party—Struggle), 45–46, 50, 57–58, 69–70, 177–78, 229–30, 234
Perkasa, Andika, 107–8, 109–10, 113
personalist parties, 60–63, 234
Pertamina state oil company, 150–51
Peru, 19–20, 21–22, 232–33
  See also Latin America
Philippines, 11, 14, 20–22, 205–6, 234–35, 245–46
piety, Muslim, 205–6, 207–8, 209–10, 219
PKB (National Awakening Party), 50, 52, 59, 223–24
  See also Muslims/Muslim groups
PKI (Indonesian Communist Party), 36, 114–15
PKS (Prosperous Justice Party), 67–69, 81, 83
police
  and the cabinet, 121, 125, 127–28, 131, 132–33, 244–45
  in democratic decline, 244–45
  managing coalitional role of, 129–33
  and the military, 113–15, 121
  politics of, 133–37, 138–39
  powers of, 120, 122–25, 127–28, 136–37
  presidential power over, 126–29
  in presidential power over local government, 167–68
  in repression of fringe Muslim groups, 130–31, 222–23
  and Tito Karnavian, 121–22, 133–37

political parties
  in accommodation of Islamic interests, 223–24
  balancing, 59–60, 64–74, 75
  benefits of broad coalitions with, 74–75
  in the cabinet, 52, 56, 58–59, 64, 65–68
  cartelization of, 8, 14–15, 243
  as channel for civil servants in the cabinet, 151–52
  in coalitional presidentialism, 9, 14–15, 232–34, 236
  in democratic decline, 17
  in executive nominations, 55, 56–59, 61–62, 63, 65, 69–75
  in the history of the presidency, 34, 36
  and the legislature, 21–22, 23–24, 82–83
  local governors as, 172–73, 179–80
  and oligarchs, 185–87, 195
  in power play with presidents, 56–57, 70–74
  powers of, 56–60
  in pre-2004 instability, 228–29
  presidential power and leverage over, 3–5, 60–65, 79–87, 229–30
  in the rise of local leaders, 177–78, 179
  size and strength of, 9, 14–15, 21–22, 232–34, 236
  See also under name of party
politicization/depoliticization
  of the bureaucracy, 25, 141, 143, 145–46, 158–59
  of the police, 125, 126–27
popularity
  of civil servants in elections, 145–46
  electoral, of Islamic groups, 213–14
  oligarchic media in sustaining, 187–88
  in political party support, 56–57, 61–62, 234
  of presidents, in power over oligarchs, 192–93
  of Risma, 178–79
  See also coattail effect; electability
popular vote, 6, 12–13, 39
populism/populists, 5, 176–77, 185, 233–34
post-authoritarian states, 13–14, 52–53, 140–41, 227–28, 242
PPP (Unity Development Party), 37, 63–64
  See also Muslims/Muslim groups
Prabowo Subianto
  as agent of coalitional presidentialism, 240
  as defense minister, 248n5
  and the military, 112
  and Muslim groups, 214
  and oligarchs, 197–98, 199–200, 202–3
  as political outsider, 6–7
  as populist oligarch, 185

Pramono Edhie Wibowo, 110
Pranowo, Ganjar, 167, 169–70
Prasetijono, Widi, 45, 109
Pratikno, 43–45
Presidential Decision 70/2002, 127
presidentialism
　defined, 6–9
　in Indonesian history, 11–13
Presidential Military Secretariat, 45
prosecutions, 19–21, 112
Puan Maharani, 89, 93, 95
punishment
　of the bureaucracy, 150–51
　loss of cabinet positions as, 230
　of Muslim groups, 211–12, 222–23, 231–32
　of oligarchs, 191, 198, 203
　of political parties, 67–68
　of presidents by parties, 69
　in stability, 240–41
Purnama, Basuki Tjahaja, 59, 84, 150–51, 190–91

qualitative and quantitative analysis, 28–29
quasi-parliamentary period, 34–35, 52–53

"rainbow coalitions," 11
Rais, Amien, 214
Razi, Fachrul, 217
reciprocity. *See* transactionalism
reconciliation initiative of 1965, 114–17
recruitment
　civil service, 143, 155, 156
　of military officers, 109–10
　by Muslim groups, 220–21
　of non-party actors, 22, 44
　of religious actors, 26
　of Risma, 176
　of Thohir, 194–95
red lines. *See* vested interests
re-election of presidents
　bureaucracy in, 150
　in Indonesia, 13–14
　local governments in, 168–69, 174
　in measuring stability, 19–21
　military in, 101
　Muslim groups in, 208–9, 213, 214, 217
　oligarchs in, 191, 196–97
　police in, 131–32
　political parties in, 57–58, 63, 71, 74
　in post-2004 stability, 2, 227, 228–29
　See also electability; elections
reform/reformist initiatives
　in broad party coalitions, 70
　bureaucratic, 25, 141, 147–48, 149–50, 154–58, 159–60
　coalition size in likelihood of, 5
　and democratic decline, 243–44
　and local government, 162, 163–64
　and the military, 100–101, 102–3, 104, 106–7, 116, 118–19, 137
　and oligarchs, 202–3
　of the Palace, 43–44
　and the police, 132–33, 136, 137
　and political parties, 56–57, 70–74
Regional Leadership Forum, 102–3
regional secretaries, 144–45, 167, 171
regions. *See* local governments and leaders
regulatory power/regulatory instruments
　in appointment of senior police officers, 127
　in banning HTI, 222
　over local governments, 171–72
　over the bureaucracy, 148, 153
　in power over oligarchs, 189–90
　of the president, post-2004, 41–42
　in presidential power over Muslim groups, 213
Religion, Ministry of, 211–12, 217, 224
religion/religious groups, 17, 26, 205–6, 223–24, 240
　See also Muslims/Muslim groups
representation, proportional, 9, 82–83
repression
　in democratic decline, 243–44
　in the history of the presidency, 38
　of LGBTI groups and citizens, 135
　by the military, 98
　of Muslim groups, 26, 207–8, 215, 219, 222–23, 224–25, 231–32
　New Order civil service in, 142–43
　police in, 122, 130–31, 134–35, 222–23
rewards
　appointments as, 45–46, 230
　for the bureaucracy, 141, 149–50
　for local governments, 169, 180
　in managing DPR coalitions, 87–88
　for the military, 24–25, 103–4, 106–7
　for Muslim groups, 211–12, 213, 217–18
　for oligarchs, 198–99, 204–5
　for police, 125, 127–29, 136–37
　for political parties, 56–59, 74
　See also favors
Rinakit, Sukardi, 46
Rini Soemarno, 147–48
RIS (Federal Republic of Indonesia), 34–35
Rismaharini, Tri, 162–63, 175–79, 249n6

rivalries
  in the bureaucracy, 156–57
  of coalition actors, in democratic decline, 243
  in coalitional stability, 229–30
  in democratic decline, 243
  inter-party, 63–64, 65–66, 229–30
  intra-Islamic, 210–11, 214, 220–21, 224–25
  in the legislature, 93, 94–95
  military-police, 113–14, 128, 131, 137
Rizieq Shihab, 123, 130, 222–23
Robison, Richard, 15–16, 183, 192–93
Romahurmuziy, Muhammad ("Romy"), 72
running-mates
  Muslim, 53, 208–10, 215, 216–17
  oligarchs as, 185, 200–201
  police preferences in, 132
  political parties in choosing, 56, 70–74
Ryacudu, Ryamizard, 105, 110–11

Said, Sudirman, 93–94
Samad, Abraham, 132
sanctions. *See* disciplining
Sarundajang, Sinyo Harry, 169
Sastrosoenarto, Hartarto, 194
scandals, finance, 91–95
security forces, 4–5, 45, 129, 138–39
  See also military/civil-military relations; police
Selvanus, Yulius, 112
semi-presidential systems, 7–8
separatists, Papuan, 135
Setgab (Joint Secretariat), 68–69
Shihab, Rizieq, 207
Simanjuntak, Maruli, 109
Siradj, Said Aqil, 222
Sirait, Maruarar, 50
Siti Nurbaya Bakar, 151–52
Sjahrir, Sutan, 34
social affairs, minister for, 178, 216
social control, 142–43
Soepomo, 33, 36–37
Soesatyo, Bambang, 95
sovereignty, 34–35
speakers, DPR, 88–90, 91–95
Sri Mulyani Indrawati, 199, 203
stability/instability
  breadth of coalition actors in, 226–28, 238–39, 241
  bureaucracies in, 141, 142, 160
  coalitional presidentialism in, 3–5, 9–10, 27
  comparative, 19–24, 232–33
  and democratic decline, 2–3, 5, 242–46

  DPR in, 78, 83, 88
  in emerging democracies, 1–3
  of hybrid and transitional presidentialism, 12–13
  Indonesian constitution in, 18, 227, 236–38
  local governments in, 161–62, 175, 180
  management of Muslim groups in, 219
  military in, 99–100, 101, 103–4
  oligarchs in, 184–85, 188
  police loyalty in, 129
  political parties in, 14, 75
  post-2004 drivers of, 236–41
  "presidential toolbox in," 3–5
  security agencies in, 138
  strategies in sustaining, 228–32
state-owned enterprises (SOEs), 127–28, 147–48, 150–51, 190, 194–95, 212–13
State Secretariat, 43–45
States of Emergency, Law on, 101–2
Strategic Reserve, 109–10, 248n4
structure, institutional and political
  of the bureaucracy, 43, 141, 143, 149–50, 153
  in comparative context, 233
  COVID-19 changes to, in democratic decline, 245–46
  of the military, 103, 105–6, 109
  New Order civil service in enforcing, 142–43
  oligarchs as members of, 195–96
  the Palace as, 43–48
  physical, of presidential institutions, 48
  role of presidents in, 32
  in stability, 236–37
Subagyo, H. S., 113
Sudi Silalahi, 43–45
Suharto
  and autocratic presidentialism, 11–12
  and bureaucratic patronage, 156
  in the history of the presidency, 36–37, 53
  in local government power, 163–64
  management of oligarchs by, 193–94
  and the military, 100, 106–7, 108–9
  and oligarchs, 188, 190–91, 196–97
  and the rise of Muslim power, 207
  in shaping expectations of the president, 32
Suhartono, 109–10
Sukarno
  and autocratic presidentialism, 11–12
  in the history of the presidency, 34–35, 52–53
  military cabinet appointments by, 106–7
  military power under, 100
  and Muslim groups, 211–12
  in shaping expectations of the president, 32
  as symbol of unity, 52–53

Surabaya, 162–63, 176–79
Suryadi, Deddy, 109
Suswantono, Bambang, 109–10
Sutanto, 131
Sutarto, Endriartono, 105, 106, 110–11
Sutiyoso, 113
Syadzily, Ace Hasan, 73–74
Syafiuddin, Irianto MS, 175
Syuhud, Marsudi, 216

Tandjung, Akbar, 89–90, 183–84
Tanjung, Chairul, 192
Tanoesoedibjo, Hary, 187–88, 191–92, 197–98
technocrats, 22, 50–52, 71, 151–52, 193–94
territorial command structure, 102–4, 111–12, 118
terrorism, 121, 122–23, 222–23
theater, political, 88, 108–9
Thohari, Hajriyanto Y., 85–86
Thohir, Erick, 147, 195, 196–98
Tikal, Klemens, 170
Tito Karnavian, 121–22, 127–28, 131–32, 133–37, 171–72, 249n4
Tjahjanto, Hadi, 45, 117
toolbox, presidential, 3–5, 27, 60–65, 90–91, 224, 229–32
transactionalism
  and the bureaucracy, 159
  in coalition-building, 49–50
  in the legislature, 89–90, 91, 95
  and local governments, 170–71, 174–75, 180–81
  and the military, 108, 111
  and the oligarchs, 198

UKP4 (Presidential Working Unit for Development Monitoring and Control), 46–47, 145
unanimity, 96
unilateralism, 6, 9–10
United States, 31, 78, 205
Urbaningrum, Anas, 92–93
Utilization of the State Apparatus and Bureaucratic Reform, Ministry of, 143, 154

vested interests
  acceptance of, in stability, 241
  of the bureaucracy, 25, 140–41, 142, 148, 153, 158–59, 160
  in democratic decline, 241, 242, 245
  of the legislature, 84–85, 96–97

of local governments, 172–73
of the military, 23–24, 112–13, 118
of Muslim groups, 206, 219
of oligarchs, 186, 202, 203
of the police, 123–24, 137
in presidential-local relations, 174–75, 179–80
of security agencies, 138–39
veto actors, 15–16, 23–24, 38, 96–97
veto power
  in balancing party coalitions, 64–65
  in coalitional presidentialism, 15–16, 24, 229
  in co-legislative authority, 40–41
  in comparative context, 23–24
  in democratic decline, 245
  in the history of the presidency, 38
  in the legislature, 96–97
  of police, 125
  of security agencies, 138–39
  in stability, 231, 237
violence
  anti-communist, 99–100, 114–17
  against ethnic-Chinese oligarchs, 190–91
  ethno-religious, 100–101, 122–23, 190–91
  and the military, 100–101, 111–12, 114–17
  against non-indigenous oligarchs, 190–91
  and police, 120, 122–23
vote shares, 6, 39, 170–71, 174, 208–9, 224–25
voting
  civil servants' right to, 152
  mobilization of, 128–29, 166, 174, 208–9, 222–23
  police in, 124, 128–29
  popular vote, 6, 12–13, 39
  vote buying, 17
  withholding of right to, 17

Wahid, Abdurrahman
  1999 election of, 39
  and the civil service, 144
  hostile relationship with police, 129
  impeachment of, 1–2, 37–38, 89–90, 101, 236–39
  and the military, 101, 102–3
  and Muslim groups, 213–14
  on Muslim groups and the Ministry of Religion, 211–12
  as transitional president, 12–13
Wanandi, Jusuf, 250n2
Wanandi, Sofjan, 189
Waseso, Budi, 126–28, 138

wealth
  of bureaucrats, 145, 158–59
  measuring, 184
  of military officers, 107–8
  of oligarchs, 182–83, 193–94
  in personalized parties, 61, 63
  of police officers, 135–36
Widjajanto, Andi, 46
Widjojo, Agus, 116
Widodo, Joko
  administration of, 45–48
  as agent of coalitional presidentialism, 13–14, 240
  and the bureaucracy, 147–49, 150–51, 152–53
  Cabinet Secretariat of, 45–46, 53–54
  coalition-building by, 49, 50–52, 231–32
  in comparative context, 234
  in democratic decline, 99–100, 118–19, 242, 244
  and the DPR, 84–85, 87–88, 94–96
  impeachment of Wahid as influence on, 236–39
  incorporation of religious actors by, 26
  and the KPK law, 74–75, 85
  and local governments, 162, 165, 166, 167–68, 170–71, 172–73, 177–78
  and the military, 99–100, 108–10, 113–17, 118–19
  as minority president, 75
  and Muslim groups, 59, 208–10, 213–14, 216–18, 220–23, 224–25
  and the NU, 53, 220–23
  and oligarchs, 186, 188, 191, 192–93, 194–95, 196, 197–98, 200–204
  and the Palace, 43–44
  and the PDI-P, 60–61
  and the police, 128–29, 131–32, 134–35
  and political parties, 57–58, 63–65, 67–75, 86–87, 229–30, 234
  and radical Islamic groups, 219, 220–23
  on reestablishment of the GBHN, 40
  reform of administrative structures by, 43–44
  residence of, 48
  and security agencies, 137
  in shaping expectations of the president, 32
  stability of rule by, 2
  State Secretariat of, 43–45
Wirahadikusumah, Agus, 103
Wiranto, 101, 104, 107–8, 112, 196, 222

Yudhoyono, Susilo Bambang
  administration of, 45–47
  as agent of coalitional presidentialism, 13–14
  and the bureaucracy, 143–44, 154, 157–58, 159
  Cabinet Secretariat of, 45–46
  on civil-military relations in stability, 101
  coalition-building by, 49–52
  in comparative context, 234
  in democratic decline, 242, 244
  and the DPR, 79–80, 84–85, 95–96
  impeachment of Wahid as influence on, 236–38
  and local governments, 167–68, 173–74, 180
  and the military, 105, 110
  as minority president, 75
  and Muslim groups, 208, 218, 224–25, 242
  and oligarchs, 202–4
  and the police, 128, 132
  as political outsider, 6–7
  and political parties, 57–60, 64–65, 67–69, 71–72, 75, 86–87, 229–30, 234
  residence of, 48
  State Secretariat of, 43–45

Printed in the USA
CPSIA information can be obtained
at www.ICGtesting.com
LVHW081810021123
762854LV00003B/381